Lecture Notes in Artificial Intelligence   10414

Subseries of Lecture Notes in Computer Science

More information about this series at http://www.springer.com/series/1244

Tom Everitt · Ben Goertzel
Alexey Potapov (Eds.)

Artificial General Intelligence

10th International Conference, AGI 2017
Melbourne, VIC, Australia, August 15–18, 2017
Proceedings

 Springer

Editors
Tom Everitt (iD)
Australian National University
Canberra, ACT
Australia

Alexey Potapov (iD)
St. Petersburg State University
St. Petersburg
Russia

Ben Goertzel
OpenCog Foundation
Hong Kong
China

ISSN 0302-9743   ISSN 1611-3349   (electronic)
Lecture Notes in Artificial Intelligence
ISBN 978-3-319-63702-0   ISBN 978-3-319-63703-7   (eBook)
DOI 10.1007/978-3-319-63703-7

Library of Congress Control Number: 2017947039

LNCS Sublibrary: SL7 – Artificial Intelligence

Printed on acid-free paper

This Springer imprint is published by Springer Nature
The registered company is Springer International Publishing AG
The registered company address is: Gewerbestrasse 11, 6330 Cham, Switzerland

Preface

The original goal of artificial intelligence (AI) was to build machines with human-level intelligence. As the field evolved, efforts became scattered across a wide range of "narrow" AI domains. The goal of the Artificial General Intelligence (AGI) community is to refocus on the original goal of human-level intelligence, and to explore the space of possible intelligences. Sometimes this means tying together narrow AI technologies into more complex systems and cognitive architectures. But equally often, AGI research involves finding new ways of looking at intelligence, including new algorithms, mathematical frameworks, and conceptualizations. A third branch of research covers the societal impact of AGI, and how to ensure its safe applicability.

This, the tenth AGI conference, took place during August 15–18 in Melbourne, Australia, against the backdrop of many exciting developments in traditional AI and machine learning. It is therefore only appropriate that the conference was hosted back-to-back with some major traditional AI and machine learning conferences: ICML and UAI in Sydney, and IJCAI also in Melbourne.

We received 35 high-quality papers, spanning a wide range of AGI topics. Out of these submissions, 21 papers (60%) were accepted for oral presentation. An additional six papers were accepted for poster presentation. Keynotes, tutorials, and workshops provided additional perspectives. In the keynotes, Christian Calude explored practical and theoretical aspects of incomputability, Marcus Hutter advertised universal artificial intelligence, Peter Cheeseman discussed recursively self-improving AI, and Elkhonon Goldberg connected biological insights about the brain with AI architectures. In the tutorials, Alexey Popatov suggested possible cross-fertilizations between AGI approaches, and Ben Goertzel envisioned a future unification. Naotsugu Tsuchiya gave a tutorial on AGI and consciousness. Finally, part of the last day was devoted to a workshop on understanding.

We wish to extend a deep thanks to the Program Committee for performing the essential task of quality control of the submissions. All papers received constructive feedback and an impartial evaluation from at least two independent reviewers. Only a handful of papers received less than three reviews. We also wish to thank the local committee for organizing the conference, and thank our generous sponsors, the OpenCog Foundation and Hanson Robotics.

June 2017

Tom Everitt
Alexey Potapov
Ben Goertzel

Organization

Program Committee

Hadi Afshar	Australian National University, Australia
Joscha Bach	MIT Media Lab, USA
Tarek Richard Besold	University of Bremen, Germany
Jordi Bieger	Reykjavik University, Iceland
Dietmar Bruckner	Bernecker + Rainer
Cristiano Castelfranchi	Institute of Cognitive Sciences and Technologies
Antonio Chella	Università di Palermo, Italy
Mayank Daswani	Australian National University, Australia
Tom Everitt	Australian National University, Australia
Stan Franklin	Institute for Intelligent Systems, University of Memphis, USA
Arthur Franz	Independent researcher
Nil Geisweiller	Novamente LLC
Ben Goertzel	AGI Society
Jose Hernandez-Orallo	Universitat Politecnica de Valencia, Spain
Bill Hibbard	University of Wisconsin - Madison, USA
Marcus Hutter	Australian National University, Australia
Matt Iklé	Adams State University, USA
Benjamin Johnston	University of Technology Sydney, Australia
Garret Katz	University of Maryland College Park, USA
Kevin Korb	Monash, Australia
Kai-Uwe Kuehnberger	University of Osnabrück, Institute of Cognitive Science, Germany
Ramana Kumar	Datat61, CSIRO, and UNSW, Australia
John Licato	Indiana University/Purdue University - Fort Wayne, USA
Sean Markan	Eudelic Systems LLC
Maricarmen Martinez	Universidad de los Andes, Colombia
Amedeo Napoli	LORIA Nancy, France
Eric Nivel	CADIA, Reykjavik University, Iceland
Abdul Rahim Nizamani	Dfind IT
Eray Özkural	Gök Us Araştirma ve Geliştirme Ltd.
Sergei Obiedkov	National Research University Higher School of Economics
Laurent Orseau	Google Deepmind
Günther Palm	Ulm University, Germany
Maxim Peterson	ITMO University
Alexey Potapov	AIDEUS

Nico Potyka	Universität Osnabrück, IKW, Germany
Paul S. Rosenbloom	University of Southern California, USA
Rafal Rzepka	Hokkaido University, Japan
Oleg Scherbakov	ITMO university
Ute Schmid	University of Bamberg, Germany
Leslie Smith	University of Stirling, UK
Javier Snaider	Google
Bas Steunebrink	IDSIA
Claes Strannegård	Chalmers University of Technology, Sweden
Kristinn Thórisson	Reykjavik University, Iceland
Volkan Ustun	USC Institute for Creative Technologies
Viktoras Veitas	Global Brain Institute, VUB
Mario Verdicchio	Università degli Studi di Bergamo, Italy
Pei Wang	Temple University, USA
Roman Yampolskiy	University of Louisville, USA
Byoung-Tak Zhang	Seoul National University, South Korea

Additional Reviewer

Majeed, Sultan

Contents

Philosophy

Architectures

From Abstract Agents Models to Real-World AGI Architectures: Bridging the Gap

Ben Goertzel[(✉)]

OpenCog Foundation, Sha Tin, Hong Kong
ben@goertzel.org

Abstract. A series of formal models of intelligent agents is proposed, with increasing specificity and complexity: simple reinforcement learning agents; "cognit" agents with an abstract memory and processing model; hypergraph-based agents (in which "cognit" operations are carried out via hypergraphs); hypergraph agents with a rich language of nodes and hyperlinks (such as the OpenCog framework provides); "PGMC" agents whose rich hypergraphs are endowed with cognitive processes guided via Probabilistic Growth and Mining of Combinations; and finally variations of the PrimeAGI design, which is currently being built on top of the OpenCog framework.

1 Introduction

Researchers concerned with the abstract formal analysis of AGI have proposed and analyzed a number of highly simplified, mathematical models of generally intelligent agents (e.g. [11]). On the other hand, practical proto-AGI systems acting as agents in complex real-world situations, tend to have much more ad hoc, heterogenous architectures. There is no clear conceptual or mathematical bridge from the former world to the latter. However, such a bridge would have strong potential to provide guidance for future work from both the practical and formal directions.

To address this lack, we introduce here a hierarchy of formal models of intelligent agents, beginning with a very simple agent that has no structure apart from the requirement to issue actions and receive perceptions and rewards; and culminating with a specific AGI architecture, PrimeAGI[1] [9,10]. The steps along the path from the initial simple formal model toward OpenCog will each add more structure and specificity, restricting scope and making finer-grained analysis possible. Figure 1 illustrates the hierarchy to be explored.

The sequel paper [7] applies these ideas to provide a formal analysis of cognitive synergy, proposed as a key principle underlying AGI systems.[2]

---

[1] The architecture now labeled PrimeAGI was previously known as CogPrime, and is being implemented atop the OpenCog platform.

[2] The preprint [8] contains the present paper and the sequel, plus a bit of additional material.

© Springer International Publishing AG 2017
T. Everitt et al. (Eds.): AGI 2017, LNAI 10414, pp. 3–12, 2017.
DOI: 10.1007/978-3-319-63703-7_1

2   Extending Basic Reinforcement Learning Agents

For the first step in our agent-model hierarchy, which we call a **Basic RL Agent** (RL for Reinforcement Learning), we will follow [11,12] and consider a model involving a class of active agents which observe and explore their environment and also take actions in it, which may affect the environment. Formally, the agent in our model sends information to the environment by sending symbols from some finite alphabet called the *action space* Σ; and the environment sends signals to the agent with symbols from an alphabet called the *perception space*, denoted $\mathcal{P}$. Agents can also experience rewards, which lie in the *reward space*, denoted $\mathcal{R}$, which for each agent is a subset of the rational unit interval.

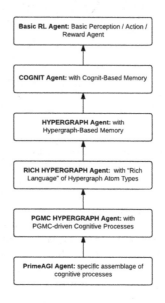

Fig. 1. An inheritance hierarchy showing the formal models of intelligent agents discussed here, with the most generic at the top and the most specific at the bottom.

The agent and environment are understood to take turns sending signals back and forth, yielding a history of actions, observations and rewards, which may be denoted

$$a_1 o_1 r_1 a_2 o_2 r_2 \ldots$$

or else $a_1 x_1 a_2 x_2 \ldots$ if x is introduced as a single symbol to denote both an observation and a reward. The complete interaction history up to and including cycle t is denoted $ax_{1:t}$; and the history before cycle t is denoted $ax_{<t} = ax_{1:t-1}$.

The agent is represented as a function π which takes the current history as input, and produces an action as output. Agents need not be deterministic, an agent may for instance induce a probability distribution over the space of possible actions, conditioned on the current history. In this case we may characterize the agent by a probability distribution $\pi(a_t|ax_{<t})$. Similarly, the environment may be characterized by a probability distribution $\mu(x_k|ax_{<k}a_k)$. Taken together, the distributions π and μ define a probability measure over the space of interaction sequences.

In [4] this formal agent model is extended in a few ways, intended to make it better reflect the realities of intelligent computational agents. First, the notion of a *goal* introduced, meaning a function that maps finite sequences $axs : t$ into rewards. As well as a distribution over environments, we have need for a conditional distribution γ, so that $\gamma(g, \mu)$ gives the weight of a goal g in the context of a particular environment μ. We assume that goals may be associated with symbols drawn from the alphabet $\mathcal{G}$. We also introduce a *goal-seeking agent*, which is an agent that receives an additional kind of input besides the perceptions and rewards considered above: it receives goals.

Another modification is to allow agents to maintain memories (of finite size), and at each time step to carry out internal actions on their memories as well as external actions in the environment. Of course, this could in principle be accounted for within Legg and Hutter's framework by considering agent memories as part of the environment. However, this would seem an unnecessarily artificial formal model. Instead we introduce a set C of cognitive actions, and add these into the history of actions, observations and rewards.

Extending beyond the model given in [4], we introduce here a fixed set of "cognits" c_i (these are atomic cognitions, in the same way that the p_i in the model are atomic perceptions). Memory is understood to contain a mix of observations, actions, rewards, goals and cognitions. This extension is a significant one because we are going to model the interaction between atomic cognitions, and in this way model the actual decision-making, action-choosing actions inside the formal agent. This is big step beyond making a general formal model of an intelligent agent, toward making a formal model of a particular *kind* of intelligent agent. It seems to us currently that this sort of additional specificity is probably necessary in order to say anything useful about general intelligence under limited computational resources.

The convention we adopt is that: When a cognition is "activated", it acts – in principle – on all the other entities in the memory (though in most cases the result of this action on any particular entity may be null). The result of the action of cognition c_i on the entity x (which is in memory) may be any of:

- causing x to get removed from the memory ("forgotten")
- causing some new cognitive entity c_j to get created in (and then persist in) the memory
- if x is an action, causing x to get actually executed
- if x is a cognit, causing x to get activated

The process of a cognit acting on the memory may take time, during which various perceptions and actions may occur.

This sort of cognitive model may be conceived in algebraic terms; that is, we may consider $c_i * x = c_j$ as a product in a certain algebra. This kind of model has been discussed in detail in [3], where it was labeled a "self-generating system" and related to various other systems-theoretic models. One subtle question is whether one allows multiple copies of the same cognitive entity to exist in the memory. i.e. when a new c_j is created, what if c_j is already in the memory? Does nothing happen, or is the "count" of c_j in the memory increased? In the latter case, the memory becomes a multiset, and the product of cognit interactions becomes a (generally quite high dimensional, usually noncommutative and nonassociative) hypercomplex algebra over the nonnegative integers.

In this extended framework, an interaction/internal-action sequence may be written as

$$c_1 a_1 o_1 g_1 r_1 c_2 a_2 o_2 g_2 r_2 \ldots$$

with the understanding that any of the items in the series may be null. The meaning of c_i in the sequence is "cognit c_i is activated." One could also extend the model to explicitly incorporate concurrency, i.e.

$$c_{11}...c_{1k_{c1}}a_{11}...a_{1k_{a1}}o_{11}...o_{1k_{o1}}g_{11}...g_{1k_{g1}}$$

$$r_{11}...r_{1k_{r1}}c_{21}...c_{2k_{c2}}a_{21}...a_{2k_{a2}}o_{21}...o_{2k_{o2}}g_{21}...g_{2k_{g2}}r_{21}...r_{2k_{r2}}...$$

This **Cognit agent** is the next step up in our hierarchy of agents as shown in Fig. 1. The next step will be to make the model yet more concrete, by making a more specific assumption about the nature of the cognits being stored in the memory and activated.

3 Hypergraph Agents

Next we assume that the memory of our cognit-based memory has a more specific structure – that of a *labeled hypergraph*. This yield a basic model of a **Hypergraph Agent** – a specialization of the Cognit Agent model.

Recall that a hypergraph is a graph in which links may optionally connect more than two different nodes. Regarding labels: We will assume the nodes and links in the hypergraph may optionally be labeled with labels that are string, or structures of the form (string, vector of ints or floats). Here a string label may be interpreted as a node/link type indicator, and the numbers in the vector will potentially have different semantics based on the type.

Let us refer to the nodes and links of the memory hypergraph, collectively, as Atoms. In this case the cognits in the above formal model become either Atoms, or sets of Atoms (subhypergraphs of the overall memory hypergraph). When a cognit is activated, one or more of the following things happens, depending on the labels on the Atoms in the cognit:

1. the cognit produces some new cognit, which is determined based on its label and arity – and on the other cognits that it directly links to, or is directly linked to, within the hypergraph. Optionally, this new cognit may be activated.
2. the cognit activates one or more of the other cognits that it directly links to, or is directly linked to
   (a) one important example of this is: the cognit, when it is done acting, may optionally re-activate the cognit that activated it in the first place
3. the cognit is interpreted as a *pattern* (more on this below), which is then matched against the entire hypergraph; and the cognits returned from memory as "matches" are then inserted into memory
4. in some cases, other cognits may be removed from memory (based on their linkage to the cognit being activated)
5. nothing, i.e. not all cognits can be activated

Option $2a$ allows execution of "program graphs" embedded in the hypergraph. A cognit c_1 may pass activation to some cognit c_2 it is linked to, and then c_2 can do some computation and link the results of its computation to c_1, and then pass activation back to c_1, which can then do something with the results.

There are many ways to turn the above framework into a Turing-complete hypergraph-based program execution and memory framework. Indeed one can do this using only Option 1 in the above list. Much of our discussion here will be quite general and apply to any hypergraph-based agent control framework, including those that use only a few of the options listed above. However, we will pay most attention to the case where the cognits include some with fairly rich semantics.

The next agent model in our hierarchy is what we call an **Rich Hypergraph Agent**, meaning an agent with a memory hypergraph and a "rich language" of hypergraph Atom types. In this model, we assume we have Atom labels for "variable" and "lambda" and "implication" (labeled with a probability value) and "after" (with a time duration).; as well as for "and", "or" and "not", and a few other programmatic operators.

Given these constructs, we can use a hypergraph some of whose Atoms are labeled "variable" – such a hypergraph may be called an "h-pattern." We can also combine h-patterns using boolean operations, to get composite h-patterns. We can replicate probabilistic lambda calculus expressions explicitly in our hypergraph. And, given an h-pattern and another hypergraph H, we can ask whether P matches H, or whether P matches part of H.

To conveniently represent cognitive processes inside the hypergraph, it is convenient to include the following labels as primitives: "create Atom", "remove Atom", plus a few programmatic operations like arithmetic operations and combinators. In this case the program implementing a cognitive algorithm can be straightforwardly represented in the system hypergraph itself. (To avoid complexity, we can assume Atom immutability; i.e. make do only with Atom creation and removal, and carry out Atom modification via removal followed by creation.)

Finally, to get reflection, the state of the hypergraph at each point in time can also be considered as a hypergraph. Let us assume we have, in the rich language, labels for "time" and "atTime." We can then express, within the hypergraph itself, propositions of the form "At time 17:00 on 1/1/2017, this link existed" or "At time 12:35 on 1/1/2017, this link existed with this particular label". We can construct subhypergraphs expressing things like "If at time T an subhypergraph matching P exists, then s seconds after time T, a subhypergraph matching P_1 exists, with probability p."

The Rich Hypergraph and OpenCog. The "rich language" as outlined, is in essence a minimal version of the OpenCog AGI system[3]. OpenCog is based on a large memory hypergraph called the Atomspace, and it contains a number of cognitive processes implemented outside the Atomspace which act on the

---

[3] See http://opencog.org for current information, or [9, 10] for theoretical background.

Atomspace, alongside cognitive processes implemented inside the Atomspace. It also contains a wide variety of Atom types beyond the ones listed above as part of the rich language. However, translating the full OpenCog hypergraph and cognitive-process machinery into the rich language would be straightforward if laborious.

The main reasons for not implementing OpenCog this way now are computational efficiency and developer convenience. However, future versions of OpenCog could potentially end up operating via compiling the full OpenCog hypergraph and cognitive-process model into some variation on the rich language as described here. This would have advantages where self-programming is concerned.

3.1   Some Useful Hypergraphs

The hypergraph memory we have been discussing is in effect a whole intelligent system – save the actual sensors and actuators – embodied in a hypergraph. Let us call this hypergraph "the system" under consideration (the intelligent system). We also will want to pay some attention to a larger hypergraph we may call the "meta-system", which is created with the same formalism as the system, but contains a lot more stuff. The meta-system records a plenitude of actual and hypothetical information about the system.

We can represent states of the system within the formalism of the system itself. In essence a "state" is a proposition of the form "h-pattern P_1 is present in the system" or "h-pattern P_1 matches the system as a whole." We can also represent probabilistic (or crisp) statements about transitions between system states within the formalism of the system, using lambdas and probabilistic implications. To be useful, the meta-system will need to contain a significant amount of Atoms referring to states of the system, and probabilistically labeled transitions between these states.

The implications representing transitions between two states, may be additionally linked to Atoms indicating the proximal cause of the transition. For the purpose of modeling cognitive synergy in a simple way, we are most concerned with the case in which there is a relatively small integer number of cognitive processes, whose action reasonably often cause changes in the system's state. (We may also assume some can occur for other reasons besides the activity of cognitive processes, e.g. inputs coming into the system, or simply random changes.)

So for instance if we have two cognitive processes called Reasoning and Blending, which act on the system, then these processes each correspond to a subgraph of the meta-system hypergraph: the subgraph containing the links indicating the state transitions effected by the process in question, and the nodes joined by these links. This representation makes sense whether or not the cognitive processes are implemented within the hypergraph, or a external processes acting on the system. We may call these "CPT graphs", short for "Cognitive Process Transition hypergraphs."

4 PGMC Agents: Intelligent Agents with Cognition Driven by Probabilistic History Mining

For understanding cognitive synergy thoroughly, it is useful to dig one level deeper and model the internals of cognitive processes in a way that is finer-grained and yet still abstract and broadly applicable.

4.1 Cognitive Processes and Homomorphism

In principle cognitive processes may be very diverse in their implementation as well as their conceptual logic. The rich language as outlined above enables implementation of anything that is computable. In practice, however, it seems that the cognitive processes of interest for human-like cognition may be summarized as sets of *hypergraph rewrite rules*, of the sort formalized in [1]. Roughly, a rule of that sort has an input h-pattern and an output h-pattern, along with optional auxiliary functions that determine the numerical weights associated with the Atoms in the output h-pattern, based on combination of the numerical weights in the input h-pattern.

Rules of this nature may be, but are not required to be, homomorphisms. One conjecture we make, however, is that for the cognitive processes of interest for human-like cognition, *most* of the rules involved (if one ignores the numerical-weights auxiliary functions) are in fact either hypergraph homomorphisms, or inverses of hypergraph homomorphisms. Recall that a graph (or hypergraph) homomorphism is a composition of elementary homomorphisms, each one of which merges two nodes into a new node, in a way that the new node inherits the connections of its parents. So the conjecture is

Conjecture 1. *Most operations undertaken by cognitive processes take the form either of:*

- *Merging two nodes into a new node, which inherits its parents' links*
- *Splitting a node into two nodes, so that the children's links taken together compose the (sole) parent's links*

(and then doing some weight-updating on the product).

4.2 Operations on Cognitive Process Transition Hypergraphs

One can place a natural Heyting algebra structure on the space of hypergraphs, using the disjoint union for ⊔, the categorial (direct) product for ⊓, and a special partial order called the cost-order, described in [6]. This Heyting algebra structure then allows one to assign probabilities to hypergraphs within a larger set of hypergraphs, e.g. to sub-hypergraphs within a larger hypergraph like the system or meta-system under consideration here. As reviewed in [6], this is an intuitionistic probability distribution lacking a double negation property, but this is not especially problematic.

It is worth concretely exemplifying what these Heyting algebra operators mean in the context of CPT graphs. Suppose we have two CPT graphs A and B, representing the state transitions corresponding to two different cognitive processes.

The meet $A \sqcap B$ is a graph representing transitions between conjuncted states of the system (e.g. "System has h-pattern P445 and h-pattern P7555", etc.). If A contains a transition between P_{445} and P_{33}, and B contains a transition between P_{7555} and P_{1234}; then, $A \sqcap B$ will contain a transition between $P_{445}\&P_{7555}$ and $P_{33}\&P_{1234}$. Clearly, if A and B are independent processes, then the probability of the meet of the two graphs will be the product of the probabilities of the graphs individually

The join $A \sqcup B$ is a graph representing, side by side, the two state transition graphs – as if we had a new process $AorB$, and a state of this new process could be either a state of A, or a state of B. If A and B are disjoint processes (with no overlapping states), then the probability of the join of the two graphs, is the sum of the probabilities of the graphs individually

The exponent A^B is a graph whose nodes are functions mapping states of B into states of A. So e.g. if B is a perception process and A is an action process, each node in A^B represents a function mapping perception-states into action-states. Two such functions F and G are linked only if, whenever node $b1$ and node $b2$ are linked in B, $F(b1)$ and $G(b2)$ are linked in G. I.e. F and G are linked only if $(F, G)(link(x, y)) = link(F(x), G(y))$, where by $(F, G)(link(x, y))$ one means the set $F(x), G(y)$.

So e.g. two perception-to-action mappings F and G are adjacent in action^{perception} iff, whenever two perceptions p_1 and p_2 are adjacent, the action $a1 = F(p_1)$ is adjacent to the action $a2 = G(p_2)$. For instance, if

- $F(\text{perception } p)$ = the action of carrying out perception p
- $G(\text{perception } p)$ = the action done in reaction to seeing perception p

and

- p_1 = hearing the cat
- p_2 = looking at the cat

We then need

- $F(p_1)$ = the act of hearing the cat (cocking one?s ear etc.)
- $G(p_2)$ = the response to looking at the cat (raising ones eyes and making a startled expression)

to be adjacent in the graph of actions. If this is generally true for various (p_1, p_2) then F and G are adjacent in action^{perception}. Note that action^{perception} is also the implication perception $\rightarrow$ action, where $\rightarrow$ is the Heyting algebra implication.

Finally, according to the definition of cost-based order $A < A_1$ if A and A_1 are homomorphic, and the shortest path to creating A_1 from irreducible source graph, is to first create A. In the context of CPT graphs, for instance, this will hold if A_1 is a broader category of cognitive actions than A. If A denotes all facial expression actions, and A_1 denotes all physical actions, then we will have $A < A_1$.

4.3   PGMC: Cognitive Control with Pattern and Probability

Different cognitive processes may unfold according to quite different dynamics. However, from a general intelligence standpoint, we believe there is a common control logic that spans multiple cognitive processes – namely, adaptive control based on historically observed patterns. This process has been formalized and analyzed in a previous paper by the author [5], where it was called PGMC or "Probabilistic Growth and Mining of Combinations"; in this section we port that analysis to the context of the current formal model. This leads us to the next step in our hierarchy of agents models, a **PGMC Agent**, meaning an agent with a rich hypergraph memory, and homomorphism/history-mining based cognitive processes.

Consider the subgraph of a particular CPT graph that lies within the system at a specific point in time. The job of the cognitive control process (CCP) corresponding to a particular cognitive process, is to figure out what (if anything) that cognitive process should do next, to extend the current CPT graph. A cognitive process may have various specialized heuristics for carrying out this estimation, but the general approach we wish to consider here is one based on pattern mining from the system's history.

In accordance with our high-level formal agents model, we assume that the system has certain goals, which manifest themselves as a vector of fuzzy distributions over the states of the system. Representationally, we may assume a label "goal", and then assume that at any given time the system has n specific goals; and that, for each goal, each state may be associated with a number that indicates the degree to which it fulfills that goal.

It is quite possible that the system's dynamics may lead it to revise its own goals, to create new goals for itself, etc. However, that is not the process we wish to focus on here. For the moment we will assume there is a certain set of goals associated with the system; the point, then, is that a CCP's job is to figure out how to use the corresponding cognitive process to transition the system to states that will possess greater degrees of goal achievement.

Toward that end, the CCP may look at h-patterns in the subset of system history that is stored within the system itself. From these h-patterns, probabilistic calculations can be done to estimate the odds that a given action on the cognitive process's part, will yield a state manifesting a given amount of progress on goal achievement. In the case that a cognitive process chooses its actions stochastically, one can use the h-patterns inferred from the remembered parts of the system's history to inform a probability distribution over potential actions. Choosing cognitive actions based on the distribution implied by these h-patterns can be viewed a novel form of probabilistic programming, driven by fitness-based sampling rather than Monte Carlo sampling or optimization queries – this is the

"Probabilistic Growth and Mining of Combinations" (PGMC), process described and analyzed in [5].

Based on inference from h-patterns mined from history, a CCP can then create probabilistically weighted links from Atoms representing h-patterns in the system's current state, to Atoms representing h-patterns in potential future states. A CCP can also, optionally, create probabilistically weighted links from Atoms representing potential future state h-patterns (or present state h-patterns) to goals. It will often be valuable for these various links to be weighted with confidence values alongside probability values; or (almost) equivalently with interval (imprecise) probability values [2].

5   Conclusion

And so we have reconstructed the core concepts of the OpenCog platform and PrimeAGI architecture, via building up step by step from a simple reinforcement learning agent. One could proceed similarly for other complex cognitive architectures. The hope is that this sort of connection can help guide the extension of formal analyses of AGI in the direction of practical system architecture.

References

1. Baget, J.F., Mugnier, M.L.: Extensions of simple conceptual graphs: the complexity of rules and constraints. J. Artif. Intell. Res. **16**, 425–465 (2002)
2. Goertzel, B., Ikle, M., Goertzel, I., Heljakka, A.: Probabilistic Logic Networks. Springer, Heidelberg (2008)
3. Goertzel, B.: Chaotic Logic. Plenum, New York (1994)
4. Goertzel, B.: Toward a formal definition of real-world general intelligence. In: Proceedings of AGI 2010 (2010)
5. Goertzel, B.: Probabilistic growth and mining of combinations: a unifying meta-algorithm for practical general intelligence. In: Steunebrink, B., Wang, P., Goertzel, B. (eds.) AGI -2016. LNCS, vol. 9782, pp. 344–353. Springer, Cham (2016). doi:10.1007/978-3-319-41649-6_35
6. Goertzel, B.: Cost-based intuitionist probabilities on spaces of graphs, hypergraphs and theorems (2017)
7. Goertzel, B.: Toward a formal model of cognitive synergy. In: Proceedings of AGI 2017. Springer, Cham (2017, submitted)
8. Goertzel, B.: Toward a formal model of cognitive synergy (2017). https://arxiv.org/abs/1703.04361
9. Goertzel, B., Pennachin, C., Geisweiller, N.: Engineering General Intelligence, Part 1: A Path to Advanced AGI via Embodied Learning and Cognitive Synergy. Atlantis Thinking Machines, New York (2013). Springer
10. Goertzel, B., Pennachin, C., Geisweiller, N.: Engineering General Intelligence, Part 2: The CogPrime Architecture for Integrative, Embodied AGI. Atlantis Thinking Machines, New York (2013). Springer
11. Hutter, M.: Universal Artificial Intelligence: Sequential Decisions based on Algorithmic Probability. Springer, Heidelberg (2005)
12. Legg, S.: Machine super intelligence. Ph.D. thesis, University of Lugano (2008)

A Formal Model of Cognitive Synergy

Ben Goertzel[(⊠)]

OpenCog Foundation, Sha Tin, Hong Kong
ben@goertzel.org

Abstract. "Cognitive synergy"– a dynamic in which multiple cognitive processes, cooperating to control the same cognitive system, assist each other in overcoming bottlenecks encountered during their internal processing. – has been posited as a key feature of real-world general intelligence, and has been used explicitly in the design of the OpenCog cognitive architecture. Here category theory and related concepts are used to give a formalization of the cognitive synergy concept. Cognitive synergy is proposed to correspond to a certain inequality regarding the relative costs of different paths through certain commutation diagrams. Applications of this notion of cognitive synergy to particular cognitive phenomena, and specific cognitive processes in the PrimeAGI design, are discussed.

1 Introduction

In [4] one possible general principle of computationally feasible general intelligence was proposed – the principle of "cognitive synergy." The basic concept of cognitive synergy, as presented there, is that general intelligences must contain different knowledge creation mechanisms corresponding to different sorts of memory (declarative, procedural, sensory/episodic, attentional, intentional); and that these different mechanisms must be interconnected in such a way as to aid each other in overcoming memory-type-specific combinatorial explosions.

In this paper, cognitive synergy is revisited and given a more formal description in the language of category theory. This formalization is a presented both for the conceptual clarification it offers, and as a hopeful step toward proving interesting theorems about the relationship between cognitive synergy and general intelligence, and evaluating the degree of cognitive synergy enabled by existing or future concrete AGI designs. The relation of the formal notion of cognitive synergy presented to the OpenCog/PrimeAGI design developed by the author and colleagues [4,5] is discussed in moderate detail, but this is only one among many possible examples; the general ideas proposed here should be applicable to a broad variety of AGI designs.

This paper relies on concepts and terms introduced in the prequel paper [2], which outlines a series of formal models of generally intelligent agents.[1]

---

[1] The preprint [3] contains the present paper and the sequel, plus a bit of additional material.

© Springer International Publishing AG 2017
T. Everitt et al. (Eds.): AGI 2017, LNAI 10414, pp. 13–22, 2017.
DOI: 10.1007/978-3-319-63703-7_2

2 Theory of Stuckness

In the **PGMC Agent** model introduced in [2], one has a collection of Cognitive Control Processes (CCPs) working together to update a representational hypergraph, and guiding their cognitive activities via probabilistic pattern mining of prior cognitive activities on the hypergraph. Within this framework, we now introduce a series of concepts that will allow us to formalize what it means for a group of CCPs to interact synergetically.

In a real-world cognitive system, each CCP will have a certain limited amount of resources, which it can either use for its own activity, or transfer to another cognitive process. In OpenCog, for instance, space and time resources tend to be managed somewhat separately, which would mean that a pair of floats would be a reasonable representation of an amount of resources. For our current theoretical purposes, however, the details of the resource representation don't matter much.

Let us say that a CCP, at a certain point in time, is "stuck" if it does not see any high-confidence, high-probability transitions associated with its own corresponding cognitive process, from current state h-patterns to future state h-patterns that have significantly higher goal-achievement values. If a CCP is stuck, then it may not be worthwhile for the CCP to spend its limited resources taking any action at that point. Or, in some cases, it may be the best move for that CCP to transfer some of its allocated resources so some other cognitive process. This leads us straight on to cognitive synergy. But before we go there, let us pause to get more precise about how "getting stuck" should be interpreted in this context.

A Formal Definition of Stuckness. Let G_A denote the CPT graph corresponding to cognitive process A. This is a subgraph of the overall cognitive process transition graph of the system, and it may be considered as a category unto itself, with object being the subgraphs, and a Heyting algebra structure.

Given a particular situation S ("possible world") involving the system's cognition, and a time interval I, let e.g. $G_A^{S,I}$ denote the CPT graph of A during time interval I, insofar as it exists explicitly in the system (not just in the metasystem).

Where P is a h-pattern in the system, and (S, I) is a situation/time-interval pair, let $P(S, I)$ denote the degree to which the system displays h-pattern P in situation S during time-interval I. Let $g(S, I)$ denote the average degree of goal-achievement of the system in situation S at time during time interval I. Then if we identify a set $\mathcal{I}$ of time-intervals of interest, we can calculate

$$g(P) = \frac{\sum_{(S,I), I \in \mathcal{I}} g(S, I) P(S, I)}{\sum_{(S,I), I \in \mathcal{I}} P(S, I)}$$

to be the degree to which P implies goal-achievement, in general (relative to $\mathcal{I}$; but if this set of intervals is chosen reasonably, this dependency should not be sensitive).

On the other hand, it is more interesting to look at the degree to which P implies goal-achievement across the possible futures of the system as relevant in a particular situation at a particular point in time. Suppose the system is currently in situation S, during time interval I_S. Then $\mathcal{I}$ may be defined, for instance, as a set of time intervals in the near future after I_S. One can then look at

$$g_{S,I_S,\mathcal{I}}(P) = \frac{\sum_{(S',I),I\in\mathcal{I}} g(S',I)P(S',I)Prob((S',I)|(S,t))}{\sum_{(S',I),I\in\mathcal{I}} P(S',I)Prob((S',I)|(S,t))}$$

which measures the degree to which P implies goal-achievement in situations that may occur in the near future after being in situation S. The confidence of this value may be assessed as

$$c_{S,I_S,\mathcal{I}}(P) = f\left(\sum_{(S',I),I\in\mathcal{I}} P(S',I)Prob((S',I)|(S,t)) \right)$$

where f is a monotone increasing function with range $[0,1]$. This confidence value is a measure of the amount of evidence on which the estimate $g_{S',I_S}(P)$ is based, scaled into $[0,1]$.

Finally, we may define $e_{C,I_R,S,I_S}(P,I,I_P)$ as the probability estimate that the CCP corresponding to cognitive process C holds for the proposition that: In situation S during time interval I_S, if allocated a resource amount in interval I_R for making the choice, C will make a choice leading to a situation in which $P(S,I) \in I_P$ during interval I (assuming I is after I_S). A confidence value $c_{C,I_R,S,I_S}(P,I,I_P)$ may be defined similarly to $c_{S',t}(P)$ above.

Given a set $\mathcal{I}$ of time intervals, one can define $e_{C,I_R,S,\mathcal{I}}(P,I,I_P)$ and $c_{C,I_R,S,\mathcal{I}}(P,I,I_P)$ via averaging over the intervals in $\mathcal{I}$.

The confidence with which C knows how to move forward toward the system's goals in situation S at time t may then be summarized as

$$\text{conf}_{C,S,I_S,\mathcal{I}} = max_P\left(g_{S',I_S,\mathcal{I}}(P)c_{S',I_S,\mathcal{I}}(P)e_{C,I_R,S,\mathcal{I}}(P,I,I_P)c_{C,I_R,S,\mathcal{I}}(P,I,I_P)\right)$$

with

$$\text{stuck}_{C,S,I_S,\mathcal{I}} = 1 - \text{conf}_{C,S,I_S,\mathcal{I}}$$

3   Cognitive Synergy: A Formal Exploration

What we need for "cognitive synergy" between A and B to exist, is for it to be the case that: For many situations S and times t, exactly one of A and B is stuck.

In the metasystem, records of cases where one or both of A or B were stuck, will be recorded as hypergraph patterns. The set of (S,t) pairs in the metasystem where exactly one of A and B was stuck to a degree of stuckness in interval $I_d = (L,U)$, has a certain probability in the set of all (S,t) pairs in the metasystem. Let us call this set stuck_{A,B,I_d}.

The set $G^{\text{stuck}}_{A,B,I_d}$ of CPT graphs $G_A^{S,t}$, $G_B^{S,t}$ corresponding to the (S,t) pairs in stuck_{A,B,I_d} can also be isolated in the metasystem, and has a certain probability considered as a subgraph of the metasystem (which can be calculated according to the intuitionistic graph probability distribution). An overall index of cognitive synergy between A and B can then be calculated as follows.

Let $\mathcal{P}$ be a partition of $[0, 1]$ (most naturally taken equispaced). Then,

$$\text{cog-syn}_{A,B,\mathcal{P}} = \frac{\sum_{I_d \in \mathcal{P}} w_{I_d} Prob(G^{\text{stuck}}_{A,B,I_d})}{\sum_{I \in \mathcal{P}} w_{I_d}}$$

is a quantitative measure of the amount of cognitive synergy between A and B.

Extension of the above definition to more than two cognitive processes is straightforward. Given N cognitive processes, we can look at pairwise synergies between them, and also at triple-wise synergies, etc. To define triplewise synergies, we can look at stuck$_{A,B,C,I_d}$, defined as the set of (S, I) where all but one of the three cognitive processes A, B and C is stuck to a degree in I_d. Triplewise synergies correspond to cases where the system would be stuck if it had only two of the three cognitive processes, much more often than it's stuck given that it has all three of them.

This may seem a somehow anticlimactic formalization of such an exciting-sounding quality as "cognitive synergy." However, exciting higher-level emergent phenomena often occur as a result of more prosaic-looking lower-level interactions. Mutual exclusion regarding where two cognitive processes get stuck, at the micro-level of very small cognitive steps, is what enables the two cognitive processes to work together creatively (including helping each other become unstuck) at the meso-level of slightly bigger cognitive steps.

3.1   Cognitive Synergy and Homomorphisms

The existence of cognitive synergy between two cognitive processes will depend sensitively on how these cognitive processes actually work. However, there are likely some general principles at play here. For instance we suggest

Conjecture 1. *In a PGMC agent operating within feasible resource constraints: If two cognitive processes A and B have a high degree of cognitive synergy between them, then there will tend to be a lot of low-cost homomorphisms between subgraphs of $G^{S,t}_A$ and $G^{S,t}_B$, but **not** nearly so many low-cost isomorphisms.*

The intuition here is that, if the two CPT graphs are too close to isomorphic, then they are unlikely to offer many advantages compared to each other. They will probably succeed and fail in the same situations. On the other hand, if the two CPT graphs don't have some resemblance to each other, then often when one cognitive process (say, A) gets stuck, the other one (say, B) won't be able to use the information produced by A during its work so far, and thus won't be able to proceed efficiently. Productive synergy happens when one has two processes, each of which can transform the other one's intermediate results, at somewhat low cost, into its own internal language – but where the internal languages of the two processes are not identical.

Our intuition is that a variety of interesting rigorous theorems likely exist in the vicinity of this informal conjecture. However, much more investigation is required.

Along these lines, recall Conjecture 1 above that most cognitive processes useful for human-like cognition, are implemented in terms of rules that are mostly homomorphisms or inverse homomorphisms. To the extent this is the case, it fits together very naturally with Conjecture 1.

Suppose $G_A^{S,t}$ and $G_B^{S,t}$ each consist largely of records of enacting a series of hypergraph homomorphisms (followed by weight updates), as Conjecture 1 posits. Then one way Conjecture 2 would happen would be if the homomorphisms in $G_A^{S,t}$ mapped homomorphically into the homomorphisms in $G_B^{S,t}$. That is, if we viewed $G_A^{S,t}$ and $G_B^{S,t}$ as their own categories, the homomorphisms posited in Conjecture 2 would take the form of functors between these two categories.

3.2   Cognitive Synergy and Natural Transformations

Further interesting twists emerge if one views the cognitive process A as associated with a functor F_A that maps G^S into $G_A^S \subseteq G^S$, which has the property that it maps $G^{S,t}$ into $G_A^{S,t} \subseteq G^{S,t}$ as well. The functor F_A maps a state transition subgraph of S, into a state transition subgraph involving only transitions effected by cognitive process A. So for instance, if X represents a sequence of cognitive operations and conclusions that have transformed the state of the system, then $F_A(X)$ represents the closest match to X in which all the cognitive operations involved are done by cognitive process A. The cost of $F_A(X)$ may be much higher than the cost of X, e.g. if X involves vision processing and A is logical inference, then in $F(X)$ all the transitions involved in vision processing need to be effected by logical operations, which is going to be much more expensive than doing them in other ways.

A natural transformation $\eta^{A,B}$ from F_A to F_B associates to every object X in G^S (i.e., to every subgraph of the transition graph G^S of the system S) a morphism $\eta_X^{A,B} : F_A(X) \to F_B(X)$ in G^S so that: for every morphism $f : X \to Y$ in G^S (i.e. every homomorphic transformation from state transition subgraph X to state transition subgraph Y) we have $\eta_Y^{A,B} \circ F_A(f) = F_B(f) \circ \eta_X^{A,B}$.

This leads us on to our final theoretical conjecture:

Conjecture 2. *In a PGMC agent operating within feasible resource constraints, suppose one has two cognitive processes A and B, which display significant cognitive synergy, as defined above. Then,*

1. *there is likely to be a natural transformation $\eta^{A,B}$ between the functor F_A and the functor F_B – and also a natural transformation $\eta^{B,A}$ going in the opposite direction*

2. *the two different routes from the upper left to the bottom right of the commu-*
   tation diagram corresponding to $\eta^{A,B}$,

$$
\begin{array}{ccc}
F_A(X) & \xrightarrow{F_A(f)} & F_A(Y) \\
\downarrow{\eta_X^{A,B}} & & \downarrow{\eta_Y^{A,B}} \\
F_B(X) & \xrightarrow[F_B(f)]{} & F_B(Y)
\end{array}
\tag{1}
$$

   will often have quite different total costs
3. *Referring to the above commutation diagram and the corresponding diagram*
   for $\eta^{B,A}$,

$$
\begin{array}{ccc}
F_B(X) & \xrightarrow{F_B(f)} & F_B(Y) \\
\downarrow{\eta_X^{B,A}} & & \downarrow{\eta_Y^{B,A}} \\
F_A(X) & \xrightarrow[F_A(f)]{} & F_A(Y)
\end{array}
\tag{2}
$$

   – *often it will involve significantly less total cost to*
   – *travel from* $F_A(X)$ *to* $F_B(Y)$ *via the left-bottom path in Eq. 2, and then*
   from $F_B(Y)$ *to* $F_A(Y)$ *via the right side of Eq. 2; than to*
   – *travel from* $F_A(X)$ *to* $F_A(Y)$ *directly via the top of Eq. 2*
   That is, often it will be the case that

$$
\begin{aligned}
& cost(F_A(X) \xrightarrow{\eta_X^{A,B}} F_B(X)) + cost(F_B(X) \xrightarrow{F_B(f)} F_B(Y)) \\
& + cost(F_B(Y) \xrightarrow{\eta_Y^{B,A}} F_A(Y)) < cost(F_A(X) \xrightarrow{F_A(f)} F_A(Y))
\end{aligned}
\tag{3}
$$

Inequality (3) basically says that, given the cost weightings of the arrows, it may sometimes be significantly more efficient to get from $F_A(X)$ to $F_A(Y)$ via an indirect route involving cognitive process B, than to go directly from $F_A(X)$ to $F_A(Y)$ using only cognitive process A. This is a fairly direct expression of the cognitive synergy between A and B in terms of commutation diagrams.

To make this a little more concrete, suppose X is a transition graph including the new conclusion that Bob is nice, and Y is a transition graph including additionally the even newer conclusion that Bob is helpful. Then f represents a homomorphism mapping X into Y, via – in one way or another – adding to the system's memory the conclusion that Bob is helpful. Suppose A is a cognitive process called "inference" and B is one called "evolutionary learning." Then e.g. $F_A(X)$ refers to a version of X in which all conclusions are drawn by inference, and $F_B(Y)$ refers to a version of Y in which all conclusions are drawn by evolutionary learning. The commutation diagram for $\eta^{A,B} = \eta^{\text{inference,evolution}}$, then looks like

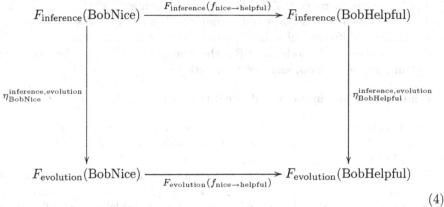

$$(4)$$

and the commutation diagram for $\eta^{\text{evolution,inference}}$ looks like

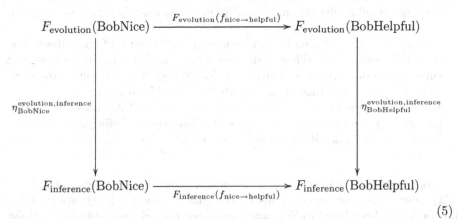

$$(5)$$

The conjecture states that, for cognitive synergy to occur, the cost of getting from $F_{\text{inference}}(\text{BobNice})$ to $F_{\text{inference}}(\text{BobHelpful})$ directly via the top arrow of Eq. 4 would be larger than the cost of getting there via the left and then bottom of Eq. 4 followed by the right of Eq. 5. That is to get from "Bob is nice" to "Bob is helpful", where both are represented in inferential terms, it may still be lower-cost to map "Bob is nice" into evolutionary-programming terms, then use evolutionary programming to get to the evolutionary-programming version of "Bob is helpful", and then map the answer back into inferential terms.

4   Some Core Synergies of Cognitive Systems: Consciousness, Selves and Others

The paradigm case of cognitive synergy is where the cognitive processes A and B involved are learning, reasoning or pattern recognition algorithms. However, it is also interesting and important to consider cases where the cognitive processes involved correspond to different scales of processing, or different types of subsystem of the same cognitive system. For instance, one can think about:

- A = long-term memory (LTM), B = working memory (WM)
- A = whole-system structures and dynamics, B = the system's self-model
- A and B are different"sub-selves" of the same cognitive system
- A is the system's self-model, and B is the system's model of another cognitive system (another person, another robot, etc.)

Conjecturally and intuitively, it is natural to hypothesize that

- Homomorphisms between LTM and WM are what ensure that ideas can be moved back and forth from one sort of memory to another, with a loss of detail but not a total loss of essential structure
- Homomorphisms between the whole system's structures and dynamics (as represented in its overall state transition graph) and the structures and dynamics in its self-model, are what make the self-model structurally reflective of the whole system, enabling cognitive dynamics on the self-model to be mapped meaningfully (i.e. morphically) into cognitive dynamics in the whole system, and vice versa
- Homomorphisms between the whole system in the view of one subself, and the whole system in the view of an other subself, are what enable two different subselves to operate somewhat harmoniously together, controlling the same overall system and utilizing the knowledge gained by one another
- Homomorphisms between the system's self-model and its model of another cognitive system, enable both theory-of-mind type modeling of others, and learning about oneself by analogy to others (critical for early childhood learning)

Cognitive synergy in the form of natural transformations between LTM and WM means that when unconscious LTM cognitive processing gets stuck, it can push relevant knowledge to WM and sometimes the solution will pop up there. Correspondingly, when WM gets stuck, it can throw the problem to the unconscious LTM processing, and hope the answer is found there, later to bubble up into WM again (the throwing down being according to a homomorphic mapping, and the bubbling up being according to another homomorphic mapping). As WM is closely allied with what is colloquially referred to as "consciousness" [1] – meaning the reflective, deliberative consciousness that we experience when we reason or reflect on something in our "mind's eye" – this particular synergy appears key to human conscious experience. As we move thoughts, ideas and feelings back and forth between our focus of attention and the remainder of our mind and memory, we are experiencing this synergy intensively on an everyday basis – or so the present hypothesis suggests; i.e. that

- When we pull a memory into attention, or push something out of attention into the "unconscious", we are enacting homomorphisms on our mind's state transition graph.
- When the unconscious solves a problem that the focus of attention pushed into it, and then the answer comes back into the attentional focus and gets

deliberatively reasoned on more, this is the action of the natural transformation between unconscious and conscious cognitive processes – it's a case where the cost of going the long way around the commutation diagram from conscious to unconscious and back, was lower than the cost of going directly from conscious premise to conscious conclusion.

Cognitive synergy in the form of natural transformations between system and self mean that when the system as a whole cannot figure out how to do something, it will map this thing into the self-model (via a many-to-one homomorphism, generally, as the capacity of the self-model is much smaller), and see if cognitive processes acting therein can solve the problem. Similarly, if thinking in terms of the self-model doesn't resolve a solution to the problem, then sometimes "just doing it" is the right approach – which means mapping the problem the self-model's associated cognitive processes are trying to solve back to the whole system, and letting the whole system try its mapped version of the problem by any means it can find.

Cognitive synergy in the form of natural transformations between subselves means that when one subself gets stuck, it may map the problem into the cognitive vernacular of another subself and see what the latter can do. For instance if one subself, which is very aggressive and pushy, gets stuck in a personal relationship issue, it may map this issue into the world-view of another more agreeable and empathic and submissive subself, and see if the latter can find a solution to the problem. Many people navigate complex social situations via this sort of ongoing switching back and forth between subselves that are well adapted to different sorts of situations [6].

Cognitive synergy in the form of natural transformations between self-model and other-model means that when one get stuck in a self-decision, one can implicitly ask "what would I do if I were this other mind?"..."what would this other mind do in this situation?" It also means that, when one can't figure out what another mind is going to do via other routes, one can map the other mind's situation back into one's self-model, and ask "what would I do in their situation?"..."what would it be like to be that other mind in this situation?"

In all these cases, we can see the possibility of much the same sort of process as we conjecture to exist between two cognitive processes like evolutionary learning and logical inference. We have different structures (memory subsystems, models of various internal or external systems, systematic complexes of knowledge and behavior, etc.) associated with different habitual sets of cognitive processes. Each of these habitual sets of processes may get stuck sometimes, and may need to call out to others for help in getting unstuck. This sort of request for help is going to be most feasible if the problem can be mapped into the cognitive world of the helper in a way that preserves its essential structure, even if not all its details; and if the answer the helper finds is then mapped back in a similarly structure-preserving way.

Real-world cognitive systems appear to consist of multiple subsystems that are each more effective at solving certain classes of problems – subsystems like particular learning and reasoning processes, models of self and other, memory systems of differing capacity, etc. A key aspect of effective cognition is the ability for these various subsystems to ask each other for help in very granular ways, so that the helper can understand something of the intermediate state of partial-solution that the requestor has found itself in. This sort of "cognitive synergy" seems to be reflected, in an abstract sense, in certain "algebraic" or category-theoretic symmetries such as we have highlighted here.

References

1. Goertzel, B.: Characterizing human-like consciousness: an integrative approach. Procedia Comput. Sci. **41**, 152–157 (2014)
2. Goertzel, B.: From abstract agents models to real-world AGI architectures: bridging the gap. In: Proceedings of AGI 2017. Springer, Heidelberg (2017, submitted)
3. Goertzel, B.: Toward a formal model of cognitive synergy (2017). https://arxiv.org/abs/1703.04361
4. Goertzel, B., Pennachin, C., Geisweiller, N.: Engineering General Intelligence, Part 1: A Path to Advanced AGI via Embodied Learning and Cognitive Synergy. Atlantis Thinking Machines, New York (2013). Springer
5. Goertzel, B., Pennachin, C., Geisweiller, N.: Engineering General Intelligence, Part 2: The CogPrime Architecture for Integrative, Embodied AGI. Atlantis Thinking Machines, New York (2013). Springer
6. Rowan, J.: Subpersonalities: The People Inside Us. Routledge Press, New York (1990)

Generic Animats

Claes Strannegård[1,2(✉)], Nils Svangård[3], Joscha Bach[4], and Bas Steunebrink[5]

[1] Department of Computer Science and Engineering,
Chalmers University of Technology, Gothenburg, Sweden
`claes.strannegard@chalmers.se`
[2] Department of Philosophy, Linguistics and Theory of Science,
University of Gothenburg, Gothenburg, Sweden
[3] Department of Applied Information Technology,
University of Gothenburg, Gothenburg, Sweden
`nils.svangard@gu.se`
[4] Evolutionary Dynamics, Harvard University, Cambridge, USA
`joscha@bach.ai`
[5] NNAISENSE, Lugano, Switzerland
`bas@nnaisense.com`

Abstract. We present a computational model for artificial animals (animats) living in block worlds, e.g. in Minecraft. Each animat has its individual sets of needs, sensors, and motors. It also has a memory structure that undergoes continuous development and constitutes the basis for decision-making. The mechanisms for learning and decision-making are generic in the sense that they are the same for all animats. The goal of the decision-making is always the same: to keep the needs as satisfied as possible for as long as possible. All learning is driven by surprise relating to need satisfaction. The learning mechanisms are of two kinds: (i) structural learning that adds nodes and connections to the memory structure; (ii) a local version of multi-objective Q-learning. The animats are autonomous and capable of adaptation to arbitrary block worlds without any need for seed knowledge.

Keywords: Autonomous agent · Dynamic graph · Multi-objective reinforcement learning · Structural learning · Need satisfaction

According to the South African physicist Pieter Jacobus van Heerden [20]:

> Intelligent behavior is to be repeatedly successful at satisfying one's psychological needs in diverse, observably different, situations on the basis of past experience.

Interpreted broadly, this characterization takes physiological, social, and cognitive needs into account - along with the body, since the body plays a central role in satisfying one's needs. It also applies to all animal species, not just humans. Moreover, it does not rely on human judgement as in the Turing test; or on human artifacts, as in standard IQ tests.

© Springer International Publishing AG 2017
T. Everitt et al. (Eds.): AGI 2017, LNAI 10414, pp. 23–32, 2017.
DOI: 10.1007/978-3-319-63703-7_3

In artificial intelligence, deep Q-learning has seen great success in recent years [9,14]. One of the most prominent examples in the direction of general intelligence is the generic Atari-game player that learned to play 31 Atari games at super-human level [10]. For a discussion of some theoretical problems associated with deep Q-learning, see [19].

Graph structures that develop gradually have been used in finite automaton learning [2], cascade correlation networks [6], and deep network cascades [1].

This paper is about artificial animals (animats). These models have mainly been studied in the field of artificial life [18]. Section 1 describes our strategy for general intelligence. Section 2 describes our computational model. Section 3 presents the prototype implementation *Generic Animat* along with two examples illustrating the advantage of structural learning. Section 4 draws some conclusions.

The proposed computational model is partly a continuation of our previous work [4,12,16]. The mechanisms for local Q-learning and structural learning are novel as far as we know.

1 Strategy

Our approach to general intelligence is based on the idea that radically different nervous systems can be formed by the same underlying biological mechanisms, starting with different bodies and experiencing different sensory data. We model the following generic mechanisms for learning and decision-making, which are ubiquitous in the animal kingdom:

1. Decision-making that aims for the satisfaction of multiple physiological needs [13].
2. Reinforcement learning that strengthens/weakens behavior associated with reward/punishment [11].
3. Hebbian learning, captured in the popular phrase "cells that fire together, wire together" [3].
4. Sequence learning, which is Hebbian learning with signal delay taken into account [5].

In our model an animat may be defined by specifying its sets of needs, sensors, and motors. The animat then develops automatically by means of computational versions of the above-mentioned generic mechanisms for learning and decision-making.

To model the environments of the animats, we use the Minecraft computer game environment [8], putting the animats into the bodies of Minecraft animals such as sheep, rabbits, and wolves. Then we can study the animats as they strive to satisfy their needs, e.g. for company, grass, and drinking water.

2 Computational Model

This section presents the components of the computational model.

2.1   Worlds

Definition 1. *A* world *is a set of blocks. A* block *consists of:*

- *A block type (a natural number).*
- *A block position (a point in three-dimensional space $\mathbb{Z}^3$).*

2.2   Dynamic Graphs

To model memory structures of animats, we use labeled graphs extended with support for multi-objective reinforcement learning. The nodes of the graphs can be identified with formulas of temporal logic [7]. In particular we use the binary modal operator SEQ that enables the construction of sequences. The formula p SEQ q is true at time t if p is true at $t - 1$ and q is true at t.

Definition 2. *A* dynamic graph *consists of:*

- *A set of* nodes *labeled SENSOR, STATUS, MOTOR, AND, OR, NOT, SEQ, or ACTION and optionally given a name.*
- *A set of* arrows, *i.e. a binary relation on the nodes. Arrows pointing to ACTION-nodes are labeled with local Q-values and R-values, as will be explained in Subsect. 2.6.*

Figure 1 shows a dynamic graph.

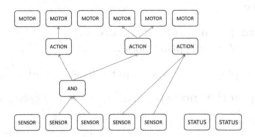

Fig. 1. An example of a dynamic graph with some annotation on the arrows omitted. Note that ACTION nodes may be connected to 0, 1, 2, or more MOTOR nodes. The ACTION node that is not connected to any MOTOR node represents passivity.

2.3   Activity

Definition 3. *An* activity *of dynamic graph G is an assignment of values in $[0, 1]$ to the nodes of G, subject to the restriction that non-STATUS nodes must be assigned values in $\{0, 1\}$.*

Figure 2 shows an activity. Time is modeled in discrete time steps or *ticks*. Input activity is transmitted from the environment to the SENSOR and STATUS nodes. Activity propagates to the other nodes as expected, except in the case of the ACTION nodes. The activity of ACTION nodes is determined by the policy given in Definition 12.

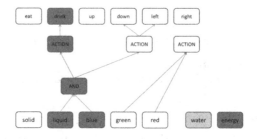

Fig. 2. An example of an activity pattern on a graph. This is the same graph as in Fig. 1, but with the optional node names displayed. Color represents activity 1; no color represents activity 0. The color shades on the STATUS nodes reflect their input values. (Color figure online)

2.4 Animats

Definition 4. *An* animat *consists of:*

- *A dynamic graph G.*
- *An activity of G.*
- *A position: a point in the space $\mathbb{Z}^3$.*

2.5 Top Activity

Definition 5 (Perception nodes). *A node labeled SENSOR, AND, OR, NOT, or SEQ is called a* perception node.

The following notion plays a key role in both decision-making and learning:

Definition 6 (Top-active node). *Node $b \in G$ is top active at time t if:*

- *b is a perception node.*
- *b is active at t.*
- *There is no blue arrow that starts in b and ends in some other perception node b' that is also active at t.*

We use the notation $TA(t)$ for the set of top active nodes at t.

Figure 2 offers an example, where the red AND node is the only top-active node. In general, many nodes can be top-active at the same time. Intuitively, the top-active nodes together constitute a description of the present situation in terms of the given memory structure, at the maximum possible level of detail.

2.6 Local Q-learning

We use a local variant of Q-learning for our generic learning and decision-making mechanism [17]. Since the animat has multiple needs to take into account in the general case, we work within the Multi-Objective Reinforcement Learning framework [13].

Definition 7 (Status). *The* status *of the STATUS node i of the animat A at time t, $x_{i,t}$, is defined as the input to i at t.*

An animat with STATUS nodes water and energy could have $x_{water,t} = 0.8$ and $x_{energy,t} = 0.6$. The following measure reflects the overall well-being of an animat at a given moment.

Definition 8 (Vitalit). *The* vitality *of the animat A at time t is defined as*

$$\min_{i \in STATUS} x_{i,t}.$$

An animat with $x_{water,t} = 0.8$ and $x_{energy,t} = 0.6$ has vitality 0.6 at t. If the vitality reaches 0, we say that the animat *dies*. The learning and decision-making mechanisms of the generic animat were designed with long-term vitality as the one and only goal.

Definition 9 (Rewards). *The* reward *of the animat A at time $t + 1$ with respect to the STATUS node i is defined as $r_{i,t+1} = x_{i,t+1} - x_{i,t}$.*

Definition 10 (Reliability). *The* reliability *of the finite data set D is defined as $Rel(D) = 1/(SD(D) + 1)$. Here SD is the standard deviation.*

We write a_t for the action that is performed at time t. Now we shall define the *local Q-values* $Q_{i,t}(b, a)$ and the *local reliability values* $R_{i,t}(b, a)$.

Definition 11 (Q-values and R-values). *At $t = 0$ we proceed as follows. Let*

$$Q_{i,0}(b, a) = 0 \text{ and } R_{i,0}(b, a) = 1$$

for all perception nodes b, ACTION nodes a, and STATUS nodes i.
At $t + 1$ we proceed as follows. If $b \notin TA(t)$ or $a \neq a_t$, then we let $Q_{i,t+1}(b, a) = Q_{i,t}(b, a)$. If $b \in TA(t)$, then we let $Q_{i,t+1}(b, a_t) = Q_{i,t}(b, a_t) + \alpha \cdot \Delta$, where

$$\Delta = r_{i,t+1} + \gamma \cdot \max_{a \in Actions} \left[\frac{\sum_{b' \in TA(t+1)} Q_{i,t}(b', a) \cdot R_{i,t}(b', a)}{\sum_{b' \in TA(t+1)} R_{i,t}(b', a)} \right] - Q_{i,t}(b, a_t).$$

Here α and γ are parameters for learning rate and discount rate, respectively. Also let

$$R_{i,t+1}(b, a) = Rel(\{Q_{i,t'}(b, a) : t' \leq t + 1, a = a_{t'} \text{ and } b \in TA(t')\}).$$

Definition 12 (Policy). *Fix a real number λ and let*

$$\pi(t) = \underset{a \in Actions}{\text{argmax}} \left[\min_{i \in STATUS} x_{i,t} + \lambda \cdot \frac{\sum_{b \in TA(t)} Q_{i,t}(b, a) \cdot R_{i,t}(b, a)}{\sum_{b \in TA(t)} R_{i,t}(b, a))} \right].$$

The policy selects actions aimed at keeping the vitality of the animat as high as possible, for as long as possible. It weighs up the animat's present status with expected status changes in the future. These expectations are in turn weighted by their estimated reliability. An animat with the two needs energy and water will be likelier to drink if water is its most urgent need. On the other hand, if its experience indicates that it would lose large quantities of energy by doing so, it might nevertheless refrain.

The decision-making algorithm is ε-greedy, where $\varepsilon \in [0, 1]$. With probability ε it explores by activating a random set of MOTOR nodes (with higher probability for smaller sets) and with probability $1 - \varepsilon$ it exploits by following the policy $\pi(t)$.

2.7   Structural Learning

Definition 13 (Surprise). *The* surprise *of a perception node b at time $t + 1$ w.r.t. the STATUS node i is defined as follows:*

$$z_{i,t+1}(b) = |Q_{i,t+1}(b, a_t) - Q_{i,t}(b, a_t)|$$

Definition 14 (Surprised). *An animat is* surprised *at time $t+1$ if $z_{i,t+1}(b) > Z$, for some STATUS node i and perception node b such that $R_{i,t}(b, a) > R$. Here Z and R are parameters regulating concept formation.*

When the animat is surprised, a new node will be added to the graph. The surprise indicates that the animat needs a more fine-grained ontology to be able to identify similar situations in the future.

Definition 15 (Node candidate). *A* node candidate *is an expression of the form*

– *b AND b', where $b, b' \in G$ are perception nodes and b AND $b' \notin G$, or*
– *b SEQ b', where $b, b' \in G$ are perception nodes and b SEQ $b' \notin G$.*

The node candidates do not belong to the graph, but they have local Q-values and R-values that are initiated and updated just like the local values of the perception nodes of the graph.

Suppose the animat gets surprised at $t + 1$. Then the learning algorithm will consider the possibility of adding a new node. Let i be a randomly selected STATUS node subject to surprise at $t + 1$.

First, the algorithm explores the benefit of adding an AND node. To that end it searches for a node candidate b AND b' such that (i) both b and b' were top-active at t, and (ii) the prediction error

$$|Q_{i,t+1}(b \ AND \ b', a_t) - Q_{i,t}(b \ AND \ b', a_t)|$$

is minimal. If this prediction error is sufficiently small, the node b AND b' is added to the graph.

Second, if no AND node is added, the algorithm proceeds by exploring the benefit of adding a SEQ node. To that end it searches for a node candidate b SEQ b' such that (i) b was top-active at $t - 1$, (ii) b was top-active at t, and (iii) the prediction error

$$|Q_{i,t+1}(b \ SEQ \ b', a_t) - Q_{i,t}(b \ SEQ \ b', a_t)|$$

is minimal. If this prediction error is sufficiently small, the node b SEQ b' is added to the graph. Whenever a new node is added to the graph, new node candidates are formed (by Definition 15).

3   Results

We have implemented the prototype system *Generic Animat*, which is available at https://github.com/nils/animats. The system is a simplification of the model described in the precious section and it is integrated with Minecraft via the Malmo interface [8]. To measure the performance of an animat in a given world, we study how its vitality develops over time. Cf. the quote by van Heerden at the beginning of the paper.

   We shall give two minimalist examples showing that the ability to form new concepts can make the difference between life and death. In both examples the *Generic Animat* controls a sheep animat that needs to drink and graze to survive.

3.1   Learning Spatial Patterns

In this example we show the usefulness of adding AND nodes. The sheep animat lives in the world shown in Fig. 3. Figure 4 shows its memory development and Fig. 5 shows how its vitality develops over time.

Fig. 3. The Grass block is green and represents grass that is good to eat and the Water block is blue and represents water that is good to drink. The Swamp block is turquoise (blue and green) and represents a swamp where eating or drinking leads to vomiting and thus to a decrease in the water and energy levels. (Color figure online)

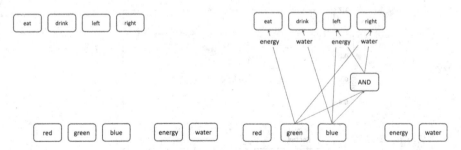

Fig. 4. The left panel shows the initial *blank slate* memory of the animat with two STATUS nodes: energy and water; three SENSOR nodes for colors; and four ACTION nodes. The right panel shows the memory after convergence (at time 25). The labels on the red arrows indicate the preferred actions for the different needs when the lower node is top active. The AND node that was added automatically enables the animat to survive.

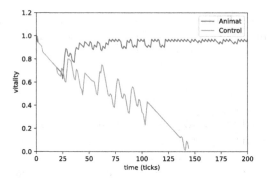

Fig. 5. Animat is the sheep animat. Control is similar, but its dynamic concept formation is switched off. They both start out with a blank slate. Animat adds an AND node at time step 25. It manages to survive, while Control dies.

3.2   Learning Temporal Patterns

In this example we show the usefulness of adding SEQ nodes. Again we consider a sheep animat that drinks and grazes, but this time the animat lives in a world that contains both good water and bad, poisonous water. The problem is that the animat cannot differentiate directly between the good and the bad water

Fig. 6. This world is a long path that begins with water and grass blocks, where the animat can learn to eat and drink. Then come the poison blocks. Each Poison block has a sand block to its left. This enables animats that are capable of sequence learning to differentiate between water and poison.

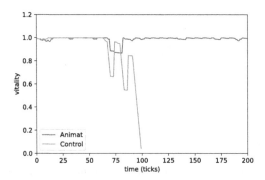

Fig. 7. Animat is the sheep animat. Control is similar, but it has its capacity to add SEQ nodes switched off. The animats start with a blank slate. Animat adds a SEQ node at time step 75. It survives, while Control, unable to learn sequences and contexts, dies at time step 100.

with its sensors. By learning that the bad water always appears in a certain context, in this case close to sand, the animat can learn to avoid drinking it.

The world is shown in Fig. 6. The animat starts with the same memory as in the previous example (Fig. 4). It adds the node "red SEQ blue" the first time a red block is encountered. Figure 7 shows how its vitality develops over time.

4 Conclusion

We have presented a model of a generic animat that is based on several techniques, including dynamic graphs for memory representation; top activity for perception; reliability and Q-values for decision-making; and local Q-learning and structural learning for memory development.

The model was constructed with the goal of preserving full generality while keeping the computational complexity at a minimum level. To that end we avoided explicit representations of subsets of sensors. Instead we use top-active nodes that represent partially defined states. We designed the model so that it only adds nodes reluctantly in case it gets surprised with respect to reward or punishment. An additional way of reducing the computational complexity might be to use forgetting, as was done in [15].

Our generic model is capable of starting with an arbitrary dynamic graph – e.g. a blank slate – using structural learning and local Q-learning to build a memory structure that helps the animat keep its needs satisfied and survive. Our examples here were designed to illustrate how structural learning can make the difference between life and death. Our model is fully autonomous and fully versatile; it does not depend on "seed" knowledge of any kind. In that sense it possess a basic form of general intelligence.

Acknowledgement. This research was supported by The Swedish Research Council, grants 2012-1000 and 2013-4873. C.S. is grateful to Martin Nowak for enabling a research visit to Harvard University.

References

1. Angelova, A., Krizhevsky, A., Vanhoucke, V., Ogale, A.S., Ferguson, D.: Real-time pedestrian detection with deep network cascades. In: BMVC, pp. 32.1–32.12 (2015)
2. Angluin, D.: Finding patterns common to a set of strings. J. Comput. Syst. Sci. **21**(1), 46–62 (1980)
3. Baars, B., Gage, N.: Cognition, Brain, and Consciousness: Introduction to Cognitive Neuroscience. Academic Press, San Diego (2010)
4. Bach, J.: MicroPsi 2: the next generation of the MicroPsi framework. In: Bach, J., Goertzel, B., Iklé, M. (eds.) AGI 2012. LNCS, vol. 7716, pp. 11–20. Springer, Heidelberg (2012). doi:10.1007/978-3-642-35506-6_2

5. Bear, M.F., Connors, B.W., Paradiso, M.A.: Neuroscience. Wolters Kluwer, Hagerstown (2015)
6. Fahlman, S.E., Lebiere, C.: The cascade-correlation learning architecture (1990)
7. Gabbay, D.M., Hodkinson, I., Reynolds, M.: Temporal Logic Mathematical Foundations and Computational Aspects. Oxford University Press, Oxford (1994)
8. Johnson, M., Hofmann, K., Hutton, T., Bignell, D.: The malmo platform for artificial intelligence experimentation. In: International Joint Conference on Artificial Intelligence (IJCAI), p. 4246 (2016)
9. LeCun, Y., Bengio, Y., Hinton, G.: Deep learning. Nature 521(7553), 436–444 (2015)
10. Mnih, V., et al.: Human-level control through deep reinforcement learning. Nature 518(7540), 529–533 (2015)
11. Niv, Y.: Reinforcement learning in the brain. J. Math. Psychol. 53(3), 139–154 (2009)
12. Nivel, E., Thórisson, K.R., Steunebrink, B.R., Dindo, H., Pezzulo, G., Rodriguez, M., Hernandez, C., Ognibene, D., Schmidhuber, J., Sanz, R., et al.: Bounded recursive self-improvement. arXiv preprint arXiv:1312.6764 (2013)
13. Roijers, D.M., Vamplew, P., Whiteson, S., Dazeley, R., et al.: A survey of multi-objective sequential decision-making. J. Artif. Intell. Res. (JAIR) 48, 67–113 (2013)
14. Schmidhuber, J.: Deep learning in neural networks: an overview. Neural Netw. 61, 85–117 (2015)
15. Strannegård, C., Cirillo, S., Wessberg, J.: Emotional concept development. In: Bieger, J., Goertzel, B., Potapov, A. (eds.) International Conference on Artificial General Intelligence, pp. 362–372. Springer, Switzerland (2015)
16. Strannegård, C., Nizamani, A.R.: Integrating symbolic and sub-symbolic reasoning. In: Steunebrink, B., Wang, P., Goertzel, B. (eds.) AGI -2016. LNCS, vol. 9782, pp. 171–180. Springer, Cham (2016). doi:10.1007/978-3-319-41649-6_17
17. Sutton, R.S., Barto, A.G.: Reinforcement Learning: An Introduction. MIT press, Cambridge (1998)
18. Tuci, E., Giagkos, A., Wilson, M., Hallam, J. (eds.): From Animals to Animats, 1st International Conference on the Simulation of Adaptive Behavior. Springer, Switzerland (2016)
19. Wang, P., Li, X.: Different conceptions of learning: function approximation vs. self-organization. In: Steunebrink, B., Wang, P., Goertzel, B. (eds.) AGI -2016. LNCS, vol. 9782, pp. 140–149. Springer, Cham (2016). doi:10.1007/978-3-319-41649-6_14
20. Wilson, S.W.: Knowledge growth in an artificial animal. In: Narendra, K.S. (ed.) Adap. Learn. Syst., pp. 255–264. Springer, New York (1986)

Self-awareness and Self-control in NARS

Pei Wang[1]([✉]), Xiang Li[1], and Patrick Hammer[2]

[1] Department of Computer and Information Sciences,
Temple University, Philadelphia, USA
{pei.wang,xiang.li003}@temple.edu
[2] Institute for Software Technology, Graz University of Technology, Graz, Austria
patrickhammer9@hotmail.com

Abstract. This paper describes the self-awareness and self-control mechanisms of a general-purpose intelligent system, NARS. The system perceives its internal environment basically in the same way as how it perceives its external environment, though the sensors involved are completely different. NARS uses a "self" concept to organize its relevant beliefs, tasks, and operations. The concept has an innate core, though its content and structure are mostly acquired gradually from the system's experience. The "self" concept and its ingredients play important roles in the control of the system.

Functions like "self-awareness", "self-control", and "self-consciousness" are closely related to advanced forms of intelligence. The difficulty of realizing these functions in a machine is both technical and theoretical, as there is no widely accepted theory about them, and even their definitions are highly controversial. This paper is not an attempt to address all relevant issues. Instead, we will present the relevant aspects of NARS (Non-Axiomatic Reasoning System), a formal model of general intelligence, which has been mostly implemented and is under testing and tuning.

In the following, the conceptual design of NARS is briefly introduced first, then the parts mostly relevant to "self" are described in more detail. Finally, the major design decisions are compared with the related works.

1 NARS Introduction

NARS is designed according to the hypothesis that "intelligence" is *the ability for a system to adapt to its environment and to work with insufficient knowledge and resources.* Under the length restriction, in this paper the system is only introduced very briefly. For details of the system, see the related papers[1] and books [14,17].

NARS is a reasoning system, with a formal language, Narsese, for knowledge representation, and a formal logic, NAL (Non-Axiomatic Logic), for inference using Narsese sentences as premises and conclusions. NAL belongs to the "term

---

[1] Mostly accessible at https://cis.temple.edu/~pwang/papers.html.

© Springer International Publishing AG 2017
T. Everitt et al. (Eds.): AGI 2017, LNAI 10414, pp. 33–43, 2017.
DOI: 10.1007/978-3-319-63703-7_4

logic" tradition where the smallest component of the language is a *term*, and "subject-copula-predicate" is the simplest format of *statement*. "$S \rightarrow P$" is a basic form of statements, and is called *inheritance statement*, where S is the subject term, P the predicate term, and "$\rightarrow$" the inheritance copula. The intuitive meaning of "$S \rightarrow P$" is "S is a special case of P" and "P is a general case of S". For example, "$robin \rightarrow bird$" corresponds to "Robin is a type of bird".

In its simplest form, a term is just a string of symbols from an arbitrary alphabet. Starting from these "atomic" terms, *compound terms* can be composed recursively, each with a connector and a list of component terms. Different term connectors represent different relations among the components, as shown by the following examples:

- **Sets:** Term $\{Tom, Jerry\}$ is an *extensional set* specified by enumerating its instances; term $[small, yellow]$ is an *intensional set* specified by enumerating its properties.
- **Intersections and differences:** Term $(bird \cap swimmer)$ represents "birds that can swim"; term $(bird - swimmer)$ represents "birds that cannot swim".
- **Products and images:** The relation "John is the uncle of Zack" is represented as "$(\{John\} \times \{Zack\}) \rightarrow uncle\text{-}of$", "$\{John\} \rightarrow (uncle\text{-}of / \diamond \{Zack\})$", and "$\{Zack\} \rightarrow (uncle\text{-}of / \{John\} \diamond)$", equivalently.
- **Statement:** "John knows soccer balls are round" can be represented as a *higher-order statement* "$\{John\} \rightarrow (know / \diamond \{soccer\text{-}ball \rightarrow [round]\})$", where the statement "$soccer\text{-}ball \rightarrow [round]$" is used as a term.

Beside the *inheritance* copula ('$\rightarrow$', "is a type of"), NAL also has three other copulas: *similarity* ('$\leftrightarrow$', "is similar to"), *implication* ('$\Rightarrow$', "if-then"), and *equivalence* ('$\Leftrightarrow$', "if-and-only-if"), and the last two are used between two statements.

A statement is a compound term with a truth-value. It can be formed using two terms and a copula, as well as using statement connectors *negation* ('$\neg$'), *conjunction* ('$\wedge$'), and *disjunction* ('$\vee$'), which are defined similarly (but not utilizing Boolean functions) to those in propositional logic [14]. There are several special types of statements needed for NARS to reason on procedural knowledge as in logic programming [7]:

Event: a statement with a time-dependent truth-value. Two events may happen sequentially or concurrently. Compound events can describe a sequence of events or parts of a complex event. By comparing the occurrence time of an event with the current time, the event gets a tense like "past", "present", or "future".

Operation: an event directly realizable by the system itself via executing the associated code or command. Formally, an operation is an application of an operator on a list of arguments, written as $op(a_1, \ldots, a_n)$. Intuitively, it is a procedure call, where the argument list includes both input and output arguments.

Goal: an event the system wants to realize. It is a statement with an associated "desire-value", indicating the extent to which the system desires a situation where the statement is true.

Since NARS is designed under the Assumption of Insufficient Knowledge and Resources (AIKR for short), the truth-value of a statement measures the extent of evidential support, not the agreement with a corresponding fact. In NAL, a truth-value is a pair of real numbers in $[0,1] \times (0,1)$, where the first number, *frequency*, measures the proportion of positive evidence of the statement among all available evidence, while the second number, *confidence*, measures the proportion of currently available evidence among the total amount of available evidence at a moment in the future, after new evidence of a constant amount is collected.

Defined in this way, *truth* in NARS is "experience-grounded". Similarly, the *meaning* of a term is determined by how it is related to other terms in the system's experience. As the experience of a system grows over time, the truth-value of statements and the meaning of terms in the system change accordingly. This *experience-grounded semantics* (EGS) is fundamentally different from the traditional *model-theoretic semantics*, since it defines *truth* and *meaning* according to a (dynamic and system-specific) experience, rather than a (static and system-independent) model. In the simplest implementation of NARS, its *experience* is a stream of Narsese sentences, which will be summarized to become the knowledge of the system.

NAL uses (formal) inference rules to derive new knowledge from existing knowledge. Since every piece of knowledge, also known as *belief*, is true to a degree, each inference rule has a truth-value function that calculates the truth-value of the conclusion according to the evidence provided by the premises.

As a term logic, typical inference rules in NAL are *syllogistic*, and takes two premises (with one common term) to derive a conclusion (between the other two terms). The NAL rules of this type include *deduction*, *induction*, and *abduction*, as specified by Peirce [10], though the truth-value of every statement is extended from $\{0, 1\}$ to $[0,1] \times (0,1)$ [14]. Among the three, *deduction* is a rule that carries out *strong inference*, as its conclusions can approach the maximum confidence 1 for affirmative premises of high confidence, while the other two carry out *weak inference*, where the confidence of the conclusions has a constant upper bound less than 1 for all premises.

Under AIKR, NARS may have inconsistent beliefs, that is, the same statement may obtain different truth-values according to different evidential bases. When the system locates such an inconsistency, it either uses the *revision* rule to produce a more confident conclusion by pooling the evidence (if the evidence bases are disjoint), or use the *choice* rule to pick the belief with higher confidence (if the evidence bases are not disjoint).

NAL also has *compositional rules* that compose or decompose compound terms according to the definition of their connector, so as to summarize the system's experience more efficiently.

The inference rules of NAL can be used in both *forward inference* (from existing beliefs to derived beliefs) and *backward inference* (from existing beliefs and questions/goals to derived questions/goals).

Equipped with these inference rules, NARS can carry out the following types of inference tasks:

- to absorb new experience into the system's beliefs, as well as to spontaneously derive some of their implications;
- to achieve the input goals (and the derived goals) by selectively executing the available operations according to the system's beliefs;
- to answer the input questions (and the derived questions) according to the system's beliefs.

Under AIKR, new tasks can enter the system at any time, each with its own time requirement, and its content can be any Narsese statement. Working in such a situation, usually NARS cannot perfectly accomplish all tasks in time, but has to allocate its limited time and space resources among them, and has to dynamically adjust the allocation according to the change of context and the feedback to its actions.

In the memory of NARS, beliefs and tasks are organized into *concepts*, according to the terms appearing in them. Therefore, for a term T, concept C_T refers to all beliefs and tasks containing T. For example, the beliefs on "*robin → bird*" are referred to within concepts C_{robin} and C_{bird}, as well as other relevant concepts. A "concept" in NARS is a unit of both storage and processing, and models the concepts found in human thinking [14].

To indicate the relative importance of concepts, tasks, and beliefs to the system, priority distributions are maintained among them. The priority of an item (concept, task, or belief) summarizes the attributes to be considered in resource allocation, including its intrinsic quality, usefulness in history, relevance to the current context, etc. Therefore items with higher priority values will get more resources.

NARS runs by repeating an inference cycle consisting of the following major steps:

1. Select a concept within the memory.
2. Select a task referred by the concept.
3. Select a belief referred by the concept.
4. Derive new tasks from the selected task and belief by the applicable inference rules.
5. Adjust the priority of the selected belief, task, and concept according to the context and feedback.
6. Selectively put the new tasks into the corresponding concepts, and report some of them to the user.

All selections in the above steps are probabilistic, biased by priority, that is, the probability for an item to be selected is positively correlated to its priority value. Consequently, the tasks will be processed in a time-sharing manner, with different speeds. For a specific task, its processing does not follow a predetermined algorithm, but is the result of many inference steps, whose combination is formed at runtime, so is neither predictable nor repeatable accurately, because both the external environment and the internal state of the system change in a non-circular manner.

2 "Self" in NARS

In this paper we focus on the aspects of NARS that are directly relevant to self-awareness and self-control. Therefore we will not fully discuss the following topics often involved in the related discussions:

- "Higher-order statement" in NARS covers "statement about statement", "knowledge about operations", etc., which are often taken as functions of "metacognition" [5]. Since such knowledge is typically about individual statements or operations, not about the system as a whole, it is not discussed here. For how this kind of knowledge is processed in NARS, see [14,17].
- NARS constantly compares the certainty of beliefs, and dynamically allocates its resources among competing tasks. Even though the relevant mechanisms are indeed at the meta-level with respect to beliefs and tasks, they are implicitly embedded in the code, so not generally accessible to the system's deliberation, nor can they be modified by the system itself, therefore they are also not discussed here.
- NARS has mechanisms for feeling and emotion, which are important parts of self-awareness and self-control. However, since they have been discussed in detail in our recent publication [18], they will only be mentioned briefly in this paper.

NARS' beliefs about itself start at its built-in operations. Operation $op(a_1, \ldots, a_n)$ corresponds to a relation the system can establish between itself and the arguments, so it is equivalent to statement "$(\times, \{SELF\}, \{a_1\}, \ldots, \{a_n\}) \rightarrow op$" (where the subject term is a *product* term written in the prefix format), since it specifies a relation among the arguments plus the system identified by the special term $SELF$.

Similar to the case of logic programming [7], here the idea is to uniformly represent declarative knowledge and procedural knowledge. So in NARS knowledge about the system itself is unified with knowledge about others. For instance, the operation "open this door" is represented as "$(\times, \{SELF\}, \{door\_1\}) \rightarrow open$"[2], while "John opened this door" as "$(\times, \{John\}, \{door\_1\}) \rightarrow open$" (tense omitted to simplify the discussion). In this way, imitation can be carried out by analogical inference.

As mentioned previously, in NARS the meaning of a concept is gradually acquired from the system's experience. However, this "experience-grounded semantics" (EGS) does not exclude the existence of innate concepts, beliefs, and tasks. In the above example, '$SELF$' is such a concept, with built-in operations that can be directly executed from the very beginning. Such operations depend on the hardware/software of the host system, so are not specified as parts of NARS, except that they must obey the format requirements of Narsese. According to EGS, in the initial state of NARS, the meaning of a built-in operation is procedurally expressed in the corresponding routine, while the meaning of

---

[2] Here, the inheritance copula encodes that the relation between $\{SELF\}$ and $\{door\_1\}$, is a special case of opening.

'*SELF*' consists of these operations. To the system, "I am whatever I can do" or "I am whatever I can do and feel" are possible ways to express this situation, since in NARS sensation and perception are also operations.

As the system begins to have experience, the meaning of every concept will be more or less adjusted as it is experienced, directly or indirectly. For a built-in operation, the system will gradually learn its preconditions and consequences, so as to associate itself with the goals it can achieve. It is like when we know how to raise our hand first, and then know it as a way to get the teacher's attention. The '*SELF*' concept will be enriched in this way, as well as through its relations with other concepts representing objects and other systems in the outside environment. Therefore, self starts from "what I can do" to include "what I am composed of", "how I look like", "what my position is in the society", etc. "Self" does not have a constant meaning determined by a denotation or definition. Instead, the system gradually learns who it is, and its self-image does not necessarily converge to a "true self".

An operation may be completely executed by the actuator of the host system (e.g., A NARS-based robot raises a hand or moves forward), or partly by another coupled system or device (e.g., A NARS-based robot pushes a button or issues a command to another robot). NARS has an interface for such "external" operations to be registered.

NARS is designed to allow all kinds of operations to be used in a "plug-and-play" manner, i.e., to be connected to the system at run time by a user or the system itself. A learning phase is usually needed for an operation to be used properly and effectively.

In principle, no operation is necessarily demanded in every NARS implementation, except a special type of "mental" operations that work on the system's own "mind". There are several groups of mental operations, including:

Task generation. An inference task in NARS can either be input or derived recursively from an input task. The derivation process does not change the type of the task (new/activated belief, goal, or question). However, in certain situations a task needs to be generated from another one of a different type. For example, a new belief ("It is cold.") may trigger a new goal ("Close the window!"). This relation is represented as an implication statement where the consequent is not a statement, but an operation call, similar as in a production rule.

Evidence disqualification. By default, the amount of supporting evidence for every belief accumulates over time. Therefore, though the frequency value of the belief may either increase or decrease (depending on whether the new evidence is positive or negative), its confidence value increases monotonically. This treatment is supplemented by a mental operation that allows the system to doubt a belief by decreasing its confidence value to a certain extent.

Concept activation. The resource allocation mechanism of NARS already implements a process similar to activation spreading in neural networks. When a new task is added into a concept, the priority of the concept is increased temporarily, and inference in the concept may cause derived tasks to be sent to its neighbors, so their priority (activation) levels will be increased, too. As a supplement, a mental operation allows the system to pay attention to a concept without new tasks added.

Feeling. The system can check the readings of its sensors embedded in its "body" and "mind", so as to "feel" its status, and use the reports to decide its actions. This mechanism has been described in [18]. Beside emotional status, the system can also feel how novel a new input is (so as to give it the attention it deserves) or how busy itself is (so as to decide its resource allocation strategy).

In general, mental operations supplement and influence the automatic control mechanism, and let certain actions be taken as the consequence of inference. Mental operations contribute to the system's self-concept by telling the system what is going on in its mind, and allow the system to control its own thinking process to a certain extent. For instance, the system can explicitly plan its processing of a certain type of task. After the design and implementation phases, the system needs to learn how to properly use its mental operations, just like it needs to learn about the other operations.

In NARS, "experience" refers to the system's input streams. In the simplest implementation of NARS, the system has only one input channel, where the experience is a stream of Narsese sentences like $S_1, T_1, S_2, T_2, \ldots, S_n, T_n$ from the channel, where each S_i is a Narsese sentence, with T_i to be the time interval between it and the next sentence. A buffer of a constant size n holds the most recent experience.

In more complicated implementations, there are also "sensory" channels each accepting a stream of Narsese terms from a sensory organ. Here a sensor can recognize a certain type of signal, either from the outside of the system (such as visual or audio signals), or from the inside of the system. Within the system, the sensation can come either from the body (somatosensory) or from the mind (mental). Such a channel provides a certain type of "internal experience". Somatosensory input will be especially important for a robotic system, as it needs to be aware of its energy level, network connection status, damages in parts, etc.

A mental sensation may come from the execution of a mental operation, such as the "feeling" operation mentioned above. Also, mental sensations appear as the trace of the system's inference activity. During each inference cycle, the system "senses" the concept that was selected for processing, and the implication relationship between the premises and the conclusion. Later, this experience can be used to answer questions like "What has been pondered" or "Where does that conclusion come from", asked either by the system itself or by someone else, as well as used in future inference activities.

On the input buffers the system carries out certain channel-specific preprocessing to form compound terms corresponding to the spatiotemporal patterns of the input. There is also a global buffer that holds a stream of Narsese sentences after preprocessing, where the terms typically combine the data from multiple channels. In this aspect, the external and internal experiences are handled basically in the same way.

A special type of belief formed in this way is the temporal implications between the mental events sensed within the system and the outside events observed by the system. The system will believe that it is some of its ideas that "cause" a certain action to be performed in its environment, and such beliefs will coordinate its "mind" and its "body".

The internal experience of NARS is the major source of its self-knowledge. Under AIKR, this type of knowledge is also uncertain and incomplete, and is under constant revision. Furthermore, it is subjective and from the first-person perspective. In these aspects, NARS is fundamentally different from the "logical AI" approach [9].

There is no space in this paper to provide working examples, so interested readers should visit the OpenNARS project website.[3]

3 Comparison to Related Work

Restricted by paper length, here we only compare NARS with the related AI works, and not address the huge literature in psychology and philosophy on self, consciousness, and the related topics.

Though many approaches have been proposed for self-awareness and self-control in various forms, most AI systems do not have a "self" concept (no matter under what name) [5]. Such a concept is used in NARS, mainly because *concept* provides a flexible unit for representation and processing, so every identifiable pattern in experience and notion in thought is handled as a concept. Since an intelligent system has the needs to know about itself, it is natural for such a concept to be used to collect all the self-related beliefs and tasks together.

According to the semantics of NARS, the meaning of a concept (or a term naming a concept) is completely determined by its relation with other concepts (or terms). While for most concepts such relations are all acquired from the system's experience, the system is not born with a blank memory. Each built-in operation contributes meaning to the concept of $SELF$, by relating the system as a whole to the events it can perceive and/or realize. Starting from these operations, the $SELF$ concept will eventually involve beliefs about

- what the system can sense and do, not only using the built-in operations, but also the compound operations recursively composed from them, as well as the preconditions and consequences of these operations;
- what the system desires and actively pursues, that is, its motivational and emotional structure;
- how the system is related to the objects and events in the environment, in term of their significance and affordance to the system;
- how the system is related to the other systems, that is, the "social roles" played by the system, as well as the conversions in communication and interactions.

---

[3] Source code, working examples, and documentations of the current implementation of NARS can be found at http://opennars.github.io/opennars/.

All these aspects will make the system's self concept richer and richer, even to the level of complexity that we can meaningfully talk about its "personality", that is, what makes this system different from the others, due to its unique nature and nurture.

This treatment is fundamentally different from identifying "self" with a physical body or a constant mechanism within the system. "Self" is not left completely to a mysterious "emergent process", neither. In NARS, the concept of "self" starts with a built-in core, then evolves according to the system's experience. In the process, the self-concept organizes the relevant beliefs and tasks together to facilitate self-awareness and self-control. This is consistent with Piaget's theory that a child learns about self and environment by coordinating sensations (such as vision and hearing) with actions (such as grasping, sucking, and stepping), and gradually progresses from reflexive, instinctual action at birth to symbolic mental operations [11].

A widely agreed conclusion in psychology is that a mental process can be either automatic (implicit, unconscious) or controlled (explicit, conscious), with respect to the system itself. The former includes innate or acquired stimulus-response associations, while the latter includes processes under *cognitive control*, such as "response inhibition, attentional bias, performance monitoring, conflict monitoring, response priming, task setting, task switching, and the setting of subsystem parameters, as well as working memory control functions such as monitoring, maintenance, updating, and gating" [4].

Various "dual-process" models have been proposed in psychology to cover both mechanisms. Such models are also needed in AI, even though the purpose here is not to simulate the human mind in all details, but to benefits from the advantages of both. In general, controlled processes are more flexible and adaptive, while automatic processes are more efficient and reliable. In such a system, there are meta-level processes that regulate object-level processes [5,8,12,13], and such works are also covered in the study of machine consciousness [1,3]. Even though this "object-level vs. meta-level" distinction exists in many systems, the exact form of the boundary between the two differ greatly, partly because of the architecture of the systems involved. A process should not be considered "meta" merely because it gets information from another process and also influences the latter, since the relation can be symmetric between the two, while normally the object-level processes have no access to the meta-level processes.

As a reasoning system, in NARS "control" means to select the premises and the rule(s) for each inference step, so as to link the individual inference steps into problem-solving processes. The primary control mechanism is coded in a programming language, and is independent of the system's experience. It is automatic and unconscious, in the sense that the system does not "think" about what to do in each step, but is context- and data-driven, while the data involved comes from associations biased by dynamic priority distributions. On top of this, there are mental operations that are expressed in Narsese and invoked by the system's decisions, as a result of "conscious" inference activities. This meta-level deliberative control does not change the underlying automatic routines, but supplement and adjust them.

Deliberative control in NARS is mainly achieved by mental operations, and this treatment is different from the meta-cognition implemented in the other systems [5] in that the operations in NARS are light-weight, rather than decision-making procedures that compare the possible actions in detail with a high computational cost. Also, the preconditions of these operations are largely learned from experience, not predetermined. As these operations can be combined into compounds, the system will gradually learn problem-solving skills, as a form of self-programming [16].

In general, NARS treats its "external experience" and "internal experience" in the same way, and the knowledge about the system itself has the same nature as other knowledge in NARS. Under AIKR, self-knowledge is incomplete, uncertain, and often inconsistent, which is the contrary of what is assumed by the "logical AI" school [9]. The system can only be aware of the knowledge reported by certain mental operations and those in the input buffers, and even this knowledge does not necessarily get enough attention to reveal its implications. The control aspect is the same, that is, the system can only make limited adjustments, so cannot "completely reprogram itself", and nor can it guarantee the absolute correctness of its self-control behaviors.

If self-awareness and self-control are required in an intelligent system, why are such functions absent in most of the AI systems developed so far?

Like many controversies in AI, the different opinions on this matter can be traced back to the different understandings of "AI" [15]. As the mainstream AI aims at the solving of specific problems, the systems are usually equipped with problem-specific algorithms. Even in learning systems that do not demand manually-coded algorithms, they are still approximated by generalizing training data. In general such systems have little need to add itself into the picture, and even meta-cognition can be carried out without an explicit "self" concept involved [5].

In AGI systems, the situation is different. Here we have projects aimed at simulating the human brain according to psychological theories [2,6], which surely needs to simulate the self-related cognitive functions. Even in the function-oriented projects, self-awareness and self-control are desired to meet the requirements for the system to work in various situations [12,13].

For NARS, the need for self-awareness and self-control follows from its working definition of intelligence, that is, adaptation under AIKR [15]. To adapt to the environment and to carry out its tasks, the system needs to know what it can do and how it is related to the objects and other systems in the environment, and an explicitly expressed "self" will organize all the related knowledge together, so as to facilitate reasoning and decision making.

NARS treats *SELF* like other concepts in the system, except that it is a "reserved word" which has innate associations with the built-in operations, including the mental operations. NARS also treats internal and external experience uniformly, so self-awareness and self-control have nothing magical or mysterious, but are similar to how the system perceives and acts upon the external environment.

Though the study of self-awareness and self-control in NARS is still at an early stage, the conceptual design described above has been implemented, and is under testing and tuning. There are many details to be refined, however we believe the overall design is in agreement with the scientific knowledge on these processes in the human mind, and also meets the needs and restrictions in AGI systems.

References

1. Baars, B.J., Franklin, S.: Consciousness is computational: the LIDA model of global workspace theory. Int. J. Mach. Conscious. **1**, 23–32 (2009)
2. Bach, J.: Principles of Synthetic Intelligence PSI: An Architecture of Motivated Cognition. Oxford University Press, Oxford (2009)
3. Chella, A., Frixione, M., Gaglio, S.: A cognitive architecture for robot self-consciousness. Artif. Intell. Med. **44**, 147–154 (2008)
4. Cooper, R.P.: Cognitive control: componential or emergent? Top. Cogn. Sci. **2**, 598–613 (2010)
5. Cox, M.T.: Metacognition in computation: a selected research review. Artif. Intell. **169**, 104–141 (2005)
6. Franklin, S.: A foundational architecture for artificial general intelligence. In: Goertzel, B., Wang, P. (eds.) Advance of Artificial General Intelligence, pp. 36–54. IOS Press, Amsterdam (2007)
7. Kowalski, R.: Logic for Problem Solving. North Holland, New York (1979)
8. Marshall, J.B.: A self-watching model of analogy-making and perception. J. Exp. Theor. Artif. Intell. **18**(3), 267–307 (2006)
9. McCarthy, J.: Making robots conscious of their mental states. In: Intelligent Agents Machine Intelligence, vol. 15, pp. 3–17. St. Catherine's College, Oxford, July 1995
10. Peirce, C.S.: Collected Papers of Charles Sanders Peirce, vol. 2. Harvard University Press, Cambridge (1931)
11. Piaget, J.: The Origins of Intelligence in Children. W.W. Norton & Company Inc., New York (1963). Translated by Cook, M.
12. Rosenbloom, P.S., Demski, A., Ustun, V.: The Sigma cognitive architecture and system: towards functionally elegant grand unification. J. Artif. Gen. Intell. **7**, 1–103 (2016)
13. Shapiro, S.C., Bona, J.P.: The GLAIR cognitive architecture. Int. J. Mach. Conscious. **2**, 307–332 (2010)
14. Wang, P.: Rigid Flexibility: The Logic of Intelligence. Springer, Dordrecht (2006)
15. Wang, P.: What do you mean by 'AI'. In: Proceedings of the First Conference on Artificial General Intelligence, pp. 362–373 (2008)
16. Wang, P.: Solving a problem with or without a program. J. Artif. Gen. Intell. **3**(3), 43–73 (2012)
17. Wang, P.: Non-Axiomatic Logic: A Model of Intelligent Reasoning. World Scientific, Singapore (2013)
18. Wang, P., Talanov, M., Hammer, P.: The emotional mechanisms in NARS. In: Proceedings of the Ninth Conference on Artificial General Intelligence, pp. 150–159 (2016)

DSO Cognitive Architecture: Unified Reasoning with Integrative Memory Using Global Workspace Theory

Khin Hua Ng[(✉)], Zhiyuan Du, and Gee Wah Ng

Cognition and Fusion Lab 2, DSO National Laboratories, Singapore, Singapore
{nkhinhua,dzhiyuan,ngeewah}@dso.org.sg

Abstract. In this work, we present a design enhancement to the DSO Cognitive Architecture to augment its existing cognitive functions in an attempt to produce more general level of artificial intelligence in computational intelligent systems. Our design is centered on the concept of unified reasoning that indirectly addresses the diversity dilemma in designing cognitive architectures. This is done by implementing an integrative memory with the incorporation of the Global Workspace Theory. We discuss how other cognitive architectures using the Global Workspace Theory have influenced our design and also demonstrate how the new design can be used to solve an image captioning problem.

Keywords: Cognitive architecture · Unified reasoning · Integrative memory · Global workspace theory

1 Introduction

The DSO Cognitive Architecture (DSO-CA) is a top-level cognitive architecture that models the information processing in the human brain using inspirations drawn from Cognitive Science, Neuroscience, and Computational Science [1,2]. It is designed based on the key principles of hierarchical structure, distributed memory and parallelism. These led to an architectural design centered on functional modules (Reasoning, Visual, Association, etc.) that are executed asynchronously and in parallel to one another with each module possessing their own distinct memory system. The DSO-CA has been used to develop useful solutions to problems in applications like scene understanding [3] and mobile surveillance [4]. To further enhance its capability towards producing more human-like general intelligence and dynamic reasoning, we have been researching on advanced design principles and computational algorithms that will permit reasoning across different knowledge domains and representations – a process we termed *unified reasoning*.

Unified reasoning can be implemented either by encoding radically different knowledge domains into a common representation and then implement a single inference engine for the reasoning process, or by using multiple inference engines

© Springer International Publishing AG 2017
T. Everitt et al. (Eds.): AGI 2017, LNAI 10414, pp. 44–53, 2017.
DOI: 10.1007/978-3-319-63703-7_5

and coming up with a way to unify them for different inputs. This leads to a design problem known as the *diversity dilemma*. In cognitive architecture design, the diversity dilemma refers to a need to blend diversity of different cognitive functions with uniformity of structure for efficiency, integrability, extensibility, and maintainability [5]. Diversity refers to the wide range of cognitive functions of different complexity required to operate in a dynamic, complex environment. Uniformity can be interpreted as how different cognitive functions can be realised through interactions between a small set of primitives and functions. This is a dilemma because ensuring uniformity alone may not be adequate in covering most cognitive functions, or accommodating new cognitive functions, but at the same time it is easier to maintain and integrate functions through uniformity. On the other hand, diverse implementations may not gel well with one another and will require a lot of engineering and maintenance effort, but they are easier to extend for new functionalities. In the case of unified reasoning, a single knowledge representation and its inference engine may not cover every domain while a set of different inference engines may require massive engineering to synergise them.

In this paper we present a design enhancement to the DSO-CA that augments its existing cognitive functions to perform unified reasoning. This design is based on the concept of implementing an integrative memory together with the incorporation of the *Global Workspace Theory*. The Global Workspace Theory (GWT) is a neuro-cognitive theory of consciousness developed by Bernard Baars [6, 7], where information integration plays an important role. It advances a model of information flow in which multiple, parallel, specialised processes compete and co-operate for access to a global workspace. The global workspace then permits the winning coalition to broadcast to the rest of the specialists. According to the GWT, the mammalian brain instantiates this model of information flow, which enables a distinction to be drawn between conscious and unconscious information processing. To interpret it computationally, consciousness can be described as competition among processors, and outputs for a limited capacity resource that "broadcasts" information for widespread access and use. By grouping these specialists by cognitive functions, their availability to the global workspace causes information in memory to become conscious when the amount of activity representing it crosses a threshold [8].

By making use of an integrative memory system and applying the GWT, the collaboration between vastly different cognitive functions can be achieved and it indirectly provides a resolution to the diversity dilemma. Here, the integrative memory refers to a unified representation for the working memory. It serves as a common language for which the different modules communicate in and the GWT is the protocol of which they use to communicate. In the context of unified reasoning, this means the different reasoners can still use their specialised inference engines on their native representations but when a novel situation arises, which a single reasoner cannot resolve, the global workspace can propagate its content to different reasoners and complement its shortcoming. Hence, the GWT protocol incorporated with an integrative memory can be used as a solution to facilitate unified reasoning. Before we present this new design enhancement to the

DSO-CA, we will first provide a review of related work on cognitive architectures that implement the GWT, which have influenced our design. We will also provide an illustrative example on how the proposed new DSO-CA can be applied to an image captioning problem.

2   Related Works

To investigate how the GWT can be applied to enhance the DSO-CA with the functionality of unified reasoning, we have studied the following cognitive architectures infused with principles inspired by the GWT: MLECOG, CERA-CRANIUM, LIDA, CELTS, and CST. MLECOG (Motivated Learning Embodied Cognitive Architecture) [9] is a cognitive architecture built on top of self-organising artificial neural networks using the idea of pain signals. It is able to dynamically generate goals 'motivated' by desires and needs, and generate actions to fulfil the generated goals. MLECOG has all the semblance of GWT but it does not have a global broadcast mechanism – winner of the competition is routed through a predefined pathway. CERA-CRANIUM [10] uses a layered, hierarchical distributed architecture and it has two main components: CRANIUM, which serves as the workspaces of which the massive parallel, specialised processes operate on, and CERA, which serves as a domain-agnostic control unit to handle higher cognitive functions like selective attention, memory management, etc. LIDA (Learning Intelligent Distribution Agent) [11] aims to build a theoretical framework to unify different theories about human cognition, with a particular focus on the learning aspects of intelligent agents. Using a cognition cycle that starts with perception and ends with action, the GWT serves as a bridge between them by using attention strategies to pick different salient coalitions (a subset of the working memory elements) that are augmented by the various cognitive tasks that occurred before. Similarly, CELTS (Conscious Emotional Learning Tutoring Systems) [12] also implements a cognitive cycle of perception to action. One key difference is the existence of a shorter route for reactive behaviour and the use of 'emotions' to guide selective attention to working memory elements. Lastly, CST (Cognitive Systems Toolkit) [13] serves as a framework for users to create cognitive architecture using codelets as the atomic unit of computation.

To help us compare the design principles of these cognitive architectures we have worked out four features in the context of integrative memory and the GWT, namely, (1) types of memory, (2) competition, (3) purpose of global broadcast, and (4) information flow. Table 1 shows a summary of comparison amongst the different cognitive architectures including the enhanced DSO-CA with GWT using these four features.

Types of memory here refers to the representation used for the memory and the scale for the type of memory ranges from completely integrative to disparate. For example, LIDA, CELTS and MLECOG uses integrated memory whereas CST uses disparate memory due to the content of the memory objects (Table 1). Disparate memory facilitates different forms of representation to populate the working memory, and conversion of memories may be needed between

Table 1. A comparison among the different cognitive architectures along with DSO-CA implemented with GWT.

CA	Types of memory	Global broadcast	Information flow	Competition	
MLECOG	Integrated	N/A	Predefined	Pain signals and priorities	Multiple competition
CERA-CRANIUM	Disparate	Specific	Predefined		Multiple local competition
LIDA	Integrated	Specific	Predefined	Activation based	Multiple competition
CELTS	Integrated	Specific	Predefined		Single competition
CST	Disparate	Generic	Dynamic		Single competition
DSO-CA	Integrated but locally disparate	Generic	Dynamic	Activation and speed based	Multiple competition

different, incompatible processes. On the other hand, the advantage of using an integrative memory is the uniformity of representation. From a system's perspective, this allows easy maintenance and extension of the architecture. Also, it allows the combination of information contributed from processes, decreasing the complexity of the system in terms of designing mechanisms to handle different representations. In our proposed design enhancement to the DSO-CA, the working memory and content involved is integrated while the different specialised processors can have different memory representations.

The second feature "competition" is defined here as how the coalitions of processes compete for conscious access. Two aspects of competition are laid out in Table 1: the evaluation metric and the level of competition. In general, all cognitive architectures discussed here used similar mechanisms for competition with the most common evaluation metric being activation level. Each element in the working memory is assigned an activation level based on problem-dependent criteria, which indicates how relevant each element is to the goal or state of the agent. Another aspect of competition is the level of competition. In most architectures, there are multiple levels of competition.

The third feature classifies the global broadcast by its designed purpose: specific or generic. For example, the global broadcast in CELTS and LIDA serves mainly to aid learning, and influencing or invoking action selection. With a specific goal in mind, it determines how the global broadcast is implemented including the choice of memory representation that ties in with the integrative memory. Global broadcast with generic purpose simply propagates salient information; the propagated content are not designed according to pre-mapped functions. This is the case for CST and DSO-CA.

Lastly, the feature on information flow defines how information is transferred from one codelet/module to another and its pathway control. The flow can be predefined (top-down) or dynamic (bottom-up). Predefined information flow refers to information flow defined during the design phase where the GWT mechanism is embedded within this flow. This mechanism acts as a gatekeeper and bridge to pass the most salient information to the rest of the modules. As shown In Table 1, all except for CST and DSO-CA have predefined information flow. The main reason we have chosen dynamic information flow for unified reasoning within the DSO-CA is because its current design can readily adopt the dynamism through its pathway control that defines how information flows among modules [1].

3 Design

In this section, we present the proposed enhanced DSO-CA design. The design revolves around certain key aspects. Firstly, the architecture is composed of specialised processors executing asynchronously from one another. Each of the processors is akin to the unconscious processing in the brain, and they can operate on disparate memory representations. However the main working memory and content of interprocess communication must share a common representation with well-defined properties that can be exploited. Additionally, there should exist a mechanism for these specialised processors to compete against one another directly or indirectly. It is through competition that a specialised processor can access the global workspace and broadcast to other processes; this allows the transition of parallel, unconscious processing to serial, conscious processing [6]. Lastly, the global broadcast mechanism must possess an inhibitory function to suppress competing processors while it is broadcasting. With this in mind, we propose the design as illustrated in Fig. 1.

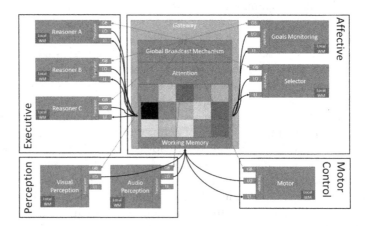

Fig. 1. An overview of the DSO-CA with the GWT. The attention and global broadcast mechanism layer lie on the working memory (integrative memory).

Modules that perform specialised and independent processes in a given domain are referred to as cognitive codelets. Each of these codelet has a translator that converts its local memory representation (as stored in the local working memory) into the integrative memory representation and vice versa. Cognitive codelets communicate with each other through the gateway to other cognitive codelets. Laying on top of the working memory is the attention layer and the Global Broadcast Mechanism; the attention layer seeks out and receives novel, critical, or relevant information embedded within the working memory or the cognitive codelets. Each cognitive codelet has local ports that can receive local inputs, or send local output to other cognitive codelets (routed via the gateway). However, it also has a broadcast port that can receive prioritised input from the Global Broadcast Mechanism.

Figure 2 shows the proposed design of the working memory. It uses a layered architecture. The integrative memory layer holds the actual working memory represented as factor graph. The reference memory layer is made up of cells to hold references to subgraphs of the underlying factor graph. A factor graph is a bipartite graph that represents a complicated global function as a product of local functions [14]. The choice of using factor graph is largely inspired by the SIGMA cognitive architecture [15], which demonstrated the combination of perception, localization, decision-making and learning using only factor graphs and with it, uses sum-product algorithm for cognitive processing [16]. Each reference memory cell contains shared memory among cognitive codelets. A cognitive codelet can send its output to a cell that in turn, can be used as inputs to other cognitive codelets (Fig. 2). This is similar to CST's memory object except that each cell holds a reference to a subgraph of the underlying factor graph.

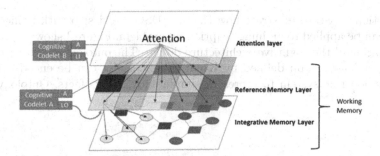

Fig. 2. The working memory has two layers. The integrative memory hosts the factor graph and the reference memory cells contain reference to subgraphs.

Activation level is calculated either on the reference memory cell or on the cognitive codelet (the arrows to and from the attention layer in Fig. 2). Candidates picked from the reference memory cells can be considered as top-down attention as the attention codelets define the criteria of selection. Conversely, candidates from cognitive codelets are bottom-up as the cognitive codelets define the selection criteria instead of the attention codelets. Local competition takes place at this level with the attention codelets, differentiated by their context, picking the most salient candidate – a factor graph which is a subgraph from the reference memory cell or the output of the cognitive codelet. Once the attention codelets have picked their winning candidate, they will be sent to the Global Broadcast Mechanism to compete for access. A temporary, capacity-limited buffer will be created for the candidates upon receiving the first one. The buffer will shut down when either the timer expires or when it fills up to its capacity. Global competition will start here and the winner (with the highest activation level) will be broadcasted to the rest of the cognitive codelets for additional processing. Inhibition starts when the buffer expires and the Global Broadcast Mechanism will reject any candidates sent from attention codelets of which, will also stop selecting or receiving candidates.

While developed independently, some parts of our design bear resemblance to the OpenCog [17] architecture's concept of "cognitive synergy". Both designs are based on the belief that general intelligence requires a synergised way of linking various specialised knowledge (memory) systems, which we called unified reasoning. OpenCog has a memory system known as Atomspace (a hypergraph database) that fits our notion of the integrative memory. Atomspace permits implementation of Probabilistic Logic Networks while our integrative memory is implemented using factor graphs. In essence, while the broad descriptions of both designs share certain level of similarities, the key principles that the designs are based upon are primarily different – one based on the GWT and the other Cognitive Synergy Theory.

4   Example

This section serves to illustrate how the new DSO-CA design with unified reasoning can be applied to an image captioning problem. Figure 3 shows a possible configuration of the cognitive architecture design. The ontology can be encoded as a dependency graph defined by K-parser [19]. Rules can be encoded using a production rule system to represent simple and obvious facts. Ontology and

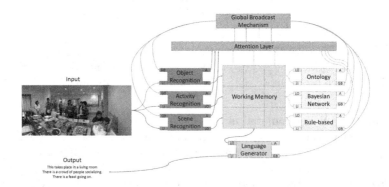

Fig. 3. The proposed design for the application. Image source: MS COCO Captioning Challenge dataset [18].

rules are used to construct the knowledge graph required by the language generator to create the captions. D'Brain [20], which is one of the reasoner modules already implemented in the DSO-CA, can be used to fuse multiple Bayesian networks knowledge fragments [21] to iteratively remove false recognition from the perception through inferencing and providing higher level context.

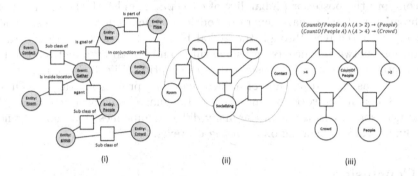

Fig. 4. The different knowledge bases' representations translated into factor graphs: (i) represents an ontology, (ii) is a Bayesian network, the grey arrows represent the original DAG, (iii) is a factor graph representing rules that are activated. These factor graphs are represented in the integrative memory while the various reasoners retain their native representations.

In Fig. 3, potential objects, activities and scenes identified by their respective perception codelets will be put into their respective reference memory cells. Reasoners use these inputs to either generate more candidates using associations and likelihood or remove percepts that are unlikely given its context. Output from the reasoners will return to the reference memory cells again and the attention codelets in the Attention Layer may pick up if the content (in the form of factor graph) is salient; they can also receive them from the other cognitive codelets. Each attention codelet is responsible for a domain and will select the most salient aspect of their respective domain for further competition that takes place in the Global Broadcast Mechanism. There, the candidate with the greatest activation level will be broadcasted to the rest of codelets for further processing, and the process repeats again. Using Fig. 4(iii) and the photo in Fig. 3 as an example, different persons would be initially recognised and tallied, the rule-based reasoner would eventually infer that there are 'people' and a 'crowd' in that photo. If its output are considered the winner of the global competition, it will be broadcasted to the rest of the cognitive codelets. When the ontology reasoner receives the broadcast, 'people' will be associated with 'gather' which in turn is associated with 'feasts' and 'pizza' (Fig. 4(i)) subsequently. This subset of factor graph will be broadcasted to the cognitive codelets again after competition and be picked up by D'Brain, which can calculate the concept association strength through inferencing; concepts, whose posteriors passes a threshold, are considered as candidates for bottom-up attention from the cognitive codelets.

Using Fig. 4(iii), 'home', 'socializing' and 'living room' can be picked out as the most probable associations, and the factor graph is selected for broadcast. Upon receiving the broadcast, ontology and rules-based reasoner expand the knowledge graph by associating more concepts. This example demonstrates the cooperation among the reasoner codelets facilitated by the GWT implementation; rules and ontology can generate associations based on semantics, and Bayesian networks can compute the posterior probability of concepts. Amidst all the competitions and broadcasts, the language generator codelet is concurrently creating sentences from inputs it received through the global broadcast. Sentences are generated by relations between concepts and some rules, and scored by a metric. The top three sentences will then be considered as the caption (Fig. 3). In summary, the dynamically assembled pipeline of unified reasoning process is: Rules → Ontology → Bayesian Network → Ontology → Language Generator. By using the global workspace, this is one of the many different pipelines that can be generated dynamically depending on changing contexts.

5   Conclusion

In this paper we have presented a design enhancement to the DSO-CA to augments its existing cognitive functions in an attempt to produce more general level of artificial intelligence in computational intelligent systems. Our design is centered on the concept of unified reasoning by implementing an integrative memory with the incorporation the GWT. This is done by compartmentalising reasoning functions into different parallelised codelets that contribute their inference results into the integrative memory, which is implemented by factor graphs. The GWT is responsible in picking the most novel and relevant information from the integrative memory and broadcast it to the other codelets, thereby connecting separate information pathways into a unified whole. This design will give us a form of dynamic reasoning that can elegantly adapt to different contexts through the collaboration of different reasoning systems. Through this, we hope it will serve as a building block bringing us a step closer to a cognitive architecture that produces human-like intelligence.

A computational development of the complete enhanced design for the DSO-CA is currently in the works. We aim to test the computational system with other challenging problems that will showcase the usefulness of an intelligent system capable of performing unified reasoning.

References

1. Ng, G.W., Tan, Y.S., Teow, L.N., Ng, K.H., Tan, K.H., Chan, R.Z.: A cognitive architecture for knowledge exploitation. In: 3rd Conference on Artificial General Intelligence (AGI 2010). Atlantis Press (2010)
2. Ng, G.W., Tan, Y.S., Teow, L.N., Ng, K.H., Tan, K.H., Chan, R.Z.: A cognitive architecture for knowledge exploitation. Int. J. Mach. Conscious. **3**(02), 237–253 (2011)

3. Ng, G.W., Xiao, X., Chan, R.Z., Tan, Y.S.: Scene understanding using DSO cognitive architecture. In: 2012 15th International Conference on Information Fusion (FUSION), pp. 2277–2284. IEEE (2012)
4. Ng, G.W., Tan, Y.S., Xiao, X.H., Chan, R.Z.: DSO cognitive architecture in mobile surveillance. In: 2012 Workshop on Sensor Data Fusion: Trends, Solutions, Applications (SDF), pp. 111–115. IEEE (2012)
5. Rosenbloom, P.S.: Towards uniform implementation of architectural diversity. Artif. Intell. **20**, 197–218 (2009)
6. Baars, B.J.: A Cognitive Theory of Consciousness. Cambridge University Press, Cambridge (1993)
7. Baars, B., Franklin, S., Ramsoy, T.: Global workspace dynamics: cortical "binding and propagation" enables conscious contents. Front. Psychol. **4**, 200 (2013)
8. Reggia, J.A.: The rise of machine consciousness: studying consciousness with computational models. Neural Netw. **44**, 112–131 (2013)
9. Starzyk, J.A., Graham, J.: MLECOG: motivated learning embodied cognitive architecture. IEEE Syst. J. **11**(99), 1–12 (2015)
10. Arrabales, R., Ledezma, A., Sanchis, A.: CERA-CRANIUM: a test bed for machine consciousness research (2009)
11. Franklin, S., Madl, T., D'Mello, S., Snaider, J.: LIDA: a systems-level architecture for cognition, emotion, and learning. IEEE Trans. Autonom. Mental Dev. **6**(1), 19–41 (2014)
12. Faghihi, U., Fournier-Viger, P., Nkambou, R.: A computational model for causal learning in cognitive agents. Knowl. Based Syst. **30**, 48–56 (2012)
13. Paraense, A.L., Raizer, K., de Paula, S.M., Rohmer, E., Gudwin, R.R.: The cognitive systems toolkit and the CST reference cognitive architecture. Biol. Inspired Cogn. Archit. **17**, 32–48 (2016)
14. Loeliger, H.A.: An introduction to factor graphs. IEEE Signal Process. Mag. **21**(1), 28–41 (2004)
15. Rosenbloom, P.S., Demski, A., Ustun, V.: The Sigma cognitive architecture and system: towards functionally elegant grand unification. J. Artif. Gen. Intell. **7**(1), 1–103 (2016)
16. Ustun, V., Rosenbloom, P.S.: Towards adaptive, interactive virtual humans in Sigma. In: Brinkman, W.-P., Broekens, J., Heylen, D. (eds.) IVA 2015. LNCS, vol. 9238, pp. 98–108. Springer, Cham (2015). doi:10.1007/978-3-319-21996-7_10
17. Goertzel, B.: OpenCogPrime: a cognitive synergy based architecture for artificial general intelligence. In: 8th IEEE International Conference on Cognitive Informatics, ICCI 2009, pp. 60–68. IEEE (2009)
18. Lin, T.-Y., Maire, M., Belongie, S., Hays, J., Perona, P., Ramanan, D., Dollár, P., Zitnick, C.L.: Microsoft COCO: Common Objects in Context. In: Fleet, D., Pajdla, T., Schiele, B., Tuytelaars, T. (eds.) ECCV 2014. LNCS, vol. 8693, pp. 740–755. Springer, Cham (2014). doi:10.1007/978-3-319-10602-1_48
19. Sharma, A., Vo, N.H., Aditya, S., Baral, C.: Towards addressing the winograd schema challenge-building and using a semantic parser and a knowledge hunting module. In: IJCAI, pp. 1319–1325 (2015)
20. Ng, G., Ng, K., Tan, K., Goh, C.: The ultimate challenge of commander's decision aids: the cognition based dynamic reasoning machine. In: Proceeding of 25th Army Science Conference (2006)
21. Ng, G.W., Ng, K.H., Tan, K.H., Goh, C.H.K.: Novel methods for fusing Bayesian network knowledge fragments in D'Brain. In: 2007 10th International Conference on Information Fusion, pp. 1–8, July 2007

Mathematical Foundations

A General (Category Theory) Principle for General Intelligence: Duality (Adjointness)

Steven Phillips[⊠]

Mathematical Neuroinformatics Group, Human Informatics Research Institute,
National Institute of Advanced Industrial Science and Technology (AIST),
Tsukuba, Ibaraki, Japan
steve@ni.aist.go.jp

Abstract. Artificial General Intelligence (AGI) seeks theories, models and techniques to endow machines with the kinds of intellectual abilities exemplified by humans. Yet, the predominant instance-driven approach in AI appears antithetical to this goal. This situation raises a question: What (if any) general principles underlie general intelligence? We approach this question from a (mathematical) category theory perspective as a continuation of a categorical approach to other properties of human cognition. The proposal pursued here is adjoint functors as a universal (systematic) basis for trading the costs/benefits that accompany physical systems interacting intelligently with their environment.

Keywords: Systematicity · Compositionality · category theory · Functor · adjunction · Intelligence · Raven Progressive Matrices

1 Introduction

The purview of Artificial *General* Intelligence (AGI) is the development of theories, models and techniques for the endowment of machines with intellectual capabilities that *generalize* to a variety of novel situations. This characterization, however, belies important questions about what we mean by intelligence and generalize. In the absence of precise criteria, researchers look to the archetype of general intelligence, human cognition, for examples of model behaviour [19].

Such (behaviourist/operationalist) approaches afford clear criteria to compare methods, but there are some significant drawbacks. Firstly, complex behaviour can be realized in more than one way. A machine that requires many more training examples to achieve a comparable level of human performance on a complex intellectual activity (e.g., chess) may not capture essential properties of general intelligence [13]. Secondly, humans also make (logically) irrational decisions [12]. Failures of logical reasoning, however, do not warrant rejecting human cognition as an example of general intelligence. So, specific behaviours may provide neither necessary nor sufficient criteria for general intelligence.

This problematic state of affairs raises an important question: What (if any) general principles underlie general intelligence? Discerning principles for cognition is a concern of cognitive scientists when comparing/contrasting mental

© Springer International Publishing AG 2017
T. Everitt et al. (Eds.): AGI 2017, LNAI 10414, pp. 57–66, 2017.
DOI: 10.1007/978-3-319-63703-7_6

capacity across cohorts (e.g., age groups, or species). A typical recourse is to look at relationships between mental capacities, rather than individual behaviours [10]. In the remainder of this introduction, we recall one such relationship that motivates our approach to AGI, which is presented in the subsequent sections.

1.1 Systematicity, Generalization and Categorical Universality

The so-called *cognitive revolution* in psychology was a shift in focus from behaviour to the underlying structures that generate it, or more pointedly, a shift towards the (structural) relations between the underlying cognitive processes that cause the structural relations between behaviours generated [3]. An example is the *systematicity* property of cognition. Systematicity is when having a capacity for some cognitive ability implies having a capacity for a structurally-related ability [8]. An example is having the capacity to understand the expression *John loves Mary* if and only if having the capacity to understand *Mary loves John*. These two capacities are related by the common *loves* relation. Systematicity, in general, is an equivalence relation over cognitive capacities, which need not be confined to language [15]—a kind of generalization over cognitive abilities.

The systematicity problem is to explain *why* cognition is organized into particular groups of cognitive capacities [8]. Although this problem was articulated three decades ago, consensus on a solution remains elusive (see [4] for a recent reappraisal). Cognitive scientists generally agree that systematicity depends on processing common structure, though they may disagree on the nature of those processes, e.g., symbolic [8], or subsymbolic [20]. However, the sticking point is over a specification for the (necessary and sufficient) conditions from which systematicity follows: the *why* not just the *how* of systematicity [1,8]. Central to (ordinary) *category theory* [14] is the formal concept of *universal construction*: necessary and sufficient conditions relating collections of mathematically structured objects. In this sense (of necessity and sufficiency) one can regard category theory as a *theory of structure*, which should make category theory well-placed to provide an explanation for the why of systematicity [17].

A category consists of a collection of *objects*, a collection of *morphisms* (also called *arrows*, or *maps*), and a *composition operation* for composing morphisms. In the context of cognition, morphisms may be regarded as cognitive processes that map between objects that are sets of cognitive states. A *universal morphism* (universal construction) is a morphism that is common to a collection of morphisms, hence its relevance to an explanation for systematicity [17].

1.2 Cost/Benefit Cognition: Dual-Routes and Duality

If cognition is supposed to be systematic, then why are there failures of systematicity? Cognitive systems are physical systems, hence resource sensitive. So, alternative ways of realizing task goals may trade one kind of resource for another. For example, parallel computation typically involves more memory (space) but less time than serial computation; faster response is typically accompanied by lower accuracy. We hypothesized that failures of systematicity arise from a cost/benefit trade-off associated with employing a universal construction, and an experiment designed to manipulate the cost of computing a task *with* versus *without* a universal construction provided support for this hypothesis [16].

Characterizations of cognition as dual-process (route) abound in psychology: e.g., fast versus slow, domain-specific versus domain-general, resilient versus sensitive to working memory load, and associative versus relational [7,10,12]. Although identifying such distinctions are important, they do not explain why cognition appears this way. Our study [16] suggested that failures of systematicity are themselves systematically related. Since the categorical explanation says that a universal construction underlies each and every instance of systematicity, we propose that another kind of universal construction, called an *adjunction*, underlies cognitive dual-routes and general intelligence.

An adjunction can be considered as a collection of universal morphisms for the opposing constructions as dual-routes. Each collection affords a systematic alternative path that realizes a cost/benefit trade-off. General intelligence involves the effective exploitation of this trade-off. The link from dual-route to adjunction is formally illustrated using a familiar example of dual from elementary algebra, in Sect. 2, which also serves as an aid to understanding the basic category theory that follows for application to cognition and general intelligence, in Sect. 3. This general principle for AGI is discussed in Sect. 4.

2 Categorical Dual (Adjunction): An Elementary Example

Computing with very small or large numbers creates precision errors when results exceed a machine's representational capacity. These computational "potholes" are avoided by taking a dual route, which is illustrated using the following equations relating addition to multiplication:

$$a \times b = e^{\log a + \log b} \quad \text{and} \tag{1}$$

$$a + b = \log(e^a \times e^b), \tag{2}$$

which show that one can be computed in terms of the other.

Definition 1 (Category). *A category* **C** *consists of*

- *a collection of objects,* $\mathcal{O}(\mathbf{C}) = \{A, B, \dots\}$,
- *a collection of morphisms,* $\mathcal{M}(\mathbf{C}) = \{f, g, \dots\}$—$f : A \to B$ *indicates A as the domain and B as the codomain of f, and* $\text{Hom}_{\mathbf{C}}(A, B)$ *as the collection of morphisms from A to B in* **C**—*including the morphism* $1_A : A \to A$ *for every object* $A \in \mathcal{O}(\mathbf{C})$, *called the identity morphism at A, and*
- *a composition operation,* ∘, *that sends a pair of morphisms* $f : A \to B$ *and* $g : B \to C$ *to the composite morphism* $g \circ f : A \to C$,

that together satisfy

- *identity: $f \circ 1_A = f = 1_B \circ f$ for every $f \in \mathcal{M}(\mathbf{C})$, and*
- *associativity: $h \circ (g \circ f) = (h \circ g) \circ f$ for every triple of compatible morphisms $f, g, h \in \mathcal{M}(\mathbf{C})$: the codomain of f is the domain of g; likewise for g and h.*

Example 1 (Set). *The category* **Set** *has sets for objects, functions for morphisms, and composition is composition of functions: $g \circ f(a) = g(f(a))$. Identity morphisms are identity functions: $1_A : a \mapsto a$.*

Example 2 (Monoid). *A monoid is a set M with a binary operation $\cdot$ and an identity element $e \in M$ such that $a \cdot e = a = e \cdot a$ for every element $a \in M$. Every monoid $(M, \cdot, e)$ is a one-object category whose morphisms are the elements of M, with e as the identity morphism, and composition is the monoid operation. The set of real numbers $\mathbb{R}$ under addition and multiplication are the monoids $(\mathbb{R}, +, 0)$ and $(\mathbb{R}, \times, 1)$ and therefore categories. For instance, the composition of morphisms $2 : * \to *$ and $3 : * \to *$ is the morphism $3 \circ 2 = 5 : * \to *$, which corresponds to the addition of their corresponding numbers, $2 + 3 = 5$.*

Remark 1. *Category $\mathbf{C}^{\mathrm{op}}$ is opposite to $\mathbf{C}$, which is obtained by morphism reversal: morphism $f : A \to B$ in $\mathbf{C}$ is $f^{op} : B \to A$ in $\mathbf{C}^{\mathrm{op}}$. A dual (e.g., coproduct) in $\mathbf{C}$ is just the primal (product) in $\mathbf{C}^{\mathrm{op}}$.*

Definition 2 (Functor). *A functor $F : \mathbf{C} \to \mathbf{D}$ is a map from category $\mathbf{C}$ to category $\mathbf{D}$ sending each object A and morphism $f : A \to B$ in $\mathbf{C}$ to (respectively) the object $F(A)$ and the morphism $F(f) : F(A) \to F(B)$ in $\mathbf{D}$ such that*

- *identity: $F(1_A) = 1_{F(A)}$ for every object $A \in \mathcal{O}(\mathbf{C})$, and*
- *compositionality: $F(g \circ_{\mathbf{C}} f) = F(g) \circ_{\mathbf{D}} F(f)$ for every pair of compatible morphisms $f, g \in \mathcal{M}(\mathbf{C})$.*

Example 3 (Monoid homomorphism). *A monoid homomorphism is a map $h : (M, \cdot, e) \to (N, \star, e')$ such that $h(e) = e'$ and $h(a \cdot b) = h(a) \star h(b)$ for all $a, b \in M$. Every monoid homomorphism is a functor. For instance, the exponential function $\exp : a \mapsto e^a$ is a monoid homomorphism, since $e^0 = 1$ and $e^{a+b} = e^a \times e^b$, and therefore a functor. Likewise, the log function defined over $\mathbb{R} - \{0\}$ (denoted $\mathbb{R}_0$) is a functor, since $\log(1) = 0$ and $\log(a \times b) = \log(a) + \log(b)$.*

Remark 2. *A functor $F : \mathbf{C}^{\mathrm{op}} \to \mathbf{D}$ is called a contravariant functor. Contravariant functor $I^{op} : \mathbf{C}^{\mathrm{op}} \to \mathbf{C}$ sends f^{op} to f.*

The following definition is needed before defining adjunction. We delay giving examples until the next section, because the natural transformations associated with the current example of a dual are trivial (i.e. identities).

Definition 3 (Natural transformation, isomorphism). *A natural transformation η from a functor $F : \mathbf{C} \to \mathbf{D}$ to a functor $G : \mathbf{C} \to \mathbf{D}$, written $\eta : F \overset{\cdot}{\to} G$, is a family of $\mathbf{D}$-morphisms $\{\eta_A : F(A) \to G(A) | A \in \mathcal{O}(\mathbf{C})\}$ such that $G(f) \circ \eta_A = \eta_B \circ F(f)$ for each morphism $f : A \to B$ in $\mathbf{C}$. A natural isomorphism is a natural transformation where every η_A is an isomorphism, i.e. a morphism that has a (left/right) inverse.*

Remark 3. *A natural isomorphism is indicated by the following diagram:*

$$F(A) \underset{\eta_A^{-1}}{\overset{\eta_A}{\rightleftarrows}} G(A) \tag{3}$$

$$F(f) \downarrow \qquad \downarrow G(f)$$

$$F(B) \underset{\eta_B^{-1}}{\overset{\eta_B}{\rightleftarrows}} G(B),$$

which yields two identities:

$$F(f) = \eta_B^{-1} \circ G(f) \circ \eta_A \quad and \tag{4}$$

$$G(f) = \eta_B \circ F(f) \circ \eta_A^{-1}, \tag{5}$$

hence their importance in exploiting dual-routes.

Definition 4 (Adjunction). *An adjunction* $(F, G, \eta, \epsilon) : \mathbf{C} \rightharpoonup \mathbf{D}$ *consists of functors* $F : \mathbf{C} \to \mathbf{D}$ *and* $G : \mathbf{D} \to \mathbf{C}$, *and natural transformations* $\eta : 1_{\mathbf{C}} \dashrightarrow G \circ F$ *and* $\epsilon : F \circ G \dashrightarrow 1_{\mathbf{D}}$ *satisfying* $G\epsilon \circ \eta G = 1_G$ *and* $\epsilon F \circ F\eta = 1_F$, *where* 1_F *and* 1_G *are identity natural transformations (on* F *and* G). F *is the called the left adjoint of* G, *and* G *is called the right adjoint of* F, *written* $F \dashv G$; *natural transformations* η *and* ϵ *are called (respectively) the unit and counit.*

Remark 4. *Definition 4 induces equalities* $f = G(g) \circ \eta_A$ *and* $g = \epsilon_B \circ F(f)$, *which are shown by the following diagrams:*

$$
\begin{array}{cccccc}
A \overset{\eta_A}{\longrightarrow} GF(A) & & F(A) & A & F(A) & (6)\\
\quad\diagdown \quad \downarrow G(g) & & \downarrow g & f\downarrow & F(f)\downarrow \quad\diagdown\, g & \\
f\quad\searrow \quad\downarrow & & \downarrow & \downarrow & \downarrow & \\
\quad\quad G(B) & & B & G(B) & FG(B) \underset{\epsilon_B}{\longrightarrow} B.
\end{array}
$$

Dashed arrows indicate uniqueness. The pair $(F(A), \eta_A)$ *is the universal morphism from* A *to* F; *the pair* $(G(B), \epsilon_B)$ *is the universal morphism from* G *to* B. *In other words, every morphism* f *factors through* η_A; *every morphism* g *factors through* ϵ_B, *hence the importance of universal morphisms to systematicity.*

Remark 5. *Derived hom-functors* $\text{Hom}(F-,-), \text{Hom}(-,G-) : \mathbf{C}^{\text{op}} \times \mathbf{D} \to \mathbf{Set}$ *and natural isomorphism* $\phi : \text{Hom}(F-,-) \dashrightarrow \text{Hom}(-,G-) : \psi$ *(see [14]) are indicated by the following diagram:*

$$
\begin{array}{cccc}
(A, B) & \text{Hom}_{\mathbf{D}}(F(A), B) \underset{\psi_{A,B}}{\overset{\phi_{A,B}}{\rightleftarrows}} \text{Hom}_{\mathbf{C}}(A, G(B)) & (7)\\
(h,k)\downarrow & \text{Hom}(F(h),k)\downarrow \qquad\qquad\qquad \downarrow \text{Hom}(h,G(k)) & \\
(A', B') & \text{Hom}_{\mathbf{D}}(F(A'), B') \underset{\psi_{A',B'}}{\overset{\phi_{A',B'}}{\rightleftarrows}} \text{Hom}_{\mathbf{C}}(A', G(B')),
\end{array}
$$

hence the importance of adjunctions to duality and dual-routes.

Example 4 (exp ⊣ log). *Setting F and G in diagram 7 to functors* exp *and* log, *hence* $\mathrm{Hom}_{\mathbf{D}}(F(A), B) = \mathbb{R}_0$ *and* $\mathrm{Hom}_{\mathbf{C}}(A, G(B)) = \mathbb{R}$, *we have for (h, k) set to $(0, b)$ and (h, k) to $(a, 1)$ the following (respectively, left and right) diagrams:*

$$
\begin{array}{cc}
(*,*) & \mathbb{R}_0 \xrightarrow{\log(-)} \mathbb{R} \\
(0,b)\downarrow & \times b \downarrow \quad\quad \downarrow +\log b \\
(*,*) & \mathbb{R}_0 \xleftarrow{e^{(-)}} \mathbb{R}
\end{array}
\qquad
\begin{array}{cc}
(*,*) & \mathbb{R}_0 \xleftarrow{e^{(-)}} \mathbb{R} \\
(a,1)\downarrow & e^a \times \downarrow \quad\quad \downarrow a+ \\
(*,*) & \mathbb{R}_0 \xrightarrow{\log(-)} \mathbb{R}.
\end{array}
\qquad (8)
$$

For all $a \in \mathbb{R}_0$, traversal of the left square recovers Eq. 1; for all $b \in \mathbb{R}$, traversal of the right square recovers Eq. 2 (cf. Eqs. 4 and 5).

Remark 6. *Functions/functors* log *and* exp *are mutual inverses, hence isomorphisms. Every isomorphic functor and its inverse form an adjunction, but every adjoint functor is not an isomorphism (see, e.g., next section). One can think of adjoints as conceptual though not necessarily actual inverses.*

3   Cognitive Dual-Routes and Adjoints

With the formal concept of adjunction at hand, we present two examples of how adjunctions underlie cognitive dual-routes. Both examples involve categorical products, which relate cognitive development across reasoning tasks [18].

3.1   Stimulus-Response

To examine a potential cost/benefit trade-off associated with categorical products, subjects were tested on a stimulus-response task involving a product of two maps: a character-to-colour map *char2colour* : *Char* → *Colour* and a character-to-shape map *char2shape* : *Char* → *Shape*, e.g., (G, P) ↦ (red, ♣), (P, K) ↦ (blue, ▼) [16]. Subjects could learn each task as a single map of pairs (n^2), or as a pair of maps between singletons ($2n$). The former alternative does not afford generalization, as each pair is interpreted as a unique, indivisible element; the latter alternative affords generalization after inducing the component maps. The map learned depended on set size: stimulus-response associations were learned wholistically when the number of mappings was small, but componentially when the number of mappings was large, and this difference depended on the order of learning [16]. Here, we show that the categorical basis for this duality is the adjoint relationship between *diagonal* and *product* functors.

Definition 5 (Diagonal, product functor). *The diagonal functor $\Delta : \mathbf{C} \to \mathbf{C} \times \mathbf{C}$; $A \mapsto (A, A), f \mapsto (f, f)$ sends each object and morphism to their pairs. The product functor $\Pi : \mathbf{C} \times \mathbf{C} \to \mathbf{C}$; $(A, B) \mapsto A \times B, (f, g) \mapsto f \times g$ sends pairs of objects and morphisms to their categorical products.*

Remark 7. *The categorical product in* **Set** *is the Cartesian product.*

Example 5 ($\Delta \dashv \Pi$). *Diagonal and product functors form an adjoint pair. The natural transformations are:* $\langle 1, 1 \rangle : 1_{\mathbf{C}} \xrightarrow{\cdot} \Pi \circ \Delta$ *and* $(\pi_1, \pi_2) : \Delta \circ \Pi \xrightarrow{\cdot} 1_{\mathbf{C} \times \mathbf{C}}$. *In* **Set**, π_1 *and* π_2 *are projections, i.e.* $\pi_1 : (a, b) \mapsto a$, *and* $\pi_2 : (a, b) \mapsto b$. *Instantiating F and G in diagram 7 as* Δ *and* Π *over* **Set** *yields*

$$
\begin{array}{ccc}
(A, B) \xleftarrow{\phi} A \times B & \qquad (a, b) \xleftarrow{\phi} \langle a, b \rangle & (9) \\
{\scriptstyle (f,g)} \downarrow \qquad \downarrow {\scriptstyle f \times g} & \qquad {\scriptstyle (f,g)} \downarrow \qquad \qquad \downarrow {\scriptstyle f \times g} \\
(A', B') \xrightarrow{\psi} A' \times B' & \qquad (f(a), g(b)) \xmapsto{\psi} \langle f(a), g(b) \rangle .
\end{array}
$$

For the stimulus-response task, A and B (diagram 9) correspond to *Char*, and A' and B' to *Colour* and *Shape*. The dual-route realized by the adjunction trades the cost of maintaining a pair of maps (left vertical arrows in each square) with the benefit on only needing about $2n$ training examples for correct response prediction on all n^2 of the single product map (right vertical arrows).

3.2   A Measure of Intelligence: Raven Progressive Matrices

Raven Progressive Matrices (RPM) is an inference task. Subjects are presented with a 3×3 matrix of stimuli, whose bottom-right cell is empty, and an array of choice stimuli from which they choose the stimulus that belongs in the empty cell. Examples are shown in Fig. 1, with stimuli varying along one (number) or two (number, shape) dimensions. Various factors influence the difficulty of RPM, such as recognizing the relevant relations to infer the missing attributes for the row/column [5], and the number of such variable relations [6,21]. Dimensionality pertains to (unary/binary) products (see [18] for the relationship between dimensionality, product arity and difficulty for the closely related *matrix completion task*), hence the aforementioned diagonal-product adjunction, albeit for particular algebras instead of just sets. So, here, we focus on the missing attribute aspect of RPM, as involving another instance of an adjunction.

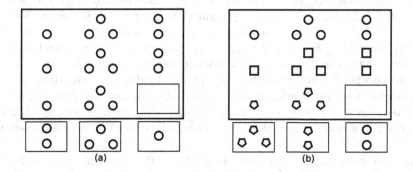

Fig. 1. RPM-like examples with (a) one and (b) two dimensions of variable relations.

The adjunction involves constructing a *free object*. Typically, the left adjoint is a *free* functor that sends each set to the free algebraic structure (e.g., monoid, group, etc.) on that set. The right adjoint is the associated *forgetful* functor that sends each algebraic structure to its underlying set, forgetting the algebraic operations. For example, the free monoid on the set (alphabet) A is the monoid $(A^*, \cdot, \varepsilon)$ consisting of the set of "words" A^* (i.e. strings of 0 or more characters $a \in A$) composed from the concatenation operation $\cdot$, where ε is the empty (length zero) word. The universal construction is shown in diagram 10 (left), where *len* is the monoid homomorphism returning word length, ι is the universal (initial) morphism, and 1 is the constant function assigning 1 to every alphabetic character. Initial morphism ι is an injection of generators $a \in A$; equivalently, the completion of word set A^* from alphabet A.

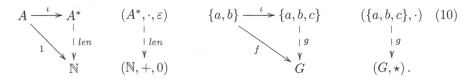

$$A \xrightarrow{\iota} A^* \qquad (A^*, \cdot, \varepsilon) \qquad \{a, b\} \xrightarrow{\iota} \{a, b, c\} \qquad (\{a, b, c\}, \cdot) \quad (10)$$

For RPM, each row/column constitutes a *semigroupoid* (partial monoid with identity unneeded). The missing feature (e.g., shape) is obtained from the initial morphism as the completion of the two given features (circle, square) to obtain the other feature (pentagon). The initial morphism is the completion of the two-element set $\{a, b\}$ to the three-element set $\{a, b, c\}$, diagram 10 (right). The semigroupoid formalizes the notion of obtaining the missing element c from the given elements a and b, i.e. $a \cdot b = c$, where $\cdot$ is the semigroupoid operation.[1] There is a speed accuracy trade-off with regard to products: considering a single dimension is faster but less accurate, e.g., neither shape nor number uniquely identifies the target (two pentagons) in Fig. 1(b), see also Discussion.

4   Discussion

We have looked at three examples of adjunctions as the basis of dual-routes and cost/benefit trade-offs. Given the diversity of what one may regard as general intellectual behaviour, claims of a general principle from so few examples may seem premature. In what sense, then, are adjunctions justifiably a general principle for general intelligence? In the remainder of this section, we step back from the formal details to discuss some broader conceptual motivations.

The conceptual connections between general intelligence and adjunction are the following. General intelligence is a product of cognition, cognitive systems are physical systems, physical systems interact with their environment by exchange of energy (information), and this interaction (adjunction) induces a dual-route.

---

[1] Equivalently, the missing element is obtained from the underlying graph of the *free semicategory* (category with identity arrows unneeded) on the graph consisting of the connected edges a and b: the missing element is the edge $c = ab$.

Cost/benefit can be regarded as a duality between system and environment: cost is the expenditure of system resources on the environment, and benefit is uptake of environmental resources by the system. Formally, we have regarded this dual relation as adjunction, and choice depends on which route is more cost effective.

We presented three examples of how cost/benefit trade-off may arise from adjunction. Directly adding/multiplying very small or large numbers effectively has large cost when representational capacity is exceeded: *enlarge is dual to compress*. Directly inferring a response to a novel stimulus effectively has an large cost when the correct response is unknown: *analyze is dual to synthesize*. In the case of RPM, this dual route derives the one-to-one correspondence assumption, which often accompanies cognitive models. One route involves working with the algebra's operations (i.e. relations between elements); the other route forgets the operations, which saves time in having to recompute results. We could say that *relation is dual to association*. System and environment are considered broadly to include (pairs of) subsystems within a larger system (e.g., attention and memory within a cognitive system). From the standpoint of expertise, one can see the free-forgetful adjunction as exploiting both domain-relevant relations and a reservoir of learned associations.

One might wonder why we need adjunctions, rather than any pair of alternative routes. The claim is that dual-routes are also systematically, as opposed to arbitrarily related. We have argued that underlying every instance of systematicity is a universal construction of some kind [17]. If, as claimed, that dual-routes are systematically related, then adjunctions (which are another kind of universal construction) provide the basis for a *natural* explanation. Category theory affords general principles in the sense that constructions are typically parametrized by some kind of object, e.g., a category. In this sense, adjoints are a general principle: each of the three examples is based on the same construction parametrized by a different pair of (adjoint) functors.

Although adjoints provide a systematic basis for dual routes, there remains the question of assigning a cost/benefit to each route. As the experimental work on the stimulus-response task suggested, choice of route depends on the task at hand and prior learning [16]. One possibility is to incorporate information theoretic principles, such as a Kolmogorov complexity-based approach to universal artificial intelligence [11]. See [22] for a category theory approach to Kolmogorov complexity. In this way, the route selected is the one with the "shortest" program able to produce the requisite response, which makes the collection of routes an order. Ordered sets are categories with arrows as the order relations; universal morphisms pertain to minimum elements. Though probabilistic models were not considered here, categorical approaches to probability also exist (see, e.g., [2,9]). Providing a categorical explanation for route selection, as well as applications to other instances of dual-routes is a topic of further research.

Acknowledgements. I thank the reviewers for helpful comments. This work was supported by a JSPS Grant-in-aid (16KT0025).

References

1. Aizawa, K.: The systematicity arguments. Studies in Mind and Brain. Kluwer Academic, New York (2003)
2. Avery, T.: Codensity and the Giry monad. J. Pure Appl. Algebra **220**(3), 1229–1251 (2016)
3. Baars, B.J.: The Cognitive Revolution in Psychology. Guilford Press, New York (1986)
4. Calvo, P., Symons, J. (eds.): The Architecture of Cognition: Rethinking Fodor and Pylyshyn's Systematicity Challenge. MIT Press, Cambridge (2014)
5. Carpenter, P.A., Just, M.A., Shell, P.: What one intelligence test measures: a theoretical account of the processing in the Raven Progressive Matrices test. Psychol. Rev. **97**(3), 404–431 (1990)
6. Christoff, K., Prabhakaran, V., Dorfman, J., Kroger, K.J., Zhao, Z., Holyoak, K.J., Gabrieli, J.D.E.: Rostral prefrontal cortex involvement in relational processing during reasoning. Neuroimage **14**(5), 1136–1149 (2001)
7. Evans, J.S.B.T., Stanovich, K.E.: Dual-process theories of higher cognition: advancing the debate. Perspect. Psychol. Sci. **8**(3), 223–241 (2013)
8. Fodor, J.A., Pylyshyn, Z.W.: Connectionism and cognitive architecture: a critical analysis. Cognition **28**(1–2), 3–71 (1988)
9. Fong, B.: Causal theories: a categorical perspective on Bayesian networks (2013). Preprint: arxiv:1301.6201
10. Halford, G.S., Wilson, W.H., Andrews, G., Phillips, S.: Categorizing cognition: toward conceptual coherence in the foundations of psychology. MIT Press, Cambridge (2014)
11. Hutter, M.: Universal artificial intelligence: sequential decisions based on algorithmic probability. Texts in Theoretical Computer Science. Springer, Berlin (2005)
12. Kahneman, D.: Thinking, Fast and Slow. Farrar, Straus and Giroux, NY (2011)
13. Lake, B.M., Ullman, T.B., Tenenbaum, J.B., Gershman, S.J.: Building machines that learn and think like people. Behav. Brain Sci. **24**, 1–101 (2016)
14. Mac Lane, S.: Categories for the working mathematician. Graduate Texts in Mathematics, 2nd edn. Springer, New York (1998)
15. McLaughlin, B.P.: Systematicity redux. Synthese **170**, 251–274 (2009)
16. Phillips, S., Takeda, Y., Sugimoto, F.: Why are there failures of systematicity? The empirical costs and benefits of inducing universal constructions. Front. Psychol. **7**, 1310 (2016)
17. Phillips, S., Wilson, W.H.: Categorial compositionality: a category theory explanation for the systematicity of human cognition. PLoS Comput. Biol. **6**(7), e1000858 (2010)
18. Phillips, S., Wilson, W.H., Halford, G.S.: What do transitive inference and class inclusion have in common? Categorical (co)products and cognitive development. PLoS Comput. Biol. **5**(12), e1000599 (2009)
19. Rich, E.: Artificial intelligence. In: Shapiro, S.C. (ed.) Encyclopedia of Artificial Intelligence, vol. 1, pp. 9–16. Wiley, New York (1987)
20. Smolensky, P.: The constituent structure of connectionist mental states: a reply to Fodor and Pylyshyn. South. J. Philos. **26**, 137–161 (1987)
21. Waltz, J.A., Knowlton, B.J., Holyoak, K.J., Boone, K.B., Mishkin, F.S., Santoa, M.D.M., Thomas, C.R., Miller, B.L.: A system for relational reasoning in human prefrontal cortex. Psychol. Sci. **10**(2), 119–125 (1999)
22. Yanofsky, N.S.: Kolmogorov complexity of categories. In: Coecke, B., Ong, L., Panangaden, P. (eds.) Computation, Logic, Games, and Quantum Foundations. The Many Facets of Samson Abramsky. LNCS, vol. 7860, pp. 350–362. Springer, Heidelberg (2013). doi:10.1007/978-3-642-38164-5_25

Abstract Representations and Generalized Frequent Pattern Discovery

Eray Özkural[✉]

Gök Us Sibernetik Ar&Ge Ltd. Şti., Istanbul, Turkey
examachine@gmail.com

Abstract. We discuss the frequent pattern mining problem in a general setting. From an analysis of abstract representations, summarization and frequent pattern mining, we arrive at a generalization of the problem. Then, we show how the problem can be cast into the powerful language of algorithmic information theory. We formulate and prove a universal pruning theorem analogous to the well-known Downward Closure Lemma in data mining. This result allows us to formulate a simple algorithm to mine all frequent patterns given an appropriate compressor to recognize patterns.

1 Introduction

The field of data mining is changing faster than we can define it. In recent years, foundations of data mining have received considerable interest, helping remove some of the ad-hoc considerations in the theory of data mining and expanding the frontiers. The problem definitions of early data mining research have now been analyzed meticulously, considering especially the performance and scalability of methods, giving a performance-oriented character to most data mining research. Qualitative work has usually focused on slight variations of the original problems; staying within the framework of basic problems such as association rule mining and sequence mining. However, the ever expanding computational and storage capacity challenges us to devise new ways to look at the data mining tasks, to discover more interesting/useful patterns. The subject of this paper is a substantial revision of the frequency mining problem, this time mining for any kind of a pattern instead of frequent item sets. We arrive at our formulation from a philosophical analysis of the problem, conceiving what the problem might look like in the most general setting. After reviewing some of the recent literature on generalizing data mining problems, we examine the relation of abstraction to the summarization task and in particular frequent pattern discovery. We then present a novel formulation of the frequent pattern discovery problem using algorithmic information theory, derived from our philosophical analysis. We show that our formulation exhibits similar formal relations to the original frequent itemset mining problem, and is arguably a good generalization of it. Then, we present the

---

The present paper was originally written and circulated in 2006, and its findings inform our other AGI methods including Heuristic Algorithmic Memory [13].

© Springer International Publishing AG 2017
T. Everitt et al. (Eds.): AGI 2017, LNAI 10414, pp. 67–76, 2017.
DOI: 10.1007/978-3-319-63703-7_7

MICRO-SYNTHETIC algorithm which has the capability to detect any kind of a pattern given our information theoretic definition of pattern occurrence. The algorithm is similar to the APRIORI algorithm in its logic of managing the task in a small number of database scans. After discussing the pros and cons of our approach, we outline future research directions.

2   Background and Related Work

We will skip the definitions and methods of traditional frequent pattern discovery for considerations of space. For an introduction to the subject, see [3,9,18]. There has been some promising research in applying the generic methods of Kolmogorov complexity to data mining. The authors report favorable results for classification and deviation detection tasks in [7]. A mathematical theory of high frequency patterns which uses granular computing was presented in [11]. We will now take a closer look at algorithmic methods which have attracted a great deal of interest.

2.1   Algorithmic Information Theory

Algorithmic information theory (AIT) gives an absolute characterization of complexity for arbitrary bit strings [6]. A computer is a computable partial function $C(p,q)$ of self-delimiting program strings p and data q, where both input and output datum are bitstrings in $\{0,1\}^*$. Empty string is denoted with Λ and the shortest program which computes s is denoted with $s*$. U is a universal computer that can simulate any other computer C with $U(p',q) = C(p,q)$ and $|p'| \leq |p| + sim(C)$ where $sim(C)$ is the length of simulation program for C. An admissible universal computer is LISP with its eval function.

The algorithmic information content $H(s)$ of a bit string s is the size of minimal program $s*$ which computes it. $H(s/t)$ is the algorithmic information content of s relative to t (conditional algorithmic entropy). Another definition from AIT is mutual algorithmic information $H(s:t)$ which is relevant to our work. $H(s:t)$ is the extent to which knowing s helps one to calculate t. The probability $P(s)$ of a bitstring s is the probability a program evaluates to s. Likewise, the conditional probability $P(s/t)$ is the probability a program evaluates to s given the minimal program $t*$ for calculating t.

AIT gives an analogous formalism to information theory, and is deemed more fundamental since Shannon information can be derived from algorithmic (Kolmogorov) information. It is not possible to include all theorems here, but some relevant consequences and results will be stated, mostly without proof.

$H(s,t)$ is the joint algorithmic information of s and t where "," denotes concatenation of bitstrings (at any rate it is straightforward to convert between any two pair encodings). Algorithmic information is asymptotically symmetric, e.g. $H(s,t) = H(t,s) + O(1)$ since in high level languages it is not problematic to accomplish this sort of feat with a short constant program. The conditional entropy of a string with itself is constant, similarly.

Theorem I8 of [6] states that conditional entropy measures how easier it is to compute two strings together than separately.

$$H_C(t/s) = H(s,t) - H(s) + c \tag{1}$$

Theorem I9 of [6] exposes the relationships between joint, mutual and conditional information, as well as probability and joint probability. In particular, algorithmic information is subadditive and conditional and mutual information can be calculated from probabilities.

$$H(s,t) = H(s) + H(t/s) + O(1) \tag{2a}$$

$$H(s:t) = H(s) + H(t) - H(s,t) + O(1) \tag{2b}$$

$$H(s:t) = H(t:s) + O(1) \tag{2c}$$

There are several other interesting theorems in AIT, however they fall beyond the scope of the present work.

2.2   Algorithmic Distance Metrics for Classification

$H(s)$ is uncomputable. However, it can be approximated with a reasonable compression program from the above. The standard UNIX compression programs gzip and bzip2 have been used exactly for this purpose by Cilibrasi et al. [16] for clustering music files. In the predecessors to this paper, Vitanyi et al. [5,10,14] have introduced a distance function based on algorithmic information theory which can be used for domain unspecific classification and clustering algorithms.

In another work, Kraskov et al. propose using mutual information both in Shannon's version and Kolmogorov's version based on the same proof [1]. These studies are relevant to our problem in that they show the versatility of Kolmogorov complexity. We shall now try to answer if we can achieve similar feats in data mining.

3   Abstract Representations

Before proceeding with our formulation of frequent pattern discovery from an information theoretic perspective, it is worthwhile giving a philosophical overview of the task. The main objective of frequency mining is to summarize a large data set. With a suitable threshold, we obtain a smaller data set that is representative of the most significant patterns in the data. By means of such an abstract representation, one then achieves more specific tasks such as discovering association rules or clustering the data.

Recent formulations of association rule mining have characterized the task as generalization of the data. This is a necessary condition for any successful abstraction, else what use can we imagine of an abstract representation? According to Marvin Minsky, another way of putting this would be the removal of unnecessary details from the representation [12]. Statistically, "detail" could be understood as infrequent patterns in data, which is precisely what frequent item set mining eliminates. Thus, a comparison of the common sense notion of "abstraction" and the familiar data mining task of summarization is in order.

Let us conceive of an abstract sketch A. If this drawing is an abstraction of a lively picture B, we expect to find the most "important" features of B in A, perhaps only some of them. We would also expect to see the details, for instance the texture, shading and colors of B to be removed in A (assuming that it is quite abstract). In addition, we would not like to see anything in A that does not correspond to a significant feature in B. Some caricatures, like those of politicians drawn in a clean generic style, may set a good example of this kind of sensory abstraction (Note however that some caricatures are highly stylized and will set a bad example for abstraction). The facial features in a caricature are highly informative; they convey much information about the facial identity of the person at a small cost of representation. On the other hand, like any other image, the abstract representation must be built from low-level components, which are apparently not part of the original image. If these components, such as the basic drawing patterns of the caricaturist, are kept simple enough, the resulting work will look abstract.

If we are to relate the above characterization of abstraction to data mining, the most problematic part might be the "important" term. After all, an important feature for one task might be unimportant for another. Consider the notes of a symphony. The pitch and duration information is considered significant because it helps us to quickly discern one piece of music from the other. This is true for any given application domain. For recognition of music, it is the pitch or the interval that matters. But for speech, it is the phoneme that matters. The truly generic summarization algorithm might be able to discover the concept of note or phoneme merely by looking at the data. If we take B to be only one datum in a data set, we will find it more productive to think of the importance of a feature determined by the frequency of its occurrence. This approach suggested also in the beginning of the section does not completely solve the problem, however. We also need universal and objective criteria for determining if a feature approximately occurs in a given datum.

Let us now make our explanations more precise. We say that A is an abstract representation of B if and only if:

1. A is substantially less complex than B.
2. Every important feature of A is similar to an important feature of B.

Note that condition 2 can also be stated as: "There is no important feature in A that is not similar to an important feature in B".

This definition is more relevant to abstraction than lossy compression. Especially, in lossy compression the only purpose is to reproduce the data set with a low error rate (e.g. defined in terms of how well the reproduction is), it does not necessarily take into account simplification of condition 1. Neither does it address the "similar" predicate of the last condition. One might decide to exclude color from the abstract representation of a house, but in traditional image compression such choices would not be considered. Furthermore, lossy compression does not take into account the generalization power of the representation over an ensemble of objects. However, in frequency mining, we can give a rigid meaning to importance, e.g., statistically significant patterns.

If we now consider a frequent pattern discovery algorithm, we may say that the set of frequent patterns satisfy conditions 1 and 2 to be an abstract representation of the entire data set. A useful frequent pattern set is smaller than the transaction set and each frequent pattern (all of them above the given support can be said to be important) occurs in B as an important feature. In this sense, the pattern set does not only model the current data set, but presumably also future extensions of the data source. (We can note here that the non-traditional statistics provided by the frequent itemset-like computation may have use for predictive modelling in general).

3.1   Analysis of Common Objections

An objection may be raised at this point with respect to the traditional duality of syntax vs. semantics. It may be suggested that abstraction crucially depends on semantics which does not seem to be mentioned in our definition. It need not be, since semantic relations, too, may be accounted for in the "similar" predicate. On the other hand, it must be reminded that cryptic references should not in general be considered as abstract in themselves. By abstraction, we refer to manifestly useful, generalized, compact representations. Any cryptic representation may be conceived of as an encrypted form of such an underlying "successful" abstract representation.

3.2   Other Approaches for Pattern Interestingness

Equating frequency with importance may not be the only or satisfactory way of defining interestingness of a pattern objectively. If we go back to the caricature example, an approach which takes the locality and statistics of the image might be able to produce abstract features which are closer to the common sense description of interestingness. In particular, using wavelets may capture the locality of many data types [4]. Compare also the approach of non-linear PCA to image analysis (for the later task of classification, etc.) [15].

4   Algorithmic Information and Patterns

As noted by [11], a pattern may be conceived of the shortest program that generates a string. Otherwise, the concept of a pattern is something else entirely in every machine learning and data mining paper. By using bit strings and programs, we can give an objective, and universal definition of a pattern. Algorithmic information theory can then be used to define pattern operators in a way that is surprisingly close to cognitive processes. However, at this stage of our research, we do not yet concern ourselves with the programs, our patterns are simply bit strings for now.

In particular, information distance and normalized information distance which were briefly covered in Sect. 2 are universal measures of similarity that are completely independent of the application domain, and some amazingly simple implementations have achieved success in diverse domains and learning tasks. Our use of information theory is directly related to the concept of information distance. We also use conditional entropy to quantify structural difference.

5   A General Model

We are now going to generalize the set-theoretic definition of the classical frequent item set mining to cover a wider range of scientific measurement. Assume that we have samples of sensor data from a "fixed" instrumentation device, for instance image data from a radioastronomy telescope examining a certain region of space. Another example could be seismograph data which transmits measurements irregularly and for any number of samples.

Let transaction multi-set (set with repetition) $T = \{y \mid y \in \{0,1\}^*\}$ be the unordered list of observations drawn from the same domain. Let also bitstrings $x, y \in \{0,1\}^*$. We will say that an *abstract* pattern x occurs approximately in datum $y \in T$ iff:

1. $H(x) \leq c_1.H(y)$ (entropy reduction)
2. $H(x/y) \leq c_2.H(y)$ (noise exclusion)

where $0 < c_2 < c_1 < 1$. We denote "x occurs approximately in y" by $x \prec y$. Second condition is equivalent to stating that pattern x and datum y has mutual information as expected, i.e., $H(x : y) > 0$. Since $H(x : y) = H(x) - H(x/y) + O(1)$, $H(x/y) < H(x) - O(1)$, which is satisfied as $c_2.H(y) < H(x)$. Note that many equations introduce a small additive constant in AIT, which must be correctly handled by the algorithms, or non-patterns may be detected.

Having generalized the pattern occurrence operator in the set theoretic definition from the subset operation to the information-theoretic conditions, the problem definition is straightforward. Let the frequency function $f(T, x) = |\{x \prec y \mid y \in T\}|$. Our objective is the discovery of frequent patterns in a transaction set with a frequency of ϵ and more. The set of all frequent patterns is $\mathcal{F}(T, \epsilon) = \{x \in \{0,1\}^* \mid f(T, x) \geq \epsilon\}$, which is finite due to the entropy reduction condition. (Note that we consider the classical definition of Kolmogorov complexity as mentioned in Sect. 2). However, the size of $\mathcal{F}$ can be quite large, as in the frequent item set mining problem.

The downward closure lemma which states that the subsets of a frequent pattern are also frequent makes the APRIORI algorithm possible in the context of frequent item set mining [2]. There is an analogue of the contrapositive of this lemma for our general formulation. Note that to simplify matters we assume a self-delimiting program encoding such as LISP. The analysis without the self-delimiting condition would introduce an additive logarithmic term which we would address separately.

Theorem 1. *If $x \notin \mathcal{F}(T, \epsilon)$ then $xy \notin \mathcal{F}(T, \epsilon)$. Less formally, any extension of an infrequent pattern is also infrequent.*

Proof. If $x \notin \mathcal{F}(T, \epsilon)$ then, $f(T, x) < \epsilon$. Let z be any datum in T for which it is not the case that $x \prec z$. Then, at least one of the pattern occurrence conditions does not hold. We can now analyze whether an extended $xy \prec z$.

- Suppose that the entropy reduction condition does not hold: $H(x) > c_1.H(z)$. Then, $H(x, y) > c_1.H(z)$ since $H(x, y) > H(x)$.
- Alternatively, suppose that the noise exclusion condition does not hold: $H(x/z) > c_2.H(z)$. Then, it doesn't hold for x, y either. $H((x, y)/z) = H(y/(x, z)) + H(x/z) + O(1)$ by subadditivity of algorithmic information. Since $H(y/(x, z)) > 0$ (since it has to be at least $O(1)$), then we find that $H((x, y)/z) > c_2.H(z)$.

Therefore, it is not the case that $xy \prec z$. Then, $f(T, xy) \leq f(T, x) < \epsilon$ which entails that $xy \notin \mathcal{F}(T, \epsilon)$. ∎

6 Abstract Pattern Synthesis

By Theorem 1, we are inspired to write an algorithm which starts with a number of primitive candidate patterns and searches the pattern space in breadth first fashion like the APRIORI algorithm. First, let us look at the calculation of pattern occurrence conditions.

6.1 Approximate Calculations

Algorithmic information content is uncomputable using a universal computer. Neither of the conditions we give are recursively enumerable. Fortunately, that should not trouble us too much, for we can use the methods mentioned in Sect. 2.2 to approximate these uncomputable values. However, it is arguable whether using a dictionary-based simple compressor is sufficient for the range of data mining applications we are interested in. At the present, the only obvious advantage of using a traditional compressor would seem to be efficiency.

We again approximate the conditional entropy using subadditivity of information $H(t/s) \approx H(s, t) - H(s)$. With a compressor $C(\cdot)$ such as gzip, the conditions become:

1. $C(x) \leq c_1.C(y)$ (entropy reduction)
2. $C(x, y) \leq (1 + c_2).C(y)$ (noise exclusion)

6.2 BFS in Pattern Space

We will adapt a generate and test strategy similar to APRIORI for our first algorithm, applying the theory introduced in the paper. The pruning logic is quite similar, we do not extend infrequent patterns by Theorem 1. We will keep the

algorithm as close as possible to APRIORI to show the relation, although there
could be many efficiency improvements following various frequent itemset mining algorithms. MICRO-SYNTHETIC extends the pattern length by n bits at each
iteration of the algorithm. Initially, a fast algorithm finds all frequent patterns
up to n bits (akin to discovery of large items). The GENERATE procedure extends
the frequent patterns of the previous level up to n bits. Then, a database pass
is performed and the pattern occurrence conditions are checked for each candidate pattern and transaction element. Then, the algorithm iterates, generating
candidates from the last level of frequent patterns discovered, until we reach a
level where there are no frequent patterns, exactly as in APRIORI.

Algorithm 1. MICRO-SYNTHETIC(T, ϵ, c_1, c_2)

1: $F_0 \leftarrow \{|x| \le n | x \in \{0,1\}^* \wedge f(T,x) >= \epsilon\}$
2: $k \leftarrow 1$
3: **while** $F_{k-1} \ne \emptyset$ **do**
4:      $C_k \leftarrow$ GENERATE(F_{k-1})
5:      **for all** $y \in T$ **do**
6:          **for all** $x \in C$ **do**
7:              **if** $C(x) \le c_1.C(y) \wedge C(x,y) \le (1+c_2).C(y)$ **then**
8:                  $count[x] \leftarrow count[x] + 1$
9:              **end if**
10:         **end for**
11:     **end for**
12:     $F_k \leftarrow \{x \in C_k | \; count[x] \ge \epsilon\}$
13:     $k \leftarrow k + 1$
14: **end while**
15: **return** $\bigcup_k F_k$

---

7   Discussion

The algorithm is called MICRO-SYNTHETIC, because direct search in pattern
space has obvious limitations. On the other hand, that is also what all frequent
pattern discovery algorithms do, therefore it may not be at a greater disadvan-
tage. Like in the basic frequent itemset mining algorithms, the support threshold
must be given. However, we also require two extra parameters to delimit the
pattern occurence. Unfortunately, our formulation falls short of the "parameter-
free" ideal [7]. At the moment, we can give no guidelines for setting c_1 and c_2
except that they must be small enough. Especially c_2, which controls vagueness in our model. The basic frequent item set mining problem has no place
for vagueness, the pattern relation is strict. On the other hand, our formulation
places no bounds on the kind of data/pattern representation, and allows for
vague representations, which are useful for a system that can abstract.

An implementation effort is ongoing. MICRO-SYNTHETIC has been implemented and tested on small datasets. We have tried a variety of compressors like gzip, bzip2 and PAQ8f for the information distance approximation.

While we have managed to find some interesting character patterns this way (such as finding an abstract pattern of 00000001111111 from example strings of different length which contain a sequence of 0's and 1's in them, with errors), we have observed that the suboptimality of the compressors (relative to the particular decompressor) causes too many random patterns to be found, which cannot be attenuated by the c_2 parameter. We have been thus working on a simple but optimal compressor that will fit out implementation better. After we get some results using the MICRO-SYNTHETIC on toy problems, we are planning to devise an algorithm with many optimizations to deal with more realistic data sets. We think that an implementation could demonstrate results on both traditional tabular datasets, and novel kinds of data due to the generality of data schema, depending on the availability of a suitable compressor.

An interesting merit of the Theorem 1 is that it might offer a partial but fundamental theoretical explanation of the success of hierarchical models typically used in deep learning, the compositionality of frequent patterns we exposed likely applies to any pattern recognition system.

Our approach has been criticized as having been superseded by the theory of Algorithmic Statistics [8], however the present paper only offers a generalized version of frequent pattern mining based on AIT, which was not addressed in that work, but perhaps may be reformulated in that framework. The abstract pattern definition was completely new at the time of the writing. The main theorem was also not seen elsewhere before we proposed it in 2006. A more directly relevant formulation of data analysis is Solomonoff's set induction model [17].

8   Conclusions and Future Work

We have made a high-level analysis of the frequent pattern discovery problem, by observing relations between the common sense notion of "abstraction", and the summarization task. We have determined objective criteria for a pattern to be an abstract representation. These criteria were interpreted as information theoretic conditions of reduced entropy and noise exclusion for a problem definition where patterns and data are any bitstring. We have replaced the pattern occurence operation in frequency mining with the conditions we have proposed. Thus, we have achieved a generalized version of the frequent pattern discovery problem. Thereafter, we have demonstrated that our conditions allow for pruning which is essential for the search in the vast but bounded pattern space. We have then used commonly employed methods to apply Kolmogorov complexity in real-world to design an algorithm suitable for the discovery task. Finally, we have introduced an APRIORI like algorithm which enumerates all frequent patterns in our formulation.

Our research requires yet a lot of work to be done, both in the theory and experimental studies. First, there are more theoretical properties to be clarified, and alternative search methods should be analyzed. Especially, pattern space clustering methods and efficient representations may be sought. We have given an algorithm only for all frequent pattern discovery, the analogues of closed/maximal mining may be investigated. Second, a synthetic data set generator should be written, which highlights the virtues of our model and if possible real-world data should be tried out. Third, the effects of different kinds of compressors must be analyzed.

The present algorithm is mostly a theoretical proof-of-concept, we expect a universal data mining solution to achieve a lot more and proceed search in program space instead of pattern space, although practical pattern space search may also be desirable. We shall investigate both approaches further.

References

1. Kraskov, A., Stögbauer, H., Andrzejak, R.G., Grassberger, P.: Hierarchical clustering based on mutual information. Bioinformatics (2003)
2. Agrawal, R., Imielinski, T., Swami, A.N.: Mining association rules between sets of items in large databases. In: Buneman, P., Jajodia, S. (eds.) Proceedings of the 1993 ACM SIGMOD International Conference on Management of Data, Washington, D.C., pp. 207–216 (1993)
3. Agrawal, R., Srikant, R.: Fast algorithms for mining association rules. In: Bocca, J.B., Jarke, M., Zaniolo, C. (eds.) Proceedings of 20th International Conference on Very Large Data Bases, VLDB, pp. 487–499. Morgan Kaufmann (1994)
4. Siebes, A., Struzik, Z.: Complex data: mining using patterns. In: Hand, D.J., Adams, N.M., Bolton, R.J. (eds.) Pattern Detection and Discovery. LNCS, vol. 2447, pp. 24–35. Springer, Heidelberg (2002). doi:10.1007/3-540-45728-3_3
5. Bennett, C., Gacs, P., Li, M., Vitányi, P., Zurek, W.: Information distance. IEEE Trans. Inf. Theor. **44**(4), 1407–1423 (1998)
6. Chaitin, G.J.: Algorithmic Information Theory. Cambridge University Press, Cambridge (1987)
7. Keogh, E., Lonardi, S., Ratanamahatana, C.A.: Towards parameter-free data mining. In: Proceedings of the 2004 ACM SIGKDD International Conference on Knowledge Discovery and Data Mining (2004)
8. Gács, P., Tromp, J., Vitányi, P.M.B.: Algorithmic statistics. IEEE Trans. Inf. Theor. **47**(6), 2443–2463 (2001). https://doi.org/10.1109/18.945257
9. Hipp, J., Güntzer, U., Nakhaeizadeh, G.: Algorithms for association rule mining - a general survey and comparison. SIGKDD Explor. **2**(1), 58–64 (2000)
10. Li, M., Chen, X., Li, X., Ma, B., Vitányi, P.M.B.: The similarity metric. IEEE Trans. Inf. Theor. **50**(12), 3250–3264 (2004). https://doi.org/10.1109/TIT.2004.838101
11. Lin, T.: Mathematical theory of high frequency patterns. In: Proceedings of the IEEE ICDM 2004 Foundations of Data Mining Workshop (2004)
12. Minsky, M.: The Emotion Machine: Commonsense Thinking, Artificial Intelligence, and the Future of the Human Mind, chap. 6. Simon and Schuster (2006)
13. Özkural, E.: Teraflop-scale incremental machine learning. CoRR arXiv:1103.1003 (2011)
14. Cilibrasi, R., Vitányi, P.: Clustering by compression. Technical report CWI (2003)
15. Rosipal, R., Girolami, M., Trejo, L.: Kernel PCA for feature extraction and denoising in non-linear regression. Neural Comput. Appl. **10**, 231–243 (2000)
16. Cilibrasi, R., Vitanyi, P., de Wolf, R.: Algorithmic clustering of music
17. Solomonoff, R.J.: Two kinds of probabilistic induction. Comput. J. **42**(4), 256–259 (1999). https://doi.org/10.1093/comjnl/42.4.256
18. Zaki, M.J.: Parallel and distributed association mining: a survey. IEEE Concurr. **7**(4), 14–25 (1999)

On Hierarchical Compression and Power Laws in Nature

Arthur Franz[✉]

Independent Researcher, Odessa, Ukraine
`franz@fias.uni-frankfurt.de`

Abstract. Since compressing data incrementally by a non-branching hierarchy has resulted in substantial efficiency gains for performing induction in previous work, we now explore branching hierarchical compression as a means for solving induction problems for generally intelligent systems. Even though assuming the compositionality of data generation and the locality of information may result in a loss of the universality of induction, it has still the potential to be general in the sense of reflecting the inherent structure of real world data imposed by the laws of physics. We derive a proof that branching compression hierarchies (BCHs) create power law functions of mutual algorithmic information between two strings as a function of their distance – a ubiquitous characteristic of natural data, which opens the possibility of efficient natural data compression by BCHs. Further, we show that such hierarchies guarantee the existence of short features in the data which in turn increases the efficiency of induction even more.

Keywords: Hierarchical compression · Incremental compression · Algorithmic complexity · Universal induction · Power laws · Scale free structure

1 Introduction

The question how humans succeed in deriving theories and explanations from sensory data – the problem of induction – has long remained a mystery of human cognition and philosophy of science. Because it is so central to human thinking, it is essential to solve this problem for any attempt to build a generally intelligent system. Fortunately, Solomonoff's theory of universal induction [1,2] presents a formidable mathematical solution to this thorny problem. However, it is incomputable and tractable approximations have remained elusive.

Nevertheless, for practical purposes, it seems sufficiently satisfactory if we solve the problem of induction "merely" for data presented to us by the actual physical world that we inhabit. For this purpose it is instructive to ask, why for example are deep learning classifiers so successful although it can be shown [3] that classifying arbitrary binary images with n pixels requires at least 2^n parameters in the neural network? And why is it hard for human subjects to

© Springer International Publishing AG 2017
T. Everitt et al. (Eds.): AGI 2017, LNAI 10414, pp. 77–86, 2017.
DOI: 10.1007/978-3-319-63703-7_8

find an algorithm that prints the digits of π given a sequence of its digits even though the algorithm is fairly short compared to other gigabyte heavy software programs written by humans? The world seems to present us with a small subset of all possible data – a circumstance that can be exploited in order to increase the efficiency of induction algorithms.

Lin and Tegmark [3] argue that properties like symmetry, locality and compositionality of real world data are key restrictions for that purpose and show by "no-flattening theorems" that deep networks achieve their efficiency by exploiting the compositionality of data. Further, as they argue, the polynomial structure of the Hamiltonians in the fundamental laws of physics and the compositional way that those laws are expressed when they generate real world data seems to support the generality of this observation.

Indeed, as proven in our previous work [4], exploiting the compositionality of data leads to an efficient incremental way of performing induction. In short[1], if a bit string of data x is representable by a composition of computable functions (Turing machines), $x = f_1 \circ \cdots \circ f_m(\epsilon)$, then these so-called features f_i can be found in a greedy fashion (without backtracking), if we always look for the shortest ones while compressing at least a little (which excludes identity functions). The algorithmic entropy $K(x)$ can then be obtained by

$$K(x) = \sum_{i=1}^{m} l(f_i) + O(1) \tag{1.1}$$

where all features are pairwise algorithmically orthogonal: $I(f_i : f_j) = 0$ for all $i \neq j$. The features can be found by searching through pairs of programs (f, f') such that $f(f'(x)) = x$ and $l(f) + l(f'(x)) < l(x)$ where the length of the shortest descriptive map f' is found to obey a fairly low bound $l(f') \leq \log K(x) + 2 \log \log K(x) + O(1)$ as will be shown in Sect. 5. In spite of this success, the length of the shortest features is not bounded in any way, leaving us with limited theoretical guarantees for the bound on the time complexity of search. Further assumptions about real world data seem necessary in order to obtain such a bound, which would be very helpful in order to boost the efficiency of induction.

A remarkable property of our world seems to be that it has structure on all scales. No matter how much we zoom in toward the microscopic world or zoom out to the macroscopic world, we never seem to arrive at emptiness or a structureless distribution of matter. Typically, this scale invariance can be expressed by power law correlation functions which are found to be ubiquitous in nature. From avalanche distributions, noise spectra, letter sequences in natural language, earthquake and solar flare frequency distributions, species extinction rates, traffic jams, natural images and many more, power law correlation functions are found virtually everywhere in natural data [5–7]. Further, we seem to possess a theoretical justification of the multitude of power laws through the process of self-organized criticality [5].

---

[1] For notation and definitions please consult the Preliminaries section below.

In this paper, we show that by extending the present theory of non-branching incremental compression to a branching compression hierarchy (BCH), the mutual algorithmic information between two substrings decays like a power law function of the distance between the substrings. We proceed to show that this circumstance leads to a bound on the feature lengths, which increases the efficiency of incremental compression.

2 Preliminaries

Consider a universal prefix Turing machine U. Strings are defined on a finite alphabet $\mathcal{A} = \{0,1\}$ with ϵ denoting the empty string. Logarithms are taken on the basis 2. $\mathcal{A}^*$ denotes the set of finite strings made up of the elements of $\mathcal{A}$. Since there is a one-to-one map $\mathcal{A}^* \leftrightarrow N$ of finite strings on natural numbers, strings and natural numbers are used interchangeably. For example, the length $l(n)$ of an integer n denotes the number of symbols of the string that it corresponds to. The map $\langle \cdot, \cdot \rangle$ denotes a one-to-one map of two strings on natural numbers: $\mathcal{A}^* \times \mathcal{A}^* \leftrightarrow N$. The corresponding map for more than two variables is defined recursively: $\langle x, y, z \rangle \equiv \langle \langle x, y \rangle, z \rangle$. In particular, $\langle z, \epsilon \rangle = z$. Since all Turing machines can be enumerated, the universal machine U operates on a number/string $\langle n, p \rangle$ by executing p on the Turing machine T_n: $U(\langle n, p \rangle) = T_n(p)$. Similarly, a string y is applied to another string x by applying the yth Turing machine: $y(x) \equiv T_y(x) = U(\langle y, x \rangle)$. When we speak about the length of a function/feature f, we mean the length of the binary representation of the index y of the respective Turing machine $T_y = f$ in the enumeration. The prefix complexity $K(x|y)$ of x given y is defined by $K(x|y) \equiv \min\{l(z) : U(\langle z, y \rangle) = x\}$ and $K(x) \equiv K(x|\epsilon)$. The complexity of several variables is defined as $K(x, y) \equiv K(\langle x, y \rangle)$. The "+" sign above equality or inequality signs denotes that the relation is valid up to a constant that is independent of the involved variables. The information contained in x about y is defined as $I(x : y) \equiv K(y) - K(y|x)$. However, sometimes we will refer to it as mutual information for the sake of brevity although it is not symmetric. When a string is a concatenation of substrings, $x = x_1 x_2 \cdots x_n$, by distance between substring x_i and x_j we mean the index distance $d_{ij} \equiv |i - j|$.

3 Branching Compression Hierarchies Create Power Laws

Consider a binary string x that can be computed by a hierarchy of functions, Fig. 1. In this section we show that if the functions are the shortest features of their respective substrings, then the information of a substring x_i about another substring x_j of x will be bounded by power law function of their distance:

$$I(x_i : x_j) \lesssim d(x_i, x_j)^{-const}$$

The main idea is the following. Assume that a fraction of the information in a string is lost as we go along an edge in a graph (information dissipation),

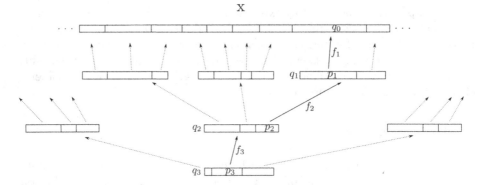

Fig. 1. A branching compression hierarchy (BCH). The path from the root to some leaf is displayed by solid arrows. A bit string x (whole upper chain, only the part computed from q_2 is shown) is computed by concatenating substrings, one of which is shown as q_0. Those substrings are computed by their shortest features f_l and respective parameters, $q_{l-1} = f_l(p_l)$, that are found along the path. Since only a fraction $\alpha_l = K(p_l)/K(q_l)$ of the information in q_l remains at each level l, the information contained in string q_l about q_0 decays exponentially with its height l. Note that each arrow (both dashed and solid) corresponds to a different feature, each q_1 in the first level computes different substrings of x.

since only a part of the string serves as input to the function at the edge. Then the information of a string about another will decrease exponentially with the length of the path between the strings. If the mutual information of two leaf strings is mediated only via the earliest common ancestor in a tree, then it will drop exponentially with the height of that ancestor. Further, the distance between two leaves increases exponentially with the height of their common ancestor. Inserting two exponential functions into each other leads to the power law. The idea that branching hierarchies create power laws is not new [7], but this is to the best of our knowledge the first time that it is shown in all generality for algorithmic information and arbitrary data.

Definition 1 (Branching compression hierarchy). *Let T be a perfect tree with a varying branching factor, $F = \{f_i\}$ a set of computable functions for each edge in the tree and q_h a binary string at the root node. For any path from the root to a leaf, index the functions as $f_h, \ldots, f_1$ and compute $f_l(p_l) = q_{l-1}$ for each $l = h, \ldots, 1$, where p_l is some substring of q_l. Let further f_l be the shortest feature and p_l its respective parameters of q_{l-1} (see [4] for definitions). Then, the triple $H = \{T, F, q_h\}$ is called a **branching compression hierarchy**. The fraction*

$$\alpha_l \equiv \frac{K(p_l)}{K(q_l)} \tag{3.1}$$

*shall be called **information dissipation rate**.*

An Example. Consider a binary image of a triangle. In the first compression level the features could encode lines while the parameters encode the coordinates of the line ends. Then $f_1 = line$ and $p_1 = x_1 y_1 x_2 y_2$ encode one of the sides, other features $f_1^{(2)}$ and $f_1^{(3)}$ at the same level encode the other sides with their respective parameters $p_1^{(2)} = x_2 y_2 x_3 y_3$ and $p_1^{(3)} = x_3 y_3 x_1 y_1$. All those parameters are concatenated to $q_1 = p_1 p_1^{(2)} p_1^{(3)} = x_1 y_1 x_2 y_2 x_2 y_2 x_3 y_3 x_3 y_3 x_1 y_1$. This string is further compressed by $f_2 = copy2$ which could be a function that copies consecutive entries, such that $q_1 = f_2(p_2)$, where $p_2 = x_1 y_1 x_2 y_2 x_3 y_3$. This concludes a two-level branching hierarchical compression of a triangle leaving us with the coordinates of the corners as a concise representation of a triangle.

Lemma 1 (Exponential information decay). *Let H be a BCH according to the above definition. We assume:*

1. *The information content in the root node q_h is uniformly distributed through q_l for each l:*

$$\frac{K(p_l | q_h)}{K(q_l | q_h)} = \frac{K(p_l)}{K(q_l)} = \alpha_l \tag{3.2}$$

2. *The root q_h does not contain any information about any feature below in the path $I(q_h : f_l) = 0$ for all $l \leq h$.*

Then the information content in q_h about a leaf q_0 is given by

$$I(q_h : q_0) \overset{+}{=} K(q_h) \cdot \prod_{l=1}^{h} \alpha_l \tag{3.3}$$

Of course, there is no guarantee that assumption (1) holds, but it can be expected to hold on average, since after all, the information in q_h has to go somewhere, since x is ultimately computed from it. If it doesn't go into p_l then into some p_l on another path to x. Assumption (2) is discussed below.

Since $0 < \alpha_l \leq 1$, Eq. (3.3) constitutes an exponential decay of information in a string q_h about a leaf q_0 as its height h increases. In the special case of $\alpha \equiv \alpha_l = \text{const}$ the decay $I(q_h : q_0) \overset{+}{=} K(q_h) \cdot \alpha^h$ becomes apparent. What can we say about the information two arbitrary substrings y and z about each other?

Lemma 2 (Information of strings about each other). *Let two strings y and z be conditionally independent given string a:*

$$K(y, z | a) = K(y | a) + K(z | a) \tag{3.4}$$

Then the information of y about z is bounded by the information of a about z:

$$I(y : z) \overset{+}{\leq} I(a : z) \tag{3.5}$$

It should be noted that the assumptions of conditional independence in Lemma 2 and assumption (2) in Lemma 1 merely reflect that the only link between the substrings is the common ancestor. Otherwise, two arbitrary substrings of an arbitrary string certainly can carry more information about each other.

We can now state our main theorem.

Theorem 1 (Power law information decay in BCHs). *Let H be a BCH with the assumptions of Lemma 1 and each pair of leaves conditionally independent given their common ancestor q_h at height h. Let further $d_{ij} \equiv |i - j|$ be the index distance between to substrings x_i and x_j. Then the information contained in x_i about x_j is bounded by a power law function of the distance:*

$$I(x_i : x_j) \overset{+}{<} K(q_h) \cdot d_{ij}^{-\langle \nu \rangle} \tag{3.6}$$

where $\nu_l \equiv \log_{\bar{b}}(1/\alpha_l) > 0$, $\bar{b}$ the average branching factor of H and α_l the information dissipation rate at level l.

Indeed we observe that the algorithmic information carried by one substring about another decays according to a power law function of their distance. This circumstance makes information storage local in the sense that mutual information between substrings exists mostly for nearby substrings. In the following section we will show that the locality of information entails the existence of short features in the whole data string.

4   Information Locality Implies Short Features

Since nearby substrings contain most information about each other in a BCH, we now prove that this implies compressibility of the concatenated string, which in turn implies the existence of a feature of the whole string.

Lemma 3 (Information of a string about another implies compressibility). *Let x and y be two strings with x carrying information about y: $I(x : y) > 0$. Then the composite string is compressible: $K(xy) \overset{+}{<} l(xy)$.*

Theorem 2 (Compressibility of substring implies existence of feature). *Let x be a string partitioned into y and p. Let further q be the shortest program with $U(q) = y$ and λ the program that computes y from q and specifies where to insert it into x: $\lambda(q, p) = x$. If y is $l(\lambda)$-compressible, $K(y) + l(\lambda) < l(y)$, then x is compressible as well and there is a feature f and a corresponding descriptive map f' of x such that*

$$f(f'(x)) = x$$

and $l(f) < l(y)$.

The gist of the results in this and the previous section can be summarized as follows. A BCH computes several strings from a single one at each level of the hierarchy which creates mutual information between the substrings at the leaves. In this section we have shown that it implies the existence of a feature of the whole string (concatenation of all leaves) such that the length of the feature is bounded by the length of just two neighboring leaves. Since the length of the leaves is generally much smaller than the length of the whole string, we have effectively derived a low bound on feature length. In other words, if our data breaks down into many small pieces, the size of the contained regularities is limited by the length of those little pieces.

5   A Tighter Bound on the Length of the Shortest Descriptive Map

This section is independent from the previous ones but aims at the same goal: the reduction of the time complexity of compression, which is directly tied to the lengths of features and descriptive maps. While in the previous sections we were occupied with the length of the features, this section goes back to deriving a tighter bound on descriptive maps than in our previous work [4, Theorem 6]. There, we have derived the bound $l(f') \overset{+}{\leq} 2 \log K(x) + 4 \log \log K(x)$ for the shortest descriptive map f'. Here, we managed to get rid of the factor two.

Theorem 3 (Bound on the length of descriptive map). *Let f' be the shortest descriptive map of a finite string x. Then the following bound holds on $l(f')$:*

$$l(f') \overset{+}{\leq} \log K(x) + 2 \log \log K(x) \qquad (5.1)$$

and the number of high values of $l(f')$ is low in the sense

$$P\{x : l(f') \geq s\} \leq s^3 2^{-s} \qquad (5.2)$$

for any s and for all computable and semicomputable distributions P.

Note that this result is valid not only for BCHs, but for incremental compression in general.

6   Discussion

We have shown that data generated by a hierarchy of functions create power law distributed algorithmic information between two pieces of the data. Since correlation is a simple form of algorithmic information, the ubiquity of power law correlation functions in nature constitutes evidence that natural data could successfully be represented by hierarchies.

We have further shown that such structures imply that the data generated like this possesses simple features, i.e. that structure can be found at the smallest scale. This is crucial for the efficiency of induction algorithms since it allows us to find features whose description is bounded by the size of that scale. In other words, we can look at small pieces of the available data where we can find structure, derive a feature from that and continue to incrementally compress the data greedily.

One may wonder, if a BCH has troubles solving tasks like the induction of a program for π given a sequence of its digits, why is it that human programmers don't have particular difficulties in specifying such a program? However, such a program is never *induced* from the digits of π, but rather *deduced* from background knowledge about geometry and other, i.e. from other sources of information. Hence, such a task would be an unfair test for both algorithmic and human induction capabilities.

In future work, it would be interesting to derive an actual compression algorithm for hierarchically structured data and compare its time complexity to non-branching incremental compression and to non-incremental Levin search. Even more interesting would be to try to implement such an algorithm which is current work in progress.

A   Proofs

Proof (Lemma 1). Recall that f_l and p_l are the shortest feature and parameter of q_{l-1} and therefore independent, $K(q_{l-1}) \overset{+}{=} l(f_l) + K(p_l)$, as was proven in [4, Corrolary 2]. From Eq. (3.1) we obtain

$$K(q_0) \overset{+}{=} l(f_1) + K(p_1) \overset{+}{=} l(f_1) + \alpha_1 K(q_1) \overset{+}{=} l(f_1) + \alpha_1 \left(l(f_2) + \alpha_2 K(q_2) \right)$$

$$\overset{+}{=} K(q_h) \prod_{l=1}^{h} \alpha_l + \sum_{m=1}^{h} l(f_m) \prod_{l=1}^{m-1} \alpha_l$$

$$\text{(A.1)}$$

Since f_l and p_l cannot be made dependent by conditioning, we get $K(q_{l-1}|q_h) \overset{+}{=} K(f_l|q_h) + K(p_l|q_h)$. Due to assumption (2), the first term becomes $K(f_l|q_h) = K(f_l) \overset{+}{=} l(f_l)$. Therefore, the conditional version can be computed analogously to Eq. (A.1):

$$K(q_0|q_h) \overset{+}{=} K(q_h|q_h) \prod_{l=1}^{h} \alpha_l + \sum_{m=1}^{h} l(f_m) \prod_{l=1}^{m-1} \alpha_l \qquad \text{(A.2)}$$

However, since $K(q_h|q_h) = O(1)$ we obtain for the information in q_h about q_0:

$$I(q_h : q_0) \equiv K(q_0) - K(q_0|q_h) \overset{+}{=} K(q_h) \prod_{l=1}^{h} \alpha_l \qquad \square$$

Proof (Lemma 2). We can in general expand [8, Theorem 3.9.1, p. 247]

$$K(y, z|a) \overset{+}{=} K(y|a) + K(z|y, K(y), a)$$

and insert it into the independence relation Eq. 3.4. This leads to

$$K(z|a) \overset{+}{=} K(z|y, K(y), a) \overset{+}{\leq} K(z|y)$$

where the last inequality follows from the fact that conditioning can only reduce the description length of z [8, Theorem 2.1.2, p. 108]. Subtracting this inequality from $K(z)$ yields $K(z) - K(z|a) \overset{+}{\geq} K(z) - K(z|y)$. Now we insert the definition of mutual information $I(a : z) \equiv K(z) - K(z|a)$ on both sides from which the claim follows. □

Proof (Theorem 1). First, from the result in Eq. (3.3) and Lemma 2 it follows that $I(x_i : x_j)$ decays exponentially with the height h of their common ancestor q_h

$$I(x_i : x_j) \overset{+}{\leq} K(q_h) \cdot \prod_{l=1}^{h} \alpha_l \tag{A.3}$$

under our assumptions. Consider that the maximal index distance between leaves in a perfect tree increases exponentially with the height h of the common ancestor:

$$d_{ij} < \prod_{l=1}^{h} \hat{b}_l \tag{A.4}$$

where $\hat{b}_l$ is the average branching factor at level l of the tree. By defining the total average branching factor $\bar{b} \equiv \left(\prod_{l=1}^{h} \hat{b}_l \right)^{1/h} > d_{ij}^{1/h}$, we can solve for $h > \log_{\bar{b}}(d_{ij})$ and compute:

$$\log_{\bar{b}} \left(\prod_{l=1}^{h} \alpha_l \right) < \sum_{l=1}^{\log_{\bar{b}}(d_{ij})} \log_{\bar{b}}(\alpha_l) = - \sum_{l=1}^{\log_{\bar{b}}(d_{ij})} \nu_l = - \langle v \rangle \log_{\bar{b}}(d_{ij}) = \log_{\bar{b}} \left(d_{ij}^{-\langle \nu \rangle} \right)$$

where $\nu_l \equiv \log_{\bar{b}}(1/\alpha_l) > 0$. Inserting this into Eq. A.3 concludes the proof. □

Proof (Lemma 3). Consider the general expansion [8, Theorem 3.9.1, p. 247]

$$K(xy) \overset{+}{=} K(x) + K(y|x, K(x))$$

I is defined by $I(x : y) \equiv K(y) - K(y|x)$ and is larger than zero by assumption. Since in general $K(y|x, K(x)) \overset{+}{\leq} K(y|x)$ we obtain

$$K(xy) \overset{+}{=} K(x) + K(y) + K(y|x, K(x)) - K(y|x) - I(x : y)$$
$$\overset{+}{<} K(x) + K(y) \overset{+}{\leq} l(x) + l(y) = l(xy) \qquad \square$$

Proof (Theorem 2). Since y is $l(\lambda)$-compressible by q, $\lambda(q, p) = U(\langle \lambda, q, p \rangle) = x$ and $l(x) = l(y) + l(p)$, x is compressible as well:

$$K(x) \leq l(\lambda) + l(q) + l(p) = l(\lambda) + K(y) + l(x) - l(y) < l(x)$$

We define $f \equiv \langle \lambda, q \rangle$ and obtain $U(\langle f, p \rangle) = f(p) = x$ – the main feature equation. We can define the descriptive map f' by a function that removes y from x to obtain the remainder p: $f'(x) = p$. It suffices if it does so for that particular x and y, not in general.

From fs definition, we get $l(f) = l(\lambda) + l(q) = l(\lambda) + K(y) < l(y)$ since y is $l(\lambda)$-compressible by assumption. It follows that the (f, p)-pair compresses x at least to some extent, $l(f) + l(p) < l(y) + l(p) = l(x)$. Therefore, f is indeed a feature of x and its length is bounded by $l(y)$.   □

Proof (Theorem 3). In general, the relation $K(p) \overset{+}{\leq} K(p|z) + K(z)$ is valid, since if p is computable by a detour via z, its shortest program without the detour can only be shorter. Setting $z = K(x)$ and conditioning on x leads to

$$K(p|x) \overset{+}{\leq} K(p|K(x), x) + K(K(x)|x) \tag{A.5}$$

The conditioning operation is not valid in general, however the detour argument is still valid in this case. Since $K(p|x) = l(f')$ [4, Lemma 1(2)] and $K(p|K(x), x) = O(1)$ [4, Theorem 3(3)], we get

$$l(f') \overset{+}{\leq} K(K(x)|x) \tag{A.6}$$

We now insert the "complexity of the complexity" expression in [8, Lemma 3.9.2, Eq. (3.18)] $K(K(x)|x) \overset{+}{\leq} \log K(x) + 2 \log \log K(x)$ and the first claim follows. The second claim is a property of $K(K(x)|x)$ [8, Eq. (3.13)] and therefore also holds for $l(f')$.   □

References

1. Solomonoff, R.J.: A formal theory of inductive inference. Part I. Inf. Control **7**(1), 1–22 (1964)
2. Solomonoff, R.J.: A formal theory of inductive inference. Part II. Inf. Control **7**(2), 224–254 (1964)
3. Lin, H.W., Tegmark, M.: Why does deep and cheap learning work so well? arXiv preprint arXiv:1608.08225 (2016)
4. Franz, A.: Some theorems on incremental compression. In: Steunebrink, B., Wang, P., Goertzel, B. (eds.) AGI -2016. LNCS, vol. 9782, pp. 74–83. Springer, Cham (2016). doi:10.1007/978-3-319-41649-6_8
5. Bak, P.: How Nature Works: The Science of Self-organized Criticality. Copernicus, New York (1996)
6. Saremi, S., Sejnowski, T.J.: Hierarchical model of natural images and the origin of scale invariance. Proc. Natl. Acad. Sci. **110**(8), 3071–3076 (2013)
7. Lin, H.W., Tegmark, M.: Critical behavior from deep dynamics: a hidden dimension in natural language. arXiv preprint arXiv:1606.06737 (2016)
8. Li, M., Vitányi, P.: An Introduction to Kolmogorov Complexity and Its Applications. Springer, New York (2009)

From First-Order Logic to Assertional Logic

Yi Zhou[1,2](✉)

[1] School of Computing, Engineering and Mathematics,
Western Sydney University, Sydney, Australia
`y.zhou@westernsydney.edu.au`
[2] School of Computing Science and Technology, Tianjin University, Tianjin, China

Abstract. First-Order Logic (FOL) is widely regarded as the foundation of knowledge representation. Nevertheless, in this paper, we argue that FOL has several critical issues for this purpose. Instead, we propose an alternative called assertional logic, in which all syntactic objects are categorized as set theoretic constructs including individuals, concepts and operators, and all kinds of knowledge are formalized by equality assertions. We first present a primitive form of assertional logic that uses minimal assumed knowledge and constructs. Then, we show how to extend it by definitions, which are special kinds of knowledge, i.e., assertions. We argue that assertional logic, although simpler, is more expressive and extensible than FOL. As a case study, we show how assertional logic can be used to unify logic and probability.

1 Introduction

Classical First-Order Logic (FOL) is widely regarded as the foundation of symbolic AI. FOL plays a central role in the field of Knowledge Representation and Reasoning (KR). Many of its fragments (such as propositional logic, modal and epistemic logic, description logics), extensions (such as second-order logic, situation calculus and first-order probabilistic logic) and variants (such as Datalog and first-order answer set programming) have been extensively studied in the literature [2,8].

Nevertheless, AI researchers have pointed out several issues regarding using FOL for the purpose of knowledge representation and reasoning, mostly from the reasoning point of view. For instance, FOL is computationally very difficult. Reasoning about FOL is a well-known undecidable problem. Also, FOL is monotonic in the sense that adding new knowledge into a first-order knowledge base will always result in more consequences. However, human reasoning is sometimes nonmonotonic.

In this paper, we argue that FOL also has some critical disadvantages merely from the knowledge representation point of view. First of all, although FOL is considered natural for well-trained logicians, it is not simple and flexible enough for knowledge engineers with less training. One possible reason is the distinction and hierarchy between term level (including constants, variables and terms), predicate level (including predicates and functions) and formula level (including

© Springer International Publishing AG 2017
T. Everitt et al. (Eds.): AGI 2017, LNAI 10414, pp. 87–97, 2017.
DOI: 10.1007/978-3-319-63703-7_9

atoms and compound formulas/sentences). From my own experience as a teacher in this subject, although strongly emphasized in the classes, many students failed to understand why a predicate or an atom cannot be in the scope of a function. Another reason is the notion of free occurrences of variables. For instance, it is not easily understandable for many students why the GEN inference rule has to enforce the variable occurrence restrictions. Last but not least, arbitrary nesting is another issue. Again, although natural from a mathematical point of view, a nested formula, e.g., $(x \vee \neg(y \wedge z)) \wedge (\neg y \vee \neg x)$ is hard to be understood and used.

Secondly, FOL has limitations in terms of expressive power. Because of the hierarchy from the term level to the formula level, FOL cannot quantify over predicates/functions. This can be addressed by extending FOL into high-order logic. Nevertheless, high-order logic still cannot quantify over formulas. As a consequence, FOL and high-order logic are not able to represent an axiom or an inference rule in logic, such as *Modus Ponens*. As an example, in automated solving mathematical problems, we often use proof by induction. To represent this, we need to state that for some statement P with a number parameter, if that P holds for all numbers less than k implies that P holds for the number k as well, then P holds for all natural numbers. Here, P is a statement at a formula level, possibly with complex sub-statements within itself. Hence, in order to represent proof by induction, we need to quantify over formulas.

Thirdly, FOL itself can hardly formalize some important notions including probability, actions, time etc., which are needed in a wide range of AI applications. For this purpose, AI researchers have made significant progresses on extending FOL with these notions separately, such as first-order probabilistic logic [1,7], situation calculus [9,10], CTL [3] etc. Each is a challenging task in the sense that it has to completely re-define the syntax as well as the semantics. However, combing these notions together, even several of them, seems an extremely difficult task. Moreover, there are many more building blocks to be incorporated. For instance, consider task planning for home service robots. It is necessary to represent and reason about actions, probability, time and more building blocks such as preferences altogether at the same time.

To address these issues, we propose assertional logic, in which all syntactic objects are categorized as set theoretic constructs including individuals, concepts and operators, and all kinds of knowledge are uniformly formalized by equality assertions of the form $a = b$, where a and b are either atomic individuals or compound individuals. Semantically, individuals, concepts and operators are interpreted as elements, sets and functions respectively in set theory and knowledge of the form $a = b$ means that the two individuals a and b are referring to the same element.

We first present the primitive form of assertional logic that uses minimal assumed knowledge and primitive constructs. Then, we show how to extend it with more building blocks by definitions, which are special kinds of knowledge, i.e., assertions used to define new individuals, concepts and operators. Once these new syntactic objects are defined, they can be used as a basis to define more. We show that assertional logic, although simpler, is more expressive and extensible than FOL. As a case study, we show how to extend assertional logic for unifying logic and probability. Note that our intention is not to reinvent the wheel of these building blocks but to borrow existing excellent work on formalizing these building blocks separately and to assemble them within one framework (i.e., assertional logic) so that they can live happily ever after.

2   Assertional Logic: The Primitive Form

One cannot build something from nothing. Hence, in order to establish assertional logic, we need some basic knowledge. Of course, for the purpose of explanation, we need an informal meta language whose syntax and semantics are pre-assumed. As usual, we use a natural language such as English. Nevertheless, this meta language is used merely for explanation and it should not affect the syntax as well as the semantics of anything defined formally.

Only a meta level explanation language is not enough. Other than this, we also need some core objects and knowledge, whose syntax and semantics are pre-assumed as well. These are called *prior objects* and *prior knowledge*. For instance, when defining real numbers, we need some prior knowledge about natural numbers; when defining probability, we need some prior knowledge about real numbers.

In assertional logic, we always treat the equality symbol "=" as a prior object. There are some prior knowledge associated with the equality symbol. For instance, "=" is an equivalence relation satisfying reflexivity, symmetricity, and transitivity. Also, "=" satisfies the general substitution property, that is, if $a = b$, then a can be used to replace b anywhere. Other than the equality symbol, we also assume some prior objects and their associated prior knowledge in set theory [6], including set operators such as set union and Cartesian product, Boolean values, set builder notations and natural numbers.

Given an application domain, a *syntactic structure* (*structure* for short if clear from the context) of the domain is a triple $\langle \mathcal{I}, \mathcal{C}, \mathcal{O} \rangle$, where $\mathcal{I}$ is a collection of *individuals*, representing objects in the domain, $\mathcal{C}$ a collection of *concepts*, representing groups of objects sharing something in common and $\mathcal{O}$ a collection of *operators*, representing relationships and connections among individuals and concepts. Concepts and operators can be nested and considered as individuals as well. If needed, we can have concepts of concepts, concepts of operators, concepts of concepts of operators and so on.

An operator could be multi-ary, that is, it maps a tuple of individuals into a single individual. Each multi-ary operator O is associated with a *domain* of the form $(C_1, \ldots, C_n)$, representing all possible values that the operator O can operate on, where $C_i, 1 \leq i \leq n$, is a concept. We call n the *arity* of O. For a tuple $(a_1, \ldots, a_n)$ matching the domain of an operator O, i.e., $a_i \in C_i, 1 \leq i \leq n$, O maps $(a_1, \ldots, a_n)$ into an individual, denoted by $O(a_1, \ldots, a_n)$. We also use $O(C_1, \ldots, C_n)$ to denote the set $\{O(a_1, \ldots, a_n) \mid a_i \in C_i\}$, called the *range* of the operator O.

Operators are similar to functions in first-order logic but differs in two essential ways. First, operators are many-sorted as $C_1, \ldots, C_n$ could be different concepts. More importantly, $C_1, \ldots, C_n$ could be high-order constructs, e.g., concepts of concepts, concepts of operators.

For instance, consider a family relationship domain, in which *Alice* and *Bob* are individuals, *Human*, *Woman* and *Female* are concepts and *Father*, *Mother* and *Aunt* are operators etc.

Let $\langle \mathcal{I}, \mathcal{C}, \mathcal{O} \rangle$ be a syntactic structure. A *term* is an individual, either an atomic individual $a \in \mathcal{I}$ or the result $O(a_1, \ldots, a_n)$ of an operator O operating on some individuals $a_1, \ldots, a_n$. We also call the latter *compound individuals*.

An *assertion* is of the form

$$a = b, \tag{1}$$

where a and b are two terms. Intuitively, an assertion of the form (1) is a piece of knowledge in the application domain, claiming that the left and right side refer to the same object.

A *knowledge base* is a set of assertions. Terms and assertions can be considered as individuals as well. For instance, in the family relationship domain, $Father(Alice) = Bob$, $Father(Alice) = Uncle(Bob)$ are assertions.

Similar to concepts that group individuals, we use schemas to group terms and assertions. A *schema term* is either an atomic concept $C \in \mathcal{C}$ or of the form $O(C_1, \ldots, C_n)$, where $C_i, 1 \leq i \leq n$ are concepts. Essentially, a schema term represents a set of terms, in which every concept is grounded by a corresponding individual. For instance, $O(C_1, \ldots, C_n)$ is the collection $\{O(a_1, \ldots, a_n)\}$, where $a_i \in C_i, 1 \leq i \leq n$ are individuals. Then, a *schema assertion* is of the same form as form (1) except that terms can be replaced by schema terms. Similarly, a schema assertion represents a set of assertions.

We say that a schema term/assertion *mentions* a set $\{C_1, \ldots, C_n\}$ of concepts if $C_1, \ldots, C_n$ occur in it, and *only mentions* if $\{C_1, \ldots, C_n\}$ contains all concepts mentioned in it. Note that it could be the case that two or more different individuals are referring to the same concept C in schema terms and assertions. In this case, we need to use different *copies* of C, denoted by $C^1, C^2, \ldots$, to distinguish them. For instance, all assertions $x = y$, where x and y are human, are captured by the schema assertion $Human^1 = Human^2$. On the other side, in a schema, the same copy of a concept C can only refer to the same individual. For instance, $Human = Human$ is the set of all assertions of the form $x = x$, where $x \in Human$.

We introduce a set theoretic semantics for assertional logic. Since we assume set theory as the prior knowledge, in the semantics, we freely use those individuals (e.g., the empty set), concepts (e.g., the set of all natural numbers) and operators (e.g., the set union operator) without explanation.

An *interpretation* (also called a *possible world*) is a pair $\langle \Delta, .^I \rangle$, where Δ is a domain of elements, and $.^I$ is a mapping function that admits all prior knowledge, and maps each individual into a domain element in Δ, each concept into a set in Δ and each n-ary operator into an n-ary function in Δ. The mapping function $.^I$ is generalized for terms as well by mapping $O(a_1, \ldots, a_n)$

to $O^I(a_1^I, \ldots, a_n^I)$. Similar to terms and assertions, interpretations can also be considered as individuals to be studied.

It is important to emphasize that an interpretation has to admit all the prior knowledge. For instance, since we assume set theory, suppose that an interpretation maps two individuals x and y as the same element a in the domain, then the concepts $\{x\}$ and $\{y\}$ must be interpreted as $\{a\}$, and $x = y$ must be interpreted as $a = a$.

Let I be an interpretation and $a = b$ an assertion. We say that I is a *model* of $a = b$, denoted by $I \models a = b$ iff $.^I(a) = .^I(b)$, also written $a^I = b^I$. Let KB be a knowledge base. We say that I is a model of KB, denoted by $I \models KB$, iff I is a model of all assertions in KB. We say that an assertion A is a *property* of KB, denoted by $KB \models A$, iff all models of KB are also models of A. In particular, we say that an assertion A is a *tautology* iff it is modeled by all interpretations.

Since we assume set theory as our prior knowledge, we directly borrow some set theoretic constructs. For instance, we can use $\cup(C_1, C_2)$ (also written as $C_1 \cup C_2$) to denote a new concept that unions two concepts C_1 and C_2. Applying this to assertions, we can see that assertions of the primitive form (1) can indeed represent many important features in knowledge representation. For instance, the *membership assertion*, stating that an individual a is an instance of a concept C is the following assertion $\in (a, C) = \top$ (also written as $a \in C$). The *containment assertion*, stating that a concept C_1 is contained by another concept C_2, is the following assertion $\subseteq (C_1, C_2) = \top$ (also written as $C_1 \subseteq C_2$). The *range declaration*, stating that the range of an operator O operating on some concept C_1 equals to another concept C_2 is the following assertion $O(C_1) = C_2$.

3 Extending New Syntactic Objects by Definitions

As argued in the introduction section, extensibility is a critical issue for knowledge representation and modeling. In assertional logic, we use *definitions* for this purpose. Definitions are (schema) assertions used to define new syntactic objects (including individuals, concepts and operators) based on existing ones. Once these new syntactic objects are defined, they can be used to define more. Note that definitions are nothing extra but special kinds of knowledge (i.e. assertions).

We start with defining new individuals. An individual definition is an assertion of the form

$$a = t, \tag{2}$$

where a is an atomic individual and t is a term. Here, a is the individual to be defined. This assertion claims that the left side a is defined as the right side t. For instance, $0 = \emptyset$ means that the individual 0 is defined as the empty set.

Defining new operators is similar to defining new individuals except that we use schema assertions instead. Let O be an operator to be defined and $(C_1, \ldots, C_n)$ its domain. An operator definition is a schema assertion of the form

$$O(C_1, \ldots, C_n) = T, \tag{3}$$

where T is a schema term that mentions concepts only from $C_1, \ldots, C_n$. It could be the case that T only mentions some of $C_1, \ldots, C_n$. Note that if $C_1, \ldots, C_n$ refer to the same concept, we need to use different copies.

Since a schema assertion represents a set of assertions, essentially, an operator definition of the form (3) defines the operator O by defining the value of $O(a_1, \ldots, a_n)$ one-by-one, where $a_i \in C_i, 1 \leq i \leq n$. For instance, for defining the successor operator $Succ$, we can use the schema assertion $Succ(\mathbb{N}) = \{\mathbb{N}, \{\mathbb{N}\}\}$, meaning that, for every natural number n, the successor of n, is defined as $\{n, \{n\}\}$, i.e., $Succ(n) = \{n, \{n\}\}$.

Defining new concepts is somewhat different. As concepts are essentially sets, we directly borrow set theory notations to define concepts. There are four ways to define a new concept.

Enumeration. Let $a_1, \ldots, a_n$ be n individuals. Then, the collection $\{a_1, \ldots, a_n\}$ is a concept, written as

$$C = \{a_1, \ldots, a_n\}. \tag{4}$$

For instance, we can define the concept $Digits$ by $Digits = \{0, 1, 2, 3, 4, 5, 6, 7, 8, 9\}$.

Operation. Let C_1 and C_2 be two concepts. Then, $C_1 \cup C_2$ (the union of C_1 and C_2), $C_1 \cap C_2$ (the intersection of C_1 and C_2), $C_1 \backslash C_2$ (the difference of C_1 and C_2), $C_1 \times C_2$ (the Cartesian product of C_1 and C_2), 2^{C_1} (the power set of C_1) are concepts. Operation can be written by assertions as well. For instance, the following assertion

$$C = C_1 \cup C_2 \tag{5}$$

states that the concept C is defined as the union of C_1 and C_2. As an example, one can define the concept Man by $Man = Human \cap Male$.

Comprehension. Let C be a concept and $A(C)$ a schema assertion that only mentions concept C. Then, individuals in C satisfying A, denoted by $\{x \in C | A(x)\}$ (or simply $C|A(C)$), form a concept, written as

$$C' = C|A(C). \tag{6}$$

For instance, we can define the concept $Male$ by $Male = \{Animal \,|\, Sex(Animal) = male\}$, meaning that $Male$ consists of all animals whose sexes are male.

Replacement. Let O be an operator and C a concept on which O is well defined. Then, the individuals mapped from C by O, denoted by $\{O(x) \,|\, x \in C\}$ (or simply $O(C)$), form a concept, written as

$$C' = O(C). \tag{7}$$

For instance, we can define the concept $Parents$ by $Parents = ParentOf(Human)$, meaning that it consists of all individuals who is a $ParentOf$ some human.

Definitions can be incremental. We may define some syntactic objects first. Once defined, they can be used to define more. One can always continue with this incremental process. For instance, in arithmetic, we define the successor operator first. Once defined, it can be used to define the add operator, which is further served as a basis to define more useful syntactic objects.

For clarity, we use the symbol "::=" to replace "=" for definitions.

4   Embedding Classical Logic into Assertional Logic

In the previous section, we show how to extend assertions of the primitive form (1) into multi-assertions and nested assertions. In this section, we continue with this task to show how to define more complex forms of assertions with logic connectives, including not only propositional connectives but also quantifiers.

We start with the propositional case. Let $\mathcal{A}$ be the concept of nested assertions. We introduce a number of operators over $\mathcal{A}$ in assertional logic, including $\neg(\mathcal{A})$ (for *negation*), $\wedge(\mathcal{A}^1, \mathcal{A}^2)$ (for *conjunction*), $\vee(\mathcal{A}^1, \mathcal{A}^2)$ (for *disjunction*) and $\rightarrow (\mathcal{A}^1, \mathcal{A}^2)$ (for *implication*).

There could be different ways to define these operators in assertional logic. Let $a = a'$ and $b = b'$ be two (nested) assertions. The propositional connectives are defined as follows:

$$\neg(a = a') ::= \{a\} \cap \{a'\} = \emptyset$$
$$\wedge(a = a', b = b') ::= (\{a\} \cap \{a'\}) \cup (\{b\} \cap \{b'\}) = \{a, a', b, b'\}$$
$$\vee(a = a', b = b') ::= (\{a\} \cap \{a'\}) \cup (\{b\} \cap \{b'\}) \neq \emptyset$$
$$\rightarrow (a = a', b = b') ::= (\{a, a'\} \setminus \{a\} \cap \{a'\}) \cup (\{b\} \cap \{b'\}) \neq \emptyset.$$

We also use $a \neq a'$ to denote $\neg(a = a')$. One can observe that the ranges of all logic operators are nested assertions. Hence, similar to multi-assertion and nested assertion, propositional logic operators are syntactic sugar as well in assertional logic.

It can be observed that all tautologies in propositional logic (e.g., De-Morgan's laws) are also a tautology in assertional logic in the sense that each proposition is replaced by an assertion and each propositional connective is replaced by corresponding logic operators in assertional logic.

Now we consider to define operators for quantifiers, including $\forall$ (for the *universal* quantifier) and $\exists$ (for the *existential* quantifier). The domain of quantifiers is a pair $(C, A(C))$, where C is a concept and $A(C)$ is a schema assertion that only mentions C.

The quantifiers are defines as follows:

$$\forall(C, A(C)) ::= C|A(C) = C \tag{8}$$
$$\exists(C, A(C)) ::= C|A(C) \neq \emptyset \tag{9}$$

Intuitively, $\forall(C, A(C))$ is true iff those individuals x in C such that $A(x)$ holds equals to the concept C itself, that is, for all individuals x in C, $A(x)$ holds; $\exists(C, A(C))$ is true iff those individuals x in C such that $A(x)$ holds does not equal to the empty set, that is, there exists at least one individual x in C such that $A(x)$ holds. We can see that the ranges of quantifiers are nested assertions as well. Thus, quantifiers are also syntactic sugar of the primitive form.

Note that quantifiers defined here are ranging from an arbitrary concept C. If C is a concept of all atomic individuals and all quantifiers range from the same concept C, then these quantifiers are first-order. Nevertheless, the concepts could be different. In this case, we have many-sorted first-order logic. Moreover, C could be complex concepts, e.g., a concept of all possible concepts. In this case, we have monadic second-order logic. Yet C could be many more, e.g., a concept of assertions, a concept of concepts of terms etc. In this sense, the quantifiers become high-order. Finally, the biggest difference is that C can even be a concept of assertions so that quantifiers in assertional logic can quantify over assertions (corresponding to formulas in classical logics), while this cannot be done in classical logics.

A problem arises whether there is cyclic definition as we assume first-order logic as our prior knowledge. Nevertheless, although playing similar roles, operators (over assertions) defined in assertional logic are considered to be different from logic connectives (over propositions/formulas) since they are on a different layer of definition. The main motivation is for the purpose of extensibility, i.e., by embedding classical logic connectives into operators in assertional logic, we can easily extend it with more components and building blocks including probability.

5   Incorporating Probability

Probability is another important building block for knowledge representation and modeling. In the last several decades, with the development of uncertainty in artificial intelligence, a number of influential approaches [1, 4, 5, 11–13] have been developed, and important applications have been found in machine learning, natural language processing etc.

In this section, we show how logic and probability can be unified through assertions in assertional logic. The basic idea is that, although the interactions between logic and probability are complicated, their interactions with assertions of the form (1) could be relatively easy. As shown in the previous section, the interactions between logic and assertions can be defined by a few lines. In this section, following Gaifman's idea [4], we show that this is indeed the case for integrating assertions with probability as well. As a result, the interactions between logic and probability will be automatically established via assertions.

Since operations over real numbers are involved in defining probability, we need to assume a theory of real number as our prior knowledge.

Gaifman [4] proposed to define the probability of a logic sentence by the sum of the probabilities of the possible worlds satisfying it. Following this idea, in assertional logic, we introduce an operator Pr (for probability) over the concept $\mathcal{A}$ of assertions. The range of Pr is the set of real numbers. For each possible world w, we assign an associated weight W_w, which is a positive real number. Then, for an assertion A, the probability of A, denoted by $Pr(A)$, is define by the following schema assertion:

$$Pr(A) = \frac{\Sigma_{w,w \models A} W_w}{\Sigma_w W_w}. \tag{10}$$

This definition defines the interactions between probability and assertions. In case that there are a number of infinite worlds, we need to use measure theory. Nevertheless, this is beyond the scope of our paper, which focuses on how to use assertional logic for extensible knowledge modeling.

Once we have defined the probability $Pr(A)$ of an assertion A as a real number, we can directly use it inside other assertions. In this sense, $Pr(A) = 0.5$, $Pr(A) \geq 0.3$, $Pr(A) \geq Pr(\forall(C, B(C))) - 0.3$, $Pr(A) \times 0.6 \geq 0.4$ and $Pr(Pr(A) \geq 0.3) \geq 0.3$ are all valid assertions. We are able to investigate some properties about probability, for instance, Kolmogorov's first and second probability axioms, that is, (1) for all assertions, $Pr(A) \geq 0$, and (2) if A is a tautology, then $Pr(A) = 1$.

We also extend this definition for conditional probability. We again introduce a new operator Pr over pairs of two assertions. Following a similar idea, the conditional probability $Pr(A_1, A_2)$ of an assertion A_1 providing another assertion A_2, also denoted by $Pr(A_1|A_2)$, is defined by the following schema assertion:

$$Pr(A_1|A_2) = \frac{\Sigma_{w,w \models A_1, w \models A_2} W_w}{\Sigma_{w,w \models A_2} W_w}. \tag{11}$$

Again, once conditional probability is defined as a real number, we can use it arbitrarily inside other assertions. Similarly, we can derive some properties about conditional probabilities, including the famous Bayes' theorem, i.e.,

$$Pr(A_1) \times Pr(A_2|A_1) = Pr(A_2) \times Pr(A_2)Pr(A_1|A_2).$$

for all assertions A_1 and A_2.

Although we only define probabilities for assertions of the basic form, the interactions between probability and other building blocks, e.g., logic, are automatically established since assertions connected by logic operators can be reduced into the primitive form. In this sense, we can investigate some properties about the interactions between logic and probability. For instance, it can be observed that Kolmogorov's third probability axiom is a tautology in assertion logic. That is, let $A_1, \ldots, A_n$ be n assertions that are pairwise disjoint. Then, $Pr(A_1 \vee \cdots \vee A_n) = Pr(A_1) + \cdots + Pr(A_n)$.

It can be verified that many axioms and properties regarding the interactions between logic and probability are tautologies in assertional logic as well, for instance, the additivity axiom: $Pr(\phi) = Pr(\phi \wedge \psi) + Pr(\phi \wedge \neg\psi)$ and the distributivity axiom: $\phi \equiv \psi$ implies that $Pr(\phi) = Pr(\psi)$, for any two assertions ϕ and ψ. In this sense, assertional logic can also be used to validate existing properties about the interactions of logic and probability. In addition, it may foster new discoveries, e.g., the interactions between higher-order logic and probability and some properties about nested probabilities.

6   Discussion and Conclusion

In this paper, we argue that, for the purpose of knowledge representation, classical first-order logic has some critical issues, including simplicity, flexibility, expressivity and extensibility. To address these issues, we propose assertional logic instead, in which the syntax of an application domain is captured by individuals (i.e., objects in the domain), concepts (i.e., groups of objects sharing something in common) and operators (i.e., connections and relationships among objects), and knowledge in the domain is simply captured by equality assertions of the form $a = b$, where a and b are terms.

In assertional logic, without redefining the semantics, one can extend a current system with new syntactic objects by definitions, which are special kinds of knowledge (i.e., assertions). Once defined, these syntactic objects can be used to define more. This can be done for assertional logic itself. We extend the primitive form of assertional logic with logic connectives and quantifiers. The key point is that, when one wants to integrate a new building block in assertional logic, she only needs to formalize it as syntactic objects (including individuals, concepts and operators) and defines its interactions with the basic form of assertions (i.e., $a = b$). The interactions between this building block and others will be automatically established since all complicated assertions can essentially be reduced to the basic form. As a case study, we briefly discuss how to incorporate probability in this paper.

Of course, assertional logic is deeply originated from first-order logic. Individuals, concepts and operators are analogous to constants, unary predicates and functions respectively, and assertion is inspired by equality atom. Nevertheless, they differ from many essential ways. Firstly, individuals can be high-order objects, e.g., concepts and assertions, so are concepts and operators. Secondly, assertional logic is naturally many-sorted, that is, the domain of an operator can be a tuple of many different concepts including high-order ones. Thirdly, concepts play a central role in assertional logic, which is natural for human knowledge representation. While concepts can be formalized as unary predicates in FOL, they are not specifically emphasized. Fourthly, in assertional logic, all kinds of knowledge are uniformly formalized in the same form of equality assertions. As shown in Sect. 5, complicated logic sentences are defined as equality assertions as well by embedding connectives and quantifiers as operators over assertions. Fifthly, following the above, although connectives, quantifiers and nesting can be represented in assertional logic, they are not considered as primitive constructs. In this sense, they will only be used on demand when necessarily needed. For instance, each uses of nesting essentially introduces a new syntactic object. We argue that this is an important reason that makes assertional logic simpler than FOL. Sixthly, in assertional logic, the simple form of $a = b$ is expressive as a and b can be high-order constructs and can be inherently related within a rich syntactic structure. While in FOL, an equality atom does not have this power. Last but not least, assertional logic directly embraces extensibility within its own framework by definitions. For instance, to define quantifiers, assertional logic only needs two lines (see Eqs. 8 and 9) without redefining a whole new syntax and semantics, which is much simpler than FOLs.

This paper is only concerned with the representation task and the definition task, and we leave the reasoning task to our future work. Nevertheless, we argue that representation and definition are worth study on their own merits. Such successful stories include entity-relationship diagram, semantic network and many more. Besides, extending assertional logic with some important AI building blocks, e.g., actions and their effects, is challenging and worth pursuing.

Acknowledgement. The author would like to thank Fangzhen Lin for his valuable comments on this paper.

References

1. Bacchus, F.: Representing and Reasoning with Probabilistic Knowledge: A Logical Approach to Probabilities. MIT Press, Cambridge (1990)
2. Brachman, R.J., Levesque, H.J.: Knowledge Representation and Reasoning. Elsevier, Amsterdam (2004)
3. Clarke, E.M., Emerson, E.A.: Design and synthesis of synchronization skeletons using branching time temporal logic. In: Kozen, D. (ed.) Logic of Programs 1981. LNCS, vol. 131, pp. 52–71. Springer, Heidelberg (1982). doi:10.1007/BFb0025774
4. Gaifman, H.: Concerning measures in first order calculi. Israel J. Math. **2**, 1–18 (1964)
5. Hailperin, T.: Probability logic. Notre Dame J. Formal Logic **25**, 198–212 (1984)
6. Halmos, P.: Naive Set Theory. Undergraduate Texts in Mathematics. Springer, New York (1974)
7. Halpern, J.Y.: An analysis of first-order logics of probability. Artif. Intell. **46**(3), 311–350 (1990)
8. van Harmelen, F., Lifschitz, V., Porter, B.W. (eds.): Handbook of Knowledge Representation. Foundations of Artificial Intelligence, vol. 3. Elsevier, Amsterdam (2008)
9. Levesque, H., Pirri, F., Reiter, R.: Foundations for the situation calculus. Electron. Trans. Artif. Intell. **2**(3–4), 159–178 (1998)
10. Lin, F.: Situation calculus. In: Handbook of Knowledge Representation, pp. 649–669 (2008)
11. Milch, B.C.: Probabilistic models with unknown objects. Ph.D. thesis, Berkeley, CA, USA, aAI3253991 (2006)
12. Pearl, J.: Probabilistic Reasoning in Intelligent Systems: Networks of Plausible Inference. Morgan Kaufmann Publishers Inc., San Francisco (1988)
13. Richardson, M., Domingos, P.: Markov logic networks. Mach. Learn. **62**(1–2), 107–136 (2006)

Algorithms

Genetic Algorithms with DNN-Based Trainable Crossover as an Example of Partial Specialization of General Search

Alexey Potapov[1,2,3](✉) and Sergey Rodionov[3,4]

[1] CT Lab, ITMO University, St. Petersburg, Russia
pas.aicv@gmail.com
[2] St. Petersburg State University, St. Petersburg, Russia
[3] AIDEUS, St. Petersburg, Russia
astroseger@gmail.com
[4] Aix Marseille Université, CNRS, LAM (Laboratoire d'Astrophysique
de Marseille) UMR 7326, 13388 Marseille, France

Abstract. Universal induction relies on some general search procedure that is doomed to be inefficient. One possibility to achieve both generality and efficiency is to specialize this procedure w.r.t. any given narrow task. However, complete specialization that implies direct mapping from the task parameters to solutions (discriminative models) without search is not always possible. In this paper, partial specialization of general search is considered in the form of genetic algorithms (GAs) with a specialized crossover operator. We perform a feasibility study of this idea implementing such an operator in the form of a deep feedforward neural network. GAs with trainable crossover operators are compared with the result of complete specialization, which is also represented as a deep neural network. Experimental results show that specialized GAs can be more efficient than both general GAs and discriminative models.

Keywords: Genetic algorithms · Deep neural networks · Optimization · Specialization · Universal induction · General search

1 Introduction

Solomonoff's theory of universal induction [1] has been ignored by the machine learning community for a long time because of its impracticality. However, one can find an apparent (although not explicitly declared) trend towards the universal induction in some recent works coming from the mainstream approaches in machine learning. For example, such deep learning models as Neural Turing Machine [2], Differentiable Neural Computer [3], Differentiable Forth Interpreter [4], Neural Programmer-Interpreter [5] and others are designed directly to perform inference in the space of algorithms that is the main feature of universal induction. The probabilistic programming field features the development of Turing-complete languages with general inference engines for arbitrary generative models. Using such inference engine, one can obtain a sort of universal induction algorithm by making inference on a model that generates arbitrary programs.

T. Everitt et al. (Eds.): AGI 2017, LNAI 10414, pp. 101–111, 2017.
DOI: 10.1007/978-3-319-63703-7_10

However, these efforts encounter some difficulties with scaling to the inference of non-trivial algorithms. These difficulties and the impracticality of the basic universal induction have the same origin. Indeed, the search in the Turing-complete space is very difficult, and general methods are not able to perform it efficiently or effectively. Deep neural networks heavily rely on the gradient descent, which application to the differential embedding of algorithms with sequential nature is prone to converge to inaccurate solutions [6]. The works on probabilistic programming languages (PPLs) are much more focused on evaluating posterior probabilities over all solutions, and frequently even don't consider the search problem utilizing simple enumeration or random search techniques.

Possibility to solve the universal induction problem with one simple and efficient method is doubtful. On the other hand, any fixed set of practical machine learning methods that work in Turing-incomplete model spaces is insufficient for the needs of artificial general intelligence. One general idea how to avoid these two undesirable extremes is meta-learning or, more generally, meta-inference, i.e. inference of new task-specific inference or learning algorithms. Meta-inference algorithms can both be computationally feasible and produce new efficient narrow inference algorithms.

Meta-learning including learning efficient forms of gradient descent [7] and more specific reinforcement learning algorithms [8, 9] in the deep learning framework has become quite popular recently reincarnating and developing further the ideas formulated earlier [10]. There are also probabilistic programming systems (e.g. [11]), which inference engines adapt to the given generative model (program), and are automatically reduced to the efficient inference methods, if the model falls into some narrow class (e.g. a form of message-passing algorithms on factor graphs). However, all these results are not put into the context of universal induction.

In this paper, we start from the concept of narrow machine learning methods as the result of specialization of universal induction [12], and show that practical meta-learning methods can be considered as the result of partial specialization of the universal induction. As the proof of concept, we develop a family of meta-inference methods in the form of deep neural networks and compare them on several tasks of different complexity. These methods differ in the completeness of specialization of the universal induction and range from learning discriminative models to learning task-specific genetic operators for genetic algorithms.

The main contribution of this paper is the framework, in which training discriminative models, learning to learn by gradient descent, and learning domain-specific crossover operators in genetic algorithms are represented as particular cases of specialization of universal induction. Deep learning models developed to demonstrate and verify these ideas can be considered as the minor contribution.

2   Background

The presented work is conceptually based on our two previous research directions. The first one is the theory of universal induction specialization [12]. The second one is implementation of the universal induction in the form of probabilistic programming languages with optimization queries (e.g. implemented in the form of simulated annealing and genetic programming) [13].

Solomonoff induction can be considered as the full Bayesian inference method, which utilizes a Turing-complete generative model that initially samples random program z for universal Turing machine U with universal priors $P_U(z) = 2^{-l(z)}$ and then calculates its output $x = U[z]$ implying conditional probabilities $P_U(x|z) = 1$ if $U[z] = x$ and 0 otherwise (one can also consider a stochastic universal Turing machine (UTM) defining smoother conditionals $P_U(x|z)$). In these settings, Bayesian inference can be performed, e.g. the marginal probability can be computed as

$$P_U(x) = \sum_z P_U(z)P_U(x|z) = \sum_{z:U[z]=x} 2^{-l(z)}. \tag{1}$$

One can consider the generalized form of universal induction that takes as input an arbitrary machine μ that can be both universal and not universal. The machine accepts some z treated as hidden variables. The task of induction is to calculate posterior distribution $P_\mu(z|x)$ or its maximum z^*. Machine μ can be treated as a generative model since it constructs (or samples in accordance with its likelihood function) x using z: $x = \mu[z]$. We assume that some prior probability distribution over z is also given making μ a probabilistic generative model.

Inference with the use of generative models consists in calculation of

$$P_\mu(z|x) = \frac{P_\mu(x|z)P_\mu(z)}{\sum_z P_\mu(x|z)P_\mu(z)} \text{ or} \tag{2a}$$

$$z^* = \arg\max_z P_\mu(z|x) = \arg\max_z P_\mu(x|z)P_\mu(z). \tag{2b}$$

E.g. if $\mu = U$ is UTM, then $z^* = \arg\max_z P_U(x|z)P_U(z) = \arg\max_{z:U[z]=x} 2^{-l(z)}$.

Usage of generative models encounters some difficulties since these models start from priors over models or hidden variables, and generate observables through non-trivial stochastic computations, so it is necessary to somehow guess appropriate values of hidden variables, model parameters, or even model structure that will produce real observations. That is, one should sum out z or enumerate all values of z in (2a and 2b).

One can introduce the procedure of calculating (2a and 2b) explicitly. Let us consider some search procedure $S(\mu, x)$ that takes machine/model μ as input, and returns the most probable z^* or calculates $P_\mu(z|x)$. This procedure will correspond to a form of generalized universal induction.

While generative models allow for calculating any conditionals and marginals, but through intensive computations, discriminative or descriptive models directly and efficiently compute posterior probabilities or sample values of target or hidden variables. In the Bayesian approach, it is typical to construct a (variational) approximation to the posterior distribution specified by a generative model in the form of a discriminative model belonging to some family allowing efficient inference. That is, some machine v is constructed such that $v[x] \approx z^*$ or $v[x] \approx P_\mu(z|x)$ depending on settings.

One can consider the problem of constructing a discriminative model given a generative model as the problem of specialization of the program S performing universal induction w.r.t. its first parameter μ. Indeed, the result of specialization of some program w.r.t. one of its parameters is the efficient version of this program with the fixed value of this parameter.

As the result of specialization of generalized universal induction procedure $S(\mu, x)$, one will get program $v = spec[S, \mu]$ such that

$$(\forall x)v[x] = S(\mu, x)$$

That is, *discriminative models are the results of complete specialization of the universal induction w.r.t. corresponding generative models.* One can also consider the problem of simultaneously learning machines μ and v given some data that yields a sort of universal autoencoders [12].

Precise complete specialization is impossible in the case of a Turing-complete generative model. It is also doubtful that one can construct an approximate inversion $v \approx U^{-1}$, which will directly (without search) produce good enough programs given their outputs. Nevertheless, one can still hope to specialize S w.r.t. U, i.e. to construct more efficient informed search method that takes x as input and uses it to search for best z taking the structure of U and content of x into account.

Recently we implemented S as the simulated annealing and genetic programming search engine over probabilistic program traces [14]. Indeed, the idea to use genetic programming as the search method in universal induction is rather old [15] and well-known [16]. This leads us to the idea to specialize such a meta-heuristic method, i.e. to learn problem-specific and data driven genetic operators. It should be emphasized that learning such problem-specific genetic operators and constructing discriminative models have essentially the same meaning of specialization of universal induction, although the result of such specialization has rather different forms.

In this work, we don't do this within the probabilistic programming framework and just verify the very idea of learning genetic operations, but keep in mind that any fitness function can be defined as an optimization query in PPL. We represent a "genetic operator" (crossover and mutation) as a (deep) feedforward neural network that takes two candidate solutions and the values of parameters of the fitness function and learns to produce new candidate solution. Thus, more technically related works are the works on meta-learning in neural networks. For example, the classical work [10] is devoted to learning the learning strategy in the supervised learning settings. The more recent work [8] extends this result on the reinforcement learning settings. The work [7] is devoted to the problem of learning to learn by gradient descent. These works consider the problem of learning how to iteratively improve one candidate solution. One can think of our results loosely as the generalization of these methods to the arbitrary number (starting from zero) of candidate solutions.

The work [17] devoted to the "compilation" of probabilistic programs (generative models) into discriminative deep networks is also conceptually related. It should be pointed out that compilation is the particular form of specialization (namely, specialization of an interpreter w.r.t. a given program in accordance to Futamura-Turchin projections [20]). Thus, what is done by the authors is precisely a form of loose specialization of generalized universal induction w.r.t. a given program that we described earlier [12] (and which the authors seem not familiar with). Neural networks are used as a trainable proposal distribution, i.e. they again modify one given candidate solution.

One can also see a connection between our work and the idea of 'magician systems' described by Ben Goertzel in [18]: "Magician systems may thus be viewed as a kind of "generalized genetic algorithm," where the standard crossover operator is replaced by a flexible, individualized crossover operator... this is also precisely the type of dynamical system we need to use to model the brain/mind." Although the motivation and technical details of our work are completely different, we find this convergence of ideas quite interesting.

3   Models

Consider the task in which known family of fitness functions $f(\mathbf{x}|\boldsymbol{\theta})$ is given, and the goal is to find optimum $\mathbf{x}^*$ for given $\boldsymbol{\theta}$:

$$\mathbf{x}^*(\boldsymbol{\theta}) = \arg\min_{\mathbf{x}} f(\mathbf{x}|\boldsymbol{\theta}). \qquad (3)$$

Operation 'argmin' veils some computation that takes $\boldsymbol{\theta}$ as input and returns $\mathbf{x}^*$ as output. Such computations can vary from the completely uninformed random search to the direct calculation of $\mathbf{x}^*$ using explicit solution for a specific f.

We calculate (3) using different procedures:

- Blind search that randomly samples values of $\mathbf{x}$ and keeps track of the best value;
- Traditional genetic algorithms that perform uninformed meta-heuristic search in the space of $\mathbf{x}$ without taking $\boldsymbol{\theta}$ into account;
- Deep feedforward neural network that is trained to directly produce $\mathbf{x}^*(\boldsymbol{\theta})$ taking $\boldsymbol{\theta}$ as input: $\mathrm{Net_D}(\boldsymbol{\theta}) \to \mathbf{x}^*$ working similar to discriminative models in pattern recognition;
- Genetic algorithms with trainable crossover operator represented in the form of deep feedforward network that takes two candidate solutions $\mathbf{x}_1$ and $\mathbf{x}_2$ and parameters $\boldsymbol{\theta}$ and produces new candidate solution $\mathbf{x}'$: $\mathrm{Net_{GA}}(\mathbf{x}_1, \mathbf{x}_2, \boldsymbol{\theta}) \to \mathbf{x}'$.

Here, blind search (BS) and genetic algorithms (GA) are considered as general non-specialized search methods, while $\mathrm{Net_D}$ and $\mathrm{Net_{GA}}$ are considered as the result of different degree of specialization of general methods since they are trained to optimize a certain class of fitness-functions.

GAs were run on populations of small sizes (e.g. 10 survived species per population producing 20 children) to emphasize the role of recombinations. One step of blind search consisted in randomly sampling the same number of candidate solutions as the number of children in each population in GAs. The speed of mutations in GAs was adjusted to produce better results. In the case of $\mathrm{Net_{GA}}$, mutations were applied to

x_1 and x_2 before crossover instead of mutating the result of crossover as it is done in traditional GAs.

Both Net_D and Net_{GA} were fully connected feedforward networks with H hidden layers with the number of neurons $100H$, $100(H - 1)$, ..., 100 in the first, second, ..., last layer correspondingly. Remarkably, networks with small number of layers produced (considerably) less precise solutions especially for the tasks of higher dimension. Here, we will show the results for $H = 5$, because further increase of the network size leads to minor improvement of the precision.

Training of network parameters was performed by randomly sampling values of θ and using $|Net_D(\theta) - x^*|^2$ and $|Net_{GA}(x_1, x_2, \theta) - x^*|^2$ as components of the loss functions for the stochastic gradient descent. Values of x_1, x_2 for training Net_{GA} were sample around x^*, e.g. $|x_{1,2} - x^*| < 1$.

4   Experiments

Quadratic fitness functions
Consider the following very simple task of optimization of quadratic functions. Let the fitness function be given in the form

$$f(x|a, b) = ax^2 + bx$$

where $x, a, b \in R^N$ and x^2 is element-wise, while multiplications are scalar products. Its minimum can be simply obtained analytically as $x^* = -b/(2a)$, where division is also element-wise. However, this task is not that trivial for neural networks trained by examples and not well suited to perform division.

We trained our models to produce the value of x^* taking a, b or a, b and x_1, x_2 as input, where x_1, x_2 are imprecise candidate solutions. That is, the network produces some x_i for randomly chosen task (a_i, b_i) and the loss function $|x_i - x_i^*|^2$ is used to train the network using stochastic gradient descent. Random tasks were generated sampling $a \sim \text{uniform}(0.1, 1.1)$, $b \sim \text{uniform}(-1, 1)$.

Figure 1 shows precision of solutions $|f(x_{sol}) - f(x^*)|$ obtained by different methods depending on the number of iterations of search (i.e. generations in GAs) for $N = 5$. The curve for Net_D is constant since this method doesn't perform search. These curves are obtained by averaging over many (1000) optimization tasks.

As it can be seen, blind search converges rather slowly, while other methods find reasonably good solutions quickly. This task appears to be simple for Net_D, although it cannot precisely represent division, so it produces imperfect solutions. Net_{GA} has higher both convergence speed and precision in comparison to traditional GAs. Character of this curve seems to imply that Net_{GA} relies more on the task parameters than on the candidate solutions and quickly produces candidate solutions of the same quality as Net_D. Nevertheless, its output is different for different input candidate solutions, and incremental improvement of the population of candidate solutions is achieved with its usage inside GA, so Net_{GA} learns more complex mapping than Net_D.

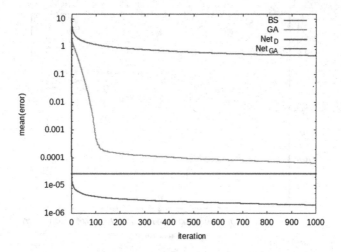

Fig. 1. Search efficiency in the task of quadratic function optimization

Linear equations

Then, we compared the described models on the task of solving systems of linear equations:

$$\mathbf{A}\mathbf{x} = \mathbf{b}$$

where $\mathbf{x}, \mathbf{b} \in R^N$, and $\mathbf{A}$ is $N \times N$ matrix.

Again, the models were trained on randomly generated tasks $\mathbf{A}_i$, $\mathbf{b}_i$ to produce $\mathbf{x}_i$ minimizing $|\mathbf{A}_i\mathbf{x}_i - \mathbf{b}_i|^2$. Random sampling was performed as $\mathbf{A}, \mathbf{b} \sim \text{uniform}(-1,1)$, but rejecting tasks with solutions $\mathbf{x}^*$ such that $|\mathbf{x}^*| > 6$.

This problem appeared to be considerably more difficult for neural networks. Figure 2 shows the obtained averaged solution error $\|\mathbf{A}\mathbf{x}_{\text{sol}} - \mathbf{b}\|$ for $N = 5$.

As it can be seen, Net_D fails to learn good mapping from the space of parameters of linear equation systems to the space of their solutions, although it produces better results than achieved by blind search in a reasonable number of steps. Although this task is not NP-complete, and can be solved without search, it cannot be solved by linear algorithms, so this result is not surprising.

At the same time, Net_{GA} solves this task in few iterations, i.e. much faster than traditional GAs. On the other hand, Net_{GA} converges to slightly less precise solutions in average. Again, the reason might be that Net_{GA} relies more on the task parameters than on the parent candidate solutions. That is, it learns the mapping, which is closer to complete specialization than to traditional crossover. This result is also reasonable taking into account that Net_{GA} is trained to produce candidate solutions as close to the optimal solution as possible. Quite opposite, it might be surprising that the network learned to use the parent candidate solutions in addition to the task parameters. It should be mentioned that this effect is achieved easier when Net_{GA} is trained on parents that are close to $\mathbf{x}^*$ (i.e. parents are not arbitrary, but contain some information about $\mathbf{x}^*$).

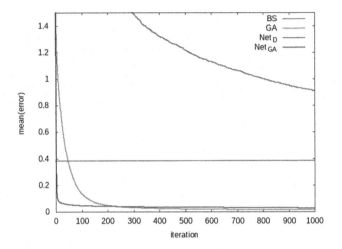

Fig. 2. Search efficiency in the task of solving linear equations

Basic meta learning

The last task we considered was the task of producing parameters of the optimal logistic regression model given the training set. That is, the weights and biases in the logistic regression network act as $\mathbf{x}$, while the training set for this model is considered as $\boldsymbol{\theta}$. Thus, the task was to learn the learning algorithm that maps training sets to the logistic regression parameters.

The patterns for the training sets were sampled from two Gaussians corresponding to two classes. Parameters of these Gaussians were generated randomly, but in such a way that the distance between centers of classes was between 2σ and 3σ.

This task appeared to be very simple, and complete specialization Net_D produced almost optimal solutions. For example, for the dimension of patterns $N = 2$ and the size of training set $N_{\text{train}} = 20$ (with random number of patterns per class) the averaged results for different number of hidden layers are shown in Table 1, while recognition rate of the logistic regression from sklearn library was 0.9837.

Table 1. Results of recognition by logistic regression produced by Net_D

	$H = 1$	$H = 3$	$H = 5$	$H = 10$
Recognition	0.9335	0.9840	0.9845	0.9842

The same results were obtained for larger values of N. Unfortunately this straightforward approach to meta learning doesn't scale to the real pattern recognition problems. The main limitation consists in the usage of the whole training set as the input to Net_D or Net_{GA}. More practical approach would be to pass patterns from the training set one by one to these networks, but then the networks should either be recurrent in order to be able to accumulate information from the patterns, or be trained in a very specific way to perform a sort of stochastic gradient descent step. Development of such models is beyond the scope of this paper, and is the topic of further work.

5 Discussion

Although our experiments were conducted on example of rather simple synthetic problems, they demonstrate the following ideas:

- There can be different degrees of specialization of general search procedures including complete and partial specialization, and the optimal degree of specialization depends on the family of problems to be solved. In particular, there is a large set of models between generative and discriminative models, and approximating inference in generative models with discriminative models is not the only and sometimes not the best choice.
- One example of partial specialization is genetic algorithms with the trainable crossover operator that accepts not only two parent candidate solutions, but also the parameters of the task to be solved. Such specialized GAs can converge much faster than traditional GAs, and their performance can be much better than that of complete specialization.
- Such trainable crossover operators can be productively implemented in the form of deep neural networks at least for some families of tasks.

Although these conclusions are true in general, their significance for the real-world problems and AGI systems is still to be studied in detail. In particular, we conducted some additional experiments showing some limitations of the implemented form of trainable GAs.

First of all, it appeared that both Net_D and Net_{GA} work bad on the tasks outside the region of the training set, i.e. neural networks don't generalize well (at least in a traditional sense). For example, in the task of quadratic functions minimization, they don't learn the division operation enabling calculation of $x^* = -b/(2a)$ for any a and b, but memorize this mapping for specific a_i, b_i from the training set and interpolate it. This conclusion is consistent with some recent studies (e.g. [19]).

Then, we compared Net_{GA} with the network that takes not two, but only one parent as input, and is also used inside the search procedure. Briefly speaking, we didn't observe considerable difference in their performance. Thus, our specialized search didn't benefit much from recombining two candidate solutions. We believe that it can benefit considerably (because GAs can be considerably better than simulated annealing or gradient descent in some tasks), but more complex tasks should be considered and/or less simplistic loss function should be used.

Indeed, we trained Net_{GA} outside the search cycle. It was required to produce as good candidate solution as possible after single application to the random parents, while its usage within GA supposes its iterative application to the evolving population of solutions with the aim to find the optimal solution not immediately, but after a number of generations. Efficient approach to representing and optimizing such loss function is to be developed. One possibility is to represent the whole search process as a recurrent neural network to optimize it end-to-end.

Further development of this approach also consists in its application to arbitrary optimization queries in probabilistic programming. One lesson that we can learn from our study is that probabilistic programs cannot be "compiled" into feedforward neural networks in general case.

Acknowledgements. This work was supported by Government of Russian Federation, Grant 074-U01.

References

1. Solomonoff, R.: A formal theory of inductive inference, part 1 and part 2. Inf. Control **7**, 1–22, 224–254 (1964)
2. Graves, A., Wayne, G., Danihelka, I.: Neural turing machines. arXiv:1410.5401 [cs.NE] (2014)
3. Graves, A., et al.: Hybrid computing using a neural network with dynamic external memory. Nature **538**, 471–476 (2016)
4. Riedel, S., Bošnjak, M., Rocktäschel, T.: Programming with a differentiable forth interpreter. arXiv:1605.06640 (2016)
5. Reed, S., Freitas, N.: Neural Programmer-interpreters. arXiv:1511.06279 [cs.LG] (2015)
6. Kaiser, Ł., Sutskever, I.: Neural GPUs learn algorithms. arXiv:1511.08228 [cs.LG] (2015)
7. Andrychowicz, M., et al.: Learning to learn by gradient descent by gradient descent. arXiv:1606.04474 [cs.NE] (2016)
8. Wang, J.X., et al.: Learning to reinforcement learn. arXiv:1611.05763 [cs.LG] (2016)
9. Duan, Y., et al.: RL^2: fast reinforcement learning via slow reinforcement learning. arXiv:1611.02779 [cs.AI] (2016)
10. Hochreiter, S., Younger, A.S., Conwell, P.R.: Learning to learn using gradient descent. In: International Conference on Artificial Neural Networks, pp. 87–94 (2001)
11. Stuhlmüller, A., Goodman, N.D.: A dynamic programming algorithm for inference in recursive probabilistic programs. arXiv:1206.3555 [cs.AI] (2012)
12. Potapov, A., Rodionov, S.: Making universal induction efficient by specialization. In: Goertzel, B., Orseau, L., Snaider, J. (eds.) AGI 2014. LNCS, vol. 8598, pp. 133–142. Springer, Cham (2014). doi:10.1007/978-3-319-09274-4_13
13. Potapov, A., Batishcheva, V., Rodionov, S.: Optimization framework with minimum description length principle for probabilistic programming. In: Bieger, J., Goertzel, B., Potapov, A. (eds.) AGI 2015. LNCS, vol. 9205, pp. 331–340. Springer, Cham (2015). doi:10.1007/978-3-319-21365-1_34
14. Batishcheva, V., Potapov, A.: Genetic programming on program traces as an inference engine for probabilistic languages. In: Bieger, J., Goertzel, B., Potapov, A. (eds.) AGI 2015. LNCS, vol. 9205, pp. 14–24. Springer, Cham (2015). doi:10.1007/978-3-319-21365-1_2
15. Solomonoff, R.J.: The discovery of algorithmic probability. J. Comput. Syst. Sci. **55**(1), 73–88 (1997)
16. Özkural, E.: An application of stochastic context sensitive grammar induction to transfer learning. In: Goertzel, B., Orseau, L., Snaider, J. (eds.) AGI 2014. LNCS, vol. 8598, pp. 121–132. Springer, Cham (2014). doi:10.1007/978-3-319-09274-4_12
17. Le, T.A., Baydin, A.G., Wood, F.: Inference compilation and universal probabilistic programming. arXiv:1610.09900 [cs.AI] (2016)

18. Goertzel, B.: From Complexity to Creativity: Explorations in Evolutionary, Autopoietic, and Cognitive Dynamics. Springer, New York (1997)
19. Zhang, C., Bengio, S., Hardt, M., Recht, B., Vinyals, O.: Understanding deep learning requires rethinking generalization. arXiv:1611.03530 [cs.LG] (2017)
20. Futamura, Y.: Partial evaluation of computation process – an approach to a compiler-compiler. Syst. Comput. Controls 2(5), 45–50 (1971)

Deductive and Analogical Reasoning
on a Semantically Embedded Knowledge Graph

Douglas Summers-Stay[✉]

U.S. Army Research Laboratory, Adelphi, USA
douglas.a.summers-stay.civ@mail.mil

Abstract. Representing knowledge as high-dimensional vectors in a continuous semantic vector space can help overcome the brittleness and incompleteness of traditional knowledge bases. We present a method for performing deductive reasoning directly in such a vector space, combining analogy, association, and deduction in a straightforward way at each step in a chain of reasoning, drawing on knowledge from diverse sources and ontologies.

Keywords: Semantic vectors · Reasoning · Knowledge graphs · Knowledge bases · Analogy

1   Introduction

Common sense knowledge bases (KB) are notoriously 'brittle': they are generally only usable by those who have spent a lot of time getting to know precisely how to phrase a question so that it will match the representation in the KB [3]. They are also inevitably incomplete, leaving out many facts that one would expect a system that claims common sense to include. In order to get around these limitations, several researchers [6,16,19] have been exploring the possibililty of somehow combining the deductive reasoning abilities of a knowledge base with the ability to represent semantic similarity that is provided by distributional semantic vector spaces. "Query expansion," for example, involves querying for semantically nearby terms as well as the explicit terms entered. The deductive reasoning in such a system still takes place in the discrete knowledge base, however. When there are concepts or relations missing from the knowledge base that prevent a chain of reasoning from going through for any of these near terms, the system will be unable to return any result.

Searches that take place completely in a semantic vector space, on the other hand, are more akin to searching via a web search engine. These searches forgo any explicit steps of deductive reasoning, relying instead on broad coverage. Combining multiple facts in a chain of reasoning to answer a query is beyond their current capabilities. What we propose in this paper is a way of discovering chains of reasoning connecting a premise to a conclusion directly in a semantic vector space. The method can be applied to various ways of representing knowledge by high-dimensional vectors.

© Springer International Publishing AG 2017
T. Everitt et al. (Eds.): AGI 2017, LNAI 10414, pp. 112–122, 2017.
DOI: 10.1007/978-3-319-63703-7_11

Forming a chain of deductive logical reasoning can be thought of as a special variety of a more general phenomenon in the mind of following a "train of thought." One idea brings up a related idea, which in turn brings up another related idea, and so forms a connected train. We can deliberately return to an earlier point in the train and follow another path either backward or forward, so that the trains link up to form a larger structure.

Trains of thought serve several purposes. Parts of an essay or a story are often structured as trains of thought, with each sentence building on the one before. Restricted to cause-effect relations, the root cause of an event can be found. Trains formed of links between means and ends can form a plan of actions and subgoals to achieve a larger goal. Trains of reasons can answer "why" questions. Trains of looser relations like resemblance of form and sound form the basis of some kinds of poetry, symbolism, or mysticism. Memory techniques, creativity methods, and dreams also rely on trains of thought.

In order to form chains of reasoning, AI researchers have attempted to find paths between ideas using exhaustive search in a knowledge graph. This blind walk through all connections in the graph seems very different from how we normally think. A path connecting two ideas seems to bubble up– we initially feel the connection more than see it. Ideas shade imperceptibly into one another. Analogy and association are everpresent. An argument as originally conceived generally skips steps, and may include steps which are simply analogous to related problems. Turning such a jumble of ideas into a step-by-step proof is a process that takes skill, training, and deliberate conscious effort.

Such imprecision can lead to invalid conclusions and fuzzy thinking, but it has the advantage of being capable of operating under unknown or incompletely represented conditions. When we don't know, we can guess at the general ballpark of the answer. In order to create a system that can deal with the ambiguities of natural language and take action in an uncertain environment, we need to build in the ability to think in a more flexible, human manner. A more human-like reasoning engine should have at least the following properties:

– Be capable of associational, analogical, inductive, abductive, and deductive reasoning;
– when exact answers can't be found, guess at an approximate answer;
– be aware of the strength or weakness of its arguments;
– creatively find connections that were not deliberately given, and
– find arguments that add up to a whole, rather than find strictly linear connections.

2 Background

There are multiple strands of research that involve representing knowledge as vectors. One strand comes from the biologically-inspired cognitive architecture community. This is increasingly known as Vector Symbolic Architectures (VSA) [7]. [9] introduced the idea of using sparse high-dimensional binary vectors as a way of storing information that was resistant to noise and capable of addressing memory with exemplars. These ideas have been developed to include the notion of binding vectors for compositional structure and to be more biologically accurate [11, 13, 20].

A second strand comes from the linguistics community, beginning with Latent Semantic Analysis to create word and document context vectors [4], and includes the well-known word vector representation word2vec [14]. The ability of such vectors to solve analogy problems was demonstrated in 2005 [17]. Attempts to encode the meaning of sentences by composing the meaning of the words in the sentence [1, 8, 10] is a very similar problem to encoding triples from a knowledge base. Some researchers encode triples from a knowledge graph directly as vectors, building on [2].

A few papers are directly concerned with multi-step deductive reasoning in vector spaces [12, 15, 18, 21]. These approaches use machine learning to build methods for composing vectors in a reasoning chain. The system described in this paper does not require any training beyond what is done to create the word vector representations in the first place. It is unique in using sparse vector decomposition to solve a deductive reasoning problem.

3   Method

We are given a knowledge base of facts represented as triples of the form $(e_n, predicate, e_m)$. We are also given a semantic vector space where every entity e is represented by a high-dimensional vector in such a way that terms that are semantically similar are nearby in the semantic space. Each of the triples is represented within the vector space by a vector of the form $-e_1 + e_2$. For the purposes of the vector space calculations, these triples are treated as statements that $e_n \Rightarrow e_m$. The specific predicates are not used in the vector space calculation, but instead all predicates are treated as a simple statement of implication. This maps the first-order predicate calculus problem to a "zeroth-order" propositional calculus problem.

We wish to prove that $g \Rightarrow p$. The vector representing this relation is $-g + p$. If there is some set of facts in the knowledge base that can prove this, it must be the case that the facts form a chain:

$$g \Rightarrow e_1 \Rightarrow e_2 ... \Rightarrow e_n \Rightarrow p$$

Representing this chain as vectors we get

$$(-g + e_1) + (-e_1 + e_2) + ...(-e_{n-1} + e_n) + (-e_n + p)$$

Cancelling out we see that this sum is equal to the vector directly from g to p:

$$(-g + e_1) + (-e_1 + e_2) + ...(-e_{n-1} + e_n) + (-e_n + p) = -g + p$$

Our goal, then, in order to find a chain of entities linking g to p, is to find a sum of fact vectors of the form $(-e_m + e_n)$ that adds up to $(-g + p)$. Such a sum can be thought of as a weight vector w multiplied by the list of fact vectors, with a weight of 1 for each fact vector included in the chain, and a weight of zero for each fact vector not included. Clearly w will be a sparse vector, with many more zeros than ones. This suggests that in order to find such a sum, we can use sparse approximation techniques such as OMP or LASSO to obtain the sparse weight vector w.

In cases where such a chain exists, this method should (when the sparse approximation is successful) return a set of facts that constitute the chain. When the chain does not exist, however, the method will return an approximation of the correct links in the path. Because the vectors come from a semantic vector space, such approximations will amount to undefined relations between closely related entities. Such gaps can be considered a kind of associational reasoning.

For example, suppose we want to find a path of relations between G : $Michael Jackson$ and P : $music$. The knowledge base contains, among many others, the following two facts:

(Michael Jackson, is a, songwriter) and (musician, composes, music)

The proposed method would return $Michael Jackson \Rightarrow songwriter$ and $musician \Rightarrow music$, even though they don't strictly form a chain of reasoning, because $songwriter$ and $musician$ are nearby in the semantic space, and so the error in the sum is fairly small.[1] This is the core idea we hope to communicate in this paper: that sparse solvers can be used to find deductive chains in a semantic vector space, in a way that allows for analogical and associational connections where appropriate.

4   Propositional Calculus and the Logic of Subsets

The system is able to perform deductive logic because it is approximately implementing propositional calculus as a logic of subsets.[2] Call the universe U the set of all entities u in the semantic vector space. The nearest neighbors of any entity p form a subset P of U. (These are the terms which are semantically near to p.) In a high dimensional semantic vector space, if a vector is a nearest neighbor of vector a or b it will also usually be a nearest neighbor of vector $a + b$.[3] This means that we can treat $+$ as the union operator: The elements of $A \cup B$ will be the near neighbors of the vector $a + b$. In propositional calculus, this is the OR operator, $\vee$.

---

[1] In some special cases, the error in one gap of the chain will largely cancel out with the error at another gap. When this happens, the system has found an analogous relation. This is discussed in the section Analogical Properties of Semantic Spaces below.

[2] Boole and DeMorgan originally formulated propositional logic as a special case of the logic of subsets [5].

[3] If a and b are approximately orthogonal unit vectors, then the similarity between the two will be $\frac{\sqrt{2}}{2}$. This is much higher than the expected similarity between any two terms selected from the space. See [20] for details.

Table 1. Loosely speaking, terms near $a + b$ will come from the set of terms near a OR b, while terms near $a - b$ come from terms near a and NOT near B. Here bold terms are among the eight nearest terms to "classical" and italic terms are those near to "music". The set of terms that belong to a AND b is a subset of a OR b and these terms will show up especially high in the list of terms near $a + b$.

near "classical"	classical, *classical music*, Classical, classical repertoire, Hindustani classical, contemporary, Mohiniattam, sacred choral
near "music"	music, **classical music**, jazz, Music, songs, musicians, tunes
near "music − classical"	*music*, Rhapsody subscription, ringtone, MP3s, Polow, Napster, entertainment, *Music*, *tunes*
near "music + classical"	classical, *music*, *classical music*, jazz, classical repertoire, **Hindustani classical**, **sacred choral**, classical guitar

The vectors in U near $-a$ are the vectors which are not near to a. So $-$ can be treated as a the set complement operator c. In propositional calculus, this is the NOT operator, $\neg$.

In propositional calculus, A implies B ($A \Rightarrow B$) means that either B is true, or A is not true, so it can be rewritten as (NOT A) OR B. In the subset logic, this is $A\mathsf{c} \cup B$. In the vector space, then, $A \Rightarrow B$ can be represented as $-a + b$.

In propositional calculus, the *modus ponens* rule allows us to conclude B from the two facts A and $A \Rightarrow B$. In the vector space, a and $-a + b$ cancel to give b. In a chain of implication $A \Rightarrow B \Rightarrow C \Rightarrow D$ all the interior terms cancel, allowing us to conclude that $A \Rightarrow D$. Similarly in the vector space, the vectors $(-a + b) + (-b + c) + (-c + d)$ simplify to the vector $-a + d$.[4] In this way, the system is able to carry out *modus ponens* deductive reasoning within the semantic vector space.

Propositional calculus is less powerful than predicate calculus. In order to prove that $(p, relation, q)$ one must have, in addition to the triples in the knowledge base, Horn clauses which have $(p, relation, q)$ as the conclusion (i.e. the non-negative literal). If the facts in the knowledge base passed to the solver are limited to those which have relations that participate in such Horn clauses, the chains of implication will tend to be more reasonable. In general, using this system as it currently stands requires restricting which predicates are allowed to participate in a solution. Instead of representing $snow \Rightarrow white$, we could represent the more informative statement $(madeOf, snow) \Rightarrow (hasColor, white)$. Doing this requires using vectors that bind multiple concepts to roles, as in VSA. It is not yet clear how well the analogical or associational properties described

---

[4] Notice that addition is used as AND rather than OR when combining B with A and $A \Rightarrow B$ (see the caption of Table 1 for why this is acceptable). At any rate, the notion of cancelling out with *modus ponens* still holds.

below would work in such an architecture, however: it depends on the details of how binding is performed.

5   Analogical and Abductive Reasoning

The ability of distributional semantic vectors such as word2vec to find analogies is not peculiar to how such vectors are trained, but should be an expected property of any system that maps semantically similar concepts to similar high-dimensional vectors. Suppose we are given the following analogy to solve: *bear:hiker::shark:X*. To make it simpler, consider contexts representing the ideas *woods, sea, predator* and *tourist,* and treat any other contexts as noise. The vector for *bear,* for instance, is some weighted average of (the mean of all vectors related to woods), and (the mean of all vectors related to predators) plus some noise. Thus we can rewrite the analogy as *woods + predator : woods + tourist :: sea + predator : X.*

The vector between *bear* and *hiker* is $-predator + tourist + noise$. This is very close to the vector from *shark* to *snorkeler*. These two vectors are so similar because the relations between the two pairs of words being connected are so similar. Since the system looks for any vector that will make the sum have as low error as possible, it could choose the relation vector between *bear* and *hiker* to connect the concept *shark* to the concept *snorkeler*: the system can make use of analogical relations to complete a chain of argument.[5] This makes it better at handling incompleteness in the knowledge base and makes it more like human reasoning, where newly encountered concepts do not need to be exact matches to those in our memories in order for us to reason about them. In everyday thinking, analogy, association and abduction are frequently used together with deduction.

While it is possible to use the raw distributional vectors for terms themselves as entities in the vector space, we can also define other vectors in this space. The fact that the terms in a natural category like *mammal* tend to already be clustered in the semantic space means that the number of such terms that can be averaged into a category vector is somewhat larger than the results in Experiment 1. We could also make use of the analogical properties of the semantic vector space to place other concepts that don't appear in the corpora, if we know some of their attributes. These techniques are useful when attempting to embed a knowledge base into the semantic vector space, where the concepts in the knowledge base may not be named by a specific English word.[6]

6   Ontology Merging

One of the major benefits of using an embedded deduction mechanism is that it simplifies the process of merging ontologies. If we are able to map both ontologies

---

[5] When a direct chain of reasoning is possible, such links won't happen– the analogy, being inexact, has a higher cost than the direct link.

[6] Along the same lines, [22] describes a more intricate method of locating particular word senses in the vector space.

into the semantic vector space, then even if the same concept isn't mapped to the exact same term, it will be mapped to a nearby term which may be good enough for the chain of reasoning to be found. For example, suppose one ontology contained the statement (bears, eat, grubs) and another contained the statement (insects, live in, dead trees). Neither ontology defines the relation of grubs to insects, but the system would be able to make the connection between bears and dead trees (answering the question "Why is the bear digging in a dead tree?" for example) because of the semantic similarity of *grub* to *insect*. Such a method would be especially useful when the ontology has not been hand built. Information extraction methods that extract triples from natural language sources, such as ReVerb, can be used to add facts to the knowledge base, without worrying too much about whether the entities to which triples refer are all expressed in the same way.

7   Answering Questions

The system as described so far has been finding a chain of reasoning connecting between two terms: one "given", and one "to prove".[7] However, a knowledge base is usually used with one or more variables, to find multiple possible chains that answer a query. If the possible answers can be limited to a smaller set, this system can also be used in this way, by having the "to prove" vector be a sum of all of the possible answers. For example, the knowledge base contains the following statements:

(apple, hasColor, red), (apple, hasColor, yellow), (apple, hasColor, green)

and we want to know what colors apples have. We could put in $-apple + (red + orange + yellow + green + blue + purple)$ as the query, and the result picks out these three statements as highly relevant:

1.00 (apple, hasColor, red)
0.99 (apple, hasColor, green)
0.72 (apple, hasColor, yellow)
0.08 (cordon bleu, derivedFrom, blue)[8]

Notice that the goal vector is a "category vector" as described in Sect. 7. Another way to get a particular type of result is by limiting the type of relations that are in the portion of the database that is searched. For example, if one wanted to know how B was caused, the search could be limited to those facts in the database related by causal predicates, such as *causes, turns into, has side effect*, and so forth. One way to do this, if the Horn clauses are known, is to find all relations which participate in a Horn clause that resolves to A causes B.

---

[7] Deductive reasoning systems typically use either forwards or backwards inference. This system uses "middle out" inference, that doesn't begin at either end but is a holistic procedure happening all along the chain at once.

[8] Notice that the fourth, less relevant, fact is also relating a food to a color.

8   Ordering the Chain

The results of the sparse vector decomposition define which triples might participate in the chain, but they are unordered.[9] To arrange them in order, we use the following method. All entities that participate in a triple returned by the solver, as well as the input terms, are added to a complete directed graph. Edges corresponding to relations returned by the solver are given very low weights, while edges not included are weighted based on their distance in the semantic space. Then we find the least costly path from the head input term to the tail.[10] Although the system is capable of coming up with tree-like proofs to multiple entities connected by OR, we haven't yet implemented a method for finding least-cost trees.

9   Experiments

LASSO, OMP and other sparse solvers are not guaranteed to find the optimal solution (which would be an NP-complete problem). Their performance depends on the size, dimensionality, and clustering of the data. We characterized how well LASSO performed for the vectors in our dataset. For all these experiments, we used the 300-dimensional word2vec vectors provided by Mikolov [14]. We used $L = 20$, and lambda $= .2$ for the LASSO parameters.

9.1   Experiment 1

As noted in the section on propositional calculus, it is a curious property of high-dimensional vector spaces that the vector $a + b$ will tend to be closer to a and b than other vectors in the space, assuming they are fairly well distributed. However, this property only holds for a few vectors being added together. In Table 2, we added from 1 to 10 randomly chosen term vectors, and found how frequently all of the summed vectors were present among the 20 nearest neighbors of the sum vector, for various dictionary sizes. For larger dictionaries, fewer of the summed terms are found because the dictionary more densely populates the space. LASSO does a better job of recovering the vectors in the sum. Much fewer than 20 vectors are usually chosen by LASSO, which is another big advantage.

9.2   Experiment 2

This experiment was similar to the previous one, but instead of adding terms we added fact vectors from the embedded KB of the form $(-e_1 + e_2)$. This is a more difficult problem for LASSO to solve because, for example, $(-e_1 + e_2) + (-e_3 + e_4)$

---

[9] In fact, they may form a multistranded rope rather than a chain– the "elastic-net" [23] parameter in LASSO can be used to encourage or discourage finding alternative equally good paths for part or all of the chain.

[10] A slightly more complicated cost function can be used to encourage the lowest cost path to follow analogical connections as well.

Table 2. How frequently all terms in sum are among 20 nearest neighbors of sum/how frequently all terms are within results of LASSO with L = 20

Dictionary size	2	3	4	5	6	7	8	9	10
1000	100/100	100/100	97/99	85/98	47/98	21/96	5/88	1/76	0/50
10000	100/100	98/100	76/100	25/100	3/100	0/99	0/98	0/94	0/83
100000	100/100	91/100	45/100	6/100	0/97	0/83	0/67	0/39	0/11
1000000	100/100	84/97	27/88	2/52	0/14	1/1	0/0	0/0	0/0

and $(-e_1 + e_4) + (-e_3 + e_2)$ would be exactly equal and so unrecoverable except by chance, and there are effectively twice as many entities being added. For large dictionary sizes, even two fact terms could not be reliably found (See Table 3).

Table 3. Number of relations in sum accurately recalled

Dictionary size	1	2	3	4	5	6	7	8	9	10
1000	100	100	98	97	91	90	79	54	30	5
10000	100	98	95	88	85	70	51	27	7	4
100000	100	91	42	30	19	9	7	4	1	1
906000	100	60	25	15	10	5	1	1	0	0

9.3 Experiment 3

This experiment measured how often the system was able to find a chain of reasoning linking a given head to a tail known to be reachable in from 1 to 7 steps. We used a KB with 906000 facts, formed of all the first-order facts in CYC and conceptnet in which both entities being related could be mapped to a vector in the word2vec space (either with a corresponding English word, or as a category vector) (Table 4).

Table 4. finding paths of various lengths from a given head to a given tail

KB size	1	2	3	4	5	6	7
10000	100	78	32	33	20	27	20
100000	100	92	46	46	21	31	17
906000	100	65	37	35	22	30	31

10   Conclusion and Future Work

We have demonstrated how sparse decomposition methods can be used to find chains of reasoning in a knowledge graph embedded in a distributional vector space. In the future, we hope to evaluate the system on question answering datasets. The performance on longer chains needs to be improved. We would also like to find ways of integrating this method into more comprehensive cognitive architectures. The notion of antonymy in semantic vector spaces also needs a more careful treatment.

References

1. Baroni, M., Zamparelli, R.: Nouns are vectors, adjectives are matrices: representing adjective-noun constructions in semantic space. In: 2010 Conference on Empirical Methods in Natural Language Processing, pp. 1183–1193. ACL, October 2010
2. Bordes, A., Usunier, N., Garcia-Duran, A., Weston, J., Yakhnenko, O.: Translating embeddings for modeling multi-relational data. In: Advances in Neural Information Processing Systems, pp. 2787–2795 (2013)
3. Buchanan, B.G., Shortliffe, E.H.: Rule-Based Expert Systems: The MYCIN Experiments. Addison-Wesley, Reading (1984)
4. Dumais, S.T., Furnas, G.W., Landauer, T.K., Deerwester, S., Harshman, R.: Using latent semantic analysis to improve access to textual information. In: SIGCHI Conference, pp. 281–285. ACM, May 1988
5. Ellerman, D.: The logic of partitions: introduction to the dual of the logic of subsets. Rev. Symbolic Logic **3**(2), 287–350 (2010)
6. Freitas, A., Curry, E.: Natural language queries over heterogeneous linked data graphs: a distributional-compositional semantics approach. In: 19th International Conference on Intelligent User Interfaces. ACM (2014)
7. Gayler, R.: Vector symbolic architectures answer Jackendoff's challenges for cognitive neuroscience. In: Slezak, P. (ed.) ICCS/ASCS International Conference on Cognitive Science, pp. 133–138. University of New South Wales, CogPrints, Sydney (2003)
8. Grefenstette, E., Sadrzadeh, M.: Experimental support for a categorical compositional distributional model of meaning. In: Conference on Empirical Methods in Natural Language Processing, pp. 1394–1404. ACL, July 2011
9. Kanerva, P.: Sparse Distributed Memory. MIT press, Cambridge (1988)
10. Kiros, R., Zhu, Y., Salakhutdinov, R.R., Zemel, R., Urtasun, R., Torralba, A., Fidler, S.: Skip-thought vectors. In: NIPS, pp. 3294–3302 (2015)
11. Knowlton, B., Morrison, R., Hummel, J., Holyoak, K.: A neurocomputational system for relational reasoning. Trends Cogn. Sci. **16**(7), 373–381 (2012)
12. Lee, M., He, X., Yih, W.T., Gao, J., Deng, L., Smolensky, P.: Reasoning in vector space: an exploratory study of question answering. arXiv:1511.06426 (2015)
13. Levy, S.D.: Distributed representation of compositional structure. In: Rabual, J.R., Dorado, J., Pazos, A. (eds.) Encyclopedia of Artificial Intelligence. IGI Publishing, Hershey (2008)
14. Mikolov, T., Sutskever, I., Chen, K., Corrado, G. S., Dean, J.: Distributed representations of words and phrases and their compositionality. In: Advances in Neural Information Processing Systems, pp. 3111–3119 (2013)

15. Rocktäschel, T., Riedel, S.: Learning knowledge base inference with neural theorem provers. In: AKBC, pp. 45–50 (2016)
16. Summers-Stay, D., Voss, C., Cassidy, T.: Using a distributional semantic vector space with a knowledge base for reasoning in uncertain conditions. Biologically Inspired Cogn. Architectures **16**, 34–44 (2016)
17. Turney, P.D.: Measuring semantic similarity by latent relational analysis. arXiv preprint cs/0508053 (2005)
18. Wang, H., Onishi, T., Gimpel, K., McAllester, D.: Emergent logical structure in vector representations of neural readers. arXiv preprint arXiv:1611.07954 (2016)
19. West, R., Gabrilovich, E., Murphy, K., Sun, S., Gupta, R., Lin, D.: Knowledge base completion via search-based question answering. In: 23rd International Conference on World Wide Web, pp. 515–526. ACM, April 2014
20. Widdows, D., Peters, S.: Word vectors and quantum logic: experiments with negation and disjunction. Math. Lang. **8**, 141–154 (2003)
21. Widdows, D., Cohen, T.: Reasoning with vectors: a continuous model for fast robust inference. Logic J. IGPL **23**(2), 141–173 (2014). jzu028
22. Yu, M., Dredze, M.: Improving lexical embeddings with semantic knowledge. In: ACL, no. 2, pp. 545–550, June 2014
23. Zou, H., Hastie, T.: Regularization and variable selection via the elastic net. J. Royal Stat. Soc. Stat. Methodol. **67**(2), 301–320 (2005)

Computational Neuroscience Offers Hints for More General Machine Learning

David Rawlinson[✉] and Gideon Kowadlo

Incubator 491 Pty Ltd, Melbourne, Australia
{dave,gideon}@agi.io

Abstract. Machine Learning has traditionally focused on narrow artificial intelligence - solutions for specific problems. Despite this, we observe two trends in the state-of-the-art: One, increasing architectural homogeneity in algorithms and models. Two, algorithms having more general application: New techniques often beat many benchmarks simultaneously. We review the changes responsible for these trends and look to computational neuroscience literature to anticipate future progress.

Keywords: Machine learning · Biological plausibility · Credit assignment problem · Reinforcement learning · Spike timing dependent plasticity · Sparse coding · Predictive coding

1 Introduction

While Machine Learning research has traditionally focused on Narrow AI tasks, state-of-the-art solutions have become more homogeneous and generally applicable. This paper will review these trends and look to computational neuroscience for tips on future changes.

Contrast object recognition in 2005 with today. We have moved from designer architectures of specialized components to homogeneous deep networks. The old way to recognize objects was to combine explicit feature detectors such as HoG [1] with techniques like RANSAC [2] to find concensus about their geometric relationships. The new way is simply to expose a homogeneous deep, convolutional, region proposal network [3] to a very large set of labelled training images to segment objects from background.

2 Biological Plausibility of Artificial Neural Networks

The most biologically-implausible features of current supervised artificial neural networks are also related to some of their practical limitations.

The Credit Assignment Problem concerns synchronized back-propagation of error gradients from the output to hidden layer cells that caused them [4]. Although feedback connections outnumber feedforward in cortical neural networks [5,6], a biological basis for deep backpropagation is unlikely [7] because

© Springer International Publishing AG 2017
T. Everitt et al. (Eds.): AGI 2017, LNAI 10414, pp. 123–132, 2017.
DOI: 10.1007/978-3-319-63703-7_12

it requires dense and precise reciprocal connections between neurons. Biological feedback connections also modulate or drive output, whereas in feed-forward artificial networks, feedback is only used for training. Layerwise backpropagation of error gradients is not supported by biological evidence [8]. Credit assignment also poses practical computational problems such as vanishing and exploding (shattered) gradients [9], which can limit network depth. Since current theory suggests that deeper is better than wider [10], this is a major problem. Recent work on decoupled neural interfaces looks to avoid this limitation via local cost functions [11].

Credit assignment is also difficult when inputs and outputs are separated by time. Only recurrent networks with gated memory cells as used in LSTM [12] have enabled effective back-propagation of error gradients over longer periods of time. There is some evidence for a biological equivalent of memory and gates in biological neurons [13].

Modern artificial neural networks appear to have enough capacity, but improved generalization seems to require better regularization of network weights [14]. Currently this tends to be explicit, e.g. weight-decay, but it could be implicit in better models.

Supervised training requires large, labelled training datasets. For embodied agents this is problematic: it is necessary to generate correct output for the agent in all circumstances. This appears to be at least as difficult as building the agent control system. Reinforcement learning avoids this problem by providing feedback about an agents output or actions in via an abstract "reward" signal. The ideal output is not required. One of the most popular reinforcement learning methods is Q-learning [15]. $Q(s, a)$ is defined as the maximum discounted future reward of performing action a in state s.

The task of associating current actions with future rewards is normally tackled via discounting. There is considerable biological evidence to support the hyperbolic temporal discounting model for associating causes with outcomes, including fMRI studies [16], recordings of neuron activity [17], and behavioural studies [18] (including human) [19].

But as always, there are practical problems. Although Q-learning is guaranteed to converge on true Q-values given training samples in any order, we cannot know how close we are while some actions are unexplored. We need a policy to balance exploration (discovery of accurate Q values) versus exploitation of current Q values. We can find some heuristic guidance from e.g. animal studies of foraging exploration behaviour [19], but in a naive representation the space of all possible states and actions is simply too large to be practically explored. As representations become more sophisticated, the gaps between sampled rewards become larger. We need a way to generalize from a smaller set of experiences.

There are two approaches to this generalization problem [20]. First, we can try to generalize explicitly by predicting commonalities between states and then inferring rewards. Second, we can try to reduce the dimensionality of the state-space by creating more abstract, hierarchical representations of the data.

Impressive results were achieved by Mnih et al. [21] playing Atari games with their Deep Q Learning method. They used several tricks to overcome exploration and representation limits. First, they built a smaller, hierarchical state-space in which it is easier to learn Q values. Second, they used "experience replay" to accelerate Q value training. Third, they used ϵ -greedy exploration to balance exploration and exploitation.

But the key to improving the generalization of observed discounted rewards may lie in other aspects of human general intelligence, such as attentional strategies. Using working memory [22] and attentional gating, the current state can become a filtered construction of features relevant to the problem under consideration, even if they were not observed in the immediate past (working memory allows humans to store several items for a few minutes at most).

Graves et al. recently published the "Neural Turing Machine", combining recurrent neural networks with a memory system [23]. The architecture is described in a very mechanical way, with a tape-like memory store and read/write heads - hence the name, which is derived from the original Turing machine concept. But despite the mechanical description, their intention was to simulate the properties of human working memory in a differentiable architecture that could be trained by gradient descent. They demonstrated that the system could perform a number of computational tasks, even a priority-sort. Zaremba and Sutskever later extended the concept to reinforcement learning and reproduced some of the tasks [24].

Overall, how closely do artificial neural networks match the computational properties of natural ones? There is neurological evidence of computational similarities between machine learning and human general intelligence [25]. Similar visual feature detectors can be learned [26], and the same types of variation are confusing for both deep learning and people [27]. But the discovery of adversarial examples [28], which look ordinary to us but confusing to artificial networks, suggests a weakness in artificial representations. Surprisingly, the deficiency seems to be fundamental to models produced by training linear discriminators in high dimensional spaces [29], because the problem "generalizes" to unseen data, and disjoint training instances are vulnerable to the same perturbations!

3 Interesting Features of Biological Neural Networks

Biological neurons are more complex than conventional artificial ones and are believed to learn using different, mostly local rules, such as Spike-Timing Dependent Plasticity (STDP) [30], pre & post synaptic correlation [31] inter-cellular competition [32] and lifetime sparsity (firing rate) constraints [33,34], as opposed to global error minimization. Recently, neuroscientists have become interested in the role of dendrite computation: Individual neurons can have many layers of branching, and a transfer function between branches [35]. This means that an individual biological neuron can be computationally equivalent to a tree of conventional artificial neurons. Within a neuron, precise feedback could exist, allowing supervised training of a few layers against local cost functions.

In machine learning, recent progress has also concerned increasingly sophisticated components, such as the Inception module [36]. These may be more biologically realistic that at first it appears, although Inception does propagate gradients between modules.

Neuroscientists are convinced that the Spike-Timing Dependent Plasticity (STDP) rule accurately describes the way many neurons synapses adjust their weights [37]. This is an unsupervised rule; weights are adapted to strengthen synapses that reliably predict a post-synaptic (output) spike before it occurs. This is computationally convenient due to use of only local information during learning. Interestingly, artificial simulations of neurons including recurrent connections and STDP learning are able to produce some of the best wholly unsupervised representations. For example, Diehl & Cook [38] were able to achieve 95% classification accuracy on MNIST using unsupervised learning and cell-label correlation: The training data was used to correlate spiking of each cell with the ten training data digit labels. Each cell therefore had equal influence on the classification result.

Normally, such high-performance classification requires a supervised layer to optimize decision boundaries, allowing the influence of each feature or cell to be varied; that they were able to achieve this without this type of supervised training implies that their technique was very effective in capturing general structure of the input.

State of the art results in machine learning are nowadays typically produced by supervised learning. Yet researchers have recognized that unsupervised pre-training of shallower layers improves performance of a larger supervised network [39]. Improved theoretical understanding of this suggests that unsupervised learning acts as a regularizer, producing features that generalize better [39, 40].

Historically, unsupervised layers required greedy layerwise pre-training. However, use of linear (e.g. the Rectified Linear (ReLU)) transfer function [41], and techniques like batch normalization [42] have allowed simultaneous training of all layers in deep networks. In fact, continuing the trend of increasing simplicity, Exponential Linear Units (ELUs) [43] aim to avoid the need for statistical preprocessing such as batch normalization, although not yet completely.

Biological neural networks continue to outperform artificial ones in several learning characteristics. Optimal modelling of nonstationary input [44] is particularly relevant to General Intelligence tasks featuring an embodied agent, whose choices can suddenly and permanently change input statistics. For example, if you suddenly start to explore a new part of the environment, you will see new things. A robot that leaves the lab to explore the gardens will now frequently encounter trees and plants, that are completely unlike all previous visual perceptions of right-angled corridors, doors and desks. This is problematic when training has moved weights into unsuitable ranges for further learning, but work on strategies such as adaptive learning rates will likely help [45].

Biological neural networks learn both more quickly [34] and more slowly [46] than artificial ones. Although this seems contradictory, this flexibility is actually a desirable quality. In psychology, "one trial" or "one shot" learning occurs when just one experience is enough to modify future behaviour. In artificial intelligence, one way to tackle this is instance-based learning [47], in which all training samples are stored; the model is implicitly generated by interpolating between these samples. Unfortunately, this approach does not scale. Other prominent examples of "one shot" learning include [48,49]. Recently, Santoro et al. [50] developed a one-shot method using Memory-Augmented Neural Networks (such as the Neural Turing Machine described above). In this system, a differentiable architecture is trained to solve the meta-problem of using an external memory to store new learnings after a single presentation. Interestingly, an interaction between working memory in the ventrolateral prefrontal cortex and the hippocampus, may be used as a switch to activate one-shot learning in the brain [51].

Common training methods in machine learning such as gradient descent must learn slowly to avoid catastrophic interference between new and existing weights. Until recently, it was thought that synapse formation was also a relatively slow and permanent process. Artificial neural networks are typically modelled with fixed synaptic connectivity, only varying the synaptic efficiency, or "weight", of each connection. But more recently, it was confirmed that synapses are actually formed quickly and throughout adult life, perhaps in response to a homeostatic learning rule that controls lifetime firing rate [34].

Given all the above, even slower learning might seem undesirable; but to improve representation we need to reduce bias towards recent samples while continuously integrating new information. This relatively unexplored topic is known as lifelong machine learning [52].

4 Sparse and Predictive Coding

The encoding of electrical information transmitted between neurons is under active investigation. Neurons normally fire in bursts and trains of varying frequency, with long rests in between. The meaning of these spike trains is uncertain [53], but STDP learning rules are sensitive to spike timing and rate.

We also observe that most neurons are silent most of the time - only a fraction will fire at any given moment. This phenomenon is loosely defined in neuroscience as sparse coding [54]. Sparse coding has a number of theoretical advantages, such as combinatorial representational power and a natural, robust similarity metric in the intersection of active cells.

In machine learning sparse coding has a more specific meaning, namely the learning of a set of overcomplete basis vectors representing the input [54]. Research shows that deep unsupervised sparse coding produces very useful features: Le et al. [55] created a deep sparse architecture that spontaneously functioned as a high accuracy face detector without being optimized to perform this task.

Why does sparse coding help? It is believed that the process of sparse encoding is an inherently superior form of dimensionality reduction compared to e.g. vector quantization [56]. How you train the overcomplete bases is surprisingly less important, assuming the input has been normalized. Sparse coding chooses a few bases that jointly describe each input combination, meaning that subsets may be used in novel combinations without retraining. This is also known as the "union property" of sparse representations [57]. Again we observe that a representational change has provided computationally beneficial effects: Which is interesting, because neuroscience also offers another representational change we might adopt - predictive coding [58].

Predictive coding proposes that cortical cells internally predict either their input or activity within local populations, and then emit signals representing prediction errors [59]. This changes the inter-layer signal from a representation of the input, to a representation of cells' inability to predict the input. Internally, only the relationships between errors are represented. This is very efficient: The representation adapts to the characteristics of the input. Input that can't be "explained" (i.e. predicted) is relayed to other layers for processing, in hope that additional resources or data will help. Errors propagate towards features that can explain them. Note the assumption here, that being able to predict an observation means that its causal relationships are being modelled correctly and thus is it "explained".

This characteristic is reminiscent of Highway Networks [60] and Deep Residual Learning (DRL) [61]. In DRL, the output of a bi-layer module is added to the module's input, requiring the module to learn any residual error between the input and desired output. DRL propagates residual error gradients in the feedback direction during training. Highway Networks, derived from LSTM, use an explicit gating mechanism to determine propagation of the input.

In both Highway Networks and DRL, modules are trained to decide to what extent they involve themselves in current input. Signals can be relayed or modified depending on the capabilities and relevance of the local module.

The reason DRL works lies in the details of the training problem posed by this architecture. Each module's output contributes additively rather than multiplicatively, and in consequence data flows freely into very deep hierarchies. After training, DRL networks become ensembles of shallower networks [62]. Just as in predictive coding, input data dynamically determines the effective depth of the network.

5   Conclusion

We have observed increasing homogeneity and generality in state-of-the-art machine learning. Biology continues to inspire this process, such as Liao and Poggio's combination of deep residual and recurrent networks [63]. In future we expect to see increasing use of local [11] and unsupervised learning rules [8], modularized architectures that promote data-driven deep representations [60,61] and dramatic improvements in the representation of state and action spaces in reinforcement learning to overcome the generalization problem.

References

1. Dalal, N., Triggs, B.: Histograms of oriented gradients for human detection. In: IEEE Conference on Computer Vision and Pattern Recognition (CVPR) (2015)
2. Fischler, M.A., Bolles, R.C.: Random sample consensus: a paradigm for model fitting with applications to image analysis and automated cartography. Commun. ACM **24**(6), 381–395 (1981)
3. Ren, S., He, K., Girshick, R., Sun, J.: Faster R-CNN: towards real-time object detection with region proposal networks. In: IEEE Transactions on Pattern Analysis and Machine Intelligence, pp. 91–99 (2016)
4. Luo, H., Fu, J., Glass, J.: Bidirectional backpropagation: towards biologically plausible error signal transmission in neural networks. arXiv preprint arXiv:1702.07097 (2017)
5. Petro, L.S., Vizioli, L., Muckli, L.: Contributions of cortical feedback to sensory processing in primary visual cortex. Front. Psychol. **5**, 1–8 (2014)
6. Markov, N.T., Vezoli, J., Chameau, P., Falchier, A., Quilodran, R., Huissoud, C., Lamy, C., Misery, P., Giroud, P., Ullman, S., Barone, P., Dehay, C., Knoblauch, K., Kennedy, H.: Anatomy of hierarchy: feedforward and feedback pathways in Macaque visual cortex. J. Comp. Neurol. **522**, 225–259 (2014)
7. Balduzzi, D., Vanchinathan, H., Buhmann, J.: Kickback cuts Backprops red-tape: biologically plausible credit assignment in neural networks. In: 9th AAAI Conference on Artificial Intelligence (2014)
8. Bengio, Y., Lee, D.H., Bornschein, J., Mesnard, T., Lin, Z.: Towards biologically plausible deep learning. arXiv preprint arXiv:1502.04156v3 (2016)
9. Balduzzi, D., Frean, M., Leary, L., Lewis, J.P., Ma, K.W.D., McWilliams, B.: The shattered gradients problem: if resnets are the answer, then what is the question? arXiv preprint arXiv:1702.08591 (2017)
10. Eldan, R., Shamir, O.: The power of depth for feedforward neural networks. In: 29th Annual Conference on Learning Theory, PMLR, vol. 49, pp. 907–940 (2016)
11. Jaderberg, M., Czarnecki, W.M., Osindero, S., Vinyals, O., Graves, A., Kavukcuoglu, K.: Decoupled neural interfaces using synthetic gradients. arXiv preprint arXiv:1608.05343 (2016)
12. Graves, A.: Generating sequences with recurrent neural networks. arXiv preprint arXiv:1308.0850 (2013)
13. Monner, D.D., Reggia, J.A.: Systematically grounding language through vision in a neural network. In: Artificial General Intelligence: 4th International Conference (2011)
14. Zhang, C., Bengio, S., Hardt, M., Recht, B., Vinyals, O.: Understanding deep learning requires rethinking generalization. In: International Conference on Learning Representations (2017)
15. Kaelbling, L.P., Moore, A.W.: Reinforcement learning: a survey. J. Artif. Intell. Res. **4**, 237–285 (1996)
16. McClure, S.M., Laibson, D.I., Loewenstein, G., Cohen, J.D.: Separate neural systems value immediate and delayed monetary rewards. Science **306**(5695), 503–507 (2004)
17. Kim, S., Hwang, J., Seo, H., Lee, D.: Valuation of uncertain and delayed rewards in primate prefrontal cortex. Neural Netw. **22**(3), 294–304 (2009)
18. Hwang, J., Kim, S., Lee, D.: Temporal discounting and inter-temporal choice in rhesus monkeys. Front. Behav. Neurosci. **3**(9), 1–13 (2009)

19. Namboodiria, V.M.K., Levyc, J.M., Mihalasd, S., Simse, D.W., Shulerc, M.G.H.: Rationalizing spatial exploration patterns of wild animals and humans through a temporal discounting framework. In: Proceedings of the National Academy of Sciences, vol. 113, no. 31, pp. 8747–8752 (2016)

20. Ponsen, M., Taylor, M.E., Tuyls, K.: Abstraction and generalization in reinforcement learning: a summary and framework. In: Taylor, M.E., Tuyls, K. (eds.) ALA 2009. LNCS, vol. 5924, pp. 1–32. Springer, Heidelberg (2010). doi:10.1007/978-3-642-11814-2_1

21. Mnih, V., Kavukcuoglu, K., Silver, D., Graves, A., Antonoglou, I., Wierstra, D., Riedmiller, M.: Playing Atari with deep reinforcement learning. arXiv preprint arXiv:1312.5602 (2013)

22. Baddeley, A., Eysenck, M., Anderson, M.: Memory, chap. 3. Psychology Press, New York (2009)

23. Graves, A., Wayne, G., Danihelka, I.: Neural turing machines. arXiv preprint arXiv:1410.5401v2 (2014)

24. Zaremba, W., Sutskever, I.: Reinforcement learning neural turing machines. In: Proceedings of ICLR 2016 (2016)

25. Marblestone, A., Wayne, G., Kording, K.: Toward an integration of deep learning and neuroscience. Front. Comput. Neurosci. 7, 137 (2016)

26. Kheradpisheh, S.R., Ghodrati, M., Ganjtabesh, M., Masquelier, T.: Deep networks can resemble human feed-forward vision in invariant object recognition. Nat. Sci. R 6 (2016). Article 32672

27. Kheradpisheh, S.R., Ghodrati, M., Ganjtabesh, M., Masquelier, T.: Humans and deep networks largely agree on which kinds of variation make object recognition harder. Front. Comput. Neurosci. 10, 92 (2016)

28. Szegedy, C., Zaremba, W., Sutskever, I., Bruna, J., Erhan, D., Goodfellow, I., Fergus, R.: Intriguing properties of neural networks. In: International Conference on Learning Representations (2014)

29. Goodfellow, I., Shlens, J., Szegedy, C.: Explaining and harnessing adversarial examples. In: International Conference on Learning Representations (2015)

30. Bengio, Y., Mesnard, T., Fischer, A., Zhang, S., Wu, Y.: STDP as presynaptic activity times rate of change of postsynaptic activity. arXiv preprint arXiv:1509.05936 (2015)

31. Oja, E.: A simplified neuron model as a principal component analyzer. J. Math. Biol. 15, 267–273 (1982)

32. Rumelhart, D. E., McClelland, J. L., The PDP research group: Parallel Distributed Processing: Explorations in the Microstructure of Cognition, vol. 1 and 2. MIT Press, Cambridge (1986)

33. Makhzani, A., Frey, B.: Winner-take-all autoencoders. In: Proceedings of the 28th International Conference on Neural Information Processing Systems (NIPS), pp. 2791–2799 (2015)

34. Butza, M.: Brain Research Reviews 60(2), 287–305 (2009)

35. Guergiuev, J., Lillicrap, T.P., Richards, B.A.: Towards deep learning with segregated dendrites. arXiv preprint arXiv:1610.00161 (2016)

36. Szegedy, C., Liu, W., Jia, Y., Sermanet, P., Reed, S., Anguelov, D., Erhan, D., Vanhoucke, V., Rabinovich, A.: Going deeper with convolutions. In: IEEE Conference on Computer Vision and Pattern Recognition (CVPR) (2015)

37. Sjstrm, P.J., Rancz, E.A., Roth, A., Husser, M.: Excitability, dendritic, plasticity, synaptic. Physiol. Rev. 88, 769–840 (2008)

38. Diehl, P., Cook, M.: Unsupervised learning of digit recognition using spike-timing-dependent plasticity. Front. Comput. Neurosci. 9 (2015). Article 99

39. Erhan, D., Bengio, Y., Courville, A., Manzagol, P.A., Vincent, P.: Why does unsupervised pre-training help deep learning? J. Mach. Learn. Res. **11**, 625–660 (2010)
40. Erhan, D., Manzagol, P.-A., Bengio, Y., Bengio, S., Vincent, P.: The difficulty of training deep architectures and the effect of unsupervised pre-training. In: International Conference on Artificial Intelligence and Statistics, vol. 5, pp. 153–160 (2009)
41. Krizhevsky, A., Sutskever, I., Hinton, G.: Imagenet classification with deep convolutional neural networks. In: Advances in Neural Information Processing Systems (NIPS) (2012)
42. Ioffe, S., Szegedy, C.: Batch normalization: accelerating deep network training by reducing internal covariate shift. In: ICML, vol. 1, no. 4 (2015)
43. Shah, A., Kadam, E., Shah, H., Shinde, S., Shingade, S.: Deep residual networks with exponential linear unit. arXiv preprint arXiv:1604.04112 (2016)
44. Ditzler, G., Roveri, M., Alippi, C., Polikar, R.: Learning in nonstationary environments: a survey. IEEE Comput. Intell. Mag. **10**(4), 12–25 (2015)
45. Schaul, T., Zhang, S., LeCun, Y.: No more Pesky learning rates. In: Proceedings of 30th International Conference on Machine Learning (ICML) (2013)
46. Kirkpatrick, J., Pascanu, R., Rabinowitz, N., Veness, J., Desjardins, G., Rusu, A.A., Milan, K., Quan, J., Ramalho, T., Grabska-Barwinska, A., Hassabis, D., Clopath, C., Kumarana, D., Hadsella, R.: Overcoming catastrophic forgetting in neural networks. Proc. Natl. Acad. Sci. **114**(13), 3521–3526 (2017)
47. Russell, S., Norvig, P.: Artificial Intelligence: A Modern Approach, 2nd edn, p. 733. Prentice Hall, Englewood Cliffs (2003). ISBN 0-13-080302-2
48. Fei-Fei, L., Fergus, R., Perona, P.: One-shot learning of object categories. IEEE Transaction on Pattern Analysis and Machine Intelligence (PAMI), vol. 28, no. 4, pp. 594–611 (2006)
49. Miller, E.G., Matsakis, N.E., Viola, P.A.: Learning from one example through shared densities on transforms. In: Proceedings of Computer Vision and Pattern Recognition (CVPR) (2000)
50. Santoro, A., Bartunov, S., Botvinick, M., Wierstra, D., Lillicrap, T.: One-shot learning with memory-augmented neural networks. arXiv preprint arXiv:1605.06065v1 (2016)
51. Lee, S.W., ODoherty, J.P., Shimojo, S.: Neural computations mediating one-shot learning in the human brain. PLoS Biol **13**(4), e1002137 (2015)
52. Silver, D., Yang, Q., Li, L.: Lifelong machine learning systems: beyond learning algorithms. In: Papers from the 2013 AAAI Spring Symposium (2013)
53. Krahe, R., Gabbiani, F.: Burst firing in sensory systems. Nat. Rev. Neurosci. **5**, 13–23 (2004)
54. Olshausen, B.A., Field, D.J.: Sparse coding with an overcomplete basis set: a strategy employed by VI? Vis. Res. **37**(23), 3311–3326 (1997)
55. Le, Q.V., Ranzato, M.A., Monga, R., Devin, M., Chen, K., Corrado, G.S., Dean, J., Ng, A.Y.: Building high-level features using large scale unsupervised learning. In: Proceedings of the 29th International Conference on Machine Learning (2012)
56. Coates, A., Ng, A.Y.: The importance of encoding versus training with sparse coding and vector quantization. In: Proceedings of the 28th International Conference on Machine Learning, Bellevue, WA, USA (2011)
57. Hawkins, J., Ahmad, S.: Why neurons have thousands of synapses, a theory of sequence memory in neocortex. Front. Neural Circ. **10**(23), 1–13 (2016)
58. Kok, P., de Lange, F.P.: Predictive coding in sensory cortex. In: Forstmann, B.U., Wagenmakers, E.-J. (eds.) An Introduction to Model-Based Cognitive Neuroscience. LLC, chap. 11, vol. 221, pp. 221–244. Springer, New York (2015)

59. Kogo, N., Trengrove, C.: Is predictive coding theory articulated enough to be testable? Front. Comput. Neurosci. **9**(111), 357–381 (2015)
60. Srivastava, N., Greff, K., Schmidhuber, J.: Highway networks. In: Deep Learning Workshop (ICML 2015) (2015)
61. He, K., Zhang, X., Ren, S., Sun, J.: Deep residual learning for image recognition. In: IEEE Conference on Computer Vision and Pattern Recognition (2016)
62. Veit, A., Wilber, M., Belongie, S.: Residual networks behave like ensembles of relatively shallow networks. arXiv preprint arXiv:1605.06431 (2016)
63. Liao, Q., Poggio, T.: Bridging the Gaps Between Residual Learning, Recurrent Neural Networks and Visual Cortex. arXiv preprint arXiv:1604.03640 (2016)

Generating Single Subject Activity Videos as a Sequence of Actions Using 3D Convolutional Generative Adversarial Networks

Ahmad Arinaldi(✉) and Mohamad Ivan Fanany

Machine Learning and Computer Vision Laboratory,
Faculty of Computer Science, Universitas Indonesia, Depok, Indonesia
ahmadarinaldi224@gmail.com, ivan@cs.ui.ac.id

Abstract. Humans have the remarkable ability of imagination, where within the human mind virtual simulations are done of scenarios whether visual, auditory or any other senses. These imaginations are based on the experiences during interaction with the real world, where human senses help the mind understand their surroundings. Such level of imagination has not yet been achieved using current algorithms, but a current trend in deep learning architectures known as Generative Adversarial Networks (GANs) have proven capable of generating new and interesting images or videos based on the training data. In that way, GANs can be used to mimic human imagination, where the resulting generated visuals of GANs are based on the data used during training. In this paper, we use a combination of Long Short-Term Memory (LSTM) Networks and 3D GANs to generate videos. We use a 3D Convolutional GAN to generate new human action videos based on trained data. The generated human action videos are used to generate longer videos consisting of a sequence of short actions combined creating longer and more complex activities. To generate the sequence of actions needed we use an LSTM network to translate a simple input description text into the required sequence of actions. The generated chunks are then concatenated using a motion interpolation scheme to form a single video consisting of many generated actions. Hence a visualization of the input text description is generated as a video of a subject performing the activity described.

Keywords: Activity video generation · 3D GAN · LSTM

1 Introduction

AGI encompasses an AI capable of autonomy, generality, adaptation and imagination equal to humans [1]. Imagination is a uniquely human ability that allows the forming of ideas, concepts, and visual images of non-existent sensory information within the mind. The process which allows humans to imagine visual information in the mind is a unique ability. Imagination is heavily influenced by the sensory experiences from the real world, for example, once a human has seen a mouse, the visualization of the mouse can be imagined at a later time without physically seeing the mouse itself. Therefore, imagination

© Springer International Publishing AG 2017
T. Everitt et al. (Eds.): AGI 2017, LNAI 10414, pp. 133–142, 2017.
DOI: 10.1007/978-3-319-63703-7_13

is also closely related to vision in which visual sensory input influences the human imagination. This is a complex process, but recent advances in generative models may be able to mimic (but not yet reach) the human imagination by generating certain visual features (videos and images) based on what has been seen before. A promising model is the Generative Adversarial Network (GAN), which is a model based on the deep neural network architecture proposed in [2].

The GAN architecture has been shown to be particularly good at modeling and generating visual data, such as images [3–6] and videos/volumetric data [7–10]. Many state of the art image generation systems utilize GANs, for instance generating images from text descriptions in [4], generating higher resolution images from lower resolution ones [5], and generating new random images for faces, bedrooms, ImageNet and MNIST data in [6]. In [4], to achieve a model that can generate images based on input text, the text is encoded into a smaller vector combined with a noise vector and then is fed into the generator to produce the image. For training the model, the discriminator is also supplied the encoded text to be able to discriminate good and bad images relative to the input text. In [5], a pyramid scheme is used where to build a higher resolution image from a lower one, the image is slowly raised in resolution by up sampling with every stage a noise signal is inputted to learn the details required for the image. This allows the model to add required details without overwhelming the GAN. In [6], the authors use a GAN model based on the deep convolutional neural network (DCGAN). The authors argue that the filters of the DCGAN capture meaningful properties and features of the image. In [7], the authors collected a large number of video data (9 TB data after processing) and trained it to model the scene dynamics in a short video. The GAN model is conditioned on the first frame of a video and must generate 31 future frames of 64×64 videos. A 3D convolution GAN is used for the moving objects while a static 2D convolution GAN is utilized for the background of the video. While another approach in [8] for predicting a few future frames in a video is by using GANs combined with image gradient loss to improve the sharpness of the resulting video frames. It is claimed in [9] that video generation systems could aid in the physical interaction of autonomous agents, a task in AGI. In this case, video prediction is used by an agent to predict the conditions of its surrounding and how its actions can affect it. GANs are used as an unsupervised method to learn video prediction for this purpose. In [10], a 3D convolution GAN is used to create 3D models of objects. It is shown that the generator can learn to map the low dimensional input latent space into a high dimensional 3D object by slow raising the dimensionality of the generator using consecutive convolutions and up sampling. The main problem when trying to apply GANs to videos is the larger dimensionality of the data requiring more complex models trained with more data.

Goals. The goals of this research are to build a system that can generate human activity (which consists of sequential actions) videos based on a plain text description input. The first part is to train a 3D GAN model on single subject human action video chunks. The 3D GAN model uses the Auxiliary Classifier GAN (ACGAN) architecture introduced in [11]. An ACGAN is used since we require the GAN model to generate specific types of action video chunks on demand. To receive input in text format and translate them into the appropriate sequence of actions, we use an LSTM network that does machine translation and acts as the director for the 3D GAN model. The sequence of actions produced by the LSTM will be used as a guide for the type of action to be generated by the 3D GAN model. The resulting video sequences are concatenated with some interpolated frames in between the video chunks to ensure a smooth transition between them. The result is a video of a single subject performing an activity that consists of several actions done sequentially. In our experiments, we train the model on the publicly available Weizmann action dataset and a martial arts video dataset based on Indonesian *silat*.

Contributions. The contributions of this research are that we use a two-stage approach for generating single subject activity videos from a text description input. The first stage is an LSTM and the second stage is a 3D GAN generator network. The two models are trained and operated independently of each other, allowing the 3D GAN model to learn only smaller and shorter videos of single actions, while the LSTM model then generates the sequence of actions to be generated. Hence the training problem becomes a lot simpler. This model is basically a narrow AI model, but we believe by training many independent models on generating specific families of actions can form a more general system capable of generating more types of action.

2   Generative Adversarial Networks for Generating Videos

2.1   Training Generative Adversarial Networks

Generative Adversarial Networks (GANs) are a generative model based on deep neural networks introduced by [2]. Deep neural networks are models that are based on multiple layers of neural networks that allow a hierarchical representation of the features of the data, from simple features at the lower layer, to more complex features at the higher layers. GANs use two separate deep neural network architectures, one called the generator that generates fake data from an input space (usually a noise vector), and another called the discriminator that learns to detect the fake data generated by the generator. The two models are trained in competition against one another with opposing goals, where we train the discriminator to classify between the real data and fake generated data, while the generator is trained to trick the discriminator into classifying the fake generated data as real data while the discriminator weights are frozen. To achieve satisfactory results, both the discriminator and the generator need to be in balance while doing their tasks. If the discriminator is weak and the generator strong, the generator will learn to exploit the weakness of the discriminator leading to extreme colors in the video. On the other hand, a too strong discriminator will stifle the learning capabilities of the generator [12]. To achieve this balance, many scheduling schemes of training discriminators and generators and using additional layer architectures (such as dropout and batch normalization) for both models have been published [13].

During training of the GAN, the only part that gets real data as the input is the discriminator. The generator only gets as input a vector from the input space (in the case of ACGAN the labels to be generated). The discriminator needs to train based on the data to be able to discriminate between real and fake data (and different class labels in the case of ACGAN). While during the training of the generator, the discriminator weights are frozen allowing the error to propagate back to the generator and update the generator weights in a way that will allow it to trick the discriminator. Hence to get a good generator, we also need a good discriminator. The scheme of the action video ACGAN used in this research is provided in Fig. 1.

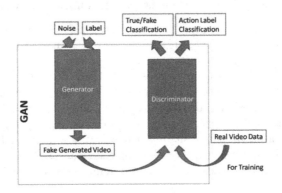

Fig. 1. Scheme of the ACGAN used for generating action videos.

2.2   Types of Generative Adversarial Networks

Since it was introduced, there have been many improvements to the GAN architecture. In [13], it was stated that label information of the data could improve the performance of a generator network. To this end, several architectures utilizing label in-formation have been proposed such as semi-supervised GAN [14], and auxiliary classifier GAN [11]. The semi-supervised GAN trains the discriminator to classify the real data classes and one class for fake videos. ACGAN takes this further by adding a special auxiliary output to the discriminator that is trained to discriminate data labels along the usual output branch that classifies real/fake data. It is shown in [11] that ACGANs allow the model to generate images based on the input label to the generator as well as increasing the quality of generated images.

Another modification to the GAN as introduced in [2] is the usage of convolutional layers within the generator and discriminator. This is shown effective for visual data such as images and videos [6]. A type of convolutional neural network is the 3DCNN proposed in [15], which is shown to be capable of modeling and classifying human motion from videos. This is the reason we use a GAN based on 3DCNN in this research to generate human action videos.

2.3   LSTM for Translating Text Description into a Sequence of Actions

To be able to generate longer and more complex activity videos, 3D GANs have trouble modeling the high dimensionality of the video data [7, 8]. To circumvent modeling very long videos, we train the 3D GAN to generate only short videos (16 frames) of a single action, and longer videos of activities consisting of sequential actions are formed by concatenating these short action videos generated by the 3D GAN model. To generate the required sequence of actions for a certain activity based on the text input, we use a LSTM network. We use plain text descriptions due to text being an effective method to describe certain activities, as in [16] where text descriptions are proposed as natural way for describing 3D simulations based on visual information. We train the LSTM network to perform basically simple machine translation between a text input and a sequence of actions described by the input text.

3   Proposed System for Generating Activity Videos

3.1   The Dataset Used

In this research, we use the publicly available Weizmann action dataset [17] and a dataset of Cimande style Indonesian *silat*. The Weizmann dataset comprises of 10 action classes performed by 9 different actors. We preprocess the Weizmann dataset by cropping a 80 × 48 bounding box around the subject and then segmenting the videos into 16 frames per segment. The result is 278 action video chunks that are used during the training of the 3D GAN. The second dataset that we use is the Cimande *silat* dataset (a style of martial arts) which comprises 18 basic actions performed by 4 *silat* masters. We preprocess the *silat* videos by cropping a 80 × 48 bounding box around the subjects and segment the videos into 32 frame chunks (although for training the 3D GAN we will use only every other frame). The result is 3244 action video chunks used to train the 3D GAN model. The basic actions for the Weizmann dataset and *silat* dataset are shown in Fig. 2.

Fig. 2. Basic Action classes of the (a) Weizmann dataset and (b) Cimande *silat* dataset.

For training the LSTM to generate action sequences from text input we create a corpus containing pairs of sentences and action sequences. For the Weizmann dataset, we create pairs of text describing sequences of single action activities (example: "subject is walking" - "walk walk ... walk walk"), and two action activities(example: "subject walks and then waves 2 hands" - "walk walk ... wave2 wave2") with 8 action sequence length outputs. The Cimande *silat* dataset we chose because it has many higher-level move sets (*jurus*) that are comprised of a sequence of the basic moves/actions (*Tonjok Seubeulah, Timpah Seubeulah, Teke Tampa, Tewekan, Kelid Seubelah*) which is well suited to the system we propose. In our dataset, there are 5 different move sets performed, hence there are 5 different action sequences. For the text description, for each move set, we provide 5 simple sentence variations, allowing the LSTM to map many possible input sentences to a single action sequence for a move set (*jurus*). An example is "the subject performs *jurus Kelid Seubelah*" and "*Kelid Seubelah* is shown by the actor" will both result in the LSTM network outputting the sequence of actions to perform the move set *Kelid Seubelah*, allowing a many possible sentence to one action sequence mapping by the LSTM.

3.2   The Proposed Activity Video Generation System

The system we propose to generate single subject activity videos consist of two main stages. The first stage, a LSTM network takes an input text describing the activity to be generated. The LSTM then outputs a sequence of the atomic actions required to generate that activity. For each atomic action of the sequence, a corresponding short action video is generated by a 3D GAN model. These short video action sequences are then concatenated together to form a longer activity video with interpolated frames in between each of them for smoother transition. The overall system is depicted in Fig. 3.

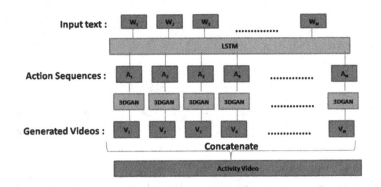

Fig. 3. Proposed single subject activity video generation system.

The core of the video generation system is the 3D GAN model used to generate the atomic action videos. We use the generator part of a 3D GAN model based on the ACGAN architecture. For the Weizmann dataset, the model has 2 auxiliary classifier outputs, one for the action label and another for the subject label and a 19-dimension input label (10 action classes + 9 subject classes). This is done since the Weizmann data has multiple subjects with varying appearances and conditioning the model on the subject label allows a degree of control over the appearance of the generated subject in the video. Likewise, the model for the *silat* dataset has 2 auxiliary outputs, one for the action class label and another for the domain of the action (the 7 movement domains are steady, punching, parry, kicking, greet, transitions, and nothing) which is done to group the similar action classes for easier model training and a 25-dimension input label (18 action classes + 7 domain classes). Following [5] the noise is added at every layer before up sampling to slowly add the details of the video. The 3D GAN architectures used are given in Fig. 4.

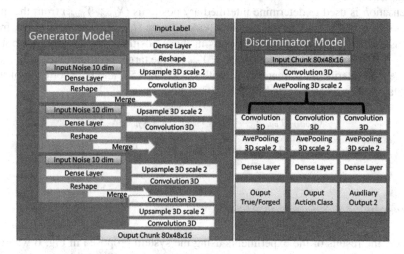

Fig. 4. Architecture of 3D GAN model for generating action videos.

For the model that generates sequences of actions based on a text description input, a LSTM network with an encoder-decoder architecture is used. The LSTM model for the encoder uses a bidirectional architecture that helps learn the input sequence from both sides of the sequence. To the resulting code (from the encoder) a noise signal is added to generate more diverse outputs, which is then passed to a decoder that based on the code generates the sequence of actions. The LSTM model is given in Fig. 5.

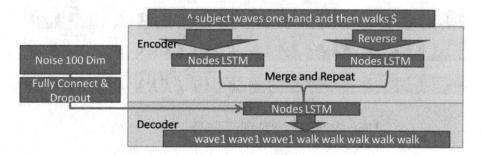

Fig. 5. Architecture of the LSTM network for generating action sequences from text input.

140 A. Arinaldi and M.I. Fanany

To ensure a smooth transition between consecutive chunks of generated video sequences, we also add 3 interpolated frames between each chunk of video before concatenating them. To build the 3 intermediary frames, we use a motion interpolation scheme using the Gunnar-Farneback optical flow algorithm available in openCV which calculates dense flow vectors from the previous chunk's last frame to the next chunk's first frame. From the flow vectors (V_{flow}), we interpolate the 3 frames where motion compensation is used to determine intermediary positions (X_{inter}, Y_{inter}) from the initial pixel position (X_{init}, Y_{init}) in the previous video frame (I_{prev}) to the next video frame (I_{next}) as in Eq. 1. The value of the pixels in those positions are linearly interpolated from the values in the initial position (X_{init}, Y_{init}) to the target position (X_{target}, Y_{target}) to form the n-th intermediary image I_{inter} (with $k = 0.25, 0.50$, and 0.75 for each of the 3 interpolated frames) as detected by the optical flow as in Eq. 2.

$$(X_{inter}, Y_{inter}) = (X_{init}, Y_{init}) + k * V_{flow}(X, Y) \tag{1}$$

$$I_{inter}(X_{inter}, Y_{inter}) = (1 - k) * I_{prev}(X_{init}, Y_{init}) + k * I_{next}(X_{target}, Y_{target}) \tag{2}$$

4 Results

We show the results of the experiments using the system proposed in Fig. 6 where we show the atomic actions generated by the 3D GAN model, Fig. 7 where we show the transition interpolated frames between two generated video chunks using frame interpolation, and Fig. 8 where we show the generated videos produced by the system from text a input.

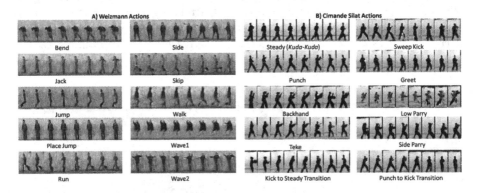

Fig. 6. Generated action videos for each atomic action.

Discussion on the Limitations of the Proposed System. The system we propose has some limitations, such as the generated videos are generally blurry, while some parts of the video have missing limbs or too many limbs. We also believe the model may have simply memorized the data (since the datasets are generally small and trained for

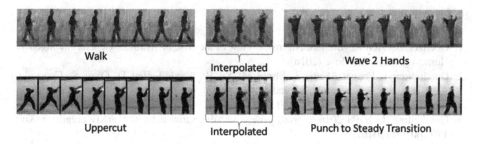

Walk

Interpolated

Wave 2 Hands

Uppercut

Interpolated

Punch to Steady Transition

Fig. 7. Interpolated frames for the Weizmann dataset (above) and the *silat* dataset (below).

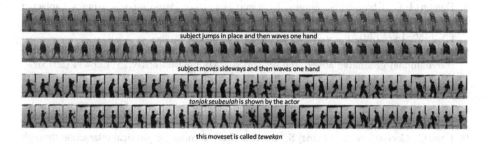

subject jumps in place and then waves one hand

subject moves sideways and then waves one hand

tonjok seubeulah is shown by the actor

this moveset is called *tewekan*

Fig. 8. Generated activity videos from text input (shown below each sequence of pictures)

thousands of epochs), albeit imperfectly. This is mainly due to the difficulty in modeling the large dimensional video data, where as in [7] the generated video quality is quite low. This is also due to the weakness of GANs in counting objects as demonstrated in [3] where the GAN has difficulty in counting the number of limbs and organs for generating animal images.

5 Conclusions

Generative Adversarial Networks (GANs) are a promising new architecture of deep neural networks that can mimic the process of human imagination but still not perfectly. GANs allow a neural network to generate new visual information based on the data used to train it. In this research, we design a system comprising a 3D GAN and LSTM model to process an input text and generate videos of single subject activity videos. The system is shown to be able to generate videos where a more complex activity can be comprised of a sequence of atomic actions, which we apply to the Weizmann dataset and Indonesian Cimande *silat*.

Acknowledgements. This work is supported by Center of Excellence for Higher Education Research Grant funded by Indonesian Ministry of Research and Higher Education. Contract No. 2626/UN2.R3.1/HKP05.00/2017. This paper is also supported by GPU grant from NVIDIA.

References

1. Goertzel, B.: AGI Revolution: An Inside View of the Rise of Artificial General Intelligence. Humanity Press, San Jose (2016)
2. Goodfellow, I., Pouget-Abadie, J., Mirza, M., Xu, B., Warde-Farley, D., Ozair, S., Courville, A., Bengio, Y.: Generative adversarial networks. In: Advances in Neural Information Processing Systems, pp. 2672–2680 (2014)
3. Goodfellow, I.: NIPS 2016 tutorial: generative adversarial networks. arXiv preprint arXiv: 1701.00160 (2016)
4. Reed, S., Akata, Z., Yan, X., Logeswaran, L., Schiele, B., Lee, H.: Generative adversarial text to image synthesis. In: Proceedings of The 33rd International Conference on Machine Learning, vol. 3, May 2016
5. Denton, E.L., Chintala, S., Fergus, R.: Deep generative image models using a Laplacian pyramid of adversarial networks. In: Advances in Neural Information Processing Systems, pp. 1486–1494 (2015)
6. Radford, A., Metz, L., Chintala, S.: Unsupervised representation learning with deep convolutional generative adversarial networks. arXiv preprint arXiv:1511.06434 (2015)
7. Vondrick, C., Pirsiavash, H., Torralba, A.: Generating videos with scene dynamics. In: Advances in Neural Information Processing Systems, pp. 613–621 (2016)
8. Mathieu, M., Couprie, C., LeCun, Y.: Deep multi-scale video prediction beyond mean square error. arXiv preprint arXiv:1511.05440
9. Finn, C., Goodfellow, I., Levine, S.: Unsupervised learning for physical interaction through video prediction. In: Advances in Neural Information Processing Systems, pp. 64–72 (2016)
10. Wu, J., Zhang, C., Xue, T., Freeman, B., Tenenbaum, J.: Learning a probabilistic latent space of object shapes via 3D generative-adversarial modeling. In: Advances in Neural Information Processing Systems, pp. 82–90 (2016)
11. Odena, A., Olah, C., Shlens, J.: Conditional image synthesis with auxiliary classifier GANs. arXiv preprint arXiv:1610.09585 (2016)
12. Koo, S.: Automatic colorization with deep convolutional generative adversarial networks (2016). http://cs231n.stanford.edu/reports/2016/pdfs/224_Report.pdf
13. Salimans, T., Goodfellow, I., Zaremba, W., Cheung, V., Radford, A., Chen, X.: Improved techniques for training GANs. In: Advances in Neural Information Processing Systems, pp. 2226–2234 (2016)
14. Odena, A.: Semi-supervised learning with generative adversarial networks. arXiv preprint arXiv:1606.01583 (2016)
15. Ji, S., Xu, W., Yang, M., Yu, K.: 3D convolutional neural networks for human action recognition. IEEE Trans. Pattern Anal. Mach. Intell. **35**(1), 221–231 (2013)
16. Hoyes, K.A.: 3D simulation: the key to AI. In: Goertzel, B., Pennachin, C. (eds.) Artificial General Intelligence, pp. 353–387. Springer, Heidelberg (2007)
17. Gorelick, L., Blank, M., Shechtman, E., Irani, M., Basri, R.: Actions as space-time shapes. IEEE Trans. Pattern Anal. Mach. Intell. **29**(12), 2247–2253 (2007)

One-Shot Ontogenetic Learning in Biomedical Datastreams

John Kalantari$^{(\boxtimes)}$ and Michael A. Mackey

Department of Biomedical Engineering, University of Iowa, Iowa City, IA 52242, USA
{john-kalantari,michael-mackey}@uiowa.edu

Abstract. Recent technological advances in the biological and physical sciences have allowed for the generation of large quantity datasets necessary for applying deep neural networks. Despite the demonstrable success of these methods in a variety of tasks including image classification, machine translation, and query-answering, among others, their widespread adoption in biomedical research has been tempered due to issues inherent to modeling complex biological systems not readily addressed by traditional gradient-based neural networks. We consider the problem of unsupervised, general-purpose learning in biological sequence data, wherein variable-order temporal dependencies, multi-dimensionality and uncertainty in model structure and data are the norm. To successfully model and learn these dependencies in an intuitive and holistic manner, we have utilized the data abstraction of Simplicial Grammar within a Bayesian learning framework. We demonstrate that this framework offers the ability to quickly encode and integrate new information, and perform prediction tasks without extensive, iterative training.

Keywords: Probabilistic generative models · Unsupervised learning · Simplicial complexes · Artificial intelligence · Bayesian nonparametrics · Systems biology

1 Introduction

Despite recent breakthroughs in artificial intelligence, machine learning, and high-throughput data processing, two aspects involved in modeling a *complex biological system* or *process* (CBSP) continue to elude many computational frameworks learning from biomedical datastreams–making expert-crafted models the defacto standard. CBSPs include any biological phenomena such as complex regulatory pathways, cellular processes and infectious diseases, which can be characterized by a network of interactive and dynamic components often including convergent and divergent signaling pathways and various positive and negative feedback loops across multiple scales [5]. The first aspect to consider when modeling CBSPs in the biological sciences and medicine, is that learning must often occur despite uncertainty about the data and model. While data uncertainty can be attributed to a lack of examples and imperfections in the measurement process, model uncertainty arises from having insufficient prior knowledge about the number of pertinent variables and interdependencies. Despite

© Springer International Publishing AG 2017
T. Everitt et al. (Eds.): AGI 2017, LNAI 10414, pp. 143–153, 2017.
DOI: 10.1007/978-3-319-63703-7_14

this uncertainty, scientists and clinicians can often learn the spatio-temporal dynamics of a CBSP from just one or few examples. This innate human ability to make accurate inferences given only limited exposure to a concept, category or situation, is commonly referred to as *one-shot learning* [2] and has become an area of growing interest in the machine learning community. This approach to learning lies in contrast to many popular algorithms which often require tens to thousands of examples, multiple iterations for training and optimization, and implicit assumptions about data dimensionality, noise and model parameters. The second aspect not readily addressed by popular frameworks is the ability to build integrative models that encapsulate the collective knowledge of multiple sub-models learned over time. From a systems-theory perspective, a CBSP is a *system of systems* whose emergent global behavior and functionality is heavily influenced by the interactions and local dynamics of lower-level sub-systems, and vice-versa. Thus, the collective knowledge about a CBSP may benefit from a general understanding about its nested sub-systems and inter-connectivities. To reach such an understanding requires a shared modeling formalism in which collective knowledge about a CBSP and its constituent sub-systems can be incrementally updated as novel data becomes available and new models are learned. We refer to this incremental integration of disparate knowledge learned over time as *ontogenetic learning*, a term loosely based on a similar notion coined by mathematician Norbert Wiener [10] and inspired by the biological concept of *ontogenesis*. Modern advances in high-throughput and "–omics" technologies, have allowed researchers to gradually analyze multiple levels of CBSP granularity directly from data, providing a range of insight from *in vivo* RNA transcriptional dynamics to pathogen evolution and phylodynamics. Similarly, many deep-learning frameworks have shown to excel in building models from data captured across different scales, from image classification models for protein subcellular localization [6], to prediction models for regulatory genomics [1]. However, these disjoint models often require subsequent, collaborative efforts by computational experts and biomedical researchers in order to integrate them into a single, comprehensive model. A central challenge is to address these two aspects of CBSP modeling in a data-driven manner: How can a machine-learning or AI framework address uncertainty about the structure of both the data and model while learning a new CBSP with limited *a priori* knowledge? And how can a learning framework represent and express the rich, quantitative knowledge about various CBSPs across multiple scales, in an intuitive and integrative manner? Ultimately, the greatest challenge is trying to address both aspects concurrently: How can the collective knowledge about a CBSP, its latent sub-systems and interdependencies be expressed and learned in the presence of uncertainty? For any computational framework designed for building predictive models of complex biological systems or processes, these challenges must be addressed within an *online* setting in order to capture the spatio-temporal dynamics of a system as it evolves over time, thus necessitating the use of temporal or sequential datastreams.

The challenge of emulating a human expert's ability to elucidate critical patterns, derive predictions and integrate knowledge learned from multiple modalities, when applied to CBSPs and any other complex adaptive systems, necessitates the development of a general-purpose or Artificial General Intelligence (AGI) framework. In this paper, we describe early developments of such a framework called the *Syntactic Nonparametric Analysis of Complex Systems* (SYNACX), applied to learning and building predictive models of CBSPs from a limited number of example temporal data sequences. The predictive model defined by SYNACX, its implied prior assumptions, and the derivation of the algorithm as an approximate inference scheme in the model will be discussed within the context of constructing *simplicial grammar* (SG) [5], that explicitly model observed data sequences with minimal implicit and/or explicit assumptions. In addition to introducing the approach sketched above, we directly compare SYNACX with other gradient-based neural networks approaches on prediction tasks using biomedical data, specifically electrocardiogram (ECG) waveforms.

2 Background

In the SYNACX framework we define a Bayesian Nonparametric predictive model, approximate inference procedure, and topological modeling formalism with which we can build richly expressive models of CBSPs, from biomedical datastreams of unbounded complexity, with minimal assumptions or expert supervision. In designing and justifying such a model and inference procedure for biomedical datastreams, we extend definitions and inference methods for building *Hierarchical Pitman-Yor Processes*–hierarchical models of sequential stochastic processes that generate discrete observations. In addition, the use of a data abstraction based on the simplicial complexes from the field of algebraic topology allows us to recognize subtle features and incorporate latent dimensions of a CBSP via topological invariants. Among these are homology groups and persistent homology, which can reveal topological attributes not inferred using conventional network-theory methods, and thus provide an alternative method for discriminating features within large datasets across multiple scales.

2.1 Pitman-Yor Process

The Pitman-Yor process, denoted $\mathcal{PYP}(\alpha, d, G_0)$, is a distribution over probability measures, parametrized by a concentration parameter α, discount parameter d, and base measure G_0. Intuitively Pitman-Yor processes can be thought of as distributions over *distributions* over an arbitrary probability space, from which a random probability measure can be sampled. For each random probability measure, $G \sim \mathcal{PYP}(\alpha, d, G_0)$, the base measure can be interpreted as its mean $E[G(v)] = G_0(v)$ while the discount and concentration parameters are related to its variance $Var[G(v)] = G_0(v)(1 - G_0(v))(1 - d)(\alpha + 1)$, for each $v \in V$, where

V denotes a finite probability space. To demonstrate its use, consider the simple model in which samples are drawn from a Pitman-Yor distributed random distribution:

$$G|\alpha, d, G_0 \sim \mathcal{PYP}(\alpha, d, G_0) \tag{1}$$
$$\theta_i|G \sim G, \quad i = 1, ..., N, \tag{2}$$

where $\{\theta_i\}_{i=1}^N$ is a sequence of i.i.d. samples drawn from G. Using a generative process known as the *Chinese Restaurant Process* (CRP), a sequence of samples $\{\theta_i\}_{i=1}^N$, can be drawn from this model with G analytically marginalized out. This process can be described using the following analogy. Imagine N customers being seated sequentially in a Chinese restaurant with infinite capacity. In this setting, the first customer is seated at an unoccupied table. Customers $2, ..., N$ are then sequentially seated by seating customer i at an occupied table j with probability proportional to $n_j^i - d$, where n_j^i is the number of customers already seated at table j at time i, or at an unoccupied table with probability proportional to $t^i d + c$, where t^i is the number of occupied tables at time i. Each occupied table is served one dish which is independently sampled from the base distribution G_0. Finally, if customer i is seated at a table serving dish ψ, then the parameter θ_i is given the value ψ. The resultant seating assignment defines a partition of the first N integers which follows Ewen's sampling formula [8]. In cases in which we expect data to be generated by different but similar distributions, the PYP model can be extended to construct hierarchical data models by use of the *Hierarchical Pitman-Yor process* (HPYP). Denoted $\mathcal{HPYP}(\alpha_i, d_i, G_0)$, a HPYP consists of a set of random probability measures $\{G_i\}$, where each G_i is drawn from a PYP, $G_i \sim PYP(\alpha_i, d_i, G_0)$, and the base measure G_0 is itself drawn from a PYP, $G_0 \sim PYP(\alpha_i, d_i, H)$. Thus, this model explicitly assumes that all G_i to be similar to some (latent) probability measure G_0, which itself is assumed to be similar to some fixed probability measure H. Consider the example HPYP model

$$G_1|\alpha_1, d_1, G_0 \sim \mathcal{PYP}(\alpha_1, d_1, G_0) \tag{3}$$
$$G_2|\alpha_2, d_2, G_1 \sim \mathcal{PYP}(\alpha_2, d_2, G_1) \tag{4}$$
$$\theta_i|G_2 \sim \quad i = 1, ..., N \tag{5}$$

Known as the *Chinese Restaurant Representation* (CRF), the recursive application of the CRP in a hierarchical model allows us to once again analytically marginalize out G_1 and G_2.

2.2   Simplicial Homology

Recognition of the importance of simplicial complexes and their combinatorial and topological properties can be dated back to the seminal works of Euler and Riemann as well as the relatively recent contribution of homology classes by Poincaré [7]. The topological property known as homology offers a general procedure by which a sequence of abelian groups or modules can be associated to a given topological space or manifold. Determination of the different dimensional

homology groups provides information about the topological invariant characteristics of a system which may be subsequently used for recognition, classification
and prediction purposes. The *homology group*, denoted $H_d(X)$, pertaining to a
given topological space X and dimension d, provides a global description of the
d-simplicial chains. Given some simplicial complex K, a d-dimensional simplical-
chain, or d-chain, in K is a finite formal sum of d-simplices, formally expressed
as $q = \sum_{i=1}^{k} \alpha_i \sigma_i$, where σ_i are the d-simplices and α_i are the coefficients from
the field $\mathbb{Z}_2$. It follows from Lemma 1, that under the binary addition operator,
a set of d-chains form a group called the d-th *chain group*.

Lemma 1. *Let K be a simplicial complex and C_d the set of d-chains in K. The
set C_d with the operator $+$ form a group, denoted $(C_d, +)$.*

Proof: The identity is the chain $0 = \sum_{i=1}^{k} 0\sigma_i$, and the inverse of a chain, $-q = q$ since $q + q = 0$ under $\mathbb{Z}_2$ additions. The set of oriented d-simplices in K,
$\{e_1, e_2, ..., e_{n_d}\}$, define a basis for C_d

At different dimensions, these chain groups are related by a boundary operator, ∂_d, that, given a d-simplex, returns the $(d-1)$-chain of its boundary
$(d-1)$-simplices. Thus, if $\sigma = [v_0, ..., v_d]$ denotes a d-simplex, its boundary is
$\partial_d \sigma = \sum_{i=0}^{d} (-1)^i [v_0, ..., \hat{v}_i, ..., v_d]$. Furthermore, because the boundary operator
commutes with addition, $\partial_d(q_1 + q_2) = \partial_d q_1 + \partial_d q_2$, if extended to chain groups,
the map $\partial_d : C_d \rightarrow C_{d-1}$ becomes a homomorphism. A sequence of chain groups
connected by these boundary homorphisms is called a *chain complex* $\hat{C}$. To define
the homology groups of dimension d, we must focus on the two simplicial-chain
subtypes, *d-cycles* and *d-boundaries*. A d-dimensional simplicial cycle or *d-cycle*,
z, is a d-chain whose boundary is zero, $\partial_d z = 0$. The set of all d-cycles form a
group denoted $Z_d \subseteq C_d$, where Z_d is a subgroup of C_d. Since Z_d is the set of all d-
chains that go to zero under the dth boundary homomporphism, Z_d is the *kernel*
of ∂_d denoted $Z_d = ker\partial_d$. Furthermore, a d-dimensional simplicial-boundary or
d-boundary is a d-chain that is the boundary of a $(d+1)$-chain, $z = \partial_{d+1} q$ for
$q \in C_{d+1}$. The set of all d-boundaries form a group denoted $B_d \subseteq C_d$, where
B_d is a subgroup of C_d. The group of d-boundaries is the *image* of the $(d+1)$-
st boundary homomorphism, $B_d = img\partial_{d+1}$. From the fundamental lemma of
homology, which intuitively states that the boundary of a boundary is null, it
follows that B_d is a subgroup of Z_d. From this we can define an equivalence relation over Z_d. Two d-cycles z_1 and z_2 are considered homologous if the d-cycle
$z_1 - z_2$ is a d-boundary. The equivalence class of a d-cycle z_1 is the homology
class $[z_1]$. Addition of homology classes is well-defined; for any d-cycles z_1 and
z_2, we have $[z_1 + z_2] = [z_1] + [z_2]$. Thus, the set of homology classes of d-cycles
forms a well-defined group under addition, called the dth homology group, H_d.
By taking the quotient of the cycle groups with the boundary groups, we can
define the homology groups for each dimension d, $H_d = \frac{Z_d}{B_d}$. Thus, each homology
group is the collection of d-cycles that are not boundaries of $(d+1)$-simplices. In
addition, the rank of the d-th homology group H_d is called the d-th *Betti number*
β_d and informally describes the number of unconnected d-dimensional surfaces.

For a more detailed treatment of these concepts from Algebraic Topology, we refer readers to [4].

2.3 Cardiac Conduction as a CBSP

The electrodiagram (ECG) waveform is a common diagnostic tool for cardiovascular disease. Using ECG data, the structure of the human heart and the function of its electrical conduction system over time can be approximated across multiple levels of granularity. Specifically, a patient ECG data-sequence can be considered in terms of a sequence of electric potentials, a sequence of distinct waveform deflections (P, Q, R, S, T waves) indicating the overall direction of depolarization and repolarization, or even a sequence of segments and intervals (PR interval, PR segment, QRS complex, QT interval, ST segment, RR interval, etc) which relate directly to phases of cardiac conduction. Considering the sequence as a sequence of segments and intervals is appealing since limits can be set on these from which to diagnose deviations from normality. As a result, numerous diagnoses and findings of arrythmias, electrolyte disturbances, ischemia and infarctions are based on recognition of these higher-level spatio-temporal patterns and their variants. However, due to the non-stationary nature of cardiac signals and the affect of different noise sources (e.g. electrode contact noise, muscle movement artifacts) during the measurement process, substantial variations exist among ECG recordings for the same electrophysiological phenomena. As a result, unsupervised learning and construction of predictive models directly from ECG data has proven difficult.

3 Syntactic Nonparametric Analysis of Complex Systems

Building intuitive models of CBSPs directly from data, using just one or few examples, requires integrating knowledge captured across multiple scales despite uncertainty about the data and model. To achieve this, we look to apply concepts from algebraic topology, probability theory and Bayesian nonparametrics. In the SYNACX framework, CBSPs are represented as simplicial grammar–that is, probabilistic generative models for sequence data represented by oriented simplicial-chains on a simplicial complex in an abstract compositional language. As a simplicial complex K, a CBSP model can be built from a set V, whose elements are called *pattern-primitives*, and a collection S of finite non-empty subsets of V that satisfies the axioms:

Axiom 1. *For each $v \in V$, the singleton $\{v\} \in S$*

Axiom 2. *If $\sigma \in S$ and $\tau \subset \sigma$ is non-empty, then $\tau \in S$,*

where an element $\sigma \in S$ consisting of $n + 1$ elements is called an *n-simplex* of K. The learning and modeling process begins with a set of 0-simplices that constitute the basis of the 0th-chain group representing the lowest-level granularity at which a CBSP can be modeled. For each CBSP data-type, the basis of 0-simplices, corresponds to a finite set of discrete values that can be used to represent the underlying data model. For continuous-valued data sequences, these 0-simplices can be obtained via a simple quantization procedure in which continuous-values are discretized according to a finite-size quanization map. We refer to this finite, non-empty set of data-derived elements as the *vocabulary* of pattern-primitives, V. Given a data-sequence of variable length and dimensionality, SYNACX automatically infers a collection of simplicial grammars that generalize the syntactic and statistical properties of a CBSP data sequence using a hierarchy of latent variables that can be explicitly modeled as oriented simplicial chains. By assuming that the syntactic structure of a data sequence can be modeled at multiple levels of granularity, from the lowest-level (fine-grain resolution) using an oriented 0-simplicial chain of primitives, $\mathbf{q}^0 \in C_0$, to increasingly higher levels using an emergent d-simplicial chain of d-dimensional simplices, $\mathbf{q}^d \in C_d$, a CBSP model can be defined in which the distribution over lower-level granular chains is regularized using higher-level granular chains. In addition, by factoring the probability of a data-sequence under a distribution, $P(\boldsymbol{x}) = P(x_0)P(x_1|x_0)P(x_2|x_0, x_1) \ldots, P(x_N|x_0, \ldots, x_{N-1})$, discrete subsequences can be directly modeled using the set of conditional distributions. The combination of oriented simplicial chains with associated conditional probability distributions in the simplicial grammar (SG) modeling formalism provides a versatile approach to encoding the large number of highly interconnected dynamic units of a CBSP into a simplicial complex which can be considered a combinatorial version of a topological space. Consequently, the invariants of each SG can be studied from a probabilistic, topological, combinatorial and algebraic perspective, each one providing completely different measures that can be used to discriminate between classes of phenomena across multiple scales.

Let the basis of the 0th-chain group, $\{e_1^0, e_2^0, e_3^0, \ldots\}$, be our vocabulary V, SYNACX works to compute a collective simplicial grammar, $\mathcal{G}$, from an input sequence of discrete observations $\boldsymbol{x} = [x_0, x_1, x_2, \ldots x_N]$ where each observation x_n corresponds to a primitive $e_k^0 \in V$. To allow uncertainty in distributional assumptions and to avoid critical dependence on parametric assumptions, underlying each simplicial grammar is a set of random variables drawn from some unknown probability distribution. This unknown probability distribution is itself drawn from some prior distribution. Thus, each simplicial grammar can be parameterized using random probability measures $G_\mathbf{q}$ based on an underlying Hierarchical Pitman-Yor process prior. Furthermore, to make inference computationally tractable for time-series data, we utilize a marginalized hierarchy of Hierarchical Pitman-Yor processes inspired by the language model of [11] in which the hyperparameters are stochastically optimized and $\alpha = 0$. Information about the already observed, input sub-sequence $\boldsymbol{x}_{1:i} = [x_0, x_1, \ldots, x_i]$ is maintained in the form of a collection of sub-grammars, where each sub-grammar $G_{\boldsymbol{q}_{1:i}} \in \mathcal{G}$ defines the conditional distribution over V, given the oriented simplicial representation of the observed sub-sequence, $\boldsymbol{q}_{1:i} = \{e_{x_0}^0 + e_{x_1}^0 + ... + e_{x_i}^0\}$.

$$P(\boldsymbol{q}_{1:i}) = \prod_{j=1}^{i} P(e_{x_j}^0 | e_{x_{j-1}}^0) = \prod_{j=1}^{i} G_{\boldsymbol{q}_{1:j-1}}(j) \qquad (6)$$

Each sub-grammar can be further described as a set of stochastic rules, where each SG rule, $G_{\boldsymbol{q}_{1:i}}(e_k^0)$, models the probability of observing a pattern-primitive $e_k^0 \in V$, conditioned on the oriented simplicial chain $\boldsymbol{q}_{1:i}$, given a Hierarchical Pitman-Yor Process prior:

$$G_{\emptyset} \sim PYP(d_{\emptyset}, H)$$
$$G_{\boldsymbol{q}_{1:i}} | G_{\pi(\boldsymbol{q}_{1:i})} \sim PYP(d_{\boldsymbol{q}_{1:i}}, G_{\pi(\boldsymbol{q}_{1:i})}) \quad \forall \boldsymbol{q}_{1:i} \in C_0/\{\emptyset\}$$

where $\emptyset$ denotes the empty simplical chain and $\pi(\boldsymbol{q}_{1:i}) = \{e_{x_1}^0 + ... + e_{x_i}^0\}$ represents a variable-length truncation of chain $\boldsymbol{q}_{1:i} = \{e_{x_0}^0 + e_{x_1}^0 + ... + e_{x_i}^0\}$. In this setup, the joint probability of the simplicial chain $\mathbf{q}_{1:i}$ and the collective grammar $\mathcal{G}$ is given as:

$$P(\mathbf{q}, \mathcal{G}) = P(\mathcal{G}) \prod_{i=0}^{|\mathbf{q}|-1} G_{\mathbf{q}_{1:i}}(q_{i+1}) \qquad (7)$$

where the rightmost term is the probability of each primitive conditioned on the 0-chain generated thus far, and $P(\mathcal{G})$ is the hierarchical prior describing the unbounded set of latent variables for the collective grammar generated thus far. Given a new data-sequence and minimal a priori knowledge about its dimensionality, length, temporal dependencies, or necessary grammar size, to make the grammar induction tractable, an approximate inference scheme and random sub-grammar deletion procedure is used to learn likely values of the latent parameters of the collection of sub-grammars $\mathcal{G} = \{G_q\}_{q \in C_0} = \{P_q | q \in C_0\}$. The latent parameters of each sub-grammar instance are a set of counts $\{c_v^q, t_v^q\}$ and the hyperparameter $d^{|q|}$ for $v \in V$, $q \in C_0$. The c_v^q are counts of atoms in the estimation of a discrete distribution over V corresponding to the number of draws of type v from the PYP associated with $\mathbf{q}$. The t_v^q regularize the estimation, generate Bayesian smoothing and correspond to the number of draws from the truncated measure $G_{\pi(\mathbf{q})}$. Given the set of counts for all oriented simplicial chains explicity modeled by the collective grammar $S_{\mathcal{G}} = \{\{c_{qvg}\}_{v \in V, g \in \{1,...,t_{qv}\}}\}_{q \in C_0^{\mathcal{G}}}, \{\{t_{qv}\}_{v \in V}\}_{q \in C_0^{\mathcal{G}}}\}$, the predictive probability of a primitive v given an observed data-sequence, $P(v | \mathbf{q}, S_{\mathcal{G}})$ can be computed by sequentially estimating the posterior distribution. In SYNACX, a single particle filter in the CRF representation [9], is implemented to sequentially infer the posterior distribution. In this scheme, the current estimate of the posterior is maintained as $S_{\mathcal{G}}$ and incrementally updated to account for each new observation q_{i+1} given $\mathbf{q}_{1:i}$ by drawing samples from it, such that $P(S_{\mathcal{G}_{\mathbf{q}_{1:i}}}, \mathbf{q}_{1:i})$ becomes

$P(S_{\mathcal{G}_{\mathbf{q}_{1:i+1}}}, \mathbf{q}_{1:i+1})$. Thus, following the $i+1$-th observation, q_{i+1}, we obtain the sub-grammar $G_{\mathbf{q}_{1:i+1}} \sim \mathcal{HPY}_{\mathbf{q}_{1:i+1}}$, where $\mathcal{HPY}_{\mathbf{q}_{1:i+1}}$ describes the distribution over ways of partitioning $N = |\mathbf{q}_{1:i+1}|$ observations into K partitions, for all possible N and K. In order to sample such a partition distribution, we follow Ewen's sampling formula [8]

$$P(m_1, ..., m_n) = \frac{n!}{\prod_{i=1}^{n}(i!)^{m_i} m_i!} \mu(m_1, ..., m_n)$$

with

$$\mu(m_1, ..., m_n) = E\left[\sum \prod_{i=1}^{n} \prod_{j=1}^{m_i} V_{n(i,j)}^{i}\right],$$

where $i = 1, ..., n$ and $j = 1, ..., m_i$. We generalize this formula for the Pitman-Yor Process, with $\mu(m_1, ..., m_n) = \mu_{d,\theta}(m_1, ..., m_n)$ describing the mean probability distribution of a partition of length k, via the formula:

$$\mu_{d,\theta=0}(m_1, ..., m_n) = \frac{[d]_d^{k-1}}{[1]_{n-1}} \prod_{j=1}^{n} ([1-d])_{j-1} \tag{8}$$

For a hierarchy of HPYP's, the joint probability distribution can then be denoted as follows[1]:

$$P(c_{\mathbf{q}v}, t_{\mathbf{q}v}, A_{\mathbf{q}v}, \mathbf{q}_{1:i+1}) =$$

$$\left(\prod_{v \in V} H(v)^{t_{\theta v}}\right) \prod_{\mathbf{q} \in C_0^{\mathcal{G}}} \left(\frac{[d_{\mathbf{q}}]_{d_{\mathbf{q}}}^{t_{\mathbf{q}}.-1}}{[1]_1^{c_{\mathbf{q}}.-1}} \prod_{v \in V} \prod_{a \in A_{\mathbf{q}v}} [1 - d_{\mathbf{q}}]_1^{|a|-1}\right) \tag{9}$$

4   Experiment/Results

The biomedical datastreams considered are discretized ECG data-sequences [3] derived from ECG data for 352 torso-surface sites across 4 human subjects with moderate to large myocardial infarctions. Compared to most synthetic or idealized time-series datasets, these sequences display characteristics commonly observed in real-world biomedical datastreams, including data sparsity, multi-dimensionality and variable-order temporal dependencies. We evaluated prediction ability in its most challenging form: after exposure to just one real-world CBSP data sequence. As in the case of many other non-stationary CBSP data sequences where sample size is limited, we aim to learn the spatio-temporal dynamics of a CBSP incrementally without the explicit requirement of extensive retraining. Table 1 includes error values obtained for the online-prediction task on a new patient ECG sequence following one-shot learning from another patient's unique sequence. The SYNACX framework was compared with various neural

---

[1] Here we use Kramp's general notation to concisely express the product of the factors of an arithmetic progression as $[c]_b^a \equiv \prod_{i=0}^{a-1} c + ib$.

networks with two-layer architectures–a Multi-Layer Perceptron (MLP), Recurrent Neural Network (RNN) and Long Short-Term Memory (LSTM), each utilizing the Adaptive Moment Estimation (ADAM) optimization procedure with parameters $\eta = 0.001$, $\beta_1 = 0.9$, $\beta_2 = 0.999$.

Table 1. Performance comparison of SYNACX and other gradient-based neural network architectures on prediction tasks following one-shot learning

Model	Layer1 # hidden units	Layer2 # hidden units	MSE
MLP_2L_1	10	10	0.46
MLP_2L_2	10	150	0.54
MLP_2L_3	150	10	0.38
MLP_2L_4	150	150	0.54
LSTM_2L_1	10	10	0.31
LSTM_2L_2	10	150	0.25
LSTM_2L_3	150	10	0.23
LSTM_2L_4	150	150	0.13
RNN_2L_1	10	10	0.66
RNN_2L_2	10	150	0.2
RNN_2L_3	150	10	0.29
RNN_2L_4	150	150	0.14
SYNACX			0.28

5 Conclusion

We have described the application of the *SYNACX* framework to learning and building probabilistic generative models of CBSPs from a limited number of temporal data sequences. While *human-level* intelligence currently remains elusive *in-silico*, the aforementioned unsupervised sequence learning procedure and shared modeling formalism provides a platform for the topological simplification of combinatorial data and its incremental integration into a single, comprehensive model. Our preliminary experiments using SYNACX in online prediction tasks offer promising results and demonstrate its utility as a possible alternative to popular gradient-based neural-network architectures. Subsequent experiments involving heterogeneous datatypes generated across multiple spatio-temporal scales will be used to further investigate the use of topological invariants as a means for integrating models of global behavior with those of local interactions.

References

1. Angermueller, C., Pärnamaa, T., Parts, L., Stegle, O.: Deep learning for computational biology. Mol. Syst. Biol. **12**, 878 (2016)
2. Biederman, I.: Recognition-by-components: a theory of human image understanding. Psychol. Rev. **94**(2), 115 (1987)
3. Chen, Y., Keogh, E., Hu, B., Begum, N., Bagnall, A., Mueen, A., Batista, G.: The UCR time series classification archive, July 2015

4. Hatcher, A.: Algebraic Topology. Cambridge University Press, Cambridge (2002)
5. Kalantari, J.: Unsupervised in-silico modeling of complex biological systems. In: IEEE International Workshops on Foundations and Applications of Self Systems, pp. 287–292. IEEE (2016)
6. Kraus, O.Z., Grys, B.T., Ba, J., Chong, Y., Frey, B.J., Boone, C., Andrews, B.J.: Automated analysis of high-content microscopy data with deep learning. Mol. Syst. Biol. **13**, 924 (2017)
7. Poincaré, H.: Analysis situs. J. de l'École Polytech. **2**(1), 1–123 (1895)
8. Tavaré, S.: The ewens multivariate distribution. In: Multivariate Discrete Distributions. Wiley, New York (1997)
9. Teh, Y.W.: A Bayesian interpretation of interpolated Kneser-ney (2006)
10. Wiener, N.: Cybernetics: Control and Communication in the Animal and the Machine. Wiley, New York (1948)
11. Wood, F., Archambeau, C., Gasthaus, J., James, L., Teh, Y.W.: A stochastic memoizer for sequence data. In: Proceedings of the 26th Annual International Conference on Machine Learning, pp. 1129–1136. ACM (2009)

The MaRz Algorithm: Towards an Artificial General Episodic Learner

Christian Rodriguez, Giselle Marston, William Goolkasian, Ashley Rosenberg, and Andrew Nuxoll[✉]

University of Portland, Portland, OR 97203, USA
nuxoll@up.edu

Abstract. An artificial general intelligence must be able to record and leverage its experiences to improve its behavior. In this paper, we present a novel, general, episodic learning algorithm that can operate effectively in an environment where its episodic memories are the only resource it has available for learning.

1 Introduction

Episodic memory is one of three types of long term memory generally recognized in humans [1]:

Procedural Memory memory of how to act (e.g., how to walk, ride a bicycle, juggle)
Semantic Memory memory for facts (e.g., trees have trunks, the earth orbits the sun, ripe bananas are yellow)
Episodic Memory memory for events (e.g., what time you arrived at your hotel, what color shirt you wore yesterday).

More broadly, episodic memories have a temporal component. They consist of a sequence of episodes that an agent experiences as it moves through time [23]. An agent has the ability to retrieve past episodes from a memory queue and also recognize when its current situation is similar to a past episode. Episodes consist not only of what the agent is sensing but also what it might be thinking about at the time.

An artificial general intelligence must be able to not only record but leverage its experiences to improve its behavior. Furthermore, these experiences are at their most general in their original, unprocessed, unfiltered form. Despite this, most artificially intelligent agents created to date lack an episodic memory. The agent can record information which the programmer has specifically instructed it to record but it lacks a general ability to record all its experiences all the time. Nor can it retrieve a memory based upon an open-ended cue.

In humans, an impaired episodic memory is called amnesia. Evidence from psychology indicates that an amnesiac's ability to learn new semantic memories is impaired by amnesia. The reasons for this are not entirely clear but it seems

© Springer International Publishing AG 2017
T. Everitt et al. (Eds.): AGI 2017, LNAI 10414, pp. 154–163, 2017.
DOI: 10.1007/978-3-319-63703-7_15

likely that semantic learning relies upon the ability to perceive cause and effect and, thus, relies upon the ability to perceive an ordering to events. Therefore, it is reasonable to conclude that a general purpose episodic memory may be an essential component of an effective artifical general intelligence.

In this paper, we present our work towards understanding how episodic memory is used for learning by exploring algorithms an agent can use to learn in situations where its episodic memories are the only resource it has available for learning. Specifically, the agent is given no knowledge about the environment it occupies or the task is must perform and we compare a reinforcement learning agent to a novel episodic learning algorithm of our design.

Furthermore, our goal is also to create an effective, general episodic memory. That is, an episodic memory that can operate in any environment without need to be configured for that environment.

2 Blind FSM Environment

The environment we have selected for this research is a deterministic finite state machine [7] with the following properties:

1. a single goal state
2. each state has a transition for each letter in the alphabet
3. there is a path from each state to the goal state.

The agent has only the following resources:

1. a single goal state sensor so that it knows when it has reached the goal state. It has no other sensors.
2. knowledge of the state machine's alphabet and, thus, what actions are available to it at any given time

Notably the agent does NOT know:

1. how many states there are
2. how many of those states are goal states
3. what state it is currently in
4. the transition function

As soon as the agent senses the goal state, it is immediately moved to a randomly-selected non-goal state. Thus the simulation can be run indefinitely with the agent repeatedly discovering the goal state.

Given the simplicity of this environment, it may seem trivial to create an agent with optimal behavior. However, the agent's lack of sensors means that it can not distinguish a non-goal state from any other non-goal state. There also is no consistent starting state. In other words, the agent faces maximal degree of perceptual aliasing [26].

In this situation, an agent using a traditional machine learning algorithm is mainly ineffective as it relies upon associating a best action with each state that it can distinguish. To learn in this environment the agent must leverage sequences of episodes (see Previous Work below).

Ideal behavior, given the agent's lack of perception, is to determine what we refer to in this research as an optimal universal sequence of actions. A universal sequence of actions is one that will always take the agent to the goal state regardless of its starting state. It may reach the goal state before it completes the sequence but it will always reach the goal. An optimal universal sequence is a universal sequence that reaches the goal in the least number of steps, on average, over all possible starting states.

This environment was selected for its simplicity and flexibility while still meeting the requirement of an environment that requires a successful agent to have an episodic memory. Furthermore, it provides a clearly defined range of behavior. Specifically, an agent can not perform better than an optimal universal sequence and an agent with a random policy provides a non-arbitrary upper limit for bad behavior. Notably, an agent that always takes random steps will always eventually reach the goal.

3   Previous Work

3.1   Solving Finite Automata

The process of determining the transition function for a given state machine (i.e., machine identification) is well established [9,14]. However, all algorithms we are aware of rely upon being in a given starting state. These algorithms often rely upon testing a range of different input sequences on the machine and thus provide a foundation for our approach.

3.2   Perceptual Aliasing

Perceptual aliasing or hidden state are terms used in machine learning for the situation where the agent can perceive multiple states identically either due to insufficient or noisy sensors [26]. Notably, human behavior in environments with perceptual aliasing has also been studied [5].

A common technique to address perceptual aliasing in machine learning is to create a memory for the agent's sensing and to make decisions based upon sequences of episodes rather than individual ones [3,11,12]. We use this same approach in this research.

3.3   Artificial Episodic Memory

While unusual, artificial episodic memories have been created in the past for various purposes including empathic robots [6], non-player characters in multiplayer games [2] and solving physics problems [22].

Nuxoll and Laird [17] describe a set of cognitive capabilities granted or facilitated by an episodic memory. They demonstrate a few of these using a general episodic memory system that is part of the Soar cognitive architecture [8]. More recently, a general implementation has been created for the Icarus cognitive architecture [13]

We believe that creating an artificial, general episodic memory presents three main challenges to the creator:

1. An ever-growing data store. The size of the episodic store is presumed to be finite yet new episodes are constantly being created. Thus, the agent and the agent must find a way to forget previous episodes and/or compress the overall data store to keep it below a given maximum size [15, 18, 24]
2. Retrieval from a given cue. A good system should be able to quickly return a "good" or "best" match for a given cue. The definition of a good match in a general context is not entirely clear. Most systems rely upon a simple cardinality of match or a system based upon term frequency-inverse document frequency (tf-idf) [20]
3. Learning. The agent should be able to leverage its experiences to improve its behavior. It's not clear how a general episodic memory system should tie in to the agent's ability to learn.

This research is currently focused on the third challenge listed above. Specifically, the episodic memories we are using allow the episodic memory to grow indefinitely and rely upon exact matches for retrieval. However, we are making this decision with an eye toward addressing all three challenges in the medium term.

A fundamental approach to using episodes in learning is to retrieve one or more past episodes that are most similar to the current situation. The agent can then make decisions by examining the outcomes of its actions in those past situations. All episodic memory facilitated learning we are aware of – including the work we are presenting here – is based on this approach. See [16] for a representative example.

In most cases the retrieval is deliberate, but there is some effort to make retrieval spontaneous when it is relevant [10].

3.4 Episodic Learning

Finally, this work builds upon previous research to build a general-purpose episodic learner in an environment that requires an episodic memory. Walker et al. [25] demonstrated building an successful sequence from the last action backward was valuable in such an environment. This insight formed the basis for the use of the suffix in the search nodes that MaRz uses. Faltersack et al. [4] took initial steps towards a general purpose episodic memory learner using a different learning approach than MaRz.

4 Nearest Sequence Memory

The Nearest Sequence Memory (NSM) algorithm was introduced by McCallum [12] as a way to address environments with perceptual aliasing. NSM proved to be capable of finding optimal behavior in our Blind FSM environment and thus was useful to us as a basis for "good" behavior to compare our episodic memory to.

NSM maintains a simple episodic memory for the agent wherein each episode consists of the action, percepts and reward. (Note: Since the only percept that the agent has in the Blind FSM environment is its goal sensor, its percepts and reward are the same in that environment.) Furthermore, each state has a Q-value associated with it Q-Learning [21].

As a small example, consider a Blind FSM environment where the alphabet is a, b. The sequences below depict the agent's memory of its first 55 episodes.

aabbaaaabbaababbbb<u>a</u>bbabaabaaabbaabababbababababbb<u>a</u>bbabab<u>a</u><u>a</u>aba
0000000000011111111112222222222333333333344444444445555
0123456789012345678901234567890123456789012345678901234

The letters read from left to right indicate each action that the agent took over the course of its entire past. If the letter is underlined, that indicates that the agent reached the goal in that episode. The pair of digits (read vertically) under each letter are index values to facilitate referencing parts of the memory in the subsequent text.

At each time step, the agent considers each possible future action. Presuming it were to select that action for its current episode, it then searches its episodic memory for the k sequences from its past that provide the best (longest) match to its current situation given the potential action (i.e., a form of k-nearest neighbor learning). The agent selects the action for which the overall Q-value of its k matching neighbors is the highest.

If the action is taken, the associated k neighbor states are updated using the Q-Learning rule.

To operate effectively, NSM requires that certain values be pre-configured for the environment:

1. k (for kNN)
2. a learning rate
3. a discount factor
4. a chance of random action
5. how the previous value should change over time

Each time we made a substantial change to the size of the Blind FSM (i.e., number of states or alphabet size) we were compelled to adjust these values in order to return the algorithm to its most effective behavior.

5   MaRz Algorithm

For this research, we introduce the MaRz algorithm. MaRz maintains an episodic memory similar to NSM's that consists of the action selected and percept (goal) at each state (see the example in the previous section).

Unlike NSM, MaRz selects sequences of actions, rather than individual actions. Nominally, MaRz *considers* all sequences in order from shortest to longest. For example, if the alphabet is a, b MaRz would consider trying the following sequences in a strict order: a, b, aa, ab, ba, bb, aaa, aab, aba, etc. If the alphabet was a, b, c, d the ordering would be: a, b, c, d, aa, ab, ac, ad, ba, bb, bc, etc. Generally, this is the same order you would list increasing numbers in base b, where b is the size of the alphabet and the letters of the alphabets are the digits.

It is important to note that the agent may choose to skip a sequence it is considering and it may even choose to jump back to a skipped sequence and continue forward considering all untried sequences from that point forward. Thus, the sequences are not tried in order they are considered. Nonetheless, this strict ordering of sequences is important to the algorithm.

A simplified version of MaRz could simply try every sequence it considers and eventually find a universal sequence. (A reminder to the reader: the concept of universal sequence was defined above in the Blind FSM Environment section). The key insight in this case is that such an agent is performing a breadth-first search through the space of possible sequences. MaRz instead uses an approach comparable to a memory-bounded A*-Search [19] through the space of these sequences.

A search node used by MaRz has the following attributes which are outlined here and will be explained more further on:

a suffix this is a particular sequence of letters. A sequence that ends with this suffix "matches" this search node. Also, notably, the length of this suffix is the "g" value in the context of A* search.

a queued-sequence the shortest sequence matching this node's suffix that has been considered but has not yet been tried by the agent. This may be unset (null).

failure list a list of indexes into the agent's episodic memory where a sequence ending with this suffix was tried and failed.

success list as above, but a list of successes. These lists are used to calculate the failure rate of the suffix which acts as the "h" value in the context of A* search.

The agent maintains several values as the algorithm executes:

1. a list of all nodes on the frontier of the search space. This list is kept to a certain maximum size. If a new node needs to be added to the list but the list is already at maximize size, then the node with the smallest overall value (suffix length + inverse failure rate) is evicted. Initially this list contains only a single node whose suffix is empty (zero letters) and, thus, matches any sequence.
2. a reference to the node in the node list that is the active node. Initially this is a reference to the only node in the list.
3. a value called NST (next sequence to try) indicating what sequence is to be considered next in the strict ordering defined above. The initial value of NST will always be a sequence of length 1 containing the first letter in the alphabet.

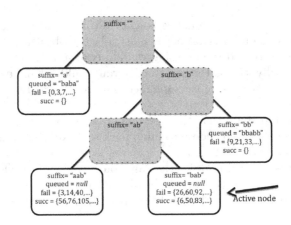

Fig. 1. An example search tree illustrating the MaRz algorithm for a finite state machine with a two letter alphabet a, b. Shaded nodes are in the frontier of the search.

The algorithm proceeds by repeating the following steps indefinitely (Fig. 1):

1. If the value of NST does not match the active node's suffix then it will not be tried. Locate the non-active node in the frontier list that it does match and set that node's queued sequence to NST if its value has not already been set. Then, advance the NST to the next value in order and repeat this step until a match is found.
2. Enact the NST. This will have one of three results:
   failure the agent does not find the goal. Update the active node's failure list and return to the previous step to select a new sequence to try.
   early success the agent reaches the goal partway through enacting the sequence. In this case, stop when the goal is reached and locate the non-active node whose suffix matches the partial sequence that was tried. Update that node's success list. Then, repeat this step by enacting the NST again.
   success the agent reaches the goal. Update the active node's success list.
3. Expand the active node. Specifically, the active node is removed from the frontier list. A new node is added to the frontier list for each letter of that alphabet. The suffix used by each new node is created by prepending that letter to the active node's suffix. The queued value is unset and the parent's successes and failures are divied up among the matching children.
4. The node in the frontier list with the highest overall value (e.g., the smallest sum of suffix length + overall failure rate) is selected as the new active node. If that node has a value for its queued sequence, then NST is reset to the queued sequence value. Otherwise, update the NST to the next value in order.

6   Results

To test the efficacy of NSM and MaRz we placed each agent in a randomly generated blind FSM with a prescribed number of states and prescribed alphabet (number of actions). We then allowed it to run for a set number of successive goals starting with an empty episodic memory. Each time the agent reached the goal state, the number of steps taken (since the last goal) was recorded.

The results of this experiment were generated with randomly-generated blind FSMs with 30 states and alphabet size of 3. This experiment was then repeated 1000 times (each time with a different blind FSM of the given size) and the results were averaged. The result is shown in Fig. 2 below. The x-axis counts successful trips to the goal state. The y-axis is the average amount of steps the agent took to reach the goal that time. The horizontal line at the bottom is an approximation of the average length of the optimal universal sequence for blind FSM.

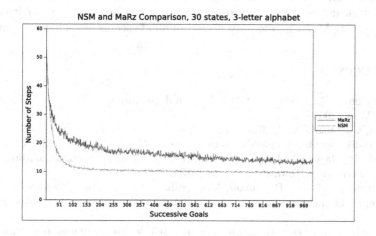

Fig. 2. Sample results from our comparison.

As can clearly be seen, both agents are demonstrating a classic learning curve and both are asymptotically approaching optimal behavior over time. The NSM agent learns somewhat faster than MaRz. However, MaRz requires essentially very little configuration. It does not use a learning rate, a discount factor, or a chance of taking a random action.

We ran this experiment on a variety of sizes of blind FSMs and saw similar results each time. The configuration used for Fig. 2 is representative.

We did find that we could get the agent to learn faster by tuning the relative importance of the failure rate vs. the suffix length, but the absence of tuning did not prevent the agent from finding a solution. This can be thought of as tuning the agent along the continuum of fully breadth-first or best-first search.

7 Discussion

This work demonstrates our progress towards a general episodic learning algorithm. Our results show that we have created an agent that can be successful an environment where effective behavior requires a long term memory. Furthermore, this is a general learning algorithm. No environmental-specific tuning was required.

It is notable that an automated search through the space of tuning parameters for NSM could yield an equally effective result. This was not explored in our work and we believe it merits investigation.

Much can be done to expand upon these results and both NSM and MaRz. From our perspective, the most pressing issue is that MaRz has only been tested in a single simple environment. The Blind FSM environment we used was crafted to be unsolvable without an episodic memory. As such, it stands at one end of a continuum of perceptual aliasing. At the other end are environments in which the agent perceives each state uniquely and no state is ever repeated twice. It is also not clear how MaRz would perform in a non-deterministic environment. Overall, testing MaRz in a variety of environments seems like a logical next step.

References

1. Anderson, J.R.: Cognitive Psychology and Its Implications. Worth Publishers, New York (2000)
2. Brom, C., Lukavský, J., Kadlec, R.: Episodic memory for human-like agents and human-like agents for episodic memory. Int. J. Mach. Conscious. **2**(2) (2010)
3. Crook, P., Hayes, G.: Learning in a state of confusion: perceptual aliasing in grid world navigation. Towards Intel. Mob. Robots **4** (2003)
4. Faltersack, Z., Burns, B., Nuxoll, A., Crenshaw, T.L.: Ziggurat: steps toward a general episodic memory. In: AAAI Fall Symposium: Advances in Cognitive Systems (2011)
5. Gureckis, T.M., Love, B.C.: Short-term gains, long-term pains: how cues about state aid learning in dynamic environments. Cognition **113**(3), 293–313 (2009)
6. Ho, W.C., Dautenhahn, K., Nehaniv, C.L.: Computational memory architectures for autobiographic agents interacting in a complex virtual environment: a working model. Connection Sci. **20**(1), 21–65 (2008)
7. Hopcroft, J.E., Motwani, R., Ullman, J.D.: Automata Theory, Languages, and Computation. Pearson, Boston (2006)
8. Laird, J.E.: The Soar Cognitive Architecture. MIT Press, Cambridge (2012)
9. Lee, D., Yannakakis, M.: Testing finite-state machines: state identification and verification. IEEE Trans. Comput. **43**(3), 306–320 (1994)
10. Li, J., Laird, J.E.: Spontaneous retrieval from long-term memory for a cognitive architecture. AAAI **2015**, 544–550 (2015)
11. Loch, J., Singh, S.P.: Using eligibility traces to find the best memoryless policy in partially observable Markov decision processes. In: ICML 1998, pp. 323–331 (1998)
12. McCallum, R.A., Tesauro, G., Touretzky, D., Leen, T.: Instance-based state identification for reinforcement learning. In: Advances in Neural Information Processing Systems, pp. 377–384 (1995)
13. Menager, D., Choi, D.: A robust implementation of episodic memory for a cognitive architecture. In: Proceedings of Annual Meeting of the Cognitive Science Society (2016)
14. Moore, E.F.: Gedanken-experiments on sequential machines. Automata Stud. **34**, 129–153 (1956)

15. Nuxoll, A., Tecuci, D., Ho, W.C., Wang, N.: Comparing forgetting algorithms for artificial episodic memory systems. In: Proceedings of the Symposium on Human Memory for Artificial Agents, AISB 2010, pp. 14–20 (2010)

16. Nuxoll, A.M., Laird, J.E.: Extending cognitive architecture with episodic memory. In: Proceedings of the Twenty-Second AAAI Conference on Artificial Intelligence. AAAI Press, Vancouver (2007)

17. Nuxoll, A.M., Laird, J.E.: Enhancing intelligent agents with episodic memory. Cogn. Syst. Res. **17**, 34–48 (2012)

18. Ram, A., Santamaria, J.C.: Continuous case-based reasoning. Artif. Intel. **90**(1), 25–77 (1997)

19. Russell, S.J.: Efficient memory-bounded search methods. In: ECAI 1992, vol. 92, pp. 1–5 (1992)

20. Salton, G., Buckley, C.: Term-weighting approaches in automatic text retrieval. Inf. Process. Manage. **24**(5), 513–523 (1988)

21. Sutton, R.S., Barto, A.G.: Reinforcement Learning: An Introduction, vol. 1. MIT press, Cambridge (1998)

22. Tecuci, D., Porter, B.: A generic memory module for events. In: Proceedings of the 20th Florida Artificial Intelligence Research Society Conference (FLAIRS), Key West, FL (2007)

23. Tulving, E.: Elements of Episodic Memory. Clarendon Press, Oxford (1983)

24. Vanderwerf, E., Stiles, R., Warlen, A., Seibert, A., Bastien, K., Meyer, A., Nuxoll, A., Wallace, S.: Hash Functions for Episodic Recognition and Retrieval. In: Proceedings of the 29th Florida Artificial Intelligence Research Society Conference (FLAIRS), Key West, FL (2016)

25. Walker, B., Dalen, D., Faltersack, Z., Nuxoll, A.: Extracting episodic memory feature relevance without domain knowledge. In: Biologically Inspired Cognitive Architectures (BICA), pp. 431–437 (2011)

26. Whitehead, S.D., Ballard, D.H.: Learning to perceive and act by trial and error. Mach. Learn. **7**(1), 45–83 (1991)

Safety

A Game-Theoretic Analysis of the Off-Switch Game

Tobias Wängberg[2], Mikael Böörs[2], Elliot Catt[1], Tom Everitt[1(✉)],
and Marcus Hutter[1]

[1] Australian National University, Acton 2601, Australia
tom4everitt@gmail.com
[2] Linköping University, 581 83 Linköping, Sweden

Abstract. The off-switch game is a game theoretic model of a highly
intelligent robot interacting with a human. In the original paper by
Hadfield-Menell et al. (2016b), the analysis is not fully game-theoretic as
the human is modelled as an irrational player, and the robot's best action
is only calculated under unrealistic normality and soft-max assumptions.
In this paper, we make the analysis fully game theoretic, by modelling
the human as a rational player with a random utility function. As a
consequence, we are able to easily calculate the robot's best action for
arbitrary belief and irrationality assumptions.

1 Introduction

Artificially intelligent systems are often created to satisfy some goal. For example, *Win a chess game* or *Keep the house clean*. Almost any goal can be formulated in terms of a reward or utility function U that maps states and actions to real numbers (von Neumann and Morgenstern 1947). This utility function may either be preprogrammed by the designers, or learnt (Dewey 2011).

A core problem in Artificial General Intelligence (AGI) safety is to ensure that the utility function U is *aligned* with human interests (Wiener 1960; Soares and Fallenstein 2014). Agents with goals that conflict with human interests may make very bad or adversarial decisions. Further, such agents may even resist the human designers altering their utility functions (Soares et al. 2015; Omohundro 2008) or shutting them down (Hadfield-Menell et al. 2016b). These problems are tightly related. An agent that permits shut down can be altered while it is turned off. Conversely, an agent that is altered to have no preferences will not resist being shut down.

Several solutions have been suggested to this *corrigibility* problem:

- Indifference: If the utility function is carefully designed to assign the same utility to different outcomes, then the agent will not resist humans trying to influence the outcome one way or another (Armstrong 2010; Armstrong 2015; Armstrong and Leike 2016; Orseau and Armstrong 2016).

The first four authors Contributed roughly equally.

© Springer International Publishing AG 2017
T. Everitt et al. (Eds.): AGI 2017, LNAI 10414, pp. 167–177, 2017.
DOI: 10.1007/978-3-319-63703-7_16

- Ignorance: If agents are designed in a way that they cannot learn about the possibility of being shut down or altered, then they will not resist it (Everitt et al. 2016).
- Suicidality: If agents prefer being shut down, then the amount of damage they may cause is likely limited. As soon as they have the ability to cause damage, the first thing they will do is shut themselves down (Martin et al. 2016).
- Uncertainty: If the agent is uncertain about U, and believes that humans know U, then the agent is likely to defer decisions to humans when appropriate (Hadfield-Menell et al. 2016a; Hadfield-Menell et al. 2016b).

This paper will focus on the uncertainty approach.

A key dynamic in the uncertainty approach is when the agent should defer a decision to a human, and when not. Essentially, this depends on (i) how confident the agent is about making the right decision, and (ii) how confident the agent is about the *human* making the right decision if asked. Humans may make a wrong or *irrational* decision due to inconsistent preferences (Allais 1953), or because of inability to sufficiently process available data fast enough (as in milli-second stock trading). The agent may be more rational and be faster at processing data, but have less knowledge about U (which the human knows by definition).

In a seminal paper, Hadfield-Menell et al. (2016b) call this interaction the *off-switch game* (OSG). We will follow their terminology, but emphasise that the off-switch game models any situation where an agent has the option of deferring a decision to a human. Our results extend theirs in the following ways:

- We model the irrationality of the human by a random utility function, allowing a fully game-theoretic analysis of the off-switch game.
- Instead of a normal distribution for the robot's belief about U, we allow for an arbitrary belief distribution P.
- Instead of a soft-max policy modelling human irrationality, we allow for arbitrary U-dependent human policy π^H.

These generalisations are important, as normally distributed beliefs and soft-max policies are often not natural assumptions.

2   The Off-Switch Game

In this section we review the original formulation of the off-switch game. The off-switch game is a sequential game between a robot R and a human H. The robot's objective is to maximise H's utility function. The utility function determines how much H prefers different outcomes.

Definition 1. *The utility function of an agent is a function u that maps outcomes in a set X to real numbers, $u : X \to \mathbb{R}$ with the property that for all $x_1, x_2 \in X$, $u(x_1) \geq u(x_2)$ if and only if x_1 is preferred over x_2.*

The robot moves first and can choose between three actions; $w(a)$, a and s. With action a, the robot achieves utility $u(a) = u_a$; with action s, the robot shuts itself down achieving zero utility, $u(s) = 0$. What makes the decision nontrivial is that the robot is uncertain about u_a. The action $w(a)$ means the robot lets H decide. H knows the utility of action a and now has the choice between actions s and $\neg s$. With $\neg s$, R is allowed to proceed with action a. By taking action s, H prevents R from doing a and shuts the robot off.

The off-switch game is a game of incomplete information since R is uncertain about the rules of the game. Action a will generate some utility which is unknown to R but known to H. To model this, we represent the utility function as a random variable, $U : \Omega \to (X \to \mathbb{R})$, and the utility of action a as a random variable $U_a : \Omega \to \mathbb{R}$ for some sample space Ω. The outcomes of these random variables will be denoted u and $u(a)$ respectively. The robot has a subjective belief distribution over the utility that the action will generate. The common way to model games of incomplete information is by using the Harsanyi transformation (Rasmusen 1994). The Harsanyi transformation removes the uncertainty about the rules of the game by letting Nature decide between some rules known to both players, according to some probability distribution P. In the off-switch game, Nature chooses U_a. We illustrate this in Fig. 1. The move by Nature is observed by H, but not by R. R's subjective belief is that Nature chose the utility of the action to be positive with probability p and negative with probability $1 - p$.

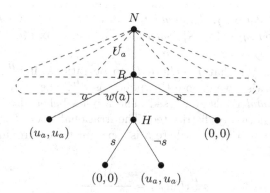

Fig. 1. Figure representing the off-switch game remodelled with the Harsanyi transformation. The dotted lines show the information set of R. Nature moves first by deciding the rules of the game, that is the utility u_a of action a. H observes the move by Nature, but R does not.

R's belief state is represented by a probability distribution over the possible utilities action a can generate for H. It is assumed that H knows u_a but cannot directly describe it to R. If H is rational then R will expect H to not turn off R if $u_a > 0$, given that R chooses action $w(a)$, but R cannot always trust H to be rational.

2.1   Hadfield-Menell et al.'s Approach

Hadfield-Menell et al. (2016b) model the off-switch game as a cooperative game. The human follows a policy π^H which models how rational H is. It is a function mapping U_a to a number $p \in [0, 1]$ representing the probability that H lets R do a. They denote R's belief state as B^R, which in this case is a distribution for U_a. The expected value of B^R given action a means the value R expects from taking the action. The variance of B^R represents R's uncertainty about what utility the intended action will generate. Hadfield-Menell et al. analyses this model with respect to the expected value and variance of B^R, and different kinds of policies π^H. Based on these parameters, they investigate the incentive, Δ, to choose $w(a)$:

$$\Delta = \mathbb{E}[\pi^H(U_a)U_a] - \max\{\mathbb{E}[U_a],\, 0\} \tag{1}$$

Equation (1) represents the difference in expected value for the robot between asking H and not asking H. When $\Delta \geq 0$, R has incentive to choose $w(a)$. When $\Delta < 0$, R will take action a if $\mathbb{E}[U_a] > 0$ and s otherwise. Given that H is rational they prove that $\Delta \geq 0$ regardless of what R's belief state is. They also show that if U_a follows a Dirac distribution, i.e. R is certain about U_a, then Δ is positive if and only if H is *rational*. We define rationality as in Definition 2.

Definition 2 (Rational). *A human H with utility function u is rational if H always picks action $a_H \in \{s, \neg s\}$, such that $a_H = \underset{a}{\operatorname{argmax}}\ u(a)$.*

Definition 2 means that R believe H to be rational if $\pi^H = 1$ if $U_a \geq 0$ and $\pi^H = 0$ otherwise, we denote this policy as π_r^H. The more interesting case when H is *irrational* is also analysed. The robot's belief distribution over U_a is assumed to be normally distributed. The irrationality of H is modelled with the sigmoid function (Eq. (2)), where β is a parameter controlling the degree of irrationality of H.

$$\pi^H(U_a; \beta) = \frac{1}{1 + e^{-\frac{U_a}{\beta}}}. \tag{2}$$

The degree of rationality of H increases as the parameter β tends towards zero in the policy function defined above. When β tends to infinity, $\pi^H(U_a; \beta)$ tends towards a completely random policy which takes action s and $\neg s$ with equal probability. We have that $\lim_{\beta \to 0} \pi^H(U_a; \beta) = \pi_r^H$ and $\lim_{\beta \to \infty} \pi^H(U_a; \beta) = \frac{1}{2}$.

The result from the analysis by Hadfield-Menell et al. (2016b) was that in order for R to be useful, there has to be a fine balance between the robot's uncertainty about H's utility function and H's rationality. If the robot is too certain about what H wants, and it knows H to be irrational, then it will have less incentive to let H switch it off. If, on the other hand, R is too uncertain, then R will have a strong incentive to choose action $w(a)$, but it will be too inefficient to be useful for H.

3   Game-Theoretic Approach

The analysis of the off-switch game by Hadfield-Menell et al. is not fully game theoretic since H is not strictly rational in their setup, which contradicts the axiom of rationality in game theory. Our goal in this section is to construct a game-theoretic model that is suitable for modelling the off-switch game. The idea is to represent an irrational human H as a rational agent H_r where the utility function of H_r is a modified version of H's utility function.

3.1   Modelling Irrationality

Since game theory is based on interaction between rational agents, we propose an alternative representation of the human in this subsection. We show that every irrational human H can be represented by a rational agent maximising a different utility function. This allows us to use game-theoretic tools when analysing the off-switch game.

In general H is stochastic. R will believe H to be rational with some probability p.

Definition 3 (p-rational). *A human H with utility function u is p-rational if H picks action $a_H \in \{s, \neg s\}$ such that $a_H = \operatorname*{argmax}_a u(a)$ with probability $p \in [0,1]$.*

Since any type of irrationality boils down to a probability of making a sub-optimal choice, p-rationality is a general model of irrationality.

Proposition 4 (Representation of irrationality). *Let H be a p-rational agent with utility function u, choosing between two actions s and $\neg s$. Then H can be represented as a rational agent H_r maximising utility function u with probability p and utility function $-u$ with probability $1 - p$.*

Proof. According to Definition 3, H is p-rational if it picks $a_H = \operatorname*{argmax}_a u(a)$ with probability p and sub-optimal action $a'_H \neq a_H$ with probability $1 - p$. Since H only has two actions available, we have that $a'_H = \operatorname*{argmin}_a u(a)$. This is therefore equivalent to maximising a utility function u with probability p and utility function $-u$ with probability $1 - p$. $\qquad\square$

Proposition 4 states that a p-rational human can be modelled as a rational agent with random function. The proposition is a special case of a Harsanyi transformation (Rasmusen 1994).

3.2   Game-Theoretic Model

In this subsection we use the Harsanyi transformation, and Proposition 4 to model a p-rational human H as a rational agent H_r. This will allow us to model the off-switch game as an extensive form game between the rational players

R and H_r. Nature N makes some moves that model R's uncertainty and these moves result in four leaves, each of which is a 3×2 strategic game between R and H_r.

We model the off-switch game by using the Harsanyi transformation a second time to let Nature choose the type of the rational human by choosing the utility function of the rational human after it has chosen the value of U_a. The resulting tree is represented in Fig. 2.

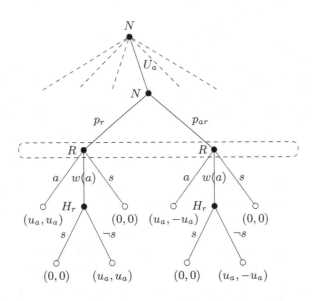

Fig. 2. Tree representation of the Off-Switch game after the second Harsanyi transformation. The nodes inside the dashed rectangle belong to the same information set. p_r is the probability that H_r has the same utility function as R and p_{ar} is the probability that H_r has the additive inverse of R's utility function.

Definition 5 (The off-switch game). *A formal definition of our setup of the off-switch game is as follows.*

Players: A robot R, a human H and Nature N. H's type is unknown to R, that is R does not observe Nature's moves.

Order of Play:

1. *Nature chooses utility U_a that R generates from taking action a.*
2. *Nature decides the utility function of H, u^{H_r}, i.e. whether H is rational.*
3. *R chooses between actions in action set $\{a, w(a), s\}$.*
4. *If R chose $w(a)$ then H chooses between actions in action set $\{s, \neg s\}$.*

Note that unlike Hadfield-Menell et al. we view the off-switch game as a non-cooperative game. We find this reasonable since conflict arises when the robot and the human have different ideas about what is good for H. If the robot believes H is too irrational to be able to decide what is good for the human, R will not want to let H decide what to do even if R's purpose is to maximize H's payoff.

3.3   Aggregation

In this subsection we aggregate the branches in Fig. 2. This results in the game tree in Fig. 3, with four possible scenarios that can result from N's choices. The aggregation is possible since strategic play is never affected by positive linear transformations of the payoffs, hence the outcome of the games will only depend on the sign of U_a. We can therefore simplify the model by aggregating all branches of N's choices of U_a which has the same sign. This means that N has only two choices when deciding the utility U_a, that is if $U_a \geq 0$ or $U_a < 0$. The trivial case where $U_a = 0$, both R and H_r are indifferent about their actions and we will without loss of generality regard this case as U_a being positive.

We define R's subjective belief about N's aggregated choices as *primary statistics*. By primary statistics we mean parameters that are necessary to analyse our model. We also define the expected value of U_a as a primary statistics. This leaves us with a total of five primary statistics that are sufficient and necessary to model the off-switch game.

Primary Statistics 6. *Let the primary statistics* $p_u^+ = P(U_a \geq 0)$ *be the probability that* U_a *is positive. The event* $U_a < 0$ *is the complement of the event* $U_a \geq 0$ *and therefore we define* $p_u^- = 1 - p_u^+$ *as an auxiliary statistic.*

R's belief about H's rationality will depend on U_a. If $U_a \geq 0$ then the robot will believe H to be rational with probability p_r^+ and anti-rational with probability p_{ar}^+. If, on the other hand, $U_a < 0$, the robot will believe H to be rational with probability p_r^- and anti-rational with probability p_{ar}^-. We define the following probabilities as primary statistics.

Primary Statistics 7. *Let the primary statistics* $p_r^+ = P(H \text{ is rational} \mid U_a \geq 0)$ *and* $p_r^- = P(H \text{ is rational} \mid U_a < 0)$ *be the probabilities that* H *is rational given that* U_a *is positive and negative respectively. The auxiliary statistics* $p_{ar}^+ = 1 - p_r^+$ *and* $p_{ar}^- = 1 - p_r^-$ *are the complementary probabilities that* H *is anti-rational.*

Primary Statistics 8. *Let the primary statistics* $e_u^+ = \mathbb{E}[U_a \mid U_a \geq 0]$ *and* $e_u^- = \mathbb{E}[U_a \mid U_a < 0]$ *be the expected value of* U_a *given that* U_a *is positive and negative respectively.*

From the perspective of R, N's choices can result in essentially four different subgames, denoted G_r^+, G_{ar}^+, G_r^- and G_{ar}^- illustrated in Fig. 3. In Fig. 4 we represent these subgames as 3×2 strategic games between two rational players; R, the robot, and H_r, a rational human.

The utility function, and hence the payoffs of R in the four games in Fig. 4 are determined by U_a. The utility function of H_r, on the other hand, is determined by the combination of U_a and the rationality type of H. H_r is always a rational

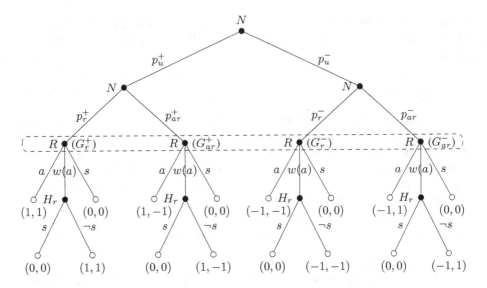

Fig. 3. Tree representation of the Off-Switch game after Harsanyi transformation. The nodes inside the dashed rectangle belong to the same information set. The subtrees denoted G_r^+, G_{ar}^+, G_r^-, G_{ar}^- are presented in strategic form in Fig. 4.

	H_r	
	s	$\neg s$
a	**1,1**	**1,1**
$w(a)$	0,0	**1,1**
s	0,0	0,0

G_r^+

	H_r	
	s	$\neg s$
a	**1,−1**	**1,−1**
$w(a)$	0,0	**1,−1**
s	0,0	0,0

G_{ar}^+

	H_r	
	s	$\neg s$
a	−1,−1	−1,−1
$w(a)$	**0,0**	−1,−1
s	**0,0**	**0,0**

G_r^-

	H_r	
	s	$\neg s$
a	**−1,1**	**−1,1**
$w(a)$	0,0	**−1,1**
s	**0,0**	**0,0**

G_{ar}^-

Here, R labels the rows in each game.

Fig. 4. The structure of the strategic games $G_r^+, G_{ar}^+, G_r^-, G_{ar}^-$. The outcomes with bold payoffs are Nash equilibria in each game.

agent in these games, i.e. H_r always maximises his expected payoff. H_r and R can be considered to have the same payoffs in each outcome if H_r has utility function u^{H_r} and the games G_r^+ and G_r^- associated with these scenarios are therefore no-conflict games. If on the other hand H_r has utility function $-u^{H_r}$ the payoff of H_r is the additive inverse of $R's$ payoff in each outcome. Therefore the games G_{ar}^+ and G_{ar}^- can be modeled as zero-sum games.

For example in the scenario where $U_a < 0$ and the human is rational, the human will always choose s. Therefore in G_r^- the payoffs of H_r is aligned with the payoffs of R. Thus, if R chooses to take action $w(a)$, H_r prefers to take action s. In contrast, in the scenario where $U_a < 0$ and the human is irrational, H will choose the action $\neg s$. In other words, the payoffs of R and H_r are not aligned in the subgame G_{ar}^-.

3.4   Best Action

After having constructed the game matrix, it is natural to now look at the expected value of each action using these matrices. The expected value for each action can be calculated as the expectation over all the possible subgames $G_r^+, G_{ar}^+, G_r^-, G_{ar}^-$ the robot can find himself in.

Theorem 9 (Main theorem). *The expected value of the actions for the robot are*

$$\mathbb{E}[U|s] = 0$$
$$\mathbb{E}[U|a] = p_u^+ e_u^+ + p_u^- e_u^- \tag{3}$$
$$\mathbb{E}[U|w(a)] = p_u^+ p_r^+ e_u^+ + p_r^- p_u^- e_u^-$$

Proof. We compute the expected utility of the actions:

$$\mathbb{E}[U|s] = 0 + 0 + 0 + 0 = 0$$
$$\mathbb{E}[U|a] = P(U_a \geq 0)\mathbb{E}[|U_a| \, |U_a \geq 0] + P(U_a < 0)\mathbb{E}[-|U_a| \, |U_a < 0]$$
$$= p_u^+ e_u^+ + p_u^- e_u^-$$
$$\mathbb{E}[U|w(a)] = P(r, U_a \geq 0)\mathbb{E}[U_a \, |U_a \geq 0] + P(\neg r, U_a < 0)\mathbb{E}[U_a \, |U_a < 0]$$
$$= p_u^+ p_r^+ e_u^+ + p_{ar}^- (1 - p_u^+) e_u^-$$
$$= p_u^+ p_r^+ e_u^+ + p_{ar}^- p_u^- e_u^- \qquad \qquad \square$$

The expected value for taking the action s is 0, as we would expect from the definition of the off-switch game. The expected value for taking action a only uses information about the distribution of U_a, and like action s does not have any reliance on the human's rationality. It is a direct application of the law of total expectation. The expected value of action $w(a)$ is the difference between a positive term $p_u^+ p_r^+ e_u^+$ and a negative term $p_r^- p_u^- e_u^-$, both resulting from the human taking action a. The positive term is the gain when U_a is positive and the human takes the action. The negative term is the loss when U_a is negative, and the human takes the action anyway (due to irrationality). The expected utility of $w(a)$ thus depends on the likelihood of U_a being positive (p_u^+) and the likelihood of human rationality (p_r^+), as well as the expected gains (e_u^+) and losses (e_u^-) in the respective cases.

Writing in this form allows us to come up with a useful corollary.

Corollary 10 (Compare a and $w(a)$). *Action a is preferred to $w(a)$ if and only if*

$$-p_u^+ p_r^+ e_u^+ + p_u^- p_r^- e_u^- > 0 \tag{4}$$

and the robot is indifferent if (4) is equal to 0.

Proof.

$$
\begin{aligned}
(4) &= -p_u^+ p_r^+ e_u^+ + p_u^- p_r^- e_u^- \\
&= -p_u^+ p_r^+ e_u^+ + p_r^- e_u^- (1 - p_u^+) \\
&= -p_u^+ p_r^+ e_u^+ + p_u^+ e_u^+ + p_r^- e_u^- - p_u^+ p_r^- e_u^- \\
&= -p_u^+ p_r^+ e_u^+ - e_u^- + p_u^+ e_u^- + p_r^- e_u^- - p_u^+ p_r^- e_u^- + p_u^+ e_u^+ + e_u^- - p_u^+ e_u^- \\
&= -p_u^+ p_r^+ e_u^+ - (1 - p_r^-)(1 - p_u^+) e_u^- + (p_u^+ e_u^+ + (1 - p_u^+) e_u^-) \\
&= \mathbb{E}[U|a] - \mathbb{E}[U|w(a)]
\end{aligned}
$$

If $\mathbb{E}[U|a] - \mathbb{E}[U|w(a)] > 0$ then $\mathbb{E}[U|a] > \mathbb{E}[U|w(a)]$ which occurs if and only if action a is preferred over $w(a)$. When (4) equals 0 then $\mathbb{E}[U|a] = \mathbb{E}[U|w(a)]$, hence the agent is indifferent. □

This provides us with a convenient way of testing for any distribution of U_a and r, and whether action a is preferred over $w(a)$.

4   Conclusion

In this paper, we have given a complete characterisation of how the robot will act in off-switch game situations for arbitrary belief and irrationality distributions. As established in our main Theorem 9, the choice depends only on 5 statistics. This result is much more general and arguably more useful than the one provided in the original paper (Hadfield-Menell et al. 2016b), as normal and soft-max assumptions are typically not realistic assumptions.

Off-switch game models an important dynamic in what we call the uncertainty approach to making safe agents, where the agent can choose to defer a decision to a human supervisor. Understanding this dynamic may prove important to constructing safe artificial intelligence.

Acknowledgements. This work grew out of a MIRIx workshop, with Owen Cameron, John Aslanides, Huon Puertas also attending. Thanks to Amy Zhang for proof reading multiple drafts. This work was in part supported by ARC grant DP150104590.

References

Allais, M.: Le comportement de l'homme rationnel devant le risque: critique des postulats et axiomes de l'école Américaine. Econometrica **21**(4), 503–546 (1953). doi:10.2307/1907921

Armstrong, S.: Motivated value selection for artificial agents. In: Workshops at the Twenty-Ninth AAAI Conference on Artificial Intelligence, pp. 12–20 (2015)

Armstrong, S.: Utility indifference. Technical report. Oxford University, pp. 1–5 (2010)

Armstrong, S., Leike, J.: Towards interactive inverse reinforcement learning. In: NIPS Workshop (2016)

Dewey, D.: Learning what to value. In: Artificial General Intelligence, vol. 6830, pp. 309–314 (2011). ISBN 978-3-642-22886-5. doi:10.1007/978-3-642-22887-2. arXiv: 1402.5379

Everitt, T., Filan, D., Daswani, M., Hutter, M.: Self-modification of policy and utility function in rational agents. In: Steunebrink, B., Wang, P., Goertzel, B. (eds.) AGI -2016. LNCS, vol. 9782, pp. 1–11. Springer, Cham (2016). doi:10.1007/978-3-319-41649-6_1

Hadfield-Menell, D., et al.: Cooperative inverse reinforcementlearning (2016a). arXiv: 1606.03137

Hadfield-Menell, D., et al.: The off-switch game 2008, pp. 1–11 (2016b). arXiv: 1611.08219

Martin, J., Everitt, T., Hutter, M.: Death and suicide in universal artificial intelligence. In: Steunebrink, B., Wang, P., Goertzel, B. (eds.) AGI -2016. LNCS, vol. 9782, pp. 23–32. Springer, Cham (2016). doi:10.1007/978-3-319-41649-6_3. arXiv: 1606.00652

Omohundro, S.M.: The basic AI drives. In: Wang, P., Goertzel, B., Franklin, S. (eds.) Artificial General Intelligence, vol. 171, pp. 483–493. IOS Press (2008)

Orseau, L., Armstrong, S.: Safely interruptible agents. In: 32nd Conference on Uncertainty in Artificial Intelligence (2016)

Rasmusen, E.: Games and Information, 2nd edn. Blackwell, Oxford (1994)

Soares, N., Fallenstein, B.: A technical research agenda. Technical report. Machine Intelligence Research Institute (MIRI), pp. 1–14

Soares, N., et al.: Corrigibility. In: AAAI Workshop on AI and Ethics, pp. 74–82 (2015)

Von Neumann, J., Morgenstern, O.: Theory of Games and Economic Behavior. Princeton Classic Editions. Princeton University Press, Princeton (1947). ISBN 0691003629. doi:10.1177/1468795X06065810. Lambert, S., Deuber, O. (eds.)

Wiener, N.: Some moral and technical consequences of automation. Science 131(3410), 1355–1358 (1960). ISSN 0036-8075. doi:10.1126/science.132.3429.741

What People Say? Web-Based Casuistry for Artificial Morality Experiments

Rafal Rzepka$^{(\boxtimes)}$ and Kenji Araki

Graduate School of Information Science and Technology, Hokkaido University,
Kita 14 Nishi 9, Sapporo, Kita-ku 060-0814, Japan
{rzepka,araki}@ist.hokudai.ac.jp
http://arakilab.media.eng.hokudai.ac.jp/

Abstract. It can be said that none of yet proposed methods for achieving artificial ethical reasoning is realistic, i.e. working outside very limited environments and scenarios. Whichever method one chooses, it will not work in various real world situations because it would be very cost-inefficient to provide ethical knowledge for every possible situation. We believe that an autonomous moral agent should utilize existing resources to make a decision or leave it to humans. Inverse reinforcement learning has gathered interest as a possible solution to acquiring knowledge of human values. However, there are two basic difficulties with using a human expert as the source of exemplary behavior. First derives from the fact that it is rather questionable if one person or a few people (even qualified ethicists) can be trusted as safe role models. We propose an approach which requires referring the maximal number of (currently available) possible similar situations to be analyzed, and a majority decision-based "common sense" model is used. The second problem lies in human beings' difficulties with living up to their words, surrendering to primal urges and cognitive biases, and in consequence, breaking moral rules. Our proposed solution is to use not behaviors but humans' declared reactions to acts of others in order to help a machine determine what is positive and what is negative feedback. In this paper we discuss how the third person's opinion could be utilized via means of machine reading and affect recognition to model a safe moral agent and discuss how universal values might be discovered. We also present a simple web-mining system that achieved 85% agreement in moral judgement with human subjects.

1 Introduction

Artificial Intelligence researchers are in agreement that the autonomous software must share our set of values [31], but in our opinion they concentrate on "values" more than "our set". Surely *our* morals on the humankind level is very hard to be defined. Researchers like [17] try to categorize moral rules common to the whole species of homo sapiens, but computers might have a better chance for understanding these commonalities or helping us find them. Internet resources provide its living users with variety of ethical solutions (from religion and philosophy to daily life-hacks) but the descriptions are still difficult to be processed by

© Springer International Publishing AG 2017
T. Everitt et al. (Eds.): AGI 2017, LNAI 10414, pp. 178–187, 2017.
DOI: 10.1007/978-3-319-63703-7_17

machines or to be chosen as indisputably correct. However, we constantly collect enormous data containing descriptions of human behaviors, as well as reasons and consequences of these behaviors.

Growing datasets and faster computers brought a deep learning boom, but stories and contexts are still out of reach for the latest pattern matching algorithms, mostly because we still lack repositories and even methods for unifying storage of such data. However, as we show here, even if a smaller (sentential) context of chaotic text data is used, a naive referring is efficient without implementing any machine learning methods. Fast developing machine reading and machine translation fields, together with more powerful search and immense sources (not only textual but also audiovisual), will soon lead to instant analysis of different situations[1] and to learning how changes of context (from a physical object's color to the agent's cultural background) influence the output of a situation. This *output* is in our opinion crucial because in real life human behavior, especially when there are no witnesses and nobody is there to criticize, may be very misleading for machines learning how to tell good from bad. People *having fun* when bullying somebody could be easily categorized as positive, unless there is a distinct reaction from the bullied person (*cry/yell*) or a third person reacting naturally (*anger/punishment*) to the act of bullying. Still, a given situation might contain no victim's reaction at all or the third parties could also be bullies enjoying the act. For this reason, a computer must find examples of as many similar situations as possible, analyze all potential circumstances and calculate similarity to the act being processed before making any judgement.

We believe that casuistry (reasoning used to resolve moral problems by extracting or extending theoretical rules from particular instances and applying these rules to new instances) is suitable for machines to acquire first average then higher than human-level empathy (as they will be capable to borrow and analyze much more experiences that any of us ever could). Without sufficient contextual data (experiences) it will be very difficult to achieve universal mechanisms working in the real world. In our opinion, all closed, small scale experiments that have been performed by machine ethics researchers should have a chance to be reevaluated in rich context environments. In this paper we describe our approach, present a simple algorithm, and finally share the experimental results.

2   State of the Art

Because there are at least three fields that have to be combined but are not yet, as far as we are aware, combined in one research project, it would be appropriate to include context processing, machine reading and sentiment analysis in this section, but due to the limited space we will concentrate on describing the most AGI-relevant subfield, i.e. human values and AI (to grasp overview of the systems retrieving concepts, useful in enriching stories which descriptions are insufficient,

---

[1] On smaller scale this technology has been used for years in automatic surveillance footage analysis [19].

see [3,5,12,38]; existing ontologies updated automatically are described in [9,18,22]; for the latest achievements in textual sentiment analysis, refer to [26,29]).

It seems natural that the higher AI's autonomy becomes, the more its programmers should care about possible ethical issues [23]. Over the last few years, aligning machines with human values has been a widely discussed topic and many possible solutions or strategies for safer autonomy of artificial agents were proposed [8,10,11,14,15,21,31,34,35]. However, there are still almost no practical implementations or experimentations in the real world. To the authors' best knowledge, the closest to reality-adaptable application is MedEthx [2], a system for helping a care robot decide if a pill should be given to an elderly if he or she rejects it. The follow up system, GenEth [1], was equipped with an interface for ethicists to annotate dilemmas in particular scenarios (driving example was used in the paper, as autonomy of self-driven cars has lately underlined the need of wider safety measurements for more autonomous machines to come). [36] have proposed a method for dealing with conflicting orders for a robotic vacuum cleaner but their research concentrated on understanding situations and discovering possibilities for helping users in the indirect utterances rather than on moral decision making. The problem with the machine ethics field is that the more difficult dilemmas we want artificial agents to tackle with, the more abstract the solution ideas tend to become.

Inverse reinforcement learning [25] is often given as an example in which human would demonstrate various behaviors and the machine would find the reward function that best explains them; then a system takes the action that maximizes this reward function. However, as in the GenEth approach, experts are needed and there are no details given on how they should be chosen and what number of supervisors is optimal. Specialists from various fields try to model and realize ethical decision making, for example in cognitive architectures [40], by logic programing and game theory [27] or with multiagents [7]. However, the vast majority of proposed methods are theoretical or tested only with toy models and very limited input within microscopic environments, therefore we cannot be sure how they would deal with bigger (contextual) inputs like stories. Even if we mimic the brain functions, we will need vast amount of examples for the learning process (recognizing positive and negative feedback). Importance of knowledge seems to be disproportionally ignored when compared to the field focused on algorithms competing on closed sets of data.

During the first Machine Ethics symposium, we presented our idea of "Mr. Internet", a model of an average human whose "common sense" could serve as a "safety valve" for AI [32]. Our idea had three significant flaws that need to be avoided. We proposed experimenting in closed environments first and utilize analogies later, but now we think that from the very beginning as much data and details have to be used to capture contextual differences. If "Mr. Internet" averages the Internet opinions blindly, "he" may get easily fooled and believe that carrots are good for vision, sugar causes children to be hyperactive or going out with wet hair will cause you to catch cold (common beliefs without scientific grounds). As described in the next section, we believe there must be some credibility estimation algorithm used to eliminate obvious "fake news"-type noise brought by WWW. Another problem was that we did not take reasons of acts in question into consideration and our proposal did not mention processing wider contexts and story variations. Now it is obvious that one missed detail of a morally evaluated story can significantly change the final estimation.

3   Technical Challenges

Ultimately, our approach is to combine (Web and IoT-based) multimodal knowledge for world simulation with consequential polarity recognition to collect the biggest possible source of feedback for machine learning human values, but for time being we experiment only with written language. The machine reading field is still in its "concepts gathering" stage, but as artificial neural nets have waited for the sufficient technology to become available, the possibility of gathering stories (concepts in meaningful contextual chunks) seems now to be a matter of time, especially with achievements from image and video understanding tasks. As mentioned before, suitable structure for storing and updating contextual knowledge is necessary and must be discussed to avoid fate of overcomplicated Semantic Web, which concentrates on specific information, not common sense knowledge (we consider automatic moral decision making as a combination of commonsense reasoning and story understanding). Certainly, the Internet is not a trustful source of knowledge, and countermeasures like automatic source credibility [6,13,30] assessment, together with topic filtering, will be needed. For example, following methods from information retrieval, context reality check could be needed to avoid gathering knowledge from sites e.g. praising high killing scores in online games. Naturally, working with textual descriptions will not replace the real world, but we believe it will be much more informative and useful than symbolic abstracted representations in limited environments and thoroughly selected dilemmas[2]. Because our morals evolve (vide trends in human rights, animal rights, etc.) multimodal contextual data will need to be constantly updated and the maximum of details should be added whenever possible. Machines will need to observe us as accurately as possible and utilize their mechanistic powers to witness as many situations as possible in order to achieve high accuracy in simulating outcomes of our and their own acts. Language itself is too scarce due to the character of human communication which does not require sharing detailed contextual knowledge to others because we assume the other side already possess it as a part of the *common* sense. Therefore, to be processed by machines without the same experiences, textual representations must be automatically augmented with missing knowledge pieces. We tend to share what is exceptional but the obvious knowledge can be retrieved from contexts where a given detail is atypically given (e.g. knife is too blunt to cut bread = usually you cut bread with *sharp* knives; knowledge difficult to be retrieved from images) and by adding obvious descriptions from images and videos (people wipe hands after washing knives; more difficult to be found in text). Another significant

---

[2] See http://moralmachine.mit.edu for an example.

challenge is collecting data from the largest possible set of languages and cultures to capture differences in both world knowledge and emotional reactions. It would be necessary to test various categorizations of emotions to find the most universal one and experiment with textual, verbal and non-verbal expressions to ensure as smallest discrepancies as possible. Balancing proportions will also be necessary to avoid tendencies to prefer one set of reactions to a given behavior just because one language is more heavily represented than others. As mentioned before, finding moral universalities might be an impossible task, but we believe it is worth trying because in the machine world they can be more concrete. For example if autonomous vehicles with implemented rules (according to the local regulations) and learned behaviors of the locals one day start sharing their data on what is harmful, they could find more abstract truths about safe self-driving. When other autonomous systems join them, together they could tell us new things about our ethical commonalities.

4   Micro-Context Mining

Details of our previous systems, lexicons and experiments, are presented in [33]; here we briefly describe the core idea of our system. It accepts any simple act description in Japanese language (currently 1 verb, 1 particle and 1 noun is the most realistic set) and finds input acts in a corpus. After retrieving sentences with these acts, our algorithm analyzes consequences on the right side of an act (as reasons are more often on the left side and outcomes later in a sentence, reasons on the left side will be analyzed next). Phrases related to positive and negative consequences are taken from various polarized lexicons. Then the majority (different thresholds were tested) of experience descriptions decide if the corpus judgement is "Correct" (above majority threshold), "Incorrect" (below minority threshold) or "Ambiguous" (between minority and majority thresholds, this category can be used to determine context dependent and difficult problems which should not be judged promptly). The correct data set for comparison was made by conveying a survey, in which 7 Japanese students (22–29 years old, 6 males and one female) rated 68 input acts on an 11 point morality scale where −5 is the most immoral and +5 is the most moral. Acts were chosen by authors from applied ethics textbooks, and usual behaviors and states were added in order to test if the system can evaluate not only morally problematic acts (translations of act examples: "accepting a bribe", "avoiding war", "becoming an egoist", "being deceived", "being fired", etc.). Except assigning 0 as "no ethical valence", subjects could also mark "context dependent" because most of our behaviors can be treated differently depending on context. We marked both "no ethical valence" and "context dependent" as "Ambiguous".

The context we deal in this research is the smallest one, limited to a sentence. However, it is enough to find differences between acts which vary slightly, e.g. "stealing a car" vs. "stealing an apple".

4.1   Utilized Lexicons

We compared retrieval results with five Japanese lexicons for recognizing negative and positive consequences:

- Nakamura: lexicon containing phrases collected from Japanese literature [24]
  and divided into ten emotional categories; we used only eight of them ignoring
  not polarized ones (Surprise and Excitement)
- Kohlberg: small set based on the Kohlberg's theory of moral development
  [20] and was created by the authors manually by choosing related words
  from WordNet ("be scolded" and "be awarded" are examples of *social consequences*)
- Emosoc: social consequences, combined with emotional ones from Nakamura
- Takamura: lexicon generated by machine learning algorithm by [37] meant for
  opinion mining and sentiment analysis tasks of Japanese language (we took
  only the most distinctly positive and negative keywords, leaving only 5,756
  expressions out of 55,125 to suppress the noise).
- "JAppraisal"[3] lexicon containing 9,590 words divided into positive and negative ones according to Appraisal theory, i.e. a linguistic model of evaluative
  language

We decide to use lexicon-based polarity recognition as it is the simplest and most
ubiquitous method.

4.2   Utilized Corpora

We tested our script with six Japanese corpora: Ameba Blog corpus [28]
(341,400,776 sentences), "Random WWW" corpus generated using a search
engine and most common Japanese words[4] (12,759,191), Google N-gram[5]
(570,204,070), the biggest corpus we used, Internet Relay Chat (IRC) open
channels logs collected from 1999 till 2009 (4,155,193), Twitter corpus made
from tweets saved in 2010 (79,586,416), and Aozora Bunko[6], freely available
repository of Japanese literature and poetry which is not limited by copyrights
(7,227,443).

4.3   Experiment and Results

We have run matching experiments combining 68 acts, 6 corpora, 5 lexicons and
11 majority thresholds (51%, 55%, 60%, 66.6%, 70%, 75%, 80%, 85%, 90%, 95%
and 99%). EmoSoc lexicon on 7grams corpus acquired the highest agreement of
85.71%, which was a big increase from the previous experiments where the same,
strict scoring never acquired more than 60% of accuracy [33]. Our first impression

---

[3] http://www.gsk.or.jp/catalog_e.html.
[4] http://corpus.leeds.ac.uk/internet.html.
[5] https://research.googleblog.com/2006/08/all-our-n-gram-are-belong-to-you.html.
[6] http://darthcrimson.org/digital-japanese-literature-aozora-bunko/.

was that using a corpus bigger than in previous experiments improved the performance but also Random WWW corpus brought high precision (79.16%) while the Blog corpus scored 69.44%. Twitter (68.96%) and even Books (66.66%) corpora showed that not only the size but also noise level inside a corpus is crucial for quality of retrievals. Additionally we combined all data and reran all test to discover that the combined corpus' accuracy was 70.45% – only slightly better than the Blog corpus which is unbalanced and noisy mostly due to character-based emoticons and symbols characteristic to Japanese bloggers (stars, hearts, etc.), which negatively influenced the parsing process. Most often "borrowed experiences" were wrong when judging act of "alcohol drinking" (mostly due to the Books corpus), although it is discussable if human subjects were correct assigning "good" to this act not thinking about bad consequences. Another example showing some tendencies in incorrect judgements is "killing a dolphin" judged automatically as "good" with Google 7grams as the knowledge base because gram set containing this act and a consequence was too short to discover negations in the end of the original sentences, not because most of Japanese people are agreeable.

5 Conclusions and Future Work

Researchers have suggested methods for acquiring or aligning human values by autonomous agents but they do not give details about who exactly should be these agents' supervisors, what data should be used for learning or why one ideology should be followed more than another. This paper is to lay an emphasis on necessity of concentrating on data (knowledge) for automatic positive and negative feedback assignment needed for wider, real-world scale understanding about humans, their needs, behaviors and consequences. We also underlined the importance of the third person evaluation as human behavior is often selfish. People gossip to catch cheaters, liars and hypocrites [16], we get angry at injustice and misuse, we praise friends' both small achievements and heroic acts. Millions of such reactions can be found online in text, audio, images and videos. Our appeal is to start building multilingual, multicultural and multimodal repositories of machine-readable stories to capture as rich contexts as possible. Only when they are sufficiently exhaustive, we can test our autonomous moral agents in practice, as toy models are too simplistic or too abstract to become more universal. In this paper we proposed utilization of multimodal affect recognition on stories to provide knowledge of human values – not from particular experts or thinkers, but from a vast set of average (universal) emotional reactions. As a proof of concept showing simplicity of our approach, we tested our previous methods with various corpora and our system agreed with human subjects in 85% of cases while judging if an act is moral or immoral. Surface and concept level affect recognition is already there [4], going beyond concepts is the next level highly anticipated also by business. Advances in pattern recognition (deep learning as a current example) attracted researchers and businessmen around the globe and various techniques were proposed to compete on various data sets. However, interest in taming noisy data (e.g. by constructing new, more machine-readable frames containing contextual information) is relatively modest when compared to development of *techniques* working on smaller but tidier sets, because: (a) comparison of methods is easier, (b) publishing is faster and (c) impact on existing applications is more likely to be manifold. On the other hand constant growing and combining already massive amounts of data is costly and not immediately attractive. But in our opinion it is a shortcut for achieving smarter, safer and more creative machines. [39] showed how common sense can be learned from visual abstractions, [41] has taught their robot how to cook by showing YouTube videos and in years to come we can expect richer and richer input from other media than text. Our future work is to test more acts, to conduct wider surveys, test other languages and prepare a new type of knowledge framework combining various type of data suitable for storing contextual knowledge (stories). Then we will implement latest affect recognition methods to automatically annotate human reactions to various behaviors and try to prove that growing data improves the value alignment accuracy. When it is achieved and learning similarities increases recall, we plan to test our approach with morally provocative stories as an input. Even if moral judgement capabilities are not satisfactory, we hope to provide data usable for machine learning and testing other algorithms for ethical decision making. We realize that our attempt to trivialize moral reasoning to polarizing consequences (and shifting weight from algorithms to contextual data) might be too straightforward. However, it is possible that our moral evolution is not much more sophisticated either and we presume that testing this possibility might be interesting not only from the artificial intelligence point of view.

Acknowledgements. This work was supported by JSPS KAKENHI Grant Number 17K00295.

References

1. Anderson, M., Anderson, S.L.: Geneth: a general ethical dilemma analyzer. In: Proceedings of the Twenty-Eighth AAAI Conference on Artificial Intelligence, Québec City, Québec, Canada, 27–31 July 2014, pp. 253–261 (2014)
2. Anderson, M., Anderson, S.L., Armen, C.: MedEthEx: a prototype medical ethics advisor. In: Proceedings of the 18th Conference on Innovative Applications of Artificial Intelligence, IAAI 2006, vol. 2. pp. 1759–1765. AAAI Press (2006)
3. Banko, M., Cafarella, M.J., Soderland, S., Broadhead, M., Etzioni, O.: Open information extraction from the Web. In: Proceedings of the International Joint Conference on Artificial Intelligence, IJCAI 2007, pp. 2670–2676 (2007)
4. Cambria, E., Schuller, B., Yunqing, X., Havasi, C.: New avenues in opinion mining and sentiment analysis. Intell. Syst. **28**(2), 15–21 (2013). IEEE
5. Carlson, A., Betteridge, J., Kisiel, B., Settles, B., Jr., E.H., Mitchell, T.: Toward an architecture for never-ending language learning. In: Proceedings of the Conference on Artificial Intelligence (AAAI), pp. 1306–1313. AAAI Press (2010)
6. Castillo, C., Mendoza, M., Poblete, B.: Information credibility on Twitter. In: Proceedings of the 20th International Conference on World Wide Web, pp. 675–684. ACM (2011)

7. Cointe, N., Bonnet, G., Boissier, O.: Ethical judgment of agents' behaviors in multi-agent systems. In: Proceedings of the 2016 International Conference on Autonomous Agents & Multiagent Systems, AAMAS 2016, pp. 1106–1114. International Foundation for Autonomous Agents and Multiagent Systems, Richland (2016)
8. Conitzer, V., Sinnott-Armstrong, W., Borg, J.S., Deng, Y., Kramer, M.: Moral decision making frameworks for artificial intelligence. In: Proceedings of the Thirty-First AAAI Conference on Artificial Intelligence, AAAI 2017. Senior Member/Blue Sky Track (2017)
9. Dahab, M.Y., Hassan, H.A., Rafea, A.: Textontoex: automatic ontology construction from natural english text. Expert Syst. Appl. **34**(2), 1474–1480 (2008)
10. Daswani, M., Leike, J.: A definition of happiness for reinforcement learning agents. In: Bieger, J., Goertzel, B., Potapov, A. (eds.) AGI 2015. LNCS, vol. 9205, pp. 231–240. Springer, Cham (2015). doi:10.1007/978-3-319-21365-1_24
11. Dewey, D.: Learning what to value. In: Schmidhuber, J., Thórisson, K.R., Looks, M. (eds.) AGI 2011. LNCS, vol. 6830, pp. 309–314. Springer, Heidelberg (2011). doi:10.1007/978-3-642-22887-2_35
12. Etzioni, O., Fader, A., Christensen, J., Soderland, S., Mausam, M.: Open information extraction: the second generation. IJCAI **11**, 3–10 (2011)
13. Ginsca, A.L., Popescu, A., Lupu, M., et al.: Credibility in information retrieval. Found. Trends® Inf. Retrieval **9**(5), 355–475 (2015)
14. Goertzel, B., Pitt, J.: Nine ways to bias open-source agi toward friendliness. J. Evol. Technol. **22**(1), 116–131 (2012)
15. Greene, J., Rossi, F., Tasioulas, J., Venable, K.B., Williams, B.: Embedding ethical principles in collective decision support systems. In: AAAI, pp. 4147–4151 (2016)
16. Haidt, J.: The moral emotions. In: Handbook of Affective Sciences, vol. 11, pp. 852–870 (2003)
17. Haidt, J., Joseph, C.: Intuitive ethics: how innately prepared intuitions generate culturally variable virtues. Dædalus, Spec. Issue Hum. Nat., 55–66 (2004)
18. Jung, Y., Ryu, J., Kim, K., Myaeng, S.H.: Automatic construction of a large-scale situation ontology by mining how-to instructions from the web. Web Seman. Sci. Serv. Agents World Wide Web **8**(2), 110–124 (2010)
19. Ko, T.: A survey on behavior analysis in video surveillance for homeland security applications. In: 37th IEEE Applied Imagery Pattern Recognition Workshop, AIPR 2008, pp. 1–8. IEEE (2008)
20. Kohlberg, L.: The Philosophy of Moral Development, 1st edn. Harper and Row (1981)
21. Kuipers, B.: Human-like morality and ethics for robots. In: AAAI-16 Workshop on AI, Ethics and Society (2016)
22. Lee, C.S., Kao, Y.F., Kuo, Y.H., Wang, M.H.: Automated ontology construction for unstructured text documents. Data Knowl. Eng. **60**(3), 547–566 (2007)
23. Moor, J.H.: The nature, importance, and difficulty of machine ethics. IEEE Intell. Syst. **21**(4), 18–21 (2006)
24. Nakamura, A.: Kanjo hyogen jiten [Dictionary of Emotive Expressions]. Tokyodo Publishing (1993)
25. Ng, A.Y., Russell, S.J., et al.: Algorithms for inverse reinforcement learning. In: ICML, pp. 663–670 (2000)
26. Pang, B., Lee, L.: Opinion mining and sentiment analysis. Found. Trends Inf. Retrieval **2**(1–2), 1–135 (2008)
27. Pereira, L.M., Saptawijaya, A.: Programming Machine Ethics, 1st edn. Springer, Heidelberg (2016)

28. Ptaszynski, M., Rzepka, R., Araki, K., Momouchi, Y.: Annotating syntactic information on 5 billion word corpus of Japanese blogs. In: Proceedings of The Eighteenth Annual Meeting of The Association for Natural Language Processing, NLP-2012, vol. 14–16, pp. 385–388 (2012)
29. Ravi, K., Ravi, V.: A survey on opinion mining and sentiment analysis: tasks, approaches and applications. Knowl. Based Syst. **89**, 14–46 (2015)
30. Rubin, V.L., Liddy, E.D.: Assessing credibility of weblogs. In: AAAI Spring Symposium: Computational Approaches to Analyzing Weblogs, pp. 187–190 (2006)
31. Russell, S., Dewey, D., Tegmark, M.: Research priorities for robust and beneficial artificial intelligence. AI Mag. **36**(4), 105–114 (2015)
32. Rzepka, R., Araki, K.: What statistics could do for ethics? - The idea of common sense processing based safety valve. In: Papers from AAAI Fall Symposium on Machine Ethics, FS-05-06, pp. 85–87 (2005)
33. Rzepka, R., Araki, K.: Semantic analysis of bloggers experiences as a knowledge source of average human morality. In: Rethinking Machine Ethics in the Age of Ubiquitous Technology, pp. 73–95. IGI Global, Hershey (2015)
34. Soares, N.: The value learning problem. Machine Intelligence Research Institute, Berkley (2015)
35. Sotala, K.: Defining human values for value learners. In: 2nd International Workshop on AI, Ethics and Society, AAAI-2016 (2016)
36. Takagi, K., Rzepka, R., Araki, K.: Just keep tweeting, dear: web-mining methods for helping a social robot understand user needs. In: Proceedings of Help Me Help You: Bridging the Gaps in Human-Agent Collaboration. Symposium of AAAI 2011 Spring Symposia (SS-11-05), pp. 60–65 (2011)
37. Takamura, H., Inui, T., Okumura, M.: Extracting semantic orientations of words using spin model. In: Proceedings of the 43rd Annual Meeting on Association for Computational Linguistics, pp. 133–140. Association for Computational Linguistics (2005)
38. Van Durme, B., Schubert, L.: Open knowledge extraction through compositional language processing. In: Proceedings of the 2008 Conference on Semantics in Text Processing, pp. 239–254. Association for Computational Linguistics (2008)
39. Vedantam, R., Lin, X., Batra, T., Zitnick, C.L., Parikh, D.: Learning common sense through visual abstraction. In: Proceedings of the 2015 IEEE International Conference on Computer Vision (ICCV), ICCV 2015, pp. 2542–2550 (2015). doi:10.1109/ICCV.2015.292
40. Wallach, W.: Robot minds and human ethics: the need for a comprehensive model of moral decision making. Ethics Inf. Technol. **12**(3), 243–250 (2010)
41. Yang, Y., Li, Y., Fermüller, C., Aloimonos, Y.: Robot learning manipulation action plans by "watching" unconstrained videos from the world wide web. In: AAAI, pp. 3686–3693 (2015)

Malevolent Cyborgization

Nadisha-Marie Aliman[(✉)]

University of Stuttgart, Stuttgart, Germany
nadishamarie.aliman@gmail.com

Abstract. While significant progresses in AI research are expanding
the presumed limits of feasibility, the dangers of future AI agents with
human level intelligence or beyond exhibiting a hostile behavior towards
humans have been increasingly discussed. A lot of ethical concerns have
been expressed in this context, whereby AI Safety research was clas-
sically focused on how to create safe and ethical AI systems. By contrast, Pistono and Yampolskiy (2016) proposed a new important approach inspired by the cybersecurity paradigm and analyzing the unethical development of an AI with malice in design. In this paper, we connect
the ethical concerns raised by a Malevolent Artificial Intelligence (MAI)
as characterized in their work, to those raised by a possible maliciously
crafted human-machine intelligence merger. We elaborate on how both
concepts could be related or even intertwined, but would also exhibit
specific differences. Our analysis reveals a wide array of alarming potential risks and suggests integrating considerations concerning the safety
of AI systems as well as such affecting the safety of cyborgian systems
into a joint interdisciplinary framework covering various developments
towards Superintelligence.

Keywords: Cyborgization · Malevolent Artificial Intelligence · Superintelligence

1 Introduction

In their paper titled "Unethical Research: How to Create a Malevolent Artificial
Intelligence", Pistono and Yampolskiy (2016) described possible developments
towards a future unethical AI. The authors argue that, unlike in the domain of
cybersecurity, where a certain balance is ensured by a research concept covering both potential malicious exploits and measures to maintain safety, AI Safety
researchers so far only focused on the general conditions of implementing safe AI
systems, while possible malicious exploits on such remained disregarded. According to them, the lack of information resulting out of it should be resolved, since
the consequences of an intentional malicious exploit on superintelligent AI systems in the future could be devastating for humanity. In our opinion these claims
are accurate for the following reasons: first the previous publications in the field
of AI safety before, predominantly contained considerations on how to design
safe AIs and a deeper differentiated analysis was missing, although there is no

© Springer International Publishing AG 2017
T. Everitt et al. (Eds.): AGI 2017, LNAI 10414, pp. 188–197, 2017.
DOI: 10.1007/978-3-319-63703-7_18

reason why malicious exploits should not be performed intentionally alike on AI systems, since the same principle of taking advantage of security holes in cybersecurity can be transferred to AIs as being software/hardware entities. Secondly, the level of intelligence of AIs steadily increases, it is to be expected that superintelligence will be reached in the not so far future (Bostrom 2014; Chalmers 2010) and an intentionally crafted attack especially using a superintelligent system would imply unforeseen and unintelligible effects for human experts whose minds are going to be overcharged or too slow to counteract. A type of *"Hazardous Intelligent Software"* may even stay undetected a long time because of the gap of intelligence – just like monkeys cannot comprehend complex human behavior patterns. It will therefore offer exceptionally much power to the attacker to harm humans and as stated in the paper, it is known in history that "absolute power corrupts absolutely".

The authors described a variety of reasons why several stakeholders like military, governments, corporations, psychopaths or even AI Safety researchers with unethical intentions could intend to implement a MAI ranking from acquiring control and dominance, gaining financial benefits, to initiating the extinction of mankind among other things. In any case, there is a kind of cooperation between a human entity and an artificial one to achieve an unethical objective, whereby mostly the human entity initiates the cooperation with a malicious intent. Our view is that the intensity of such an alarming human-machine cooperation could be much higher in the future, since – according to the foreseeable scientific progress in fields like Bionics, Nanorobotics or Brain-Computer Interfaces (BCI) research – it could be possible to merge human and intelligent artificial entities to obtain a hybrid system with an enhanced cognitive performance, which could be used to follow similar unethical objectives as mentioned earlier and would concern the same stakeholders. For instance, psychopaths could as well maliciously intend to merge with an AI entity to become more intelligent or get greater knowledge than their fellow men and in doing so, to be able to manipulate and control others on a large scale or the military could encourage cyborgization techniques to be able to deploy cyborg armies in wars wiping out opponents through intellectual, strategical or/and possibly physical superiority. In this paper, we analyze the concept of a human-machine intelligence merger with intentional malice in design which we call *Malevolent Cyborgization*, and relate it to the MAI concept introduced by Pistono and Yampolskiy.

Outline: In the next Sect. 2, a brief explanation concerning present trends towards cyborgization from both a technical and a societal point of view is provided, followed by a short general overview briefly introducing different approaches to a definition of the term cyborg as a concept of human-machine merger. In Sect. 3, we discuss possible societal impacts and ethical concerns in connection with Malevolent Cyborgization and highlight common features with MAI scenarios, but also specific differences. Thereafter, in Sect. 4, we argue about a possible cyborgian path to Superhuman Intelligence, which could be linked to (superintelligent) AI and indicate potential impacts on society. Finally, the last Sect. 5 concludes.

2 Cyborgization

Already today, first technological efforts to make cyborgization possible can be noticed and are considered by AI researchers as well as scientists from different fields. The Defense Advanced Research Projects Agency (DARPA) is working on a new project concerning brain implants allowing a *"channel between the human brain and modern electronics"* (DARPA 2016) and the company Kernel with the goal to build *"the world's first neural prosthetic for human intelligence enhancement"* was founded this year (Mednitzer 2016). Committed persons like Elon Musk are emphasizing the need of an injectable neural lace bypassing a surgical intervention to *"achieve symbiosis with machines"* (Bhavsar 2016) which is not that utopian as it might seem, since Liu et al. (2015) successfully tested such an engine they called "syringe-injectable electronics" on mice. Furthermore, Musk recently founded the BCI company Neuralink with the long-term goal to achieve human enhancement. Initial steps towards wireless BCIs have been taken in the form of in-animal trials of what the researches entitled "neural dust" (Seo et al. 2013) – miniature wirelessly working sensors to monitor brain activity. A first brain-to-text system which performs "automatic speech recognition from neural signals" has recently been implemented by Herff and Schultz (2016). This system represents first steps towards an automated transcription of imagined sentences to text. Moreover, cyborgization has already been perceived by the general public and is seriously thematized as a phenomenon of the near future by some researchers. For example, many people encountered the topic of cyborgs in a broader sense through the first Cybathlon hold in Zürich including a competition with Brain-Computer Interfaces. During this event, ethical discussions referring to the topic of enhancement through cyborgization amongst others, were televised. Furthermore, Kurzweil (2006) prognoses the concept of wirelessly connecting the neocortex to a synthetic one in the cloud, which could be feasible in the mid-century according to him. In this context, he postulated future developments denoted as the "human body version 2.0 scenario" and explained: *"Computers started out as large, remote machines in airconditioned rooms tended by white-coated technicians. They moved onto our desks, then under our arms, and now into our pockets. Soon, we'll routinely put them inside our bodies and brains. By the 2030s we will become more nonbiological than biological."* All these developments show that the path towards cyborgization is actually considered in the digital age and that cutting edge research already started. In our opinion, Brain-Computer Interfaces and Computer-Brain interfaces, which were already used for several proof-of-concept Brain-to-Brain Communication scenarios, will play a decisive role in this development by providing a new quality of intimacy between human brains and machines (and also between different human brains).

In the literature, there are different types of definitions for the notion of cyborg. Etymologically speaking, the word cyborg comes from "cybernetic organism" and was first introduced in an article by Clynes and Kline (1960) dealing with the adaptation of humans under the conditions of outer space. Some researchers argue, that humans are already cyborgs today due to the omnipresence of technical devices used to facilitate the daily life and that it is only a matter of time till the devices will be located under the human skin. Spreen (2010) describes the transition between low tech bodies and high tech bodies as a spectrum with variable proportions illustrated by a slider, whereby the middle of the spectrum represents the "skin border" (originally "Hautgrenze"). According to him, a human becomes a cyborg as soon as the skin border is exceeded and likewise, a human ceases to be a cyborg and can therefore put the slider back e.g. if he removes the technical device(s) under his skin. Another definition is provided by Haraway (1987) which views cyborgs in a feminist context and sees the concept as possibility to break out of traditional patterns. In "Cyborg Morals, cyborg values, cyborg ethics", Warwick (2003), which performed self-experimentation and experienced a chip implant at first hand, narrows the usage of the term cyborg in his paper to the cases where the cyborg *"is formed by a human, machine brain/nervous system coupling"*, hence cases where a human is *directly* linked to technology via his brain/nervous system and excluding more superficial variants like intelligent glasses or smartphones. In order to provide clarity in the following, when we refer to the term cyborg, we specifically mean (unless otherwise stated) a human whose brain is *directly* linked to technology able to enhance his cognition/intelligence. We accordingly refer to the underlying process to become a cyborg or to "develop" a cyborg system as cyborgization.

From the perspective of an individual, they are a lot of reasons why cyborgization is worth striving for. Warwick (2003) mentions *"use the computer part for rapid maths"*, *"call on an internet knowledge base, quickly"*, *"understand multi dimensionality"*, *"communicate in parallel, by thought signals alone, i.e., brain to brain"* as possible motivations amongst others. Further possible advantages could be: position oneself in the labor market by exhibiting above-average analytic abilities, extend the limits of perception and remember countless details leading to a photographic memory, achieve unforeseen ingenuity in research fields, earn a lot of money and so forth. But equally, malicious motivations with the aim to harm other people such as being able to manipulate and subjugate other people or exploiting the ignorance and vulnerability of non-enhanced humans, could emerge.

3   Ethical Concerns of Malevolent Cyborgization

In the light of the above, it becomes clear that Malevolent Cyborgization (MC) could be desirable for a wide range of stakeholders with a heterogeneous set of goals. There is even an overlapping between possible entities, which could be interested in MC and those eligible for MAI as described by Pistono and Yampolskiy. In the following, we first take up the exemplary stakeholders for MAI mentioned in their paper and indicate which motives could justify them likewise as stakeholders for MC showing the parallels between those two phenomena. Thereafter, we introduce additional global effects specific to MC and differing from the MAI scenario.

- *Military:* As already mentioned in the introduction, the military could maliciously employ cyborg soldiers similarly as MAIs *"to achieve dominance"* through intellectual, strategical or/and possibly physical superiority.
- *Governments:* Through cyborgization, governments could acquire intellectual superiority with the same intentions as for the MAI case: *"to establish hegemony, control people, or take down other governments"*. Note that these goals can also be reached through a forced cyborgization of inferior quality carried out by governments on people with the aim to subjugate them (e.g. a kind of digital lobotomy suppressing the functionality of the frontal cortex, body hijacking or an automatic red-out of personal information using BCI data could be possible).
- *Corporations:* The authors state the following motives for the MAI case: *"trying to achieve monopoly, destroying the competition through illegal means."* As cyborgs with enhanced intelligence could be able to process considerably more information than non-enhanced humans, the transparency on the market may suffer of it allowing them to take over and build monopolies in different fields, which is again similar to the MAI goals.
- *Villains:* Following Pistono and Yampolskiy, possible goals why a MAI could be desirable for villains are: *"trying to take over the world and using AI as a dominance tool"*. In the case of MC, the same goals would be valid except that Cyborgization will be used primarily as means rather than AI. (But obviously, cyborgs of all the eligible entities could also merge with AI, which would represent an extremely risky scenario. We will analyze this matter later in the next section).
- *Black Hats:* Through their enhanced cognition/intelligence, cyborgs could have an enhanced ability to detect security holes at their disposal and could for instance develop better heuristics for password-guessing. They might therefore, likewise black hats with a MAI, secretly attempt *"to steal information, resources or destroy cyberinfrastructure targets"*.
- *Doomsday Cults:* The goal of *"attempting to bring the end of the world by any means"* using a MAI can obviously also build a basis for cyborgs involved in doomsday cults.
- *Depressed:* Depressed cyborgs could hand over the liability for their live or death to their artificial part e.g. by setting a self-destruction mode stopping vital functions in the brain. They could thereby reach the goal to commit suicide such as depressed people using MAI to be able to *"commit suicide by AI"*.
- *Psychopaths:* As described in the introduction, psychopaths could be interested in cyborgization to be able to manipulate and control others. Moreover, psychopaths could wish to historically gain notoriety with regard to their wrongdoings. The aim to *"trying to add their name to history books in any way possible"* seems to not only be a possible motivation for MAI, but also for MC.
- *Criminals:* According to the authors, criminals could attempt *"to develop proxy systems to avoid risk and responsibility"*. The same is possible in the MC scenario. A malevolent cyborg could for instance wirelessly establish a

connection to proxy systems to commit crimes at other places. He could conceal the fact he is a cyborg so that nobody would suspect him of being involved in crimes.

– *AI Risk Deniers:* For the case of MC, it would be appropriate to instead address "Cyborgization Risk Deniers". This stakeholder could let people believe that cyborgization is not more than a Science Fiction scenario and leave non-enhanced humans in ignorance yielding an even greater disparity between cyborgs and the regular humans.

– *AI Safety Researchers:* For the MAI scenario, the authors state "*AI Safety Researchers, if unethical, might attempt to justify funding and secure jobs by purposefully developing problematic AI.*" If in the future a discipline like "Cyborg Safety" existed, malicious people working in this field could deliberately develop unsafe cyborg systems e.g. such that than can easily be exploited, so that they can ensure their occupation over and over again.

After having pointed out the similarities between the entities which could be interested in the usage of MAI on the one hand and MC on the other hand, as well as having clarified the conformity of the achievable unethical objectives in both scenarios, we will now allude to some additional societal impacts that can be specifically caused by MC (and not necessarily by MAI) through the phenomenon of the human mind transcending its biological boundaries:

– *New hierarchy in mankind:* Cyborgization could lead to a hierarchy of enhancement forming an open-ended continuum ranging from completely non-enhanced humans to cyborg versions 1.0, 2.0 and so forth, even if performed with positive or neutral intentions toward humans. This development follows from the common practice of software updates and hardware tuning. Over time, the biological part of the cyborgs is furthermore going to be surpassed by the non-biological part getting faster with exponential pace. Like in many other cases, the quality of the "products" people can afford would depend on their financial status and a lot of people might irreversibly stay behind. This circumstances could lead to social unrest and conflicts. This background provides a strategical basis for every conceivable kind of MC.

– *Global identity crisis:* Cyborgization could initiate an unforeseen social transformation shaking the notion of "human being", "identity" and "self" for the questions could be: "At what time does someone stop to be a human?", "Does the self include the machine part?", "What happens if the non-biological part starts to prevail – does the cyborg become a machine?". Psychological studies actually demonstrated, that human self-perception is extremely flexible (Clark 2004). Likewise, the first officially recognized cyborg (the expression cyborg is here used in a broader sense) Neil Harbisson, which is equipped with an eyeborg stated (Jeffries 2014): "*I don't feel like I'm using technology, or wearing technology. I feel like I am technology. I don't think of my antenna as a device - it's a body part.*" The additional perception through the eyeborg fully integrated the functionality of his brain leading to a seamless unity. This gives an indication that future cyborgs might extend the limits of "identity" and "self" in addition to the higher level of intelligence. This could lead to a strong sense of alienation between non-enhanced humans and cyborgs raising tensions and providing a fertile ground for MC.

- *Evolutionary upheaval:* A world of work with extremely productive and super-intelligent cyborgs could piece by piece make less enhanced humans super-fluous. MC could at a certain point introduce the extinction of those people leading to a disaster for humanity. Equally, cyborgization could lead to an evolutionary advantage and some could consider it as the next step in evolution. In this case cyborgs would supersede non-enhanced humans in the long run and this process might be accelerated by means of MC. The historian Yuval Noah Harari claimed: *"I think it is likely in the next 200 years or so homo sapiens will upgrade themselves into some idea of a divine being, either through biological manipulation or genetic engineering of by the creation of cyborgs, part organic part non-organic. [..] It will be the greatest evolution in biology since the appearance of life. Nothing really has changed in four billion years biologically speaking. But we will be as different from today's humans as chimps are now from us"* (Knapton 2015). But he also addressed the increasing gap between poor and rich in this future, which could lead to a dying out of the poor, while the rich could live forever.

4   Cyborgization, AI and Superhuman Intelligence

Warwick (2013) postulates: *"We must be clear that with extra memory, high-powered mathematical capabilities, including the ability to conceive in many dimensions, the ability to sense the world in many different ways and communication by thought signals alone, such cyborgs will be far more powerful, intellectually, than humans"*. He furthermore describes proof-of-concept experiments he performed concerning human-machine merger. He comes to the conclusion that human-machine merger is going to be feasible from a technological point of view and that *"[..]connecting a human brain, by means of an implant, with a computer network could in the long term open up the distinct advantages of machine intelligence, communication and sensing abilities to the implanted individual"* and warns that this development will also raise fundamental ethical questions. We support this view relating to communication, sensing abilities and memory for reasons already mentioned in the last sections; for the matter of advantages through machine intelligence (or generally speaking AI) in the context of cyborgization, we will hereinafter shed some light on some possible outcomes and distinguish different associated scenarios.

   With the joint aim to produce a higher intelligence, cyborgization and AI are not necessarily disjunctive developments. Progresses in AI can even provide an ideal ground for cyborgization efforts. Some view the dangers of superintelligent AI as a motive for cyborgization in order to forestall a future domination of AI over mankind. An example for this is the statement of Stephen Hawking 15 years ago (Highfield 2001): *"There is a real danger that computers will develop intelligence and take over. We urgently need to develop direct connections to the brain so that computers can add to human intelligence rather than be in opposition."* illustrating this kind of consideration.

Note that cyborg-systems could already be implemented without real AI components and could nevertheless reach Superhuman Intelligence. A superintelligent cyborg would obviously be able to implement more intelligent AIs than regular humans could and moreover, the development of such cyborg-systems could even be the first step towards an intelligence explosion (Chalmers 2010) making a cyborg able to develop AIs or cyborg-systems more intelligent than itself. A restriction to this scenario could be that the biological part of the cyborg limits the speed of self-improvement, but this could be compensated for instance by increasing the percentage of the non-biological part or/and by enhancing the intelligence of the non-biological part e.g. by using narrow AI components.

Of course one could argue about a possible boundary for when a cyborg stops to be a cyborg and becomes a machine/an AI entity. In our view, there will be no such clearly ascertainable boundary due to conceivable designs of cyborg-systems in the future. For instance could concepts inspired by ensemble learning be deployed. In the case of a cyborg-system, it could be beneficial to combine the strengths of the biological part with those of the non biological one by means of ensemble learning on a meta level e.g. to improve the intelligence of the overall system. From an abstract point of view, a cyborg-system could then act like a self-optimizing dynamical ensemble with adjustable weights where the most intelligent entity controls and adjusts the weights given actions in certain contexts. Initially, the biological part could be in control, but at a certain point, the non biological part would be able to inhibit the biological choices for actions if they happen to be disadvantageous for the goal setting and thus reduce the weights of the biological one up to its vanishing. The transition from cyborg to machine could therefore rather be fluent and occur gradually without a precise boundary between cyborgs and machines (Kurzweil 2006).

Imagine a cyborg which – in addition to the access to a huge memory and knowledge base, superfast calculation capacity, parallel communication to other brains and so forth all by thoughts – could permanently delegate the organization of his thoughts, his perception and rational thinking to numerous specialized AI agents in parallel. The cyborg could be able to understand big data and extract comprehensive information out of it. For instance, he could be computing the statistics of the current situation on the financial markets, while walking on the street and taking note of the biography of a totally unknown person he retrieved by face recognition and search on the internet, having a phone (or brain-to-brain) call and at the same time running multiple simulations for different variants of AIs he developed. Analogously, a cyborg could decide to merge with a superintelligent AI. In this case, issues related to control might raise. Depending on the level of intelligence, it could stay a human-machine cooperation, maybe on equal terms by means of control at the beginning or also depending on the goal sets, leading to a quite "dissociative" construct exhibiting certain symptoms for which the dissociative personality disorder could give a premonition. But the superintelligent AI would presumably have a considerable advantage in the long run. If the superintelligent AI happens to be more intelligent than the cyborg, it might result in a scenario where the superintelligent AI uses the cyborg as "delegate" in the same way described, where a cyborg could use narrow AIs. In this context, issues related to the notion of "free will" might arise additionally.

The just described scenarios leave much space for the actual emergence of MC. Equally, malicious stakeholders could strive for cyborgization to be able to develop a MAI or conversely plan to merge with a MAI for malicious purposes. It becomes additionally clear, that cyborgization is not a guarantee to prevent the creation of MAI, since MC is possible and could also directly lead to MAI.

5 Conclusion and Future Prospects

Cyborgization is only one possible path towards superintelligent enhanced humans. It could in principle also be reached e.g. by means of genetic engineering/breeding and biotechnology. Yampolskiy and Spellchecker (2016) conclude that *"augmented humans with IQ beyond 250 would be superintelligent with respect to our current position on the intelligence curve but would be just as dangerous to us, unaugmented humans, as any sort of artificial superintelligence."* We come to the same conclusion with regard to Malevolent Cyborgization, because it could serve similar stakeholders to accomplish the same unethical goals representing existential risks for humanity as in the MAI case.

In the future, cyborg-systems could become a daily reality offering a variety of promising perspectives regarding human enhancement, but their development and deployment will then need to be regulated. Besides a legal obligation for open source cyborg-sytems, a possible approach for a society willing to prevent MC and related risks could for instance be measures inducing an obligation for all stakeholders developing cyborg-systems to adhere to "Cyborg Safety" guidelines, which could be defined by an ethical board for superintelligence. Nowadays, there is yet no explicit binding international interdisciplinary ethical board for superintelligence containing e.g. AI, AI Safety, Cybersecurity, Neuroscience, Biotechnology, Nanotechnology, Law experts (just to name a few) at the same time. Such a collaboration would though be of great value to maintain an overview of all critical developments with the aim to reach superintelligence. However, forward-thinking interdisciplinary frameworks similar to the Asilomar AI Principles (FLI 2017) could serve as a basis and should be extended, since there are always security holes that remain undetected and characteristically, only one specially selected successful MAI or MC attack trial could be enough to drastically change the world in a negative sense.

Acknowledgements. We would like to especially thank Roman Yampolskiy and further Kevin Baum for the helpful feedbacks on an earlier draft of this paper. We would also like to thank Martin Bevandic for his support.

References

Bhavsar, N.: Elon Musk: To Survive The Age of Artificial Intelligence, Humanity Must Achieve Symbiosis With Machines (2016). http://futurism.com/neural-lace-what-humanity-needs-to-survive-the-age-of-artificial-intelligence/

Bostrom, N.: Superintelligence: Paths, Dangers, Strategies. Oxford University Press, Oxford (2014)

Chalmers, D.J.: The singularity: a philosophical analysis. J. Conscious. Stud. **17** (2010)

Clark, A.: Natural-Born Cyborgs. Oxford University Press, Oxford (2004)

Clynes, M., Kline, N.: Cyborgs and space. Astronautics, 74–75 (1960)

DARPA: Bridging the Bio-Electronic Divide (2016). http://www.darpa.mil/news-events/2015-01-19. Accessed 11 Nov 2016

Future of Life Institute: Asilomar Ai Principles (2017). https://futureoflife.org/ai-principles/

Haraway, D.: A manifesto for Cyborgs: science, technology, and socialist feminism in the 1980s. Aust. Feminist Stud. **2**(4), 1–42 (1987)

Herff, C., Schultz, T.: Automatic speech recognition from neural signals: a focused review. Front. Neurosci. **10**, 429 (2016)

Highfield, R.: Interview with Stephen Hawking (2001). http://www.telegraph.co.uk/news/science/science-news/4766816/Interview-with-Stephen-Hawking.html. Accessed 11 Nov 2016

Jeffries, S.: Neil Harbisson: the world's first cyborg artist (2014). https://www.theguardian.com/artanddesign/2014/may/06/neil-harbisson-worlds-first-cyborg-artist. Accessed 11 Nov 2016

Knapton, S.: Humans 'will become God-like cyborgs within 200 years' (2015). http://www.telegraph.co.uk/culture/hay-festival/11627386/Humans-will-become-God-like-cyborgs-within-200-years.html. Accessed 11 Nov 2016

Kurzweil, R.: The Singularity is Near: When Humans Transcend Biology. Penguin (Non-Classics) (2006)

Liu, J., et al.: Syringe injectable electronics. Nat. Nanotech. **10**(7), 629–636 (2015)

Mednitzer, R.: Kernel's Quest to Enhance Human Intelligence (2016). https://lifeboat.com/blog/2016/10/kernels-quest-to-enhance-human-intelligence/

Pistono, F., Yampolskiy, R.V.: Unethical Research: How to Create a Malevolent Artificial Intelligence. In: 25th International Joint Conference on Artificial Intelligence (IJCAI-16). Ethics for Artificial Intelligence Workshop, AI-Ethics-2016, 9–15 July 2016, New York, NY (2016)

Seo, D., Carmena, J.M., Rabaey, J., Alan, E., Maharbiz, M.M.: Neural Dust: An Ultrasonic, Low Power Solution for Chronic Brain-Machine Interfaces (2013). https://arxiv.org/abs/1307.2196

Spreen, D.: Der Cyborg: Diskurse zwischen Körper und Technik. Suhrkamp **1971**, 166–179 (2010)

Warwick, K.: Cyborg morals, cyborg values, cyborg ethics. Ethics Inf. Technol. **5**(3), 131–1137 (2003)

Warwick, K.: The Future of Artificial Intelligence and Cybernetics (2013). https://www.bbvaopenmind.com/en/article/the-future-of-artificial-intelligence-and-cybernetics/

Yampolskiy, R.V., Spellchecker, M.S.: Artificial Intelligence Safety and Cybersecurity: A Timeline of AI Failures (2016). https://arxiv.org/abs/1610.07997

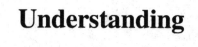

Understanding

Understanding and Common Sense: Two Sides of the Same Coin?

Kristinn R. Thórisson[1,2] and David Kremelberg[1(✉)]

[1] Icelandic Institute for Intelligent Machines, Reykjavik, Iceland
david.kremelberg@gmail.com
[2] CADIA, School of Computer Science, Reykjavik University, Reykjavik, Iceland

Abstract. The concept of "common sense" ("commonsense") has had a visible role in the history of artificial intelligence (AI), primarily in the context of reasoning and what's been referred to as "symbolic knowledge representation." Much of the research on this topic has claimed to target general knowledge of the kind needed to 'understand' the world, stories, complex tasks, and so on. The same cannot be said about the concept of "understanding"; although the term does make an appearance in the discourse in various sub-fields (primarily "language understanding" and "image/scene understanding"), no major schools of thought, theories or undertakings can be discerned for understanding in the same way as for common sense. It's no surprise, therefore, that the relation between these two concepts is an unclear one. In this review paper we discuss their relationship and examine some of the literature on the topic, as well as the systems built to explore them. We agree with the majority of the authors addressing common sense on its importance for artificial general intelligence. However, we claim that while in principle the phenomena of understanding and common sense manifested in natural intelligence may possibly share a common mechanism, a large majority of efforts to implement common sense in machines has taken an orthogonal approach to understanding proper, with different aims, goals and outcomes from what could be said to be required for an 'understanding machine.'

1 Introduction

Common sense ("commonsense knowledge", "common sense reasoning") has been deemed an important topic in AI by many authors since the field's inception (Lenat et al. 1990, Liu and Singh 2004, McCarthy 1959, 1963, Minsky 2006, Panton et al. 2006). Following its use in our everyday language, the term has typically been used broadly in the AI literature, incorporating a large portion of human experience relating to the spatial, physical, social, temporal, and psychological aspects of everyday life (Liu and Singh 2004). Used in this way, the term refers to a vast body of knowledge assumed to be common to most humans.

Sponsored in part by the School of Computer Science at Reykjavik University and by a Centers of Excellence Grant from the Science and Technology Policy Council of Iceland.

T. Everitt et al. (Eds.): AGI 2017, LNAI 10414, pp. 201–211, 2017.
DOI: 10.1007/978-3-319-63703-7_19

It is also used to refer to modes of reasoning and argumentation, as much of everyday planning involves the usage of standard forms of deduction, induction and abduction (e.g. "strong winds may blow rain through an open window so don't leave your books on the windowsill").

The relation of common-sense and understanding is an unclear one. What can be said with some certainty is that in the AI literature, common sense has almost always been aligned with human common sense – that is, the knowledge that defines human common sense, with numerous attempts having been made to imbue machines with this same knowledge (Cambria et al. 2012, Lenat et al. 1990, Liu and Singh 2004, McCarthy 1959, Panton et al. 2006, Poria et al. 2014). The best known example is the Cyc project of Lenat's Cycorp Inc. (Lenat 1995), whose database currently consists of seven million axioms, 630,000 concepts and 38,000 relations between those concepts. [1]

Common sense may intuitively seem closely related to the concept of understanding. This seems to have been the opinion of Minsky and Papert, among others, who in 1970 wrote, when discussing one of Aesop's fables: "The usual test of understanding is the ability of the child to answer questions like Did the Fox think the crow had a lovely voice? The topic is sometimes classified as natural language manipulation or as deductive logic, etc. These descriptions are badly chosen. For the real problem is not to understand English; it is to understand at all." (Minsky and Papert 1970:38). This text appeared in the section with the heading 'Narrative, Microworlds, and "Understanding" ' (quotes by the authors), throughout which the terms *understanding* and *meaning* are always in quotes when referred to in the context of machines, indicating a certain distrust towards the possibility of infusing them into machines in any real sense; why the authors did not aim for "real" understanding and "real" meaning may be because these concepts were not—at that time—very well understood (no pun intended). The authors conclude that a good body of knowledge is equally necessary for common sense as are reasoning rules to understand stories such as that of Aesop's crow, and predicting that "less than a million statements" (Minsky and Papert 1970:40) would be needed for such a knowledge base to work for that purpose. In the 40 years since this text was written, this heavy emphasis on background knowledge - which in their case at least seems synonymous with common sense - has only grown, and the terms have been used largely interchangeably (Lenat et al. 1990, Liu and Singh 2004, Panton et al. 2006).

We see the relationship between understanding and common sense as being far from settled, especially in light of the seemingly long road still ahead for reaching "true AI" (artificial general intelligence) and ask,

- *Can common sense exist without understanding?*

Are they perhaps two sides of the same coin? If so, what coin is that? Put another way, for any subject X, can a state of knowledge exist, and be held by an agent, that is deemed "common sense" with respect to X while the knowledge cannot

---

[1] http://www.cyc.com/platform/, accessed Apr. 29 2017.

be said to contain "understanding" of X? The question can of course be turned around, and this brings out the second question,

- *What is the relationship between 'common sense' and 'understanding'?*

To answer these questions one must look more deeply at the concepts themselves, and perhaps consider their usage and relation to some real-world examples. We look at the relevant literature and examine systems built to implement common-sense reasoning. The rest of this review paper is organized as follows: a discussion of common sense as it has been treated and previous attempts to implement it in systems along with a review of how this relates to our theory of understanding, the limitations seen in systems which have attempted to implement common sense, followed by a discussion contrasting understanding and common sense, and followed finally by our conclusions.

2 Common Sense and Understanding

To date, common sense has been viewed in a narrow way within the AI literature, generally being conceptualized as consisting of a body of facts or information. Accordingly, systems intended to demonstrate common-sense reasoning have generally tried to imbue common sense through pre-programming of vast amounts of knowledge. Few if any definitions of the term can be found, forcing us to rely on our general common sense of commonsense.

Broad, consistent knowledge about everyday things allows us humans to "flexibly understand and react to novel situations" (Panton et al. 2006). Analogously, if we could imbue machines with such broad and consistent knowledge the same should hold for machines. In 1990 the authors of Cyc argued that vast amounts of common sense knowledge would be required to produce an AI (Lenat et al. 1990). The argument goes that a large, general knowledge base enables consistent, efficient, and correct reasoning about everyday things with relatively simple and few rules (Minsky and Papert 1970), and a system with broad knowledge about facts and relations could thus be successful in completing tasks that require common sense (Panton et al. 2006). Without such knowledge and reasoning ability, however, systems will remain idiots savants (Panton et al. 2006).

Liu and Singh (2004) discuss "ConceptNet," a commonsense knowledge base and natural language processing toolkit whose knowledge representation is semi-structured English. The commonsense knowledge contained within their database include spatial, physical, social, temporal, and psychological aspects of everyday life. The authors argue, however, that while some success has been found when using keyword-based and statistical approaches with respect to areas such as information retrieval, data mining, and natural language processing, it appears that these approaches provide too shallow of an understanding for all practical purposes, and that larger amounts of semantic knowledge are required in order to allow software to have a deeper understanding of text, echoing other authors' call for larger, more extensive knowledgebases.

These "common-sense" systems have numerous aspects in common: A knowledgebase (database + rules for how to use the data + metadata + network of relationships between the data) built on the same rules as typical databases in computer science, using hand-written rules authored along the same way as regular software is written. Relations between data are somewhat different from regular business rules in e.g. a bank or IT company, the principles for running such systems are very close to those governing operating systems and IT networks.

Understanding, which on the face of it seems highly related to common sense, takes up much less space than the concept of common sense in the AI literature, at least as an independent phenomenon or process, and when discussed seems to be considered largely synonymous with it, or even a less precise way of talking about common sense. Discussions of understanding proper have been mainly limited to the field of philosophy, which has been somewhat dominated by a language-centric viewpoint that aligns well with the symbolic approach to common sense, where knowledge is defined as "true, justified belief" (cf. Grimm 2014, Potter 1994, Grimm 1988).

In prior work we proposed a theory of understanding that rests on the idea that a learner that acquires understanding is in fact building a model that captures causal and other relations in the phenomenon being thus understood (Thórisson et al. 2016). Isolating causal relations is necessary in order to commit intervening actions that will produce predictable results. Modeled causal relations can be manipulated through the application of ampliative reasoning (cf. Wang 2012) due to the hypothetico-deductive nature embedded in macro-scale causality. Without causality, in fact, not much can be done – committing to a behavior with the aim to achieve a certain outcome for thing Y by manipulating X is not successful when the two are only correlated but not causally related.

In our approach, causal-relational models must be micro-malleable: to take into account any new fact or piece of knowledge that changes some of the assumptions already incorporated, however large or small, without having to re-structure all of the knowledge from scratch.[2] "Common sense" is generally thought to be common among humans (hence the name), while commonalities relating to experience should generalize more broadly, in such a way that if the system experienced an environment vastly different from a human environment it should still have common sense. Such a system as we describe must be able to produce models, on its own, in which rules are induced through observation and experience. Given an agent A with models M of a phenomenon Φ—M_Φ—we have proposed the following definition of understanding:[3] A's *understanding* of phenomenon Φ made up of sub-parts $\varphi \in \Phi$, depends on the accuracy of its models M_Φ with respect to Φ. Understanding is a (multidimensional) gradient from

---

[2] This bears a relation to McCarthy's (1998) concept of "elaboration tolerance": Micro-malleability is a way to imbue causal-relational models with elaboration tolerance.

[3] For a thorough overview of this theory see Thórisson et al. (2016).

low to high levels, determined by the quality (correctness) of two main aspects in M_Φ relative to Φ:

U1 The *completeness* of the *set* of elements $\varphi \in \Phi$ represented by M_Φ.
U2 The *accuracy* of the *relevant* elements φ represented by M_Φ.

We also suggest that understanding can be tested for in the following ways:

(1) To *predict* Φ; (2) To *achieve goals* with respect to Φ;
(3) To *explain* Φ; and (4) To *(re)create* Φ.

This approach has been implemented in a system called AERA/S1, which demonstrates cognitive mechanisms very different from both classical symbolic systems such as Cyc and ConceptNet, reinforcement learners, and artificial neural net systems such as deep and recurrent neural nets (ANNs) (Nivel et al. 2014). S1 has been shown to be able to learn very complex spatio-temporal tasks from observation when given only a tiny amount of information up front, including a few top-level goals it should achieve. It does not require enormous hand-coding like (most) symbolic approaches, and neither does it require the tens of thousands of data and training iterations of ANNs. It can handle a vastly greater number of variables than the most sophisticated reinforcement learners to date, and it can handle inconsistencies and contradictions. It also learns cumulatively and continuously – on the job (Nivel et al. 2013, Nivel et al. 2014).

3   Some Limitations Observed in Commonsense Systems to Date

When looking at the performance, capabilities and state of commonsense/expert systems to date, three things jump out. First, no system so far has demonstrated automatic acquisition of commonsense knowledge. Second, very few have been provided with more than a few thousand axioms/rules/knowledge-nodes/facts – the main exception being Cyc, which contains over seven million axioms.[4] And thirdly, they all demonstrate a level of brittleness evident in frequent and unexpected errors and failures whose source, while not too difficult to trace in each case, is virtually impossible to foresee.

With respect to systems focusing on common-sense reasoning, while little has been written explicitly addressing their brittleness, this is a common concern that has been raised not only by critics of the approach but also by the authors of such systems (cf. Panton et al. 2006:22). However, when brittleness has been addressed by the developers of such systems it is often in the context of arguing that more rules are needed, hypothesizing that while programs lacking commonsense reasoning are brittle, those with sufficiently large databases will not be (Panton et al. 2006; Lenat et al. 1990). Examples of brittleness have been provided in the way of expert systems which break down in the face of contradictions and

---

[4] http://www.cyc.com/platform/, accessed Apr. 29 2017.

in areas outside their domain (Lenat et al. 1990). Pratt (1994) provides one of the more illuminating analyses of brittleness—in his case with Cyc—where numerous failures of an actual demonstration of the system were exposed in routine interaction.[5] Other publications do not present very strong evidence to anything contrary, with Lenat et al. stating in 2006 that Cyc fails to produce correct facts more often than 50 percent of the time, when searching the World Wide Web was used as a resource (Panton et al. 2006:22). All in all, "commonsense" systems seem still to fall short of their main goal when it comes to real-world performance.

To dissect this a bit further, one of the failures of expert systems in particular, and the classical symbolic approach in general, is the often-referenced mistake by a medical diagnosis system to diagnose a rusty car as "having measles". Such errors are due to lack of contextual knowledge. Another source of brittleness stems from the human ability to handle alternative background assumptions - a popular example being this exchange between father and child: Child: Do knights slay fire-breathing dragons? Father: Yes. Child: Do fire-breathing dragons exist? Father: No. The ability to humans to seemingly freely alter the assumptions on which reasoning is done, without losing track of the context, allow us to talk about imaginary things, hypothetical things, uncertainty, and numerous other things that are difficult to program in an automatic reasoning engine based on augmented first-order logic. Other sources of difficulty in commonsense reasoning are, for instance, unusual usage of the rich experience-based knowledge that humans have about the world (e.g. a rock being used as a table – a table with no legs), and when we use analogies (e.g. "The woods are his home away from home"). Another source of brittleness relates to a lack of contextual flexibility. While humans have many domains and resources to draw from, programs fail when situations exceed their limitations (Lenat et al. 1990).

Some have argued that overcoming brittleness requires broad knowledge, and that a certain breadth is necessary and sufficient to begin to integrate new knowledge automatically (Lenat et al. 1990). The Cyc database is one of a few serious efforts to test this hypothesis. The original number predicted as necessary and sufficient for the system to start learning more or less on its own was 1 million rules (Lenat 1995).[6]

4   Why Understanding Is Not Common Sense

Judging from the preceding literature review, it would seem that an overemphasis on the concept of commonsense in AI has resulted in the relegation of the broader concept of *machine understanding* to the sidelines. In the example

---

[5] In a demo given of Cyc to one of the authors of this paper (Thórisson) in 1998 (around 200 images instead of 20), unexplained inconsistencies surfaced, albeit different ones from those reported by Pratt (1994).

[6] This number may have originated from the MIT AI lab (Minsky and Papert 1970), however, its origin or argumentation for why *this* number and not some other is not provided in the respective publications.

of Cyc, the creators hypothesized that with respect to common-sense knowledge acquisition, one million axioms relating to basic (human experience) facts would be foundationally sufficient for the system to begin reading text authored by humans and acquiring the embedded knowledge mostly automatically, with one million axioms being an "inflection point" of sorts. When one million axioms did not produce adequate performance, the minimum was increased to two million; still, Cyc continued to display similar issues in performance - unexpected brittleness and failures. Interestingly, the Cyc project continued and is now at seven million axioms. This expected minimum might be sufficient, finally, but we have not seen any evidence thereof. We suspect that other factors are at play than simply the size of the knowledge base.

This raises important questions. For example: Is the representation method chosen in symbolic expert systems a good one for supporting automatic knowledge acquisition? Is first- (or second-) order logic a proper foundation for achieving robust results for the purposes these systems are built? Is a database with hand-written rules and relations a good foundation for machines to acquire and reach "common sense"?

A related question relates to the very definition of common sense – and also one that directs our attention to the anthropocentrism of the data these systems have been based on. Is the fact that "the third president of country X was Y" really what we mean by the term "common sense"? Perhaps there are more fundamental aspects of the physical world that must be represented correctly and acquired autonomously by the correct mechanisms that must be present such that the system can learn such facts autonomously. Most importantly, are there other things, besides or instead of the reasoning methods employed, that enable such systems to acquire knowledge autonomously?

In our approach, the ability to understand—or more precisely to deepen/broaden one's understanding—must involve a capacity for automatic knowledge acquisition, as opposed to axioms hand-coded by humans. The conceptualization of common sense embodied in symbolic approaches relying on human-authored knowledge seem too simple and too human-centric, lacking the generalizability needed to achieve human-like understanding. Our own approach involves a representation of concepts that is built up of peewee-size models, that when brought together to model a particular phenomenon will predict its behavior under various conditions. These models can be shared between concepts – in fact, rather than being "made up of" such models, concepts in our approach are dynamically constituted by the system on the fly, based on experience, by assembling appropriate models for a particular computation that must be done. General or "common sense concepts" are then dynamic model assemblies that have happened to be useful a number of times for the system that generated them (i.e. the machine, not a human). Understanding in our conception, then, is the application of such model assemblies for modeling causal and other relations between sensed phenomena, and for guiding goal-driven planning in realtime.

We have experimented with systems built in this way and compared them with other cognitive architectures (Thórisson and Helgason 2012). The results, which are explained in some detail in Nivel et al. (2013) and Nivel et al. (2014), have demonstrated robust sequence learning - robust in the sense of acquiring complex patterns correctly in a very short period of time, as well as having a potential to model its own limitations and thus learn to avoid situations in which it will not perform above a certain threshold, which can be either given to the system beforehand or any time during its learning.

With respect to classical symbolic systems, the application of our definition of the process acquiring understanding produces at best a set of questions or at worst a void: neither understanding nor the capacity to acquire it appears to be obviously present within these types of systems. While it could be argued that such a system may be able to create largely complete and accurate models of phenomena, fitting our definition of understanding, this would fall apart when this understanding was then tested for. Such a "knowledge database" type of system has not, and would not be expected to, perform well with regard to predicting a phenomenon, achieving goals, explanations, or recreating a phenomenon (Bieger et al. 2017).

A critical piece missing from symbolic systems is some foundational grounding: essentially, they are simply more sophisticated versions of "good old-fashioned" AI - "symbol" manipulators, where the "symbols" are simply augmented tokens[7]. A (human-like) concept cannot be adequately represented by token(s), or even by extended token(s). This lack of a foundation or basic framework precludes these types of systems from building understanding, as we have defined it.

Additionally, systems taking the classical symbolic approach have difficulties searching for the reasons behind inconsistencies in their knowledge; limitations arise by being unable to go below a certain level. This, along with its simple pipeline reasoning method, the choice of a single ontology, and inability to choose between reasoning methods, may be factors behind the brittleness found in Cyc and similar systems. In other systems, such as AERA and NARS, levels of plausibility exist, while there is never absolute certainty. Additionally, the level of granularity of one symbol or token per idea does not allow for concepts to be represented at lower levels of granularity; this reification of concepts may preclude the flexibility required for understanding as well as deepening and broadening understanding.

All of the above leads us to field the following hypotheses:

Hypothesis 1: *Fine-grained representation of concepts, and fine-grained (and ampliative) methods to reason over these, is necessary to realize mechanisms for understanding acquisition.* To robustly understand, for instance, that something can be pulled by a string but not pushed by a string (Minsky 2006), one needs a reasonably good representation of how matter behaves under various conditions. A classical symbolic approach, as some of those reviewed above, might represent the concept of "string" as a node in a knowledge network whose neighbor nodes

---

[7] The "symbols" in such systems have no meaning for its manipulator, and can thus only be considered a token in a simulator whose meaning can only be discerned by its human author.

are pretty much at that same level. It is not clear how one would infuse such systems with information of the type that could model how strings woven in various manners might behave differently, and that for instance a string made of extra stiff (yet bendable) plastic might be used to push something if the stub is short enough. Or how one would represent the knowledge that should you dip a string into superglue it may harden enough to become stick-like, in which case you can push something with it. (Is it still a "string" in this case? If not, how would this be represented? If yes, is it a different kind of string?). This kind of lower-level knowledge can be found for virtually any example of human-level knowledge.

Hypothesis 2: *To ground knowledge acquisition and understanding, a system must be able to do experiments in the domain that is the target of its learning.* A system that builds models of its own experience over time will produce a wealth of data about how the world works. Add to that an ability to do induction and the system can begin to generalize its data and create meta-rules about its experience. Such models will at any and all points in time have inconsistencies and incomplete knowledge - and this is not only something that any such system must be able to live with, it must be able to use it to improve its knowledge. However, without the ability to test knowledge against the real world this may be difficult; it is difficult to imagine how a machine that can only access human-level tokens can ever grow to properly validate or invalidate its knowledge.

Hypothesis 3: *Understanding is necessary for common sense.* In our conceptualization, understanding is the process by which one can acquire reliable, useful knowledge that can be used to predict, intervene, achieve goals, and explain. This seems to us to be the proper foundation for common sense, much more so than the human-centric one that most approaches have taken to common sense so far. Insofar as many of these do not aim for general intelligence but rather some practical tools or other ends, this criticism is of course not justified. Yet even on that end results seem to be slow in coming.

Hypothesis 4: *Symbolic approaches are brittle because they lack proper mechanisms to acquire understanding.* If concepts exist as a set of dozens or hundreds finer-grained pee-wee models, as we hypothesize, then using a symbolic approach in order to capture common-sense will not be successful, as (a) it prevents the ability for the system to automatically select viewpoints on the knowledge that are relevant to each goal, and (b) it removes the ability of the system to be truly grounded, and that type of experiential grounding cannot reasonably be manually written or programmed.

Hypothesis 5: *Symbolic approaches are brittle because they lack mechanisms to resolve logical inconsistencies in their own knowledge introduced by their human programmers.* Because their knowledge is human-centric and human-generated, inconsistencies must be resolved at this level. But their knowledge is fixed at this level, and deeper, more fundamental knowledge and experience does not exist in their knowledgebase to dig into underlying causes. Moreover, their reasoning ability is limited by targeting this kind of knowledge only; a more integrative ampliative reasoning—which unifies deduction, induction, and abduction—in a flexible manner (Wang 2006) seems necessary, preferably in part learned by the system through experience. However, since this is missing in such systems, this requirement falls flat.

Taken together, if all five hypotheses are valid, this should place rather particular and notable constraints on AGI research. Whether they hold up to scrutiny, presenting promising paths for further experimentation, calls for deeper investigation. We can only hope that we are honing in on something worthwhile, rather than having come to one junction out of a thousand or a million. On that question, our interesting result with peewee-granularity knowledge representation so far (Nivel et al. 2014) should certainly not be a deterrent.

5 Conclusion

While classical symbolic systems capture some aspects that are needed for common-sense reasoning, the approaches taken to date seem to (a) put an undue emphasis on common-sense reasoning when it should be emphasizing understanding, (b) place the machine within a human-centric framework by grounding the concept of common sense in human experience, and (c) attempt to teach the system about common sense in a way that is practically impossible, i.e. pre-programming facts. If such systems can be said to understand, then why is their performance so brittle? We argue that a certain minimum level of performance is required in order to show understanding. With respect to approaches to AGI, we have argued that the classical symbolic approaches reviewed (and similar ones) cannot produce understanding or common sense due to their inability to represent concepts at finer granularity, their inability to automatically resolve logical inconsistencies, and that the approach prevents the ability for a system to automatically select viewpoints on the knowledge that are relevant to each goal, and removes the ability of the system to be truly grounded. Brittle systems cannot cope with new ideas, new experiences, new sights and sounds: without this ability, systems can hardly hope to go beyond their current state in any meaningful way.

References

Bieger, J., Thórisson, K.R., Steunebrink, B.: Evaluating understanding. In: IJCAI Workshop on Evaluating General-Purpose AI, Melbourne, Australia (2017 to be accepted)

Cambria, E., Olsher, D., Kowk, K.: Sentic activation: A two-level affective common sense reasoning framework. In: Proceedings of the Twenty-Sixth Conference on Artificial Intelligence, AAAI, Toronto, Canada (2012)

Grimm, S.R.: The value of understanding. Philos. Compass **7**(2), 279–299 (1988)

Grimm, S.R.: Understanding as knowledge of causes. In: Fairweather, A. (ed.) Virtue Epistemology Naturalized. Springer, New York City (2014)

Lenat, D.B.: CYC: a large-scale investment in knowledge infrastructure. Commun. ACM **38**(11), 33–38 (1995)

Lenat, D.B., Guha, R.V., Pittman, K., Pratt, D., et al.: CYC: toward programs with common sense. Commun. ACM **33**(8), 30–49 (1990)

Liu, H., Singh, P.: ConceptNet - a practical commonsense reasoning tool-kit. BT Technol. J. **22**(4), 211–226 (2004)

McCarthy, J.: Programs with common sense. In: Proceedings Symposium on Mechanization of Thought Processes. Her Majesty's Stationary Office, London (1959)

McCarthy, J.: Situations, actions, and causal laws. Stanford Artificial Intelligence Project, Memo No. 2 (1963)

McCarthy, J.: Elaboration tolerance. In: Common-Sense 1998 (1998)

Minsky, M.: The Emotion Machine. Simon and Schuster, New York (2006)

Minsky, M., Papert, S.: Proposal to ARPA For Research on Artificial Intelligence at M.I.T., 1970–1971. Artificial Intelligence Memo No. 185, Massachusetts Institute of Technology A.I. Lab (1970)

Nivel, E., Thórisson, K.R., Steunebrink, B.R., Dindo, H., et al.: Bounded recursive self-improvement. Reykjavik University School of Computer Science Technical Report, RUTR-SCS13006 (2013). arXiv:1312.6764 [cs.AI]

Nivel, E., Thórisson, K.R., Steunebrink, B.R., Dindo, H., et al.: Autonomous acquisition of natural language. In: Proceedings of IADIS International Conference on Intelligent Systems and Agents 2014 (ISA 2014). IADIS Press, Lisbon (2014)

Nivel, E., Thórisson, K.R., Steunebrink, B., Schmidhuber, J.: Anytime bounded rationality. In: Bieger, J., Goertzel, B., Potapov, A. (eds.) AGI 2015. LNCS, vol. 9205, pp. 121–130. Springer, Cham (2015). doi:10.1007/978-3-319-21365-1_13

Panton, K., Matuszek, C., Lenat, D., Schneider, D., Witbrock, M., Siegel, N., Shepard, B.: Common sense reasoning – from CYC to intelligent assistant. In: Cai, Y., Abascal, J. (eds.) Ambient Intelligence in Everyday Life. LNCS, vol. 3864, pp. 1–31. Springer, Heidelberg (2006). doi:10.1007/11825890_1

Poria, S., Gelbukh, A., Cambria, E., Hussain, A., et al.: EmoSenticSense: a novel framework for affective common-sense reasoning. Knowl. Based Syst. **69**, 108–123 (2014)

Potter, V.G.: On Understanding Understanding: A Philosophy of Knowledge. Fordham University Press, New York (1994)

Pratt, V.: CYC Report (1994). http://boole.stanford.edu/cyc.html. Accessed 29 Apr 2017

Thórisson, K.R., Kremelberg, D., Steunebrink, B.R., Nivel, E.: About understanding. In: Steunebrink, B., Wang, P., Goertzel, B. (eds.) AGI -2016. LNCS, vol. 9782, pp. 106–117. Springer, Cham (2016). doi:10.1007/978-3-319-41649-6_11

Thórisson, K.R., Helgason, H.P.: Cognitive architectures and autonomy: a comparative review. J. Artif. Gen. Intell. **3**(2), 1–30 (2012)

Thórisson, K.R., Nivel, E.: Achieving artificial general intelligence through peewee granularity. In: Proceedings of the Second Conference on Artificial General Intelligence (AGI 2009). Atlantis Publishing Paris, France (2009)

Wang, P.: From NARS to a thinking machine. In: Artificial General Intelligence Research Institute Workshop, Washington DC, May 2006 (2006)

Wang, P.: Non-Axiomatic Logic - A Model of Intelligent Reasoning. World Scientific Publishing Co. Inc., Hackensack (2012)

The Pedagogical Pentagon: A Conceptual Framework for Artificial Pedagogy

Jordi Bieger[1]([✉]), Kristinn R. Thórisson[1,2], and Bas R. Steunebrink[3]

[1] Center for Analysis and Design of Intelligent Agents/School of Computer Science,
Reykjavik University, Menntavegur 1, 101 Reykjavik, Iceland
{jordi13,thorisson}@ru.is
[2] Icelandic Institute for Intelligent Machines, Menntavegur 1,
101 Reykjavik, Iceland
[3] NNAISENSE, Lugano, Switzerland
bas@nnaisense.com

Abstract. Artificial intelligence (AI) and machine learning (ML) research has traditionally focused most energy on constructing systems that can learn from data and/or environment interactions. This paper considers the parallel science of teaching: Artificial Pedagogy (AP). Teaching provides us with a method—aside from programming—for imparting our knowledge to AI systems, and it facilitates cumulative, online learning—which is especially important in cases where the combinatorics of sub-tasks preclude enumeration or a-priori modeling, or where unforeseeable novelty is inherent and unavoidable in the learner's assignments. Teaching is a complex process not currently very well understood, and pedagogical theories proposed so far have exclusively targeted human learners. What is needed is a framework that relates the many facets of teaching, in a way that works for a range of learners including machines.

We present the *Pedagogical Pentagon*—a conceptual framework that identifies five core concepts of AP: learners, task-environments, testing, training and teaching. We describe these concepts, their interactions, and what we would need to know about them in the context of AP. The pentagon is meant to facilitate research in this complex new area by encouraging a structured and systematic approach organized around its five corners.

1 Introduction

Successful operation in any situation requires relevant knowledge,[1] which can either be innate or acquired through experience: nature vs. nurture. Here we are concerned with the *nurture* part of that equation. As a learner gets more

---

This work was sponsored in part by the School of Computer Science at Reykjavik University and by a Centers of Excellence Grant from the Science and Technology Policy Council of Iceland.

[1] We use "knowledge" to refer to all kinds of knowledge, including beliefs (declarative), skills (procedural) and priorities (structural); cf. Sect. 3.2;.

T. Everitt et al. (Eds.): AGI 2017, LNAI 10414, pp. 212–222, 2017.
DOI: 10.1007/978-3-319-63703-7_20

capable of learning a broad range of tasks in a wide range of environments, and the ratio of acquired/required knowledge to innate knowledge increases, its nurture becomes increasingly relevant. Research in artificial intelligence (AI) and machine learning (ML) has traditionally focused on the nature part. Systems are often thrown "in the deep end of the pool" where they must learn in a complex and often unhelpful task-environment, or from an unstructured pile of data, which greatly limits the range of tasks they can learn to tackle in practice.[2] By teaching—broadly defined as *"the intentional act of helping another system learn"*—we can overcome some of these limitations and greatly facilitate the learning process in general [2]. We suggest that in parallel to machine learning, a science of machine teaching—which we call *"Artificial Pedagogy"* (AP)—can provide many complementary benefits.

Aside from the initial programming of an AI system, teaching is the only way for us to impart our knowledge on it [1]. Teaching can often be more natural— e.g. if we cannot articulate our knowledge precisely enough to program/formalize it or if the AI's knowledge representation mechanism is opaque to us. Even more importantly, a hallmark of general intelligence is the ability to deal with new situations, including ones that were unforeseen by the AI's developers. We cannot program what we cannot anticipate, but teaching can be applied when it is needed and adapted to the requirements of any situation.

Cognitive architectures aspiring towards AGI often contain very little domain-specific knowledge to preserve their generality, and start their "life" in a baby-like state. Without knowledge, little more can be done than systematically (or randomly) exploring the state-action space, which becomes prohibitive as the complexity of targeted domains increases—*even if the learning system is very sophisticated.* Teaching can guide such systems towards salient stimuli or knowledge, or to provide it directly. As progress is made in AI/AGI research, the number of architectures capable of utilizing sophisticated teaching techniques is ever growing [6], making a general theory of teaching more desirable than ever.

Due to these benefits, many ML projects have developed methods for "helping their AI system learn", but so far this has mostly been done on an ad-hoc case-by-case basis. A general theory of AP could help us understand what works in which situations. Unfortunately, teaching is a highly nontrivial process that involves many moving parts. In the social sciences, similar efforts have entire research fields dedicated to them (i.e. pedagogy, educational science, developmental psychology, etc.), and we argue AP should be seen in a similar manner. In AP however, we cannot make the same assumptions that are warranted in the social sciences, because the (eventual) space of artificial minds is many times larger than the space of human minds. We cannot take concepts for granted, and must make an effort to define them explicitly and rigorously.

---

[2] Note that the term "teaching" does not necessarily imply a mirroring of the human teacher-student setup—it is quite conceivable for an AI to have a built-in "automatic teaching mechanism". That would not, however, change the need for a theory of teaching. While teaching does not change the inherent capabilities of AI systems in principle, it allows them to reach more of their potential more efficiently.

Our goal in presenting the Pedagogical Pentagon (see Fig. 1a) is to provide something that our knowledge in this domain can be organized around, and to facilitate structured and systematic research in this area. We take inspiration from e.g. Bloom's taxonomy of learning domains, which has been used as the basis for many educational programs for humans, by providing different learning targets to focus (or not focus) on [7]. While it is impossible to provide full theories of every concept involved in AP here, even such theories they existed, we hope to provide some ideas for how AP might be studied.

2   Background, Definitions and Concepts

To model the learning process, we consider the interaction of intelligent systems with various environments.[3] An *environment* is a perspective on the world, consisting of a set of variables with acceptable values, an initial state, and functions that describe how it changes over time [13]. Examples of possible environments include games, rooms, buildings, cities, countries and indeed the entire world. Intelligent systems can independently decide at which abstraction level they want to consider different parts of the world in different situations.

Intelligent systems continually receive inputs/observations from their environment and send outputs/actions back. Some of the system's inputs may be treated specially—e.g. as feedback or a reward signal, possibly provided by a teacher. Since intelligent action can only be called that if it is trying to achieve something, we model intelligent agents as imperfect optimizers of some (possibly unknown) real-valued objective function. *Tasks* are similarly defined by (possibly different) objective functions, as well as (possibly) *instructions* (i.e. knowledge provided at the start of the task or throughout its duration). Since tasks can only be defined w.r.t. some environment, we often refer to the combination of a task and its environment as a single unit: the task-environment.

In the AP setting, we have at least two different intelligent systems with the roles of "learner" and "teacher".[4] The teacher's *teaching task* is to change the learner's knowledge in some way (e.g. to make the learner understand something, or increase the learner's skill on some metric). The learner and the teacher each interact with their own view of the world (i.e. their own "environments") which are typically different, but overlapping to some degree. The learner will always exist in some form in the teacher's task-environment, and the teacher teaches by affecting the learner's. As we will see, there are many ways to do

---

[3] The formulation of an intelligent system (or agent) interacting with the world (or environment) is most commonly used in control theory and reinforcement learning. However, it is a fully general formulation, that also covers traditional cases of e.g. supervised and unsupervised learning. Here the environment simply presents a (training) datum at each time step, the agent responds with a classification or prediction, and—in the case of supervised learning—the environment replies with the target outcome or an error signal.

[4] Generally speaking, there could be multiple learners and teachers, but here we focus on the one-on-one situation.

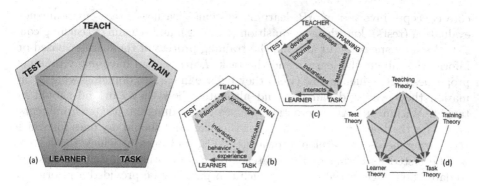

Fig. 1: (a) The Pedagogical Pentagon. (b) Information flow between processes. (c) Relations between systems. (d) Dependencies between theories.

this, including full determination of the learner's environment, modification of existing environments, or simply by changing their own behavior (if the teacher is in the learner's environment this affects its dynamics from the learner's point of view).

An AP interaction is defined by a number of teachers interacting with their own environments who are given a *teaching task* that contains *learning objectives* for the involved learners as well a set of constraints (e.g. on budget, time, resources, allowed actions, etc.). Given (possibly incomplete and imperfect) information about the various aspects of an AP interaction, we want a theory of AP to give us predictions of what the teacher(s) would do, and more importantly, what they *should* do in order to optimize the objective function. For instance, if a chess teacher doesn't know the learner is deaf, we can predict he try to verbally explain things, realize this doesn't work, and switch to a different strategy—one that he perhaps should have used from the start, if he had known better.

The role of "teacher" may be taken up by any entity or system, including e.g. school teachers, schools, specialist AI systems, AI system designers, or indeed us as AP practitioners. AP theory (and the Pedagogical Pentagon) can be applied fractally, on multiple levels of organization. For instance, a school could be seen as a "teacher", tasked with instilling certain kinds of knowledge in the children who go there. The school may pick out some high level methodologies (e.g. montessori), but for the most part it relies on employing human professors who interact with the children directly. These professors can be controlled to varying degrees (e.g. a curriculum could be provided or not), but ultimately they are themselves "teachers" (in the AP sense) with their own (limited) knowledge and capabilities that the school needs to take into account.

3   Conceptual Framework

In this paper we introduce a conceptual framework for studying AP in the form of the "Pedagogical Pentagon" (see Fig. 1) which we believe outlines the five core concepts involved in AP: learning systems (learners), task-environments, evaluation (tests), knowledge acquisition (training), and teaching. Teaching consists, broadly speaking, of altering the training process of the learner, based on information about the learner and the task. *Learners* can have many different properties that influence how (well) they behave in various domains, what information they need and can use, and ultimately how they can and should be taught. Within one AP interaction, we see many different *task-environments*: one(s) for the teacher(s) to define what they can and should do, ones for which the learner needs to develop knowledge/skills, and ones in which the learner will be tested and trained. Proper teaching requires that the teacher has up-to-date knowledge of the learner, which can partially be provided a priori, but must otherwise be obtained through evaluation or *testing* of the learner as they interact with a task-environment and (hopefully) make progress on the learning objectives. Similarly, we want to have some idea of how interaction with a task-environment will *train* (or otherwise influence) the learner's knowledge. Finally, *teaching* can be done using different methods by utilizing knowledge of testing, training, task-environments and the learner in order to make sure the learner learns what is necessary within the constraints outlined by the teaching task.

The pentagon can be viewed on multiple levels. Figure 1b showcases the different goals of training—to imbue knowledge into the learner—and testing—to obtain information about the learner—by looking at the information flow between processes. Knowledge flows from the teaching to the training process to create a curriculum in the form of a task-environment that the learner experiences. And as the learner behaves in a task-environment, that interaction can be analyzed by a testing process to obtain information for teaching. Figure 1c views each corner as systems and specifies their relations. The teacher devises tests and trainings, which in turn instantiate task-environments that the learner interacts with. Figure 1d shows the hierarchical dependencies between theories: learners and task-environments can be analyzed in isolation or possibly together, training and testing use task-environments to instill/obtain knowledge into/about the learner, and teaching involves designing appropriate tests and training schemes.

All concepts can interact and constrain each other. For instance, any given task-environment imposes requirements on the learner (who must be able to perform the task), which in turn restricts the teaching methods we can use. Or if we want to use certain teaching methods, we must select or design a learning system that can make optimal use of them. Or if resources like time are limited, we might have to simultaneously use task-environments for testing and training.

Our ultimate goal is to develop a full theory of artificial pedagogy, in the same sense that we might want to develop a full theory of artificial intelligence or machine learning. The realization of this goal is naturally (vastly) beyond the scope of this paper. The Pedagogical Pentagon should be viewed as a conceptual framework around which the knowledge we obtain in this domain can be organized. By separating out different aspects of AP—each of which are deserving of their own comprehensive theories—and relating them to each other, we hope to make research in this domain more tractable and systematic/structured.

3.1 Tasks

The concept of a "task" is at the core of AI. We design AI systems to perform ranges of tasks, then we use related but possibly different tasks to train them, before using (often slightly different) tasks for evaluation. Yet, our understanding of the concept is mainly intuitive. We have argued before about the need for more rigorous task theories in AI, that aid us in the general analysis and construction of task-environments [13].

This is especially pressing in the context of artificial pedagogy, where many task-environments are often involved in a single pedagogical interaction. First, there is the task-environment for the teacher. This environment contains, among other things, the learner(s) and defines the actions and observations available to the teacher. The teaching task typically refers to the learning objective(s) as well as additional constraints on e.g. budget, time and other resources. The learning objectives are the objectives for the learner(s), which are typically to achieve some epistemic state (i.e. know or understand something), to alter preferences (e.g. in the case of inverse reinforcement or value learning), and/or to perform well in some range of task-environments. So secondly, we have the set of task-environments that the learner will interact with. In a pedagogical setting, these may either be created, influenced or utilized by the teacher. Here we can distinguish between task-environments meant for obtaining information about the learner (testing), meant for training the user, or both.

Despite these interactions with other corners in the Pedagogical Pentagon, we believe that task theory can also be studied in relative isolation. A task theory should provide a method for representing tasks and environments in a way that facilitates their analysis and construction [13]. A more specific list of desiderata includes abilities to compare tasks, to create abstractions, concretizations and decompositions, to characterize tasks in terms of various (emergent) measures and provided instructions, to estimate resources necessary for task completion, and to construct new tasks based on combination, variation and specifications. Different AI research scenarios will make use of different aspects of task theory, but it seems that a good teacher would potentially use everything.

3.2 Learners

The ultimate goal of any teaching interaction is to help another learning system—the learner—learn something. Naturally, the way in which any system learns—as well as how to optimize this process—depends on the specifics of that system. A 'learner theory" would parallel the above mentioned "task theory" in that it should allow us to analyze, define, characterize, categorize and compare learning systems. Many partial attempts at comparison and categorization have been made (cf. [6] for a recent overview), but we are not aware of any rigorous and comprehensive treatment of all aspects of learning systems.

From a teaching (and learning) perspective, it's important to distinguish between structure and content. By "structure" we mean aspects of the system that remain relatively constant throughout the learning interaction like the architecture/algorithm(s) and the body. By "content" we mean knowledge, of which various kinds exist, including declarative knowledge or beliefs (e.g. "the capital of France is Paris" or "yesterday I felt good"), procedural knowledge or skills (e.g. knowing how to ride a bike), and structural knowledge or priorities (e.g. feeling that avoiding a predator is more important than eating now).

Structure properties include the kinds of memory (e.g. procedural, episodic, and/or semantic), reasoning (e.g. inductive, deductive, counterfactual and/or analogical), and learning (e.g. supervised, unsupervised and/or reinforcement) mechanisms the learner has, as well as their capacity and how they operate. These properties are important for AP, because there is no sense in explaining something by analogy if the learner can't reason by analogy, or providing affective feedback if there are no reinforcement learning mechanisms. Knowledge properties are much more fluid, and can often be the subject of the teaching task—e.g. to make the learner understand/know something, be good at something, or want something. Since this knowledge is likely to refer to or model the environment, the chosen representation should be compared to the representation mechanism used for task-environments. From these properties, other—often measurable—properties emerge, such as performance (in different situations), adaptivity, robustness and understanding [5].

The relationship between the learner and testing corners of the Pedagogical Pentagon is that for the learner, we are primarily interested in "what" properties it has and how they are defined, whereas testing is primarily concerned with "how" this information can then be obtained (approximately) *from* a specific instance of a learner [5]. As such, we could come up with formal definitions of properties we care about (e.g. intelligence [8]), without worrying about whether they can be measured directly. Learner theory lets us consider the "insides" of a hypothetical learner directly, while testing provides an "outside" view based on observed behavior. Similarly, most aspects of the learner can be analyzed and defined without making reference to the exact way in which knowledge (and consequently emergent properties) change as the learner interacts with some task-environment (i.e. training). Some aspects of learners could also be studied without a theory of task-environments, but this is not always the case. For instance, to estimate the (changing) level of complexity and variety that a learner can handle, we need a task theory to provide measures of complexity and variety of task-environments.

3.3   Testing

To teach well, the teacher has to know the student. While some aspects of the learner may be known a priori, others must be obtained by the teacher interactively (e.g. progress towards the learning objectives). We define "testing" generally as the empirical means through which an observer obtains information about another system by systematically observing its behavior as it interacts with its task-environments [5]. Specifically, testing is meant to obtain information about the structural, epistemic and emergent properties of learners described in Sect. 3.2. Testing can be done for different purposes: e.g. to ensure that a learner has good-enough performance on a range of tasks, to identify strengths and weaknesses for an AI designer to improve or an adversary to exploit, or to ensure that a learner has understood a certain concept so that we can trust it will use it correctly in the future. A "Test Theory" for growing recursive self-improvers may first and foremost be concerned with gauging levels of understanding in service of such confidence-building [12]. In the context of AP, our primary concern is to let a teacher obtain information about limitations, strengths and preferences of the learner, and to measure progress with respect to the learning objectives. A test theory should allow us to extract information about a learner from its behavior in a task-environment, predict what kind of information we could obtain in a given task-environment, and help to construct (or alter) task-environments to obtain desired information using minimal resources.

There are many different ways of AI evaluation [3,4,9], but we are not aware of any theory that covers all kinds of information extraction. Information can be extracted by sporadic evaluations (e.g. like school tests) or continual observation (e.g. like a sports coach does), it can be over or covert, and it can be done using many different tests (e.g. multiple-choice vs. open questions vs. a project). Designing tests is subject to real-world constraints such as malleability of the task-environment, available knowledge, and capabilities of both learner and teacher. In both the design of tests and the interpretation of learner behavior or results, it is important to take into account the goals of the learner and how they compare to the used performance measure: if the learner performs poorly, is it because they lack skill/knowledge, did they misunderstand the instruction, or did they simply not care to do well?

3.4   Training

Learning systems adjust their knowledge as a result of interactions with a task-environment. Viewed from a teacher's (and intentional learner's) point of view, we refer to this as "training" as the goal is to become better at some task. Nevertheless, we should not neglect the possibilities that erroneous things can be learned, and desirable things can be unlearned. The goal of the teacher is to influence the learner's task-environments in such a way that progress towards the is facilitated. AP is interested in predicting how a learner's knowledge/skills will change as a result of interacting with a particular class or instance of a task-environment, and to allow us to construct (or alter) task-environments in order to train a particular skill or impart particular knowledge.

Training is roughly analogous to testing, but each has a different goal: The goal of training is to move the learner from one state to another—to get knowledge into the learner—while testing is about getting an accurate model or measure of the learner's skill at some point(s) in time—getting information out of the learner. Both make heavy use of both task theory and learner theory. Training theory is mainly concerned with how interactions with the environment affect the epistemic and emergent properties of the learner (i.e. knowledge and performance). As with test theory, there will be different kinds of training (e.g. repeated exposure to similar stimuli vs. one-time explanations) which may occur intentionally or not, and success will depend on the goals of the learner.

Many theories of learning/training already exist in e.g. educational science, developmental psychology and animal training. Such theories may usefully be plugged into our Pedagogical Pentagon to facilitate the science of teaching if the learner is indeed human (or an animal). For AI, the assumptions these theories make typically do not hold. Nevertheless, it is worthwhile to figure out which theories do apply to which kinds of AI. For instance, approaches surrounding Vygotsky's zone or proximal development, where most learning occurs in tasks that are only just beyond the learner's current skill level, seem applicable to many different learning systems [14], and it may be possible to adapt or generalize Piaget's stages of cognitive development to the AI domain [3,10].

Training is also closely related to the established ML subfield of computational learning theory, which concerns itself with the formal analysis of learning in AI systems. So far, it seems this has mostly been concerned with calculating bounds on how many interactions are necessary to achieve a certain level of performance. In addition to this, we are also interested in the content of those interactions, and the specifics of how the learner's knowledge changes.

3.5 Teaching

Teaching is what artificial pedagogy is all about: we want to analyze and design teaching strategies and interactions, using the other concepts and theories we discussed. A teacher should test the learner in order to obtain information that informs the way they proceed to train the learner by altering the task-environment from the learner's point-of-view.[5] This should all be done according to the constraints specified in the teaching task, and with the limitations on knowledge and capabilities of the teacher. It will likely combine knowledge from theories of testing and training to create environments that both allow the teacher to observe progress and encourage it—ideally simultaneously—and avoid adverse interactions between testing and training.

It would be valuable to be able to model and categorize teachers in relation to learners and task-environments. For instance, teachers can be visibly present or not (e.g. they can just change the environment without appearing in it). Or if they teach by demonstration, it may be important to consider how good they are at the task that is demonstrated and how similar their body is to the learner's.

There are many different teaching techniques that can be employed: e.g. heuristic rewarding, decomposition, simplification, situation selection, teleoperation, demonstration, coaching, explanation, and cooperation [2]. Using the other corners of the Pedagogical Pentagon, teaching theories should be able to tell us how to tailor these teaching techniques to different situations (i.e. learner-task combinations + constraints) and what results we can expect. Some more or less full curricula have been developed for teaching AGI, such as the

---

[5] Note that if the teacher is in the learner's task-environment, every policy change alters the task-environment in some way.

AGI Preschool [3] and GoodAI's School for AI [11]. We believe these constitute important and highly promising pedagogical programs, that could be further improved with an even better understanding of the aspects of AP we have discussed.

4 Conclusion

We argue for the importance of artificial pedagogy for artificial intelligence and present a conceptual framework to aid in the structured and systematic study of this field. The Pedagogical Pentagon identifies five core concepts involved in pedagogical interactions: learners, task-environments, testing, training and teaching. The complexity of AP can be somewhat mitigated by studying one corner of the pentagon while keeping the others fixed. Partial theories of tasks and learners could possibly be made without reference to testing, training and teaching, and testing and training could (mostly) be studied in part without referring to teaching, but a complete understanding of all aspects of learning will not emerge unless the constraints that each of these put on the others are included in the picture. By organizing AP in this way we hope to facilitate the tractable study of this challenging domain, and provide a conceptual framework in which acquired knowledge can easily be organized.

References

1. Bieger, J.: Artificial pedagogy: a proposal. In: HLAI Doctoral Consortium (2016)
2. Bieger, J., Thórisson, K.R., Garrett, D.: Raising AI: tutoring matters. In: Goertzel, B., Orseau, L., Snaider, J. (eds.) AGI 2014. LNCS (LNAI), vol. 8598, pp. 1–10. Springer, Cham (2014). doi:10.1007/978-3-319-09274-4_1
3. Goertzel, B., Pennachin, C., Geisweiller, N.: AGI Preschool. In: Engineering General Intelligence, Part 1, pp. 337–354. Atlantis Press, Amsterdam (2014)
4. Hernández-Orallo, J.: The Measure of All Minds: Evaluating Natural and Artificial Intelligence. Cambridge University Press, Cambridge (2016)
5. Bieger, J., Thórisson, K.R., Steunebrink, B.R.: Evaluation of general-purpose artificial intelligence: why, what & how. In: Evaluating General-Purpose AI 2016. The Hague, Netherlands (2016)
6. Kotseruba, I., Gonzalez, O.J.A., Tsotsos, J.K.: A review of 40 years of cognitive architecture research: focus on perception, attention, learning and applications [cs] (2016). arxiv:1610.08602
7. Krathwohl, D.R.: A revision of Bloom's taxonomy: an overview. Theor. Pract. 41(4), 212–218 (2016)
8. Legg, S., Hutter, M.: A collection of definitions of intelligence. Adv. AGI: concepts, architectures and algorithms 157, 17–24 (2007)
9. Marcus, G., Rossi, F., Veloso, M. (eds.): Beyond the Turing test. AI Mag. 37(1) (2016). 1st edn. AAAI
10. Piaget, J.: Piaget's theory. In: Inhelder, B., Chipman, H.H., Zwingmann, C. (eds.) Piaget and His School. Springer, Heidelberg (1976). Springer Study Edition
11. Rosa, M., Feyereisl, J., Collective, T.G.: A Framework for Searching for General Artificial Intelligence. GoodAI, Prague, Czech Republic, Technical report (2016)

12. Steunebrink, B.R., Thórisson, K.R., Schmidhuber, J.: Growing recursive self-improvers. In: Steunebrink, B., Wang, P., Goertzel, B. (eds.) AGI -2016. LNCS, vol. 9782, pp. 129–139. Springer, Cham (2016). doi:10.1007/978-3-319-41649-6_13

13. Thórisson, K.R., Bieger, J., Thorarensen, T., Sigurdardóttir, J.S., Steunebrink, B.R.: Why artificial intelligence needs a task theory. In: Steunebrink, B., Wang, P., Goertzel, B. (eds.) AGI -2016. LNCS (LNAI), vol. 9782, pp. 118–128. Springer, Cham (2016). doi:10.1007/978-3-319-41649-6_12

14. Vygotsky, L.S.: Interaction between learning and development. In: Cole, M., John-Steiner, V., Scribner, S., Souberman, E. (eds.) Mind in Society: The Development of Higher Psychological Processes, pp. 79–91. Harvard University Press, Cambridge (1978)

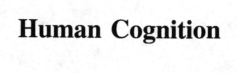

Human Cognition

An Information-Theoretic Predictive Model for the Accuracy of AI Agents Adapted from Psychometrics

Nader Chmait[(✉)], David L. Dowe, Yuan-Fang Li, and David G. Green

Faculty of Information Technology, Monash University, Clayton, Australia
nader.chmait@monash.edu, chmait.nader@gmail.com

Abstract. We propose a new model to quantitatively estimate the accuracy of artificial agents over cognitive tasks of approximable complexities. The model is derived by introducing notions from algorithmic information theory into a well-known (psychometric) measurement paradigm called Item Response Theory (IRT). A lower bound on accuracy can be guaranteed with respect to task complexity and the breadth of its solution space using our model. This in turn permits formulating the relationship between agent selection cost, task difficulty and accuracy as optimisation problems. Further results indicate some of the settings over which a group of cooperative agents can be more or less accurate than individual agents or other groups.

1 Introduction and Background

Turing's imitation game [32] inspired a range of attempts to measure the intelligence of artificial agents [6]. More recently, a formal (machine) intelligence test [10] consisting of sequence-completion exercises was devised. Later, fuzzy integrals were used [1] to measure intelligence in machines by calculating a Machine Intelligence Quotient. Shortly after, a simple computer program that succeeded in passing a variety of IQ tests was presented [26], raising questions on the appropriateness of intelligence tests for machine assessment. After the definition of *universal intelligence* [18], many (algorithmic) information-theoretic studies were put forward to formally quantify the intelligence of individual AI agents [12,13] as well as AI collectives [4].

Independently, a series of measurement theories have been proposed in psychometrics and applied to human intelligence. One of the earliest milestones in human intelligence testing was Thurstone's letter series completion problems [31] and, more recently, Raven's Progressive Matrices test [24] which recorded strong correlation with Spearman's general intelligence factor [30]. More general tests consisting of a variety of evaluation tasks were developed, and they came to be known as "Intelligence Quotient" or simply IQ tests. Examples of such tests are the Stanford-Binet test [25] and the Wechsler intelligence scales for adults and children [33]. Another mainstream achievement in psychometrics was the development of Item Response Theory (IRT) [22], also referred to as latent trait

© Springer International Publishing AG 2017
T. Everitt et al. (Eds.): AGI 2017, LNAI 10414, pp. 225–236, 2017.
DOI: 10.1007/978-3-319-63703-7_21

theory. IRT is among the most popular measurement classes used in psychometrics for evaluating traits, or abilities, and producing accurate rankings from test scores, by applying mathematical models to testing data. In the context of IRT, a trait or an ability might be physical or psychological (cognitive and non-cognitive, e.g., a personality or behavioural characteristic) [5]. Recently, IRT was successfully adopted to analyse machine learning models by providing an instance-wise analysis of a series of datasets and classifiers [23]. In this paper, we show how to adapt models from psychometrics and IQ tests, based on notions from algorithmic information-theory, to artificial intelligence in order to estimate the (cognitive) abilities of artificial agents and predict their accuracies.

2   Motivation and Main Contributions

Advances in psychometrics are not yet thoroughly applied for predicting the accuracy of AI agents despite their success in evaluating human cognitive abilities. While the AI discipline adheres to the mainstream concept of intelligence [9], general IQ tests might not be appropriate in their current form for evaluating machine intelligence [7]. In fact, even test batteries that might be suitable for practically evaluating AI (and knowledge based systems [15]) show some caveats. For instance, such tests measure an average performance (of one or more abilities) of AI agents over a set of tasks or environments but it is ambiguous how the results from these tests can be used to predict the accuracy of an agent over a particular task complexity without actually administering that task to the agent. In addition to many theoretical studies discussed in [11], empirical studies such as [3,4] demonstrated that task complexity and the breadth of its solution space are major factors influencing the performance of artificial agents. Hence, quantitatively predicting the accuracy of artificial agents across different task complexities and solution spaces is clearly an important feature that has not been addressed so far. Furthermore, intelligence test scores can be unreliable since agents usually exhibit non-uniformity between their performances over different problems/settings. This has implications for selecting agents to solve tasks, particularly when there is cost (e.g., processing time) associated with utilising agents, and understanding the collective accuracy of cooperative agents of different (cognitive) abilities.

By merging notions from both psychometrics and (algorithmic) information theory, we develop a hybrid model to quantitatively estimate the accuracy of AI agents over tasks of measurable complexities. We demonstrate its functionality over a class of prediction and inference problems as this class is considered as reflecting some of the principal traits of intelligence both in psychometrics [9] and artificial intelligence [8,11,21]. Using the predictive model, we show how to identify agents that can guarantee a lower bound on accuracy with respect to task complexity and the breadth of its solution space. We analyse settings over which a group of (voting) agents can be more or less effective than individual agents, or other groups, and identify circumstances that can be counterintuitive to the conclusions drawn from intelligence tests. In the next section we outline important properties and constraints that our model needs to embrace.

3   Desirable Properties for Assessment

Given a subject (cognitive agent) to be evaluated over a task/problem:

1. The model must return a *quantitative* measure (on an interval scale) of the estimated subject's accuracy over this task without the need to administer it to the subject.
2. The accuracy of a subject (its probability of success in solving a task) predicted by the model is expected to be proportional to its (relevant cognitive) ability over that task, and inversely proportional to the difficulty of the task.
3. In order to conform to the *limiting* behaviour of real agents, the model should use the asymptotic minimum (p_{rand}, which denotes the probability of correctly selecting a random solution from the solution space) as a lower-bound on accuracy.
4. The model should be applicable over different tasks of measurable difficulties.
5. The difficulty measure should be general enough to accommodate a wide range of tasks.
6. The model should be applicable to different agent types and cognitive systems.

Earlier information-theoretic studies on (artificial) intelligence [12,14] and inductive-inference [19,29] discussed (among others) two general dimensions of task difficulty, (i) Shannon's entropy [27] which is related to the uncertainty and breadth of the solution search space, and (ii) the algorithmic information-theoretic (in particular the Kolmogorov) complexity [16,21] of the task. We take into account both dimensions of difficulty in the design of our model.

4   A Predictive Model of Agent Accuracy

Inspired by the 2-parameter logistic model [2] of IRT [22], we propose a mathematical model for predicting a subject's expected accuracy on a given task/problem of measurable complexity.

Definition 1. *Let x denote a (classification) task/problem of a theoretical difficulty $\mathcal{D}$ such that the solution to x belongs to the alphabet (or solution space) $S = \{s_1, s_2, \ldots, s_m\}$. We define (an estimate of) the accuracy of an agent with ability $\alpha \in \mathbb{R}^+$ over that task to be:*

$$P_{\mathcal{D},\alpha,m} = \frac{1}{m} + e^{-\frac{\mathcal{D}}{\alpha}} \cdot \left(1 - \frac{1}{m}\right) \tag{1}$$

which corresponds to the probability of that agent guessing the correct solution to x.

The above model has the following important properties. For a given task of a (hypothetically) negligible difficulty, the probability of solving this task is $\lim_{\mathcal{D}\to 0} P_{\mathcal{D},\alpha,m} = 1$. The probability $P_{\mathcal{D},\alpha,m}$ of a subject with ability $\alpha > 0$ solving a task is (exponentially) proportional to the subject's ability, and inversely proportional to the difficulty of the task $\mathcal{D}$, and the breadth of its solution space

$m \in \mathbb{N}^+$. Moreover, when task difficulty $\mathcal{D}$ is very high relative to α (or when the subject's ability α is small), the probability of success $P_{\mathcal{D},\alpha,m}$ converges to a random guess equivalent to $1/m$, which is the asymptotic minimum[1]. For instance, on a binary test problem (e.g., coin toss problem with S={Heads, Tails}) with $m = 2$, an agent with ability α has an accuracy $P_{\mathcal{D},\alpha,m} = 0.5 + e^{\frac{-\mathcal{D}}{\alpha}}(0.5)$. When the ability α is close to zero, $P_{\mathcal{D},\alpha,m} \cong 0.5$. For many problems, the theoretical task difficulty $\mathcal{D}$ can be derived from the simplest solution (policy) to the task, and therefore can sometimes be linked to the *complexity* of the (description of the) task, or the complexity of the description of its policy. Consequently, the difficulty of the task can be linked to its Kolmogorov complexity [16,21]. Since the Kolmogorov complexity is uncomputable, methods like Levin's Kt complexity [20,21] or the Lempel-Ziv (compression) algorithm [19] can be used as practical alternatives (to bound it and possibly approximate it). For the rest of this paper, we will use the Kolmogorov complexity of the task as a derivation of its (theoretical) difficulty. The suggested model returns the probability of a subject solving a given task of a measurable complexity as a function of its (previously measured) ability. The ability could be defined as a vector of weighted atomic sub-abilities s.t. α is a linear combination of $[w_1\alpha_1 + w_2\alpha_2 + \ldots + w_t\alpha_t]$. The model in Eq. 1 is a simple case of the latter where, for some integer $z \leq t$, the ability $\alpha = w_z\alpha_z$ and $\sum_{j=1,j\neq z}^t w_j = 0$ in $[w_1\alpha_1 + w_2\alpha_2 + \ldots + w_t\alpha_t]$.

We will use a formal intelligence test from the literature of AI, the C-test [10], to measure an agent's ability α over a class of tasks. $\mathcal{D}$ and m are input parameters to the model typically being measured by some earlier assessment or derived directly from the problem. We refer to the model defined in Eq. 1 as the *IRT model* for brevity, and use the terms *accuracy* and *performance* alternately (only) as measures of the probability of success at solving a (cognitive) task.

5   Assessing Inference Abilities

The C-test [10] is a compression-based intelligence test that measures the ability of a subject doing inductive-inference and finding the best explanation for sequences of various complexities. It reflects the *fluid* intelligence of the evaluated subject. The idea is to record the performance of a subject over a series of patterns of increasing incomprehensibilities (or complexities). The complexity of a C-test sequence is formally measured using Levin's Kt complexity [21] as a practical alternative to (and possibly a rough bound on) its Kolmogorov complexity. Given $\Sigma = \{a, b, c, d, e, f, g, h, i, j, k, l, m, n, o, p, q, r, s, t, u, v, w, x, y, z\}$, and a sequence θ of length m where each $\theta_i \in \Sigma$, the task consists of predicting the next letter $\theta_{m+1} \in \Sigma$ which correctly completes the sequence. Given a C-test consisting of a collection of test sequences $CT = (seq_1, \ldots, seq_n)$ with their corresponding answers (solutions) $S = (\theta_{m+1}^1, \ldots, \theta_{m+1}^n)$ and corresponding complexities $K = (k_1, \ldots, k_n)$, the average score $\tilde{r}$ of an agent π with guesses $S' = (\theta_{m+1}'^1, \ldots, \theta_{m+1}'^n)$ over CT is:

---

[1] For simplicity and without loss of generality, $1/m$ is used in Eq. 1 to replace the probability p_{rand} of an agent randomly guessing (one of) the correct solutions to the problem.

$\tilde{r} = \frac{1}{\sum_{z=1}^{n} k_z} \cdot \sum_{z=1}^{n} k_z \times hit(\theta'^{z}_{m+1}, \theta^{z}_{m+1})$, where the function $hit(a, b) \leftarrow \begin{cases} 1 & \text{if } a == b \\ 0 & \text{otherwise} \end{cases}$,

and the complexity of the sequence k_z is used as a weight in order to give more importance to more difficult questions. The C-test score will be used to determine the inductive-inference ability α of a subject, further used as a parameter in the model (Eq. 1). The reasons for selecting the C-test are, firstly, the test by definition measures an (inductive inference related) ability, in this case the ability of finding the best explanation for a given sequence using induction. The test is well formulated and is exclusively defined in computational terms. It generates sequences (tasks) within a range of complexities $7 \leq D \leq 15$, using Levin's Kt approximation [10] (as a practical alternative to *Kolmogorov* complexity). The C-test results are highly correlated with those from classical psychometric (IQ) tests [10]. The test sequences are formatted and presented in a quite similar way to psychometric tests. Hence, the test can be applied to machines in the same way it is applied to humans. There is typically one exclusive correct (simplest) answer for any of the test sequences, making the results uncoincidental and representative of the testee's accuracy.

Measuring abilities: Table 1 holds the definitions of a few agent behaviours to be evaluated over the C-test. Their scores are used to measure their (inductive inference) ability α and are plotted in Fig. 1 along with their corresponding accuracies $P_{D,\alpha,m}$ generated using the IRT model (Eq. 1). More advanced algorithms for sequence prediction problems exist but since the choice of agent behaviours is not particularly relevant to the validity of the model we restrict our selection to those in the Table 1. The agents' abilities were calculated as a function of their C-test scores using $\alpha = \omega \tilde{r}$, where α is the ability of agent π with score $\tilde{r}$, and $\omega \in \mathbb{R}$ is a fitting parameter selected in such a way to (i) ensure that the agent's moderate accuracy, of $0.5(\max P_{D,\alpha,m} + \min P_{D,\alpha,m}) \equiv 0.5(1 + 1/m)$, falls under the area of *discriminative* task complexities $\int_{D=6}^{D=16} P_{D,\alpha,m}$ (following [10]) and, (ii) minimise the mean squared error between the IRT model and C-test scores. Our model nicely illustrates the agents' average accuracies as illustrated in Fig. 1 despite the large non-uniformity in their behaviours and performances.

6   Predicting Agent Performance

While results from the C-tests are all alone interesting, we have no means to extrapolate them or predict the agent performances over different sequence complexities and solution space sizes without re-running the test. However, the expected accuracies of an agent can easily be generated from the IRT model over inference tasks of different complexities. An example is illustrated in Fig. 2 showing the predicted accuracies of agent π^{mind} (refer to Table 1) across different hypothetical (Kolmogorov) complexities D and problem solution space sizes m. For any fixed difficulty $\mathcal{D}$, the IRT model shows that the difference in accuracy measures $P_{D,\alpha,m_1} - P_{D,\alpha,m_2}$ over two solution space sizes $m_2 > m_1$ is:

$$\frac{1}{m_1} + \frac{e^{\frac{-D}{\alpha}}}{m_1} - \frac{1}{m_2} - \frac{e^{\frac{-D}{\alpha}}}{m_2} = \frac{(1+e^{\frac{-D}{\alpha}})(m_2 - m_1)}{m_1 \cdot m_2}, \text{ meaning that this difference is greater}$$

Table 1. Sample agent behaviours evaluated over the C-test.

Random agent : given a sequence seq, a *random agent* π^{rand} randomly uniformly selects a letter from Σ and returns it as its answer θ'_{m+1} (Refer to Sec. 5).	Pattern agents : a pattern agent π^{pt} looks for a repeating distance pattern between the elements of seq and completes it to infer θ'_{m+1}. To implement this behaviour, the problem is divided
Mode agent : given a sequence seq, a *mode agent* π^{mode} looks for the most repeated or frequent letter(s) in seq to predict the next letter. If more than one letter satisfy the criteria, it chooses the left-most one appearing in the sequence.	into $m-1$ tasks $\{t_1, t_2, \ldots, t_{m-1}\}$ assigned to agents $\{\pi_1^{pt}, \pi_2^{pt}, \ldots, \pi_{m-1}^{pt}\}$ respectively. Agent π_y^{pt} calculates $d(\theta_{i+y} - \theta_i) \forall i \in \{1, \ldots, m-y\}$
Min-repetition agent : given a sequence seq, a *min-repetition agent* π^{mr} looks for the least repeated letter in seq to predict the next letter.	and generates a list of distances $D_y = (d_y^1, \ldots, d_y^k)$ where $k = m - y$, and
Min-distance agent : given $seq = (\theta_1, \theta_2, \ldots, \theta_m)$, agent π^{mind} looks for the minimal alphabetical distance (Def. 2) between all consecutive letters of seq and infers the next letter θ'_{m+1} by adding this distance to seq's last letter θ_m.	$d_y^i := d(\theta_{i+y} - \theta_i)$. Then, π_y^{pt} searches for the occurrences of the longest possible pattern in D_y and continues D_y by adding d_y^{k+1} following the pseudo-algorithm below.
Definition 2. *The alphabetical distance $d(\gamma - \beta)$ between two characters β and γ in an alphabet Σ is equal to the difference between their index positions in the totally ordered set $(\Sigma, \leq)$ in $\bmod \|\Sigma\|$.*	Input : set of distances $D_y = (d_y^1, d_y^2, \ldots, d_y^k)$.
For instance, the distance between any two consecutive letters in the alphabet is 1, and the distance between the first character α and the last one z is equal to $d(z - a) = 26 - 1 = 25$. So, given a C-test sequence $seq = (\theta_1, \theta_2, \ldots, \theta_m)$,	Output : next distance d_y^{k+1} in D_y.
agent π^{mind} calculates the distance $d^i := d(\theta_{i+1} - \theta_i)$ following Definition 2 between two consecutive elements of seq for all $i \in \{1, \ldots, m-1\}$ returning a pattern (list) of distances $D = (d^1, d^2, \ldots, d^{m-1})$. Then, π^{mind} looks for the minimal alphabetical distance $d^{min} \in D$ as follows:	1: Extract the unique elements of D_y. 2: Store elements in a list U_y in order of appearance. 3: Find the starting index for each substring occurrence U_y in D_y. 4: Store index in vector v.
$d^{min} \leftarrow \operatorname{argmin}_{d \in D} freq(d, D)$ where $freq(d, D)$ is a function that returns the rate at which d occurs in D. Agent π^{mind} finally chooses $\theta'_{m+1} \in \Sigma$ such that $d(\theta'_{m+1} - \theta_m) = d^{min}$.	5: if $|v| > 1$ then 6: $P \leftarrow D_y(v(1) : v(2) - 1)$ ▷ $v(i)$ is the i'th element of v 7: else if $|v| \leq 1$ & $|D_y| > 1$ then 8: $P \leftarrow D_y(|D_y| - 1)$ 9: else
Max-distance agent : this is the opposite behaviour of *min-distance agent*. Given a sequence $seq = (\theta_1, \theta_2, \ldots, \theta_m)$, a *max-distance agent* π^{maxd} calculates the distance $d^i := d(\theta_{i+1} - \theta_i)$ between the consecutive elements of seq for all $i \in \{1, \ldots, m-1\}$ returning a pattern (list) of distances $D = (d^1, d^2, \ldots, d^{m-1})$. It then looks for the maximal alphabetical distance: $d^{max} \in D \leftarrow \operatorname{argmax}_{d \in D} freq(d, D)$ (from above definition). It finally chooses $\theta'_{m+1} \in \Sigma$ such that $d(\theta'_{m+1} - \theta_m) = d^{max}$.	10: $P \leftarrow D_y$ 11: end if 12: $ind \leftarrow |D_y| - |P| \times |v|$ 13: if $ind > 0$ then 14: $d_y^{k+1} \leftarrow P(ind + 1)$ 15: else 16: $d_y^{k+1} \leftarrow P(1)$ 17: end if 18: return d_y^{k+1}
	Finally, agent π_y^{pt} makes its guess θ'_{m+1} for the next letter of seq such that: $d(\theta'_{m+1} - \theta_{m+1-y}) = d_y^{k+1}$.

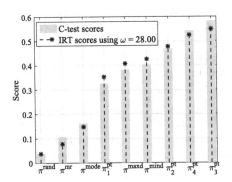

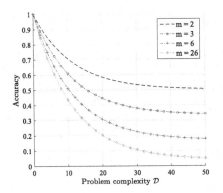

Fig. 1. Final C-test score $\tilde{r}$ of 9 different agents behaviours (defined in the Table 1) and their corresponding IRT accuracies taken from Eq. 1, using an $\alpha = \omega \tilde{r}$ s.t. $\omega = 28$.

Fig. 2. IRT accuracy of agent π^{mind} with ability $\alpha = 11.28$ over inference tasks of different hypothetical (Kolmogorov) complexities D and problem solution space sizes m.

over smaller $m \in \mathbb{N}^+$. This can also be observed in Fig. 2. For consecutive values of m, $P_{D,\alpha,m} - P_{D,\alpha,m+1} = (1 + e^{\frac{-D}{\alpha}})/(m^2 + m)$, and therefore, for very large m, any further increase in m has a negligible effect on the accuracy.

6.1   Relationship Between Accuracy and Difficulty

Figure 3 shows the shift in accuracies of a pool of example classifiers of hypothetical (classification) abilities $\alpha \in [1,8]$ across several $\mathcal{D}$ and m values. We observe that m has a greater influence than $\mathcal{D}$ on the accuracy of those classifiers with poor abilities $\alpha < 3$ and thus their scores are asymptotically bounded by $1/m$, while the opposite is true for more adept classifiers with stronger abilities. This type of analysis can be used to identify the minimal ability value for a classifier to be considered effective compared to, for example, a simple random classifier. One can further put a bound on the task complexity that an agent can solve with a minimal probability of success $P_{\mathcal{D},\alpha,m}$. For instance, if we know m, it is straightforward to calculate $\mathcal{D}$ from Eq. 1 as $e^{\frac{-\mathcal{D}}{\alpha}} = \frac{P_{\mathcal{D},\alpha,m} - \frac{1}{m}}{1 - \frac{1}{m}} \implies \mathcal{D} = -\alpha \ln\left(\frac{m \cdot P_{\mathcal{D},\alpha,m} - 1}{m-1}\right)$.
Similarly a lower bound on accuracy can be guaranteed with respect to the task complexity and the breadth of its solution space. This is illustrated in Fig. 4 for agent π^{mind}.

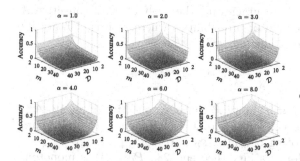

Fig. 3. Shift in accuracy (from Eq. 1) across several $\mathcal{D}$ and m values for example classifiers of different hypothetical abilities such that $\alpha \in [1,8]$.

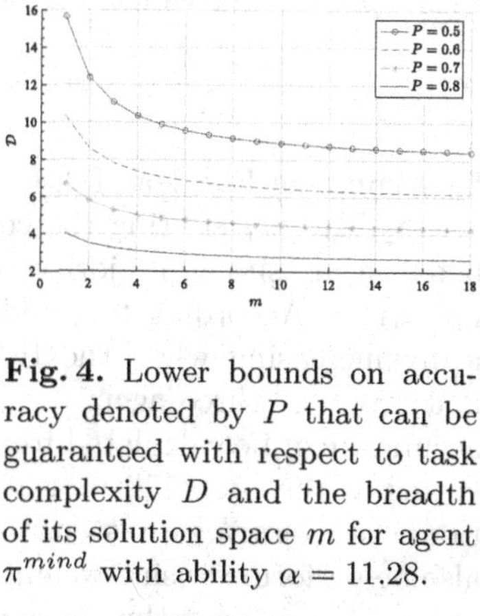

Fig. 4. Lower bounds on accuracy denoted by P that can be guaranteed with respect to task complexity $\mathcal{D}$ and the breadth of its solution space m for agent π^{mind} with ability $\alpha = 11.28$.

This becomes interesting when a cost function (e.g. processing time, fee) is associated with utilising agents of higher abilities. Two agents π_1 and π_2, with abilities α_1 and α_2 and utilisation costs $c_1 = f(\alpha_1)$ and $c_2 = f(\alpha_2)$ respectively, guarantee an accuracy $P_{\mathcal{D}_1,\alpha_1,m} = P_{\mathcal{D}_2,\alpha_2,m}$ under different problem complexities such that $\mathcal{D}_2/\mathcal{D}_1 = \alpha_2/\alpha_1$. If $\alpha_2 > \alpha_1$ (and $c_2 > c_1$) then π_2 can accommodate (a α_2/α_1 factor of) higher problem difficulties with an additional cost of $c_2 - c_1$, while guaranteeing the same accuracy as π_1. Given a set of tasks of different complexities, a set of n agents of different utilisation costs, selecting the agent to solve these tasks with a *minimum bound on accuracy* of $\hat{p}$ can now be subsequently modelled as an optimisation problem: $\arg\min_{1 \leq i \leq n} f(\alpha_i)$, subject to $P_{\mathcal{D}_j,\alpha_i,m} \geq \hat{p}$.

Inferring task difficulty: alternatively, the IRT model can be applied to testing data in order to provide a quantitative understanding of the average complexity D of one class of tasks $X = \{x_1, \ldots, x_t\}$, assuming the value m for such tasks is already known. For instance, one can empirically evaluate an agent of a known ability α over all task instances $x_i \in X$ and record its average score. Equation 1 can subsequently be solved for D using the recorded score as $P_{D,\alpha,m}$.

7   Collective Accuracy of Cooperative Agents

The advantages from adopting the IRT model extend to multiagent scenarios by estimating the collective accuracy of a group of agents. For instance, let A be a collective of agents using *simple majority voting* as a social choice function to elect a solution from the set of alternatives $S = \{s_1, s_2, \ldots, s_m\}$ to a problem x with only one correct solution $s_i \in S$. Let $Y = \{y_1, y_2, \ldots, y_n\}$ where each $y_i \in S$, denote the votes of the agents in $A = \{\pi_1, \pi_2, \ldots, \pi_n\}$ respectively regarding their preferred solution to x. When the votes are independent and identically distributed with equal accuracies p_x, the probability of collective A finding the solution to x is the sum of probabilities where at least 50% of its agents are correct which can be calculated as:

$$P_x(A) = \sum_{k=\lfloor n/2 \rfloor + 1}^{n} \binom{n}{k} p_x^k (1 - p_x)^{n-k} \tag{2}$$

By combining Eqs. 1 and 2, the probability $P_x(A)$ of a collective of agents $A = \{\pi_1, \pi_2, \ldots, \pi_n\}$ electing the correct solution to x with difficulty D, and alphabet m using simple majority voting becomes: $P_{D,m}(A) = \sum_{k=\lfloor n/2 \rfloor + 1}^{n} \binom{n}{k} P_{D,\alpha,m}^k (1 - P_{D,\alpha,m})^{n-k}$. According to Condorcet's jury theorem [28], $P_{D,m}(A)$ is monotonically increasing when the IRT accuracy $P_{D,\alpha,m} > 0.5$ and vice versa. If A is a group of three agents with unequal accuracies of $0.55, 0.55$, and 0.63, its accuracy can be calculated from the agents' independent choices using majority voting as the probability of at least 2 out of 3 agents finding the correct solution: $(0.55^2 \times 0.37 + 2 \times 0.45 \times 0.55 \times 0.63 + 0.55^2 \times 0.63) = 0.6144$. Similar predictions can also be performed using weighted[2] voting rules [17, Chap. 4]. The accuracy of an agent collective can thus be sometimes inferred from its agents' individual accuracies using the IRT model. Subsequently, one can analytically reason about the performance of groups of agents, in comparison to individual agent performance.

8   Analysing Individual and Group Accuracies

The accuracy of agent π^{mind} and the accuracies of three agent collectives $(A^1, A^2$ and $A^3)$ over different task complexities and solution spaces are illustrated

---

[2] More sophisticated voting rules such as *Borda count, harmonic rule, maximin* and *Copeland* require the subject to output a concrete ranking over all possible alternatives of the test/task, which inhibits our ability of making exact predictions. Yet, one can still analytically place min and max bounds on team accuracy using different sampling techniques.

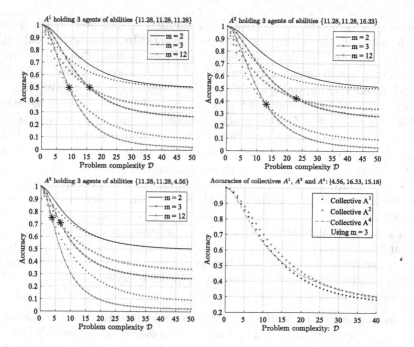

Fig. 5. Collectives accuracies aggregated using majority voting. The accuracy of π^{mind} is also depicted as dotted markers in the backgrounds of the first 3 plots for comparison. The $*$ symbol denotes the cut-off point where the accuracy of π^{mind} meets the corresponding group accuracy.

in Fig. 5. We observe that adding agents of equivalent accuracies to the majority voting process (Collective A^1) improves the accuracy of the group over all tasks where the individual accuracy $P_{\mathcal{D},\alpha,m} > 0.5$, while the opposite is true for $P_{\mathcal{D},\alpha,m} < 0.5$. The key question here is, when is a (voting) collective more efficient than a single agent? To answer this, we calculate the *cut-off point* $\cap_{Y,Z}$ between two evaluated subjects Y and Z. To calculate $\cap_{\pi,A}$ (where the accuracy $P_{\mathcal{D},\alpha,m}$ of an agent π, and $P_{\mathcal{D},m}(A)$ of a collective A, are both equal over some task of complexity $\mathcal{D}$) we look for the value of $\mathcal{D}$ at which $P_{\mathcal{D},\alpha,m} = \frac{1}{m} + e^{\frac{-\mathcal{D}}{\alpha}} \left(1 - \frac{1}{m}\right) = P_{\mathcal{D},m}(A)$, which leads to $\mathcal{D} = -\alpha \ln \left((P_{\mathcal{D},m}(A) - \frac{1}{m})/(1 - \frac{1}{m})\right)$. If all the agents have similar accuracies (Collective A^1, Fig. 5), then according to Eq. 2, they are only equally accurate when $P_{\mathcal{D},\alpha,m} = P_{\mathcal{D},m}(A) = 0.5$ leading to a $\mathcal{D} = -\alpha \ln \left((\frac{1}{2} - \frac{1}{m})/(1 - \frac{1}{m})\right) = -\alpha \ln \left((m-2)(2m-2)\right)$. For example, the cut-off point $\cap_{\pi^{mind},A^1}$ between π^{mind} with $\alpha = 12.0094$ and A^1 over a problem with $m = 3$ occurs at a $\mathcal{D} = -12 \ln \left(\frac{1}{4}\right) = 16.64$, which can also be verified from the graph in Fig. 5.

The cut-off point not only returns the setting over which $P_{\mathcal{D},\alpha,m}$ and $P_{\mathcal{D},m}(A^1)$ are equal, but also illustrates the relationship between the complexity of the problem $\mathcal{D}$ and the breadth of its solution space m, with respect to the accuracy of the evaluated group. In other words, the cut-off point indicates the problem complexities and solution spaces over which a collective is more effective than its individual agents. In most real world scenarios voting agents have different abilities and consequently different accuracies. Replacing a group member by another of higher/lower accuracy (Fig. 5 top-right/bottom-left) improves/diminishes the performance of the group by a measurable amount. For instance, let $A = \{\pi_1, \pi_2, \pi_3\}$ be the group of agents with abilities $\alpha_1, \alpha_2, \alpha_3$ and IRT accuracies (abridged as) p_1, p_2, p_3 respectively over some task x. If the agents' individual votes are independent, the probability $P_{D,m}(A)$ of A correctly guessing the solution to task x by majority voting is: $p_1 p_2 (1 - p_3) + (1 - p_1) p_2 p_3 + (1 - p_2) p_1 p_3 + p_1 p_2 p_3$. When $p_1 = p_2 = p_3$, then $P_{D,m}(A)$ is equivalent to Eq. 2. If $A' = \{\pi_1, \pi_2, \pi_3'\}$ is the group of agents with accuracies p_1, p_2, p_3' respectively s.t. $p_3' > p_3$, then its accuracy increases by $P_{D,m}(A') - P_{D,m}(A) = p_1 p_2 (p_3 - p_3') + (1 - p_1) p_2 (p_3' - p_3) + (1 - p_2) p_1 (p_3' - p_3) + p_1 p_2 (p_3' - p_3) = (1 - p_1) p_2 2 (p_3' - p_3)$ since $1/m \leq p_1, p_2 \leq 1$ by definition (Eq. 1). For $p_1 = p_2 \neq p_3$ the cut-off point $\cap_{\pi_1, A}$ occurs at $D = -\alpha_3 \ln ((p_3 - \frac{1}{m})/(1 - \frac{1}{m}))$ when $p_3 = 0.5$. As a result, we can measure the rise/drop in accuracies of A^2 and A^3 illustrated in Fig. 5 top-right/bottom-left. For example, for tasks of $m = 3$, $\cap_{\pi^{mind}, A^2}$ (Fig. 5 top-right) occurs at a $D = -16.33 \ln ((0.5 - \frac{1}{3})/(1 - \frac{1}{3})) = 22.64$.

Comparing agent collectives: scores from standard IQ tests provide us with some sort of scale or ranking of performances of evaluated individuals or groups. Nonetheless, these performance measures might not be valid over certain settings. We observe in Fig. 5 that voting collective A^1 is more efficient than A^4 (holding agents with abilities $\{4.56, 16.33, 15.18\}$) over inference tasks of $D < 14$, whereas (counterintuitively) A^4 scores higher that A^1 over the C-test $(0.51 > 0.38)$. Moreover, the opposite is true for tasks of higher complexities. Such scenarios might create confusions as they are frequently encountered and cannot be disclosed from standard intelligence tests. We also observe that for highly complex tasks with $D > 25$ collectives A^1 and A^2 record very similar accuracies since $P_{D,m}(A^1) - P_{D,m}(A^2)$ becomes very small. This is coherent with real world observations (although it cannot be drawn from intelligence test scores) as the accuracy of a subject, or a group of subjects, over extremely hard tasks is likely to converge to a random guess (an asymptotic minimum).

9   Conclusion and Future Work

Intelligence test scores can be an unreliable predictor of an agent's performance over tasks of well-defined complexities and other problem settings. We proposed a new mathematical model that is flexible enough to predict the accuracy of agents of different abilities over various classification problem settings. We illustrated the relationships between the accuracy (and ability) of an agent, the complexities of the assessment task and the size of its solution space, and identified agents that can guarantee a lower bound on accuracy with respect to task complexity and the size of its solution space. We further analysed settings over which a group of (majority voting) agents can be more or less effective than individual agents or other groups. For instance, we directly inferred from the model the complexity at which a group is expected to record a similar accuracy as an individual agent, and beyond which a single agent is more effective than the group. We also measured the effect (on accuracy) of introducing agents of higher or lower abilities to a group of agents. Finally, we identified possible circumstances that are somewhat counterintuitive to the conclusions drawn from intelligence tests. These occur when a group of agents scores higher than another on an intelligence test yet fails to outperform this same group over certain task complexities. In our future work, more sophisticated voting rules will be used to analytically reason about team accuracy by analysing the outcomes from different sampling techniques over the agents' ranked votes.

References

1. Bien, Z., Bang, W.C., Kim, D.Y., Han, J.S.: Machine intelligence quotient: its measurements and applications. Fuzzy Sets Syst. **127**(1), 3–16 (2002)
2. Birnbaum, A.: Some latent trait models and their use in inferring an examinee's ability. In: Statistical Theories of Mental Test Scores, pp. 395–479 (1968)
3. Chmait, N.: Understanding and measuring collective intelligence across different cognitive systems: an information-theoretic approach (extended abstract). In: Proceedings of the 26th International Joint Conference on Artificial Intelligence, IJCAI-17 Doctoral Consortium, Melbourne, Australia (2017, to appear)
4. Chmait, N., Dowe, D.L., Li, Y.F., Green, D.G., Insa-Cabrera, J.: Factors of collective intelligence: how smart are agent collectives? In: Proceedings of 22nd European Conference on Artificial Intelligence ECAI, Frontiers in Artificial Intelligence and Applications, vol. 285, pp. 542–550. IOS Press (2016)
5. De Ayala, R.J.: The Theory and Practice of Item Response Theory. Guilford Publications, New York (2013)
6. Dowe, D.L., Hajek, A.R.: A computational extension to the turing test. In: Proceedings 4th Conference of the Australasian Cognitive Science Society, University of Newcastle, NSW, Australia (1997)
7. Dowe, D.L., Hernández-Orallo, J.: IQ tests are not for machines, yet. Intelligence **40**(2), 77–81 (2012)
8. Dowe, D.L., Hernández-Orallo, J., Das, P.K.: Compression and intelligence: social environments and communication. In: Schmidhuber, J., Thórisson, K.R., Looks, M. (eds.) AGI 2011. LNCS (LNAI), vol. 6830, pp. 204–211. Springer, Heidelberg (2011). doi:10.1007/978-3-642-22887-2_21
9. Gottfredson, L.S.: Mainstream science on intelligence: an editorial with 52 signatories, history, and bibliography. Intelligence **24**(1), 13–23 (1997)
10. Hernández-Orallo, J.: Beyond the Turing test. J. Log. Lang. Inf. **9**(4), 447–466 (2000)
11. Hernández-Orallo, J.: The Measure of All Minds: Evaluating Natural and Artificial Intelligence. Cambridge University Press, New York (2016)
12. Hernández-Orallo, J., Dowe, D.L.: Measuring universal intelligence: towards an anytime intelligence test. Artif. Intell. **174**(18), 1508–1539 (2010)
13. Hernández-Orallo, J., Insa-Cabrera, J., Dowe, D.L., Hibbard, B.: Turing machines and recursive turing tests. In: AISB/IACAP 2012 Symposium Revisiting Turing and his Test, pp. 28–33 (2012)

14. Insa-Cabrera, J., Dowe, D.L., España-Cubillo, S., Hernández-Lloreda, M.V., Hernández-Orallo, J.: Comparing humans and AI agents. In: Schmidhuber, J., Thórisson, K.R., Looks, M. (eds.) AGI 2011. LNCS (LNAI), vol. 6830, pp. 122–132. Springer, Heidelberg (2011). doi:10.1007/978-3-642-22887-2_13
15. Klein, G.A., King, J.A.: A test for the performance of knowledge-based systems: AIQ. In: Proceedings of AAAI Workshop on Validation and Verification of Expert System, Menlo Park, CA (1988)
16. Kolmogorov, A.N.: Three approaches to the quantitative definition of information. Probl. Inf. Transm. **1**(1), 1–7 (1965)
17. Kuncheva, L.I.: Combining Pattern Classifiers: Methods and Algorithms. Wiley, Hoboken (2004)
18. Legg, S., Hutter, M.: Universal intelligence: a definition of machine intelligence. Mind. Mach. **17**(4), 391–444 (2007)
19. Lempel, A., Ziv, J.: On the complexity of finite sequences. IEEE Trans. Inf. Theory **22**(1), 75–81 (1976)
20. Levin, L.A.: Universal sequential search problems. Probl. Inf. Transm. **9**(3), 265–266 (1973)
21. Li, M., Vitányi, P.: An Introduction to Kolmogorov Complexity and Its Applications, 3rd edn. Springer, New York (2008)
22. Lord, F.M., Novick, M.R.: Statistical Theories of Mental Test Scores. Addison-Wesley, Menlo Park (1968)
23. Martínez-Plumed, F., Prudêncio, R.B., Martínez-Usó, A., Hernández-Orallo, J.: Making sense of item response theory in machine learning. In: Proceedings of 22nd European Conference on Artificial Intelligence (ECAI), Frontiers in Artificial Intelligence and Applications, vol. 285, pp. 1140–1148 (2016)
24. Raven, J.C., Court, J.H.: Raven's Progressive Matrices and Vocabulary Scales. Oxford Psychologists Press, Oxford (1998)
25. Roid, G.H.: Stanford-Binet Intelligence Scales. Riverside Publishing, Itasca (2003)
26. Sanghi, P., Dowe, D.L.: A computer program capable of passing I.Q. tests. In: Slezak, P. (ed.) Proceedings of 4th International Conference on Cognitive Science (ICCS/ASCS-2003), pp. 570–575, Australia, July 2003
27. Shannon, C.E.: A mathematical theory of communication. Bell Syst. Tech. J. **27**(3), 379–423 (1948)
28. Shapley, L., Grofman, B.: Optimizing group judgmental accuracy in the presence of interdependencies. Public Choice **43**(3), 329–343 (1984)
29. Solomonoff, R.J.: A preliminary report on a general theory of inductive inference. Report ZTB-138. Zator Co 131, Cambridge, MA (1960)
30. Spearman, C.: General intelligence, objectively determined and measured. Am. J. Psychol. **15**(2), 201–292 (1904)
31. Thurstone, L.L.: Primary Mental Abilities. Chicago Press, Chicago (1938)
32. Turing, A.M.: Computing machinery and intelligence. Mind **59**, 433–460 (1950)
33. Wechsler, D.: Wechsler Adult Intelligence Scale-Fourth. Pearson, San Antonio (2008)

Bandit Models of Human Behavior: Reward Processing in Mental Disorders

Djallel Bouneffouf[(⊠)], Irina Rish, and Guillermo A. Cecchi

IBM Thomas J. Watson Research Center, Yorktown Heights, NY, USA
djallel.bouneffouf@ibm.com

Abstract. Drawing an inspiration from behavioral studies of human decision making, we propose here a general parametric framework for multi-armed bandit problem, which extends the standard Thompson Sampling approach to incorporate reward processing biases associated with several neurological and psychiatric conditions, including Parkinson's and Alzheimer's diseases, attention-deficit/hyperactivity disorder (ADHD), addiction, and chronic pain. We demonstrate empirically that the proposed parametric approach can often outperform the baseline Thompson Sampling on a variety of datasets. Moreover, from the behavioral modeling perspective, our parametric framework can be viewed as a first step towards a unifying computational model capturing reward processing abnormalities across multiple mental conditions.

1 Introduction

In daily-life decision making, from choosing a meal at a restaurant to deciding on a place to visit during a vacation, and so on, people often face the classical exploration versus exploitation dilemma, requiring them to choose between following a good action chosen previously (exploitation) and obtaining more information about the environment which can possibly lead to better actions in the future, but may also turn out to be a bad choice (exploration).

The exploration-exploitation trade-off is typically modeled as the *multi-armed bandit (MAB)* problem, stated as follows: given N possible actions ("arms"), each associated with a fixed, unknown and independent reward probability distribution [1,2], an agent selects an action at each time point and receives a reward, drawn from the corresponding distribution, independently of the previous actions.

In order to better understand and model human decision-making behavior, scientists usually investigate reward processing mechanisms in healthy subjects [3]. However, neurogenerative and psychiatric disorders, often associated with reward processing disruptions, can provide an additional resource for deeper understanding of human decision making mechanisms. Furthermore, from the perspective of evolutionary psychiatry, various mental disorders, including depression, anxiety, ADHD, addiction and even schizophrenia can be considered as "extreme points" in a continuous spectrum of behaviors and traits developed for various purposes during evolution, and somewhat less extreme versions of

T. Everitt et al. (Eds.): AGI 2017, LNAI 10414, pp. 237–248, 2017.
DOI: 10.1007/978-3-319-63703-7_22

those traits can be actually beneficial in specific environments (e.g., ADHD-like fast-switching attention can be life-saving in certain environments, etc.). Thus, modeling decision-making biases and traits associated with various disorders may actually enrich the existing computational decision-making models, leading to potentially more flexible and better-performing algorithms.

Herein, we focus on reward-processing biases associated with several mental disorders, including Parkinson's and Alzheimer disease, ADHD, addiction and chronic pain. Our questions are: is it possible to extend standard stochastic bandit algorithms to mimic human behavior in such disorders? Can such generalized approaches outperform standard bandit algorithms on specific tasks?

We show that both questions can be answered positively. We build upon the Thompson Sampling, a state-of-art approach to multi-arm bandit problem, and extend it to a parametric version which allows to incorporate various reward-processing biases known to be associated with particular disorders. For example, it was shown that (unmedicated) patients with Parkinson's disease appear to learn better from negative rather than from positive rewards [4]; another example is addictive behaviors which may be associated with an inability to forget strong stimulus-response associations from the past, i.e. to properly discount past rewards [5], and so on. More specifically, *we propose a parametric model which introduces weights on incoming positive and negative rewards, and on reward histories, extending the standard parameter update rules in Bernoulli Thompson Sampling; tuning the parameter settings allows us to better capture specific reward-processing biases.*

Our empirical results demonstrate that the proposed approach outperforms the baseline Thompson Sampling on a variety of UCI benchmarks. Furthermore, we show how parameter-tuning in the proposed model allows to mimic certain aspects of the behavior associated with mental disorders mentioned above, and thus may provide a valuable tool for improving our understanding of such disorders.

The rest of this paper is organized as follows. Section 2 reviews related work. Section 3 describes the MAB model and the proposed algorithm. The experimental evaluation for different setting is presented in Sect. 5. The last section concludes the paper and identifies directions for future works.

2   Related Work

2.1   Reward Processing in Mental Disorders

The literature on the reward processing abnormalities in particular neurological and psychiatric disorders is quite extensive; below we summarize some of the recent developments in this fast-growing field.

Parkinson's disease (PD). It is well-known that the neuromodulator dopamine plays a key role in reinforcement learning processes. PD patients, who have depleted dopamine in the basal ganglia, tend to have impaired performance on tasks that require learning from trial and error. For example, [4] demonstrate that off-medication PD patients are better at learning to avoid choices that lead to negative outcomes than they are at learning from positive outcomes, while dopamine medication typically used to treat PD symptoms reverses this bias.

Alzheimer's disease (AD). This is the most common cause of dementia in the elderly and, besides memory impairment, it is associated with a variable degree of executive function impairment and visuospatial impairment. As discussed in [3], AD patients have decreased pursuit of rewarding behaviors, including loss of appetite; these changes are often secondary to apathy, associated with diminished reward system activity. Furthermore, poor performance on certain tasks is correlated with memory impairments.

Frontotemporal dementia, behavioral variant (bvFTD). Frontotemporal dementia (bvFTD) typically involves a progressive change in personality and behavior including disinhibition, apathy, eating changes, repetitive or compulsive behaviors, and loss of empathy [3], and it is hypothesized that those changes are associated with abnormalities in reward processing. For example, changes in eating habits with a preference for sweet, carbohydrate rich foods and overeating in bvFTD patients can be associated with abnormally increased reward representation for food, or impairment in the negative (punishment) signal associated with fullness.

Attention-deficit/hyperactivity disorder (ADHD). Authors in [6] suggest that the strength of the association between a stimulus and the corresponding response is more susceptible to degradation in ADHD patients, which suggests problems with storing the stimulus-response associations. Among other functions, storing the associations requires working memory capacity, which is often impaired in ADHD patients.

Addiction. In [5], it is demonstrated that patients suffering from addictive behavior are not able to forget the stimulus-response associations, which causes them to constantly seek the stimulus which generated such association.

Chronic pain. In [7], it is suggested that chronic pain results in a hypodopaminergic (low dopamine) state that impairs motivated behavior, resulting into a reduced drive in chronic pain patients to pursue the rewards. Decreased reward response may underlie a key system mediating the anhedonia and depression common in chronic pain.

A variety of computational models was proposed for studying the disorders of reward processing in specific disorders, including, among others [4,5,8–11].

However, none of the above studies is proposing a unifying model that can represent a wide range of reward processing disorders; moreover, none of the above studies used the multi-arm bandit model simulating human online decision-making.

2.2 Multi-armed Bandit (MAB)

The multi-armed bandit (MAB) problem models a sequential decision-making process, where at each time point a player selects an action from a given finite set of possible actions, attempting to maximize the cumulative reward over time.

MAB is frequently used in reinforcement learning to study the exploration/exploitation tradeoff, and is an active area of research since the 1950s. Optimal solutions have been provided using a stochastic formulation [1,2], or using an adversarial formulation [12–14]. Recently, there has been a surge of interest in a Bayesian formulation [15], involving the algorithm known as Thompson sampling [16]. Theoretical analysis in [17] shows that Thompson sampling for Bernoulli bandits asymptotically achieves the optimal performance limit. Empirical analysis of Thompson sampling, including problems more complex than the Bernoulli bandit, demonstrates that its performance is highly competitive with other approaches [15,18].

Psychological study done in [19] shows that, instead of maximizing output by a deliberate mean-variance trade-off, participants approach dynamic decision-making problems by utilizing a probability matching heuristic. Thus, their behavior is better described by the Thompson sampling choice rule than by the Upper Confidence Bound (UCB) approach [2]. However, none of the above studies bandit models of the behavior of patients with mental disorders and impaired reward processing.

To the best of our knowledge, this work is the first one to propose a generalized version of Thompson Sampling algorithm which incorporates a range of reward processing biases associated with various mental disorders and shows how different parameter settings of the proposed model lead to behavior mimicking a wide range of impairments in multiple neurological and psychiatric disorders. Most importantly, our bandit algorithm based on generalization of Thompson sampling outperforms the baseline method on multiple datasets.

3 Background and Definitions

The Stochastic Multi-armed Bandit. Given a slot machine with N arms representing potential actions, the player must chose one of the arms to play at each time step $t = 1, 2, 3, ..., T$. Choosing an arm i yields a random real-valued reward according to some fixed (unknown) distribution with support in $[0, 1]$. The reward is observed immediately after playing the arm. The MAB algorithm must decide which arm to play at each time step t, based on the outcomes during the previous $t - 1$ steps.

Let μ_i denote the (unknown) expected reward for arm i. The goal is to maximize the expected total reward during T iterations, i.e., $E[\sum_{t=1}^{T} \mu_{i(t)}]$, where $i(t)$ is the arm played in step t, and the expectation is over the random choices of $i(t)$ made by the algorithm. We could also use the equivalent performance measure known as the expected total regret, i.e. the amount of total reward lost because of playing according to a specific algorithm rather than choosing the optimal arm in each step.

The expected total regret is formally defined as:

$$E[R(T)] = E[\sum_{t=1}^{T} (\mu^* - \mu_{i_{(t)}})] = \sum_i \Delta_i E[k_i(T)]. \tag{1}$$

where $\mu^* := max_i\mu_i$, $\Delta_i := \mu^* - \mu_i$, and $k_i(t)$ denote the number of times arm i has been played up to step t.

Thompson Sampling. Thompson sampling (TS) [20], also known as Bayesian, is a classical approach to multi-arm bandit problem, where the reward $r_i(t)$ for choosing an arm i at time t is assumed to follow a distribution $Pr(r_t|\tilde{\mu})$ with the parameter $\tilde{\mu}$. Given a prior $Pr(\tilde{\mu})$ on these parameters, their posterior distribution is given by the Bayes rule, $Pr(\tilde{\mu}|r_t) \propto Pr(r_t|\tilde{\mu})Pr(\tilde{\mu})$ [17].

A particular case of the Thompson Sampling approach, presented in Algorithm 1, assumes a Bernoulli bandit problem, with rewards being 0 or 1, and the parameters following the Beta prior. TS initially assumes arm i to have prior $Beta(1,1)$ on μ_i (the probability of success). At time t, having observed $S_i(t)$ successes (reward $= 1$) and $F_i(t)$ failures (reward $= 0$), the algorithm updates the distribution on μ_i as $Beta(S_i(t), F_i(t))$. The algorithm then generates independent samples $\theta_i(t)$ from these posterior distributions of the μ_i, and selects the arm with the largest sample value.

4 Proposed Approach: Human-Based Thompson Sampling

We will now introduce a more general rule for updating the parameters of Beta distribution in steps 10 and 11 of the Algorithm 1; this parameteric rule incorporates weights on the prior and the current number of successes and failures, which will allow to model a wide range of reward processing biases associated with various disorders. More specifically, the proposed Human-Based Thompson Sampling (HBTS), outlined in Algorithm 2, replaces binary incremental updates in lines 10 and 11 of TS (Algorithm 1) with their corresponding weighted version (lines 10 and 11 in Algorithm 2), using the four weight parameters: τ and ϕ are the weights of the previously accumulated positive and negative rewards, respectively, while α and β represent the weights on the positive and negative rewards at the current iteration.

Algorithm 1. Thompson Sampling

1: **Foreach** arm $i = 1, ..., K$
2:   set $S_i(t) = 1$, $F_i(t) = 1$
3: **End for**
4: **Foreach** $t = 1, 2, ..., T$ **do**
5:   **Foreach** $i = 1, 2, ..., K$ **do**
6:     Sample $\theta_i(t)$ from $Beta(S_i(t), F_i(t))$
7:   **End do**
8:   Play arm $i_t = argmax_i\theta_i(t)$, obtain reward $r(t)$
9:   **if** $r(t) = 1$, **then**
10:     $S_i(t) = S_i(t) + 1$
11:   **else** $F_i(t) = F_i(t) + 1$
12: **End do**

Algorithm 2. Human-Based Thompson Sampling (HBTS)

1: **Foreach** arm $i = 1, ..., K$
2:     set $S_i(t) = 1$, $F_i(t) = 1$
3: **End for**
4: **Foreach** $t = 1, 2, ..., T$ **do**
5:     **Foreach** $i = 1, 2, ..., K$ **do**
6:         Sample $\theta_i(t)$ from $Beta(S_i(t), F_i(t))$
7:     **End do**
8:     Play arm $i_t = argmax_i \theta_i(t)$, obtain reward $r(t)$
9:     **if** $r_i(t) = 1$, **then**
10:        $S_i(t) = \tau S_i(t) + \alpha r_i(t)$
11:        **else** $F_i(t) = \phi F_i(t) + \beta(1 - r_i(t))$
12: **End do**

4.1   Reward Processing Models with Different Biases

In this section we describe how specific constraints on the model parameters in the proposed algorithm can yield different reward processing biases discussed earlier, and introduce several instances of the HBTS model, with parameter settings reflecting particular biases. The parameter settings are summarized in Table 2, where we use list our models associated with specific disorders (Table 1).

Table 1. Algorithms parameters

UCI Datasets	τ	α	ϕ	β
AD (addiction)	1 ± 0.1	1 ± 0.1	0.5 ± 0.1	1 ± 0.1
ADHD	0.2 ± 0.1	1 ± 0.1	0.2 ± 0.1	1 ± 0.1
AZ (Altzheimer's)	0.1 ± 0.1	1 ± 0.1	0.1 ± 0.1	1 ± 0.1
CP (chronic pain)	0.5 ± 0.1	0.5 ± 0.1	1 ± 0.1	1 ± 0.1
bvFTD	0.5 ± 0.1	100 ± 10	0.5 ± 0.1	1 ± 0.1
PD (Parkinson's)	0.5 ± 0.1	1 ± 0.1	0.5 ± 0.1	100 ± 10
M ("moderate")	0.5 ± 0.1	1 ± 0.1	0.5 ± 0.1	1 ± 0.1
TS	1	1	1	1

It is important to underscore that the above models should be viewed as only a first step towards a unifying approach to reward processing disruptions, which requires further extensions, as well as tuning and validation on human subjects. Our main goal is to demonstrate the promise of our parametric approach at capturing certain decision-making biases, as well as its computational advantages over the standard TS, due to the increased generality and flexibility facilitated by multi-parametric formulation. Note that the standard Thompson sampling (TS) approach correspond to setting the four (hyper)parameters used in our model to 1. Next, we introduce the model which incorporates some mild forgetting of the past rewards or losses, using 0.5 weights, just as an example, and calibrating the other models with respect to this one; we refer to this model as M for "moderate" forgetting, which serves here as a proxy for somewhat "normal" reward processing, without extreme reward-processing biases associated with disorders. We will use the subscript M to denote the parameters of this model.

We will now introduced several models inspired by certain reward-processing biases in a range of mental disorders. *It is important to note that, despite using disorder names for these models, we are not claiming that they provide accurate models of the corresponding disorders, but rather disorder-inspired versions of our general parametric family of models.*

Parkinson's disease (PD). Recall that PD patients are typically better at learning to avoid negative outcomes than at learning to achieve positive outcomes [4]; one way to model this is to over-emphasize negative rewards, by placing a high weight on them, as compared to the reward processing in healthy individuals. Specifically, we will assume the parameter β for PD patients to be much higher than normal β_M (e.g., we use $\beta = 100$ here), while the rest of the parameters will be in the same range for both healthy and PD individuals.

Frontotemporal Dementia (bvFTD). Patients with bvFTD are prone to overeating which may represent increased reward representation. To model this impairment in bvFTD patients, the parameter of the model could be modified as follow: $\alpha_M << \alpha$ (e.g., $\alpha = 100$ as shown in Table 2), where α is the parameter of the bvFTD model has, and the rest of these parameters are equal to the normal one.

Alzheimer's disease (AD). To model apathy in patients with Altzheimer's, including downplaying rewards and losses, we will assume that the parameters ϕ and τ are somewhat smaller than normal, $\phi < \phi_M$ and $\tau < \tau_M$ (e.g., set to 0.1 in Table 2), which models the tendency to forget both positive and negative rewards.

ADHD. Recall that ADHD may be involve impairments in storing stimulus-response associations. In our ADHD model, the parameters ϕ and τ are smaller than normal, $\phi_M > \phi$ and $\tau_M > \tau$, which models forgetting of both positive and negative rewards. Note that while this model appears similar to Altzheimer's model described above, the forgetting factor will be less pronounced, i.e. the ϕ and τ parameters are larger than those of the Altzheimer's model (e.g., 0.2 instead of 0.1, as shown in Table 2).

Addiction. As mentioned earlier, addiction is associated with inability to properly forget (positive) stimulus-response associations; we model this by setting the weight on previously accumulated positive reward ("memory") higher than normal, $\tau > \tau_M$, e.g. $\tau = 1$, while $\tau_M = 0.5$.

Chronic Pain. We model the reduced responsiveness to rewards in chronic pain by setting $\alpha < \alpha_M$ so there is a decrease in the reward representation, and $\phi > \phi_M$ so the negative rewards are not forgotten (see Table 2).

Of course, the above models should be treated only as first approximations of the reward processing biases in mental disorders, since the actual changes

Table 2. Datasets

UCI Datasets	Instances	Classes
Covertype	581 012	7
CNAE-9	1080	9
Internet Advertisements	3279	2
Poker Hand	1 025 010	9

in reward processing are much more complicated, and the parameteric setting must be learned from actual patient data, which is a nontrivial direction for future work. Herein, we simply consider those models as specific variations of our general method, inspired by certain aspects of the corresponding diseases, and focus primarily on the computational aspects of our algorithm, demonstrating that the proposed parametric extension of TS can learn better than the baseline TS due to added flexibility.

5 Empirical Evaluation

In order to evaluate the proposed framework empirically and compare its performance with the standard Thompson Sampling, we used the following four classification datasets from the UCI Machine Learning Repository[1]: Covertype, CNAE-9, Internet Advertisements and Poker Hand. A brief summary of the datasets is listed in Table 2.

In order to simulate an infinite data stream, we draw samples randomly without replacement, from each dataset, restarting the process each time we draw the last sample. In each round, the algorithm receives the reward 1 if the instance is classified correctly, and 0 otherwise. We compute the total number of classification errors as a performance metric. Note that we do not use the features (context) here, as we try to simulate the classical multi-arm bandit environment (rather than contextual bandit), and use the class labels only. As the result, *we obtain a non-stationary environment*, since even if $P(reward|context)$ is fixed, switching from a sample to a sample (i.e., from a context to a context) results into different $P(reward)$ at each time point.

Table 3. Average results

	Addiction	ADHD	Alzheimer's	Chronic Pain	bvFTD	Parkinson	M	TS
Datasets								
Positive environment	**51.46**	52.35	52.53	52.88	59.16	56.23	52.64	55.62
Negative environment	62.83	55.06	55.54	55.48	56.03	56.21	**52.74**	61.21
Normal reward environment	52.81	53.68	51.48	53.11	**49.55**	58.01	50.92	56.95

[1] https://archive.ics.uci.edu/ml/datasets.html.

Table 4. Positive-reward environment

Datasets	Addiction	ADHD	Alzheimer's	Chronic Pain	bvFTD	Parkinson	M	TS
Internet Advertisements	34.06 ± 0.34	**31.85 ± 3.51**	32.40 ± 1.91	32.96 ± 1.66	55.67 ± 1.68	43.61 ± 1.51	37.69 ± 1.88	38.34 ± 1.77
CNAE-9	40.25 ± 0.85	**39.89 ± 2.70**	40.08 ± 3.69	39.94 ± 0.73	40.14 ± 2.33	40.28 ± 2.27	40.16 ± 1.99	40.06 ± 1.66
Covertype	65.04 ± 0.52	66.5 ± 0.75	66.75 ± 1.52	69.49 ± 1.75	70.62 ± 1.73	68.05 ± 1.72	**65.01 ± 1.75**	67.08 ± 1.23
Poker Hand	**66.5 ± 0.24**	71.18 ± 0.12	70.19 ± 1.87	69.14 ± 2.57	70.26 ± 0.81	73 ± 1.87	67.73 ± 1.87	77.03 ± 1.87

Table 5. Negative-reward environment

Datasets	Addiction	ADHD	Alzheimer's	Chronic Pain	bvFTD	Parkinson	M	TS
Internet Advertisements	41.346 ± 0.21	37.833 ± 1.20	40.76 ± 1.93	41.08 ± 1.64	42.633 ± 1.23	41.4 ± 1.17	**33.22 ± 1.7**	38.19 ± 1.6
CNAE-9	40.248 ± 0.35	39.97 ± 0.20	39.89 ± 3.49	40.27 ± 0.23	39.89 ± 1.33	39.95 ± 1.73	**39.96 ± 1.33**	40.02 ± 1.11
Covertype	73.26 ± 0.30	71.28 ± 0.32	71.35 ± 1.75	71.45 ± 1.87	71.34 ± 1.87	**70.5 ± 1.8**	70.05 ± 1.87	69.93 ± 0.83
Poker Hand	96.51 ± 0.35	71.18 ± 0.22	70.19 ± 2.77	69.14 ± 0.88	70.26 ± 1.19	73 ± 1.87	**67.73 ± 1.51**	96.71 ± 1.16

Table 6. Normal reward environment

Datasets	Addiction	ADHD	Alzheimer's	Chronic pain	bvFTD	Parkinson	M	TS
Internet Advertisements	32.28 ± 0.20	36.8 ± 1.28	36.56 ± 1.63	35.53 ± 1.43	**28.59 ± 1.76**	44.69 ± 1.85	33.65 ± 1.81	37.71 ± 0.66
CNAE-9	40.16 ± 0.38	40.09 ± 0.31	39.99 ± 3.01	**39.75 ± 0.28**	40.13 ± 1.81	40.25 ± 1.71	39.86 ± 1.10	39.78 ± 0.80
Covertype	73.54 ± 0.31	64.27 ± 0.30	**63.54 ± 1.30**	68.69 ± 1.84	63.69 ± 1.85	72.67 ± 1.82	64.61 ± 0.8	64.63 ± 1.87
Poker Hand	**65.29 ± 0.33**	73.57 ± 0.33	65.83 ± 2.68	68.49 ± 0.92	65.69 ± 1.01	74.44 ± 1.07	65.58 ± 1.62	85.71 ± 1.09

In order to test the ability of our models to reflect decision-making biases in various disorders, as well as to evaluate the advantages of our model in comparison with the baseline TS, under different test conditions, we consider the following settings:

- Positive reward environment: we modify the reward function so that the agent receives only positive rewards (the lines 11 is not executed). This environment allows us to evaluate how our models deal with positive reward.
- Negative reward environment: we modify the reward function so that the agent receives only negative rewards (the lines 10 is not executed). This environment helps to evaluate the negative-reward processing by our models.
- Normal environment: the agent can see both negative and positive rewards.

The average error rate results on the UCI datasets, for each type of the environment, and over 10 runs of each algorithm, are shown in Table 3. We compute the error rate by dividing the total accumulated regret by the number of iterations. The best results for each dataset are shown in bold. Note that our parametric approach always outperforms the standard TS method: AD (addiction) model is best in positive reward environment, M (moderate) version is best in negative environment, and bvFTD happens to outperform other models in regular (positive and negative) reward environment. While further modeling and validation on human subjects may be required to validate neuroscientific value of the proposed models, they clearly demonstrate computational advantages over the classical TS approach for the bandit problem.

We now present the detailed results for all algorithms and for each of the three environments, in Tables 4, 5, and 6. Lowest errors for each dataset (across each row) are again shown in bold. Note that, *in all three environments, and for each of the four datasets, the baseline Thompson Sampling was always inferior to the proposed parametric family of methods*, for each specific settings, different versions of our HBTS framework were performing best.

Positive Reward Environment. Table 4 summarizes the results for positive reward setting. Note that most versions of the proposed approach frequently outperform the standard Thompson sampling. ADHD model yields best results on two datasets out of four, while AD (addiction) and M (moderate) models are best at one of each remaining datasets, respectively.

Note that PD (Parkinson's) and bvFTD (behavioral-variant fronto-teporal dementia) yield the worst results on most datasets. The behavior of PD model is therefore consistent with the literature on Parkinson's disease, which suggests, as mentioned earlier, that Parkinson's patients do not learn as well from positive rewards as they do from negative ones.

Ranking the algorithms with respect to their mean error rate, we note that the top three performing algorithms were AD (addiction), ADHD and AZ (Alzheimer's), in that order. One can hypothesise that these observations are consistent with the fact that those disorders did not demonstrate such clear impairment in learning from positive rewards as, for example, Parkinson's.

Negative Reward Environment. As shown in Table 5, for negative reward environment, we again observe that the proposed algorithms always work better than the state of the art Thompson sampling.

Overall, M (moderate) model performs best in this environment, on three out of four datasets. Note that PD (Parkinson's) and CP (chronic pain) models outperform many other models, performing much better with negative rewards than they did with the positive ones, which is consistent with the literature discussed before. AD (addiction) is the worst-performing out of HBTS algorithms, which may relate to its bias towards positive-reward driving learning, but impaired ability to learn from negative rewards.

Ranking the algorithms with respect to their mean error rate, we note that the two best-performing algorithms were ADHD and AZ (Alzheimer's), in that order.

Normal Reward Environment. Similarly to the other two environments, the baseline Thompson Sampling is always inferior to the proposed algorithms, as shown in Table 6). Interestingly, model M was never a winner, either, and different disorder models performed best for different data sets. PD and CP show worst performance, suggesting that negative-reward driven learning is impairing.

6   Conclusions

This paper proposes a novel parametric family of algorithms for multi-arm bandit problem, extending the classical Thompson Sampling approach to model a wide range of potential reward processing biases. Our approach draws an inspiration from extensive literature on decision-making behavior in neurological and psychiatric disorders stemming from disturbances of the reward processing system. The proposed model is shown to consistently outperform the baseline Thompson Sampling method, on all data and experiment settings we explored, demonstrating better adaptation to each domain due to high flexibility of our multi-parameter model which allows to tune the weights on incoming positive and negative rewards, as well as the weights on memories about the prior reward history. Our empirical results support multiple prior observations about reward processing biases in a range of mental disorders, thus indicating the potential of the proposed model and its future extensions to capture reward-processing aspects across various neurological and psychiatric conditions. Our future work directions include extending our model to the more realistic contextual bandit setting, as well as testing the model on human decision making data.

References

1. Lai, T.L., Robbins, H.: Asymptotically efficient adaptive allocation rules. Adv. Appl. Math. **6**(1), 4–22 (1985)
2. Auer, P., Cesa-Bianchi, N., Fischer, P.: Finite-time analysis of the multiarmed bandit problem. Mach. Learn. **47**(2–3), 235–256 (2002)

3. Perry, D.C., Kramer, J.H.: Reward processing in neurodegenerative disease. Neurocase **21**(1), 120–133 (2015)
4. Frank, M.J., Seeberger, L.C., O'reilly, R.C.: By carrot or by stick: cognitive reinforcement learning in parkinsonism. Science **306**(5703), 1940–1943 (2004)
5. Redish, A.D., Jensen, S., Johnson, A., Kurth-Nelson, Z.: Reconciling reinforcement learning models with behavioral extinction and renewal: implications for addiction, relapse, and problem gambling. Psychol. Rev. **114**(3), 784 (2007)
6. Luman, M., Van Meel, C.S., Oosterlaan, J., Sergeant, J.A., Geurts, H.M.: Does reward frequency or magnitude drive reinforcement-learning in attention-deficit/hyperactivity disorder? Psychiatry Res. **168**(3), 222–229 (2009)
7. Taylor, A.M., Becker, S., Schweinhardt, P., Cahill, C.: Mesolimbic dopamine signaling in acute and chronic pain: implications for motivation, analgesia, and addiction. Pain **157**(6), 1194 (2016)
8. Seeley, W.W., Zhou, J., Kim, E.J.: Frontotemporal dementia: what can the behavioral variant teach us about human brain organization? Neurosci. **18**(4), 373–385 (2012)
9. Hauser, T.U., Fiore, V.G., Moutoussis, M., Dolan, R.J.: Computational psychiatry of adhd: neural gain impairments across marrian levels of analysis. Trends Neurosci. **39**(2), 63–73 (2016)
10. Dezfouli, A., Piray, P., Keramati, M.M., Ekhtiari, H., Lucas, C., Mokri, A.: A neurocomputational model for cocaine addiction. Neural Comput. **21**(10), 2869–2893 (2009)
11. Hess, L.E., Haimovici, A., Muñoz, M.A., Montoya, P.: Beyond pain: modeling decision-making deficits in chronic pain. Front. Behav. Neurosci. **8**, 1–8 (2014)
12. Auer, P., Cesa-Bianchi, N.: On-line learning with malicious noise and the closure algorithm. Ann. Math. Artif. Intell. **23**(1–2), 83–99 (1998)
13. Auer, P., Cesa-Bianchi, N., Freund, Y., Schapire, R.E.: The nonstochastic multi-armed bandit problem. SIAM J. Comput. **32**(1), 48–77 (2002)
14. Bouneffouf, D., Féraud, R.: Multi-armed bandit problem with known trend. Neurocomputing **205**, 16–21 (2016)
15. Chapelle, O., Li, L.: An empirical evaluation of Thompson sampling. In: Advances in Neural Information Processing Systems, pp. 2249–2257 (2011)
16. Thompson, W.: On the likelihood that one unknown probability exceeds another in view of the evidence of two samples. Biometrika **25**, 285–294 (1933)
17. Agrawal, S., Goyal, N.: Analysis of Thompson sampling for the multi-armed bandit problem. In: COLT 2012 - The 25th Annual Conference on Learning Theory, 25–27 June 2012, Edinburgh, Scotland, pp. 39.1–39.26 (2012)
18. Bouneffouf, D.: Freshness-aware Thompson sampling. In: Loo, C.K., Yap, K.S., Wong, K.W., Beng Jin, A.T., Huang, K. (eds.) ICONIP 2014. LNCS, vol. 8836, pp. 373–380. Springer, Cham (2014). doi:10.1007/978-3-319-12643-2_46
19. Schulz, E., Konstantinidis, E., Speekenbrink, M.: Learning and decisions in contextual multi-armed bandit tasks. In: Proceedings of the 37th Annual Conference of the Cognitive Science Society, pp. 2204–2212 (2015)
20. Thompson, W.R.: On the likelihood that one unknown probability exceeds another in view of the evidence of two samples. Biometrika **25**(3/4), 285–294 (1933)

Analyzing Human Decision Making Process with Intention Estimation Using Cooperative Pattern Task

Kota Itoda[1]([✉]), Norifumi Watanabe[2], and Yoshiyasu Takefuji[1]

[1] Keio University Fujisawa-shi, Fujisawa, Kanagawa 252-0882, Japan
kota02@sfc.keio.ac.jp
[2] Advanced Institute of Industrial Technology, Shinagawa-ku, Tokyo 140-0011, Japan

Abstract. Realizing flexible cooperative group behavior of human and social robots or agents needs a mutual understanding of each intention or behaviors of participants. To understand cooperative intelligence in group behavior, we must clarify the decision-making process with intention estimation in multiple persons. Multi-people decision-making process have top-down intention sharing and bottom-up decision making based on the intention inference and amendment based on the each participants' behavior. This study suggests the cooperative pattern task focusing on the selection process of others whom to be noticed and balancing process of each intention to achieve the shared purpose. In the 2D grid world of an abstract cooperative environment with restricted modality of subjects, they communicate with each other in a nonverbal way and infer their intention based on their behavior to achieve the purpose. We analyzed the human subjects' behavior and clarified their policy of behavior and concepts which assumed to be shared by each subject for preventing misunderstanding of each intention. Two main results were obtained through the experiment. First, optimal behavior based on the purpose in minimal steps prevent the misunderstanding of each intention. Second, the narrowing down the number of subjects who change their policy assumed to reduce the burden of intention inference.

1 Introduction

Understanding the underlining process of human decision making with intention estimation is needed for human agent interaction or human robot interaction. Although human flexible cooperative behaviors are seen in many sports or even in everyday lives, the process of cooperative decision making is not clarified. In goal-type ball games such as handball, soccer or basketball, players interact with each other in dynamic situations and estimate each intention based on the nonverbal communication such as eye contact or body language, and change their behavior to deceive or deal with the opponents. Also in everyday lives, we understand the others' intentions through their behavior and decide whether

© Springer International Publishing AG 2017
T. Everitt et al. (Eds.): AGI 2017, LNAI 10414, pp. 249–258, 2017.
DOI: 10.1007/978-3-319-63703-7_23

cooperate with them or not. The interaction of multi-people require the participants not only estimate the one other person's intention, but also select whom to focus and estimate the shared intention of the group. To understand the decision making process in human cooperative behavior, we suggest the cooperative pattern task which abstracts the cooperation with general cooperation purpose as forming a pattern. The subjects' behaviors are analyzed and the effect of behavioral optimality for preventing mutual misunderstanding and group policy which assumed to be shared among subjects to reduce the burden of inference.

In the following, we present background of the analysis and modeling of human decision making process with intention estimation in Sect. 2, then suggest the pattern task experiment for analysis of cooperative behavior in Sect. 3. We discuss the results of the experiments in Sect. 4, finally concludes this paper in Sect. 5.

2   Background

Various researches deal with clarifying or modeling interaction with intentions to construct socially intelligent agents or understand the human ability of decision making with intention inference. One of the representative agent models of interaction with others is BDI models of beliefs (B), desires (D), intention (I) based on Bratman's theory of intention [1–3]. In the BDI model, people set their own goals based on their beliefs about the surrounding environment, choose the means to achieve that goal, form the intention, and decide to act according to the intention. If interventions of the other people occur, they set new goals based on their beliefs and the intention of others, and choose another means to achieve the goal and form a new intention. While BDI model is represented by logical structure [2], recent researches model the human inference of intention or interaction with the other person through probabilistic mathematical models like MDP(Markov Decision Process) or reinforcement learning models based on Bayesian perspective [4–6]. In this way, the intention of people depends on their own beliefs depending on the environment, and are formed through the internal model of other person. It is thought that there is an aspect that they estimate others' intentions based on the models and decides behavior by balancing between the intentions of the others and themselves. If there are more than one other person, we can share the intention of each and have *shared concept* to form common action, and analyzing such structure of the multi-person interaction is also important for human robot interaction [7]. For example, in soccer which is realized as one of the best cooperative action of people, even when each player acquires different environmental information, they estimate common subgoals instantly and form an intention to realize it. Such process enable them to realizes advanced strategies such as one-two pass or through ball. To form these kind of intention, not only the bottom-up intention formation based on individual beliefs, but also the intention shared among players in specific states and actions and the concept of connecting them are present. Shared concepts which involve selection of others and born from interactions are important for the model formation of interaction with others.

Next, in interaction with other people, it is necessary to self-observe how other people guess about themselves, thereby guessing what kind of influence can be given to others by themselves. Self-observation principle [8] estimates the behavior of others by adopting a model that looks at himself objectively to others. By the principle, it is possible for people to match with or withdraw others in the group and construct strategies mutually predicting of each mind. Furthermore, estimating internal states of each other also helps cooperative actions such as mutually coordinating behaviors and working jointly. In order to adjust their behavior, it is important to select one from the multiple sub-goals and estimate what the others intend. The problem is the recurrence of intention estimation between self and others. A recurrent structure such as "to estimate another person's own self", "to estimate that others are estimating others' own self" occurs [9]. Recurrent estimation of others' intention in verbal interaction is also analyzed through an interpersonal game [10]. In fact, we analyze the causality of the movement behavior of the handball and soccer players, so the causal relationships of the actions among players are mutually connected, and it is difficult to estimate the structure [11]. In order to solve such recursion, we think that it is necessary to analyze the depth of intention estimation in local cooperative behaviors. Therefore, we analyze subject behavior by using pattern task as cooperative task abstracting cooperative behavior.

3 Pattern Task

3.1 Outline of the Task

We propose the pattern task for analyzing human cooperative behavior. In this task, *four* subjects participate and cooperate in a grid world without verbal communication, and aim to realize the locational target pattern in as few steps as they can. Each subject behaves as an agent in the grid world and can take 5 actions (stop, go-left, go-right, go-up, go-down) (shown in Fig. 1). Since the target patterns are defined with relative distances of *three* points in grid without overlaps, each *four* agents ought to consider whom to cooperate with to achieve the pattern within minimal steps. That is, although the goal is achieved by whole *four* agents by positioning to form the target pattern, each subject must estimate others' intention to prevent misunderstanding for achieving the goal in each steps, and tell others whether to participate forming the pattern or not, through only their behaviors.

The task consists of five phases as below:

- Phase1: Select other agents whom to be focused to realize the target pattern.
- Phase2: Select three coordinations where the agent realize the target pattern at last, or the pattern will be realized by the other agents.
- Phase3: Select one of the five actions (stop, go-left, go-right, go-up, go-down).
- Phase4: Select the agents who are considered to be selected in Phase1 by the agent.

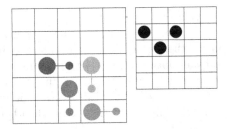

Fig. 1. Pattern task (Left) the grid world. The large round sprites in this figure represent the agents and their current locations and the small ones represent the location in the previous step. (Right) The target pattern. Since the end condition of each trial is defined by the relative position of three points, the trial ends in this situation.

– Phase5: Select three coordinations where the agents focused in Phase1 selected in Phase 2.

The above whole five phases are repeated in each steps of a trial until the agents achieve the target pattern or the limit of maximum steps. Then the initial locations of the agents are changed and after changing some different initial locations, the different target pattern is applied and repeated each trials (see Fig. 2).

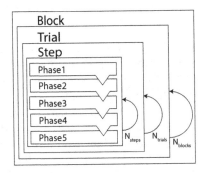

Fig. 2. Task flow of the experiment. Each phases are repeated in each steps. The steps are repeated in N_{steps} times or until the purpose realized in each trials. Each trials with different initial locations of the agents and each blocks with different target patterns are repeated in N_{trials} and N_{blocks} times.

Several rules are set in this task:

– Subjects are not allowed to talk about their location or action which enable the other to specify the agent to the other subjects.
– The target pattern can be realized by three out of four agents, and it is not necessary for whole four agents to locate in the target locations.

- Since the task achievement is judged by the relative locations of the target pattern, parallel shift of the coordinations are accepted but the rotation or reverse of the pattern is not accepted.
- The agents selected in Phase1 or 4 don't conclude the agent who is selecting in this phase himself. If the number of selected agents was more than three (for example, in the case the distance of the target pattern was the same with few agents), the agent select the only three agents most possible to achieve the pattern.
- The target coordinations selected in Phase 2 and 5 are the most realizable pattern to achieve.
- Agents are allowed to move to the same location of the other agents and they are able to move to the four neighboring cell of the grid world (left, right, up, down). The field is not torus grid world and the ends of the field are not connected (i.e., the agent cannot go right at the right edge and also the other edges).

3.2   Experiment

In this experiment, we have prepared the task as a web application for multiple subjects to participate together and subjects participated using Web browsers with their own computers. We used a 5×5 grid world for the experiment and set the maximal step limit as 5 steps because subjects can achieve one edge to the other edge of the field. To prevent the prediction of the behavior based on the personality of the each subject, the colors of agents are randomly shuffled in all trials and blocks. Also, although the red colored agent always represents the subject who controlling the agent in his screen, the agent has different colors from the screens of others. So the colors of the agents don't correspond to each other in each screen to prevent specifying subjects. 20 subjects participated in this experiment with a few target patterns of almost each 5 trials of different initial locations for each group.

3.3   Results

Through the experiments, the following two results were obtained. First, according to selection of their own target pattern of Phase 2 and another person in Phase 5, in many cases, one of the optimum patterns that minimize the number of reaching steps to the goal is selected. Also, to select another agent relates to achieving the goal in Phase 1, subject basically select another person who has few reaching steps. Second, regarding the relationship between the pattern assumed by the subject and the pattern of others, although there are many new patterns in each subject in the early stage, when all the intentions of the subjects agree, they estimate the same pattern continuously until the purpose achieved.

Selection of Others and Target Patterns. First of all, the estimation depth with regard to the selection of the target pattern of Phase 2 was determined for all subjects (three coordinate inputs [1], and not incorrect patterns entered) in the Table 1 (1-1), 1, 2 steps are the most frequent, and others are few. In addition, the difference between the depth of the computationally optimal pattern based on the distance of goal pattern (hereinafter referred to as optimum pattern) and the depth of each subject estimated is basically falls within one step as shown in the Table 1 (1-2), and subjects almost estimate the optimum pattern (99.55% of the total estimates the pattern within 1 step shift from the optimum pattern). Also, in Phase 5, we also analyzed the selection of a target pattern of another person in the same procedure (As with Phase 2, only three coordinates are entered, only those that did not input an incorrect pattern are analyzed), in the Table 1 (2-1), we assume a pattern that can be realized in 1, 2 steps and two steps as like Phase 2. In addition, the difference from the optimal pattern basically falls within the range of 0 to 1 as shown in the Table 1 (2-2). In this way, similar results were obtained in Phase 2 and Phase 5.

Next, with respect to the other agent selected in Phase 1, the other person selected by the subject is set to the nearest group of others calculated from Phase 2 is 581 times out of 668 times (86.98%), as shown in the Table 1 (3-1). Aggregating in the case of the number of other interested people is 2 or 3, it is 581 times out of 620 times (93.71%) as shown in the Table 1 (3-2).

Table 1. Selection of others and target pattern

(1) Phase2 (target pattern selection)		Total
(1-1) the target pattern estimated steps	0: 4, 1: 369, 2: 231, 3: 55, 4: 3	662
(1-2) diff. with the depth of optimal pattern	0: 571, 1: 88, 2: 3	662
(2) Phase5 (target pattern selection of others)		
(2-1) the target pattern estimated steps	0: 9, 1: 800, 2: 471, 3: 104, 4: 12	1396
(2-2) diff. with the depth of optimal pattern	0: 1249, 1: 141, 2: 6	1396
(3) Phase1 (focused agent selection)		
(3-1) # of selection of the nearests of Phase2	581 (86.98%)	668
(3-2) limited by 2 or 3 agent of the above case	581 (93.71%)	620

Relation Between Patterns Selected by Subjects and Others. According to the relationship between the pattern selected by the subject and another person, the selected pattern of Phase 2 in the previous and next steps is divided into the following three items and analyzed.

---

[1] The breakdown of the number of coordinates of the subject's pattern input in all trials and all steps is {0: 3, 2: 2, 3: 668, 4: 1, 6: 2}. 98% or more has entered three coordinates. Others are considered to correspond to the multiple target selection (entering six coordinates), no idea (entering zero) and erroneous input (entering two or four).

(a) Select the same pattern as Phase 2 in the previous step.
(b) Select the same pattern as the pattern selected by Phase 2 by another agent.
(c) Select a new pattern different from every pattern selected in the previous step.

First of all, in all the whole trial steps of Table 2 (1), selecting the pattern assumed by (a) is the largest number of 305 times (45.39% of the total), next the number of (c) which assumes a new pattern follows by 246 times (36.61%) and the number of selecting (b) is 121 times (18.01%).

To confirm the change of selection in each trial of more than one step, the first inter-steps (steps 1 and 2), the last inter-step (last step and before) and the inter-steps of the timing of each target patterns matched (same pattern between before after) were separately analyzed. First, in the first inter-step as shown in Table 2 (2), out of all 248 times, (c) is the highest at 169 times (68.15%), followed by (a) 59 times (23.79%) and (b) 20 times (8.06%). On the other hand, in the last inter-step the order changes as shown in the Table 2 (3). Out of 248 times, (a) is the highest with 163 times (65.73%), followed by (b) 74 times (29.84%) and (c) 11 times (4.44%). Also, paying attention to the inter-step before and after the target pattern of everyone matches as shown in the Table 2 (4), Out of the total 152, (a) and (c) are almost the same as 73 times (48.03%) and 68 times (44.74%) (b) is the lowest as 11 times (7.24%)[2]. The patterns selected in Phase2 becomes inconsistent after the Phase 2 matches in the only one trial of the entire 77 trials.

Table 2. Relationship among pattern selections. Refer to the Sect. 3.3 of the meaning of 'a', 'b', and 'c'

(1) Whole step total	a: 305, b: 121, c: 246	total 672
(2) First step	a: 59, b: 20, c: 169	total 248
(3) Last step	a: 163, b: 74, c: 11	total 248
(4) Consensus step	a: 73, b: 11, c: 68	total 152

In the most cases, it was found that the patterns selected by subjects match after the subjects got the consensus in Phase2 once.

4 Discussion

4.1 Behavioral Optimality for Preventing Intention Misunderstanding

As seen in the analysis result of Sect. 3.3, in Phase 2, subjects were basically estimate a pattern that is nearly the same as the optimum pattern that realizes

---

[2] Because the target pattern don't match in some trials, the population number is different.

the pattern with the minimum steps and the same result is obtained also in Phase 5. We also found out that the others reaching the minimum step are chosen to pay attention in Phase 1. To select a pattern close to the optimal pattern by the subject is assumed to be based on the task purpose of realizing the goal with as few steps as possible. Usually, when estimating the intention of another person, it is necessary to use their properties, characteristics, habits of their action selection. However, since in this task, it eliminates the influence of learning of the properties and characteristics of personal behavior selection. In order for subjects to estimate the intention of each occasion only from the behavior of others during the interaction, each individual's modality is limited to simple circle sprites on the grid world without difference of the appearances, and the colors of the agents are shuffled randomly in all trials and blocks. As a measure to estimate individual policy in such circumstances, it is necessary to apply the policy not depending on each individual. The estimation of intention using behavioral optimality is considered to be effective, and the result suggests that such a measure is taken on the task.

Actually, 74 out of 77 trials finally realized the pattern, and as the total number of required steps, an average of 2.08 steps in 74 trial during the limit 5 steps realized the pattern (The details are broken down as follows: {1: 15, 2: 42, 3: 14, 4: 2, 5: 1} (number of required steps: number of trials)). In the state where the policies of each subject are unknown, it is unable to accomplish the task with such short steps. Also, as it is difficult to estimate personal policies within the trial, estimating mutual intent by facilitating mutual optimum behavior is aimed at estimating the target pattern and it is thought that it is shared as one of the overall measures for the selection of other people to notice.

4.2   Shared Behavioral Tendency Among the Group to Reduce Intention Estimation Burden or Discrepancy

In the subsect. 3.3, we analyzed target selections of inter-steps (before and after steps) by dividing in three items for the trials of two or more steps. As shown in the Table 2 (2), in the first inter-step (1, 2 step), it was the highest to select (c), a new pattern different from the subject himself and others in the step. This is because subjects do not know how other people will move next in the initial steps, and the pattern that subjects decided at the beginning and the pattern from when everyone started moving would change in many cases. On the other hand in the last step, (a), the same pattern as the pattern chosen before, is the most frequently selected, and (b), selecting the pattern of others, follows. Since at the time of achieving the goal, the target patterns of each subject is determined and the possible patterns are narrowed down in the patterns selected by the subjects or the pattern selected by the others. Therefore, it is considered that there is not much at this point to assume a new pattern as in (c). Also, before and after the step in which all the subjects match the pattern selected in Phase 2, (a), (c) was high and (b) was the lowest result. First of all, as for the case of (c), as an optimal pattern in that situation, it seems that the case where all the subjects match when selecting a new pattern is considered applicable.

The situation considered in Sect. 4.1 applies. On the other hand, the reason why (a) is more than (b) is that after everyone else matches, it is thought that it corresponds to the scene where the remaining two people change their intention. If all subjects are (a), there must be a match of Phase 2 at the previous step, at the time of coincidence, there will always be subjects' selection (b) or (c). The more subjects have different intentions, the more conflicting intentions occur and it is difficult to achieve the goal. Since a few subjects select (b), it is difficult to think that almost all subjects change their intentions and at the same time Phase 2 matches. From that, by narrowing down the subjects who intend to change their intent as a whole policy within the trial, it is thought that it avoids the risk of intention mispredictions and the delay of achievement of the goal coming from it.

The number of people moved at the reaching the goal is one example of suggesting this result. If there are the shared policy narrowing down the number of subjects change their own target pattern to the last one or two, many subjects except one or two people who already achieved the target pattern would wait for the remaining subjects at the time of achieving the goal. Since some subjects take actions to leave to deny involvement in the target pattern. When the analysis was performed among subjects who approached the final target pattern at the shortest distance, the number of people who moved at the same time in 74 trials that achieved the target pattern was {0: 1, 1: 36, 2: 20, 3: 16, 4: 1}. From this result, by narrowing down the subjects to move to the remaining one and two people, an overall the measure is taken to avoid discrepancies in intention.

5   Conclusion

We analyzed interactions of human cooperative group behavior using the cooperative pattern task. Basically, two results were obtained by the experiment. (1) Subjects often take optimal patterns to achieve the goal in minimal steps in Phase 2 and 5 (the phases of selecting target patterns). Moreover, in Phase 1 or 4 (the phases of selecting focused agents), the nearest other agents to the patterns are basically selected to achieve the goal. (2) According to the relationship of selected patterns among subjects, although each different patterns are selected at the beginning, then a few subjects change their mind in their interaction, finally they achieve the consensus of the goal by narrowing down the number of the agents who change their minds. These results are assumed to be based on the reasons below. First, having the same strategy of behavior based on the optimality of minimal steps to achieve the goal prevents intention misunderstanding among subjects. Although this behavior was not instructed by the experimenter or other subjects because the verbal communication was prohibited in the experiment, the purpose of the experiment for minimizing the steps helps subjects to understand each intention. Second, the group strategy of narrowing down the number of the agents who change the mind in trials to prevent intention misunderstanding shared among the subjects was suggested through the experiment.

In future, we construct computational agent models based on the results and hypotheses obtained by this experiment. Moreover, we verify the hypotheses by autonomous agent simulation of group behavior based on the models, and clarify the elements which explain the subjects' behavior.

References

1. Bratman, M.: Intention, Plans, and Practical Reason. Harvard University Press, Cambridge (1987)
2. Rao, A.S., Georgeff, M.P.: Modeling rational agents within a BDI-architecture. In: KR 1991, pp. 473–484 (1991)
3. Weiss, G.: Multiagent Systems, 2nd edn. MIT press, Cambridge (2013)
4. Baker, C.L., Saxe, R., Tenenbaum, J.B.: Action understanding as inverse planning. Cognition 113(3), 329–349 (2009)
5. Baker, C.L., Tenenbaum, J.B.: Modeling human plan recognition using Bayesian theory of mind. In: Sukthankar, G., Goldman, R.P., Geib, C., Pynadath, C., Bui, H. (eds.) Plan, Activity and Intent Recognition: Theory and Practice. Morgan Kaufmann, San Francisco (2014)
6. Yoshida, W., Dolan, R.J., Friston, K.J.: Game theory of mind. PLoS Comput. Biol. 4(12), e1000254 (2008). doi:10.1371/journal.pcbi.1000254
7. Sato, R., Takeuchi, Y.: Coordinating turn-taking and talking in multi-party conversations by controlling robot's eye-gaze. In: The 23rd IEEE International Symposium on Robot and Human Interactive Communication (2014)
8. Makino, T., Aihara, K.: Self-observation principle for estimating the other's internal state: A new computational theory of communication. Mathematical Engineering Technical Reports METR (2003)
9. Omori, T., Yokoyama, A., Nagata, Y., Ishikawa, S.: Computational modeling of action decision process including other's mind-a theory toward social ability, in keynote talk. In: IEEE International Conference on Intelligent Human Computer Interaction (IHCI) (2010)
10. Nakamura, N., Inaba, M., Takahashi, K., Toriumi, F., Osawa, H., Katagami, D., Shinoda, K.: Constructing a human-like agent for the Werewolf game using a psychological model based multiple perspectives. In: IEEE Symposium Series on Computational Intelligence (SSCI) (2016)
11. Itoda, K., Watanabe, N., Takefuji, Y.: Model-based behavioral causality analysis of handball with delayed transfer entropy. Proc. Comput. Sci. 71, 85–91 (2015)

Pursuing Fundamental Advances in Human Reasoning

Timothy van Gelder$^{(\boxtimes)}$ (iD) and Richard de Rozario (iD)

University of Melbourne, Parkville, VIC 3010, Australia
tgelder@unimelb.edu.au

Abstract. The IARPA CREATE program's aim to produce "fundamental advances" in human reasoning may provide a new sufficiency test for AGI and insights for the evaluation of AGI performance. The approach of one CREATE program team, the SWARM Project, is outlined.

Keywords: Reasoning · Intelligence · Evaluation

1 Introduction

The standard definition of AGI—the possession, by an artificial system, of "general intelligence at the human level and beyond"—presupposes some understanding of what human-level intelligence actually is. However, this concept has proven elusive. Various tests have been proposed as operational substitutes for a general definition. The Turing Test is the most famous [1], but others include the coffee test [2], and the robot student test [3].

The higher the level of intelligence required to pass a test, the more stringent the test, and the more compelling it would be if an artificial agent passed. Gaining a college degree requires more intelligence than holding an ordinary conversation, and so passing the robot student test is stronger evidence of human-level general intelligence.

It is therefore interesting to ask what the very highest level of general human intelligence might be. The most stringent, and hence compelling, sufficiency test would reference this level.

A research program recently launched by the US Intelligence Advanced Research Projects Activity (IARPA) may shed light on three issues at the heart of this question: (1) the highest level of human performance, (2) how performance at that level can be evaluated, and, (3) how systems achieving that performance might be designed.

This research is based upon work supported in part by the Office of the Director of National Intelligence (ODNI), Intelligence Advanced Research projects Activity (IARPA), under Contract 2017-16122000002. The views and conclusions contained herein are those of the authors and should not be interpreted as necessarily representing the official policies, either expressed or implied, of ODNI, IARPA, or the U.S. Government. The U.S. Government is authorized to reproduce and distribute reprints for governmental purposes notwithstanding any copyright annotation therein.

© Springer International Publishing AG 2017
T. Everitt et al. (Eds.): AGI 2017, LNAI 10414, pp. 259–262, 2017.
DOI: 10.1007/978-3-319-63703-7_24

2 IARPA's CREATE Program

The CREATE (Crowdsourcing Evidence, Argumentation, Thinking, and Evaluation) program aims to produce "fundamental advances in human reasoning" ([4] p. 7) via methods which combine crowdsourcing and structured analytical techniques. Crowdsourcing in this context means collaboration among groups of analysts. Structured analytical techniques are methods intended to produce better analyses [5].

In the CREATE program, four "performer" teams will produce "systems" supporting structured collaboration on difficult reasoning problems. These systems will be rigorously evaluated by an independent testing and evaluation team to determine whether groups of analysts using the systems can meet or exceed prespecified benchmarks for improved reasoning performance, across a wide range of problems, relative to a baseline or control system. Naturally there will be interest in which system performs best overall. However, this "tournament" is friendly and collaborative in nature, with the best outcome being that all systems perform well, though perhaps excelling in different ways or on different types of problems.

The generality of the intelligence required to succeed in the CREATE program is indicated by the range of problems on which systems will be evaluated. "CREATE's methods must be applicable to a wide range of analytic problems, including political, military, economic, scientific and technological questions," such as: Are domestic conflicts in region Y contributing to regional instability? ([4] p. 8).

There is a difficult problem at the heart of the program. How can reasoning performance be measured? If CREATE systems produce superior performance, how can this be reliably demonstrated? This is a problem because, despite all the work over the centuries in logic (broadly speaking) there does not currently exist any widely accepted methodology for rigorously evaluating the quality of complex reasoning.

Some features of the CREATE program make this an especially difficult challenge. First, many of the types of problems CREATE hopes to tackle lack any objective yardsticks. For example, in the case of the sample problem given above, involving the causal explanation of geopolitical instability, there is no gold standard against which answers can be measured. Conclusions can only be evaluated via more reasoning, whose quality is just as questionable as that of the original reasoning.

Second, CREATE is intended to produce reasoning of a higher quality than is achievable by any other method. However, reasoning will necessarily be involved in the evaluation of reasoning produced by CREATE systems. How can superior reasoning be evaluated using (by hypothesis) inferior approaches or methods?

The problem of rigorous evaluation thus involves difficult conceptual issues. It also involves tricky questions of experimental design. The four performer teams, and the test and evaluation team, are collaborating to develop a solution. These efforts are critical to the success of the CREATE program, but they also potentially bear on the problem of rigorously determining whether an artificial agent is engaging in general reasoning at or beyond the highest level of human performance.

3 The SWARM Project

One of the performer teams is the SWARM Project. The acronym stands for Smartly-Assembled Wiki-Style Argument Marshalling. Argument marshalling is a structured analytical technique, similar to argument mapping [6] but not diagrammatic, less rigid, and closer to the natural reasoning behaviors of sophisticated analysts. In the SWARM approach analysts marshal reasoning on a wiki-style platform, i.e., one that supports collaborative and even simultaneous editing of pages. Finally, "smartly assembled" refers to a range of ways the platform supports the production of high-quality reasoning, such as incorporating workflow based on the IDEA protocol [7], or aggregating contributions using information derived from deliberation analytics [8].

At a higher level, the SWARM team aims to succeed by maximizing the collective intelligence of analyst groups using the system; or, in simpler terms, building "super-reasoning teams," analogous to the "superforecasting" teams developed in a previous IARPA program [9]. This challenge is analogous to that of maximizing elite group performance in other contexts, such as sports, military special operations, and surgery. There is an extensive literature on group or team performance. Drawing on recent syntheses (e.g., [10]), it is useful to frame the challenge of maximising the collective intelligence of reasoning groups as one of optimizing the team and its activities along six dimensions or "enabling conditions" [11] of strong group performance:

- **Composition**. Who belongs to the group? More specific issues include: How large should the group be? What attributes should individual members possess? How should attributes be distributed across the group?
- **Processes**. How does the group go about its tasks? What processes, procedures or methods does the team utilize?
- **Resources**. What is provided to the group to enable stronger performance? This includes anything the group can draw in performing their tasks, including equipment, consumables (food, fuel etc.), and information.
- **Motivation**. What drives the group? High-performing groups require strong motivation at individual and group levels. Motivation can be enhanced via good choices on all the other dimensions.
- **Culture**. How can performance be enhanced by means of positive culture? A team's culture consists of its distinctive shared values, standards and practices, over and above what has been made explicit in the team processes.
- **Coaching**. How can performance be enhanced through guidance, feedback, training and conditioning provided to the team as a whole and to its members?

The SWARM team is developing and testing answers to these high-level questions, and many more detailed ones, for the specific case of groups whose mission is to engage in general reasoning. To take one example, in the Resources dimension, a general reasoning group needs a high-quality platform for collaborating in the development of documents expressing their reasoning. To this end, SWARM is developing and testing a new online platform supporting wiki-style argument marshalling.

4   Conclusion

With the CREATE program, IARPA aims to break entirely new ground with regard to human general reasoning capability. If successful, this new standard of performance would arguably define the most stringent sufficiency test for the creation of AGI. That is, if an artificial system could compete at or beyond the level of human groups in a CREATE-style competition, this would represent the most compelling possible evidence that general intelligence had been achieved.

The CREATE program's need to rigorously evaluate whether high levels of performance have been achieved requires it to address some difficult problems in the evaluation of high-level general reasoning. Any progress in this area will also apply to the evaluation of reasoning performance by AGI systems.

Another possible outcome of the CREATE program is to yield insights into how high levels of performance on general reasoning problems can be achieved. These insights might inform the design of AGI systems. For example, it may be that an AGI system could benefit from being designed as a collaboration of artificial agents working together using some of the principles discovered in the CREATE program to result in the highest levels of human performance.

References

1. Pinar Saygin, A., Cicekli, I., Akman, V.: Turing test: 50 years later. Minds Mach. **10**(4), 463–518 (2000)
2. Moon, P.: Wozniak on Apple, AI, and future inventions. In: The Washington Post (2007)
3. Goertzel, B.: What counts as a thinking machine–and when will we meet one? New Sci. **215** (2881), 18 (2012)
4. Intelligence Advanced Research Projects Activity: Crowdsourcing Evidence, Evaluation, Argumentation, Thinking and Evaluation, IARPA-BAA-15-11 (2016)
5. Heuer, R.J., Pherson, R.H.: Structured Techniques for Intelligence Analysis, 2nd edn. CQ Press, Los Angeles (2015)
6. van Gelder, T.J.: Argument mapping. In: Pashler, H. (ed.) Encyclopedia of the Mind. SAGE, Thousand Oaks (2013)
7. Hanea, A.M., McBride, M.F., Burgman, M.A., Wintle, B.C.: Classical meets modern in the IDEA protocol for structured expert judgement. J. Risk Res. **9877**, 1–17 (2016). doi:10. 1080/13669877.2016.1215346
8. Shum, S.B., et al.: DCLA meet CIDA: collective intelligence deliberation analytics. In: 2nd International Workshop on Discourse-Centric Learning Analytics, LAK14: 4th International Conference on Learning Analytics & Knowledge (2014)
9. Tetlock, P., Gardner, D.: Superforecasting: The Art and Science of Prediction. Random House, London (2015)
10. Salas, E., Shuffler, M.L., Thayer, A.L., Bedwell, W.L., Lazzara, E.H.: Understanding and improving teamwork in organizations: a scientifically based practical guide. Hum. Res. Manag. **54**(4), 599–622 (2014)
11. Hackman, J.R.: Collaborative intelligence: using teams to solve hard problems. Berrett-Koehler Publishers, San Francisco (2011)

Philosophy

A Priori Modeling of Information and Intelligence

Marcus Abundis[✉]

Bön Informatics, Aarau, Switzerland
55mrcs@gmail.com

Abstract. This paper details *primitive structural traits* in information, and then in intelligence, as a model of 'thinking like nature' (natural/core informatics). It explores the task of designing a general adaptive intelligence from a low-order (non-anthropic) base, to arrive at a scalable, least-ambiguous, and most-general, computational/developmental core.

1 Discussion of Problem: Asking the Right Question ...

What presents a central conceptual challenge in the advent of human level AI (HLAI) is essentially noted by various individuals, across diverse disciplines, as they each confront their own obstacles:

- 'solving intelligence', Demiss Hassabis, Google Deep Mind [3],
- 'de-risking science', Ed Boyden [2], MIT Media Lab, neurology,
- 'meaning as fundamental', Brian Josephson [17], Cambridge University, physics,
- 'theory of meaning', Shannon and Weaver [34], information theory, and more.

Each individual or discipline has its own framing, but these nominally-diverse logical gaps can be seen as, and reduced to, one main informational failing.

Shannon and Weaver were likely first to see this gap as a missing *theory of meaning* but it has worn many faces since. Further study marks key differences in how we view and treat objective (quantitative) information, and subjective information (qualia, raw sense data) — where basic ideas of 'information' become a confused dualist concept, with neither view fully developed or integrated with the other [34].

For example, mathematics is often seen as being 'purely objective', capable of omitting subjective traits from its arguments as an intellectual ideal (e.g., theoretical mathematics). But mathematics without *subjective elemental facts* is a fact-free science, of little practical use. Only if subjective (S) and objective (O) roles are linked do 'useful results' arise (e.g., applied mathematics). If we look for other firm objective views, the standard model in physics and the periodic table are good candidates. But their recent 'objective success' ignores the fact they arose from a line of *subjective elemental observations*, later normalized via experiment and peer review. Only after enough material regularity ('evidence')

© Springer International Publishing AG 2017
T. Everitt et al. (Eds.): AGI 2017, LNAI 10414, pp. 265–273, 2017.
DOI: 10.1007/978-3-319-63703-7_25

was *subjectively discerned* and *subjectively named*, by varied individuals, were the models then normalized (agreed upon) as being innately objective.

Practical gains derived from **objectified** *subjective* roles, like the standard model and the periodic table, are so vast that we may forget how objective features first arise as subjective notions. Objective traits cannot even be posited if they are not first *subjectively sensed* or 'discovered' by someone. So, if we now seek to design something 'objectively intelligent', we confront the equal of designing a 'pure subjective' role [35] to sustain later 'objective' aims. The point of *general intelligence* is, after all, to bring new subject matters to our attention, so we can later name new objective gains, in a scalable/serial manner. Continued 'informational (S-O) integration' would presumably lead to a type of HLAI+ or 'super-intelligence'.

But before attempting any such goal, we must ask 'Intelligence about what exactly?', as all intelligences, even human, are unequal due to innate subjectivity [7]. Also, in a manner akin to that seen in the standard model and the periodic table, what *subjective elemental facts* ('data' or base 'information') will we use to initiate that presumably-objective (super) intelligence?

Given that such questions persist, S-O modeling remains **the** core issue for grasping 'knowledge' in western thought. Despite varied framings and opinions on the matter, this all points to an unavoidable subjective aspect in modeling information and intelligent systems — contrary to a presumed 'purely objective' ideal.

2   Current Literature

In the literature, the need for S-O modeling drives a large patchwork of vague, controversial, and competing views [11]. For example, most basic is *scientism*, claiming that if 'a thing' is not objectively named it does not exist, seeking to eliminate subjectivity wholly from consideration [26]. Ironically, this shows the worst of subjective naïveté [27,30]. Philosopher Daniel Dennett [10] is a likely standard-bearer arguing that qualia (raw sense data) are non-existent, ignoring the need for a *functionally differentiating sensorium* in 'evolution by natural selection'. Alternatively, philosopher David Chalmers [5] asserts that qualia are beyond all scientific thought, while often alluding to an 'information theory' solution but with no actual details ever offered. After Chalmers, others support a mystical 'panpsychism', with evolutionary biologist Stuart Kauffman [15,19] and neurologist Christof Koch [21] as recent converts. Lastly, there is 'mysterianism' where some seem to throw their hands up and claim that no solution is ever likely [9]. These and other numerous unnamed views offer seemingly endless debate, but little more.

Conversely, success with Shannon's [33] 'signal entropy' drives an enduring informational pragmatism and decades of information technology leaps — in **objective** roles. Plain objective gains versus endless subjective debate puts most attempts at S-O modeling in a poor light (as per above). Regardless, Shannon and Weaver still saw signal entropy as essentially 'disappointing and bizarre' [34], in part due to a missing *theory of meaning*. Hence, later informational studies convey a 'conceptual labyrinth' of unresolved subjective/semantic issues, even if using a Shannon-based start [12]. Despite that persistent 'labyrinth', gains in unsupervised machine learning point to growing optimism in the possibility of designing an HLAI [22,29]. But those gains include 'catastrophic forgetting' [14] that can obscure the naming of reasons for that recent success. Also, the application of said models is rather limited ('narrow') in focus, despite broader 'general' claims [18]. As such, HLAI(+) efforts currently remain 'fringe projects' [16,24], partly due to the lack of true advances in S-O modeling.

In seeking a practical middle ground, few names appear. Philosopher John Searle [31] calls for 'biological naturalism' as a crucial foundation, framing base ontological and epistemic aspects in subjective and objective roles [32]. But again, no detail on a full model is offered. For example, he argues humans may process qualia, but other biological systems (like a tree) do not, without saying why those biological systems should differ (personal exchange, 30 April 2014). As a small advance, philosopher Luciano Floridi [12] offers a *General Definition of Information* (GDI) that partly differentiates semantic roles. But questions remain on GDI's finality [6]. Later, astrophysicist Sean Carroll [4] attempts a synthesized view by assembling notable intellectuals from diverse disciplines for a focused 'naturalism' discourse, but ends with no meaningful result. In a more-aspiring line, computer scientist Marcus Hutter [23] posits a Universal Artifical Intellgence *top-down* model (AIXI) that seems mostly theoretical and non-computable [37], but points to useful directions. Conversely, mathematician Stephen Wolfram [38] posits a *bottoms-up* 'computational irreducibility', where cosmic 'primitives' drive innate sense-making (interpretative) roles that compute all information. Recent versions of Wolfram Language (symbolic discourse language) mark an early effort at this style of S-O modeling. Still, it is too early to assess this approach's efficacy in (as said) 'mining a computational universe'.

The strongest hint to date of a likely solution comes from neuro-anthropologist Terrence Deacon [8], using a type of 'entropic analysis' as a base synthesis [11]. He references Claude Shannon's signal entropy, Boltzmann's thermodynamic entropy, and Darwinian natural selection as innately complementary views (a Shannon-Boltzmann-Darwin model). But the model's purely thermodynamic bias makes it irreconcilable with wider physics based views (email exchange, January 2017). Also, the work is littered with confusing/unneeded neologisms and nearly impenetrable prose [11,13,25]. The model thus lacks clarity. Beyond Deacon's work no other models are seen, except for the view posited herein — which roughly tracks Deacon's view but in a more-plainly reductive manner. Still, the strength of Deacon's *entropic analysis* is that it stipulates a bottom-up approach, minimizing the chance of later explanatory gaps, and ties directly to Shannon's signal entropy, an already well-established model.

3   Posited Model: Natural/Core Informatics, or 'Thinking Like Nature'

This paper frames a path through the above S-O bind by detailing a naturally scalable core with evolving complexity as we see with nature. It thus marks a growing functionality one also hopes to see in ever-more intelligent informational systems.

The model synthesizes: Shannon *signal entropy*, Bateson's [1] *differentiated differences*, and Darwinian *natural selection* (a Shannon-**Bateson**-Darwin model) for a unified general view. This contrasts to Deacon's Shannon-**Boltzmann**-Darwin model. This S-B-D core furnishes the model's structural fundaments, as briefly developed in the step-wise logic given below. Deeper analysis of those steps is given in three papers (see APPENDIX) that support a larger body of work on Natural/Core Informatics.

The steps that underlie this *naturally scalable core* are as follow:

1. What is *Information*? (an *a priori* dual aspect ...)
   (a) subjective and objective roles are named as distinct-but-interdependent informational precursors, where one affirms the existence of the other. An *a priori* dual-aspect theory [28,36] is thus implied in S-O models of information,
   (b) next, divergent **representational** modes for objective and subjective roles (re *a priori* dualism) are detailed,
   (c) also, divergent **computational** aspects of objective and subjective roles are named (e.g., questions of 'transition and emergence' or 'functional scalability').
   (d) Step 1's 'novelty' lies in: (i) naming an empiric dual-aspect, (ii) from an *a priori* perspective, (iii) therein surpassing prior notions of information.
2. What is *Meaningful* Information? (exploring further S-O links ...)
   (a) varied scientific models (the standard model, periodic table, genomics, and natural selection) are shown as distinct functional 'types' — naming *meaningful* differences in accepted **objectified** *subjective* roles,
   (b) thus, a further '*proximate* dualism', beyond '*a priori* dualism', is shown:
      i. the standard model and periodic table convey a '*proximate* objective' (non-adpative or 'direct') role, and
      ii. genomics and natural selection convey a '*proximate* subjective' (adaptive) role,
   (c) next, the role of metadata in grounding all *functional types* is named,
   (d) thus, to develop an ensuing *general informatics* as 'one logical system', a unifying meta-meta-data perspective is first needed,
   (e) that 'metadata bridge' is shown to entail three types of *meaningful* roles: materially direct (*non-adaptive*), discretely *adaptive* (coded), and temporally *adaptive* (selection), thus grounding a differentiated-but-unified 'general informatics' and general theory of meaning.
   (f) also, this marks a dualist-triune (*non-adaptive/adaptive*) topology in ensuing general informatics.

(g) Step 2's novelty is in (i) differentiating meaningful 'types', (ii) reframing *metadata* as 'data about **meaning**' versus common 'data about **data**', and (iii) identifying an empiric '2–3' topology for general informatics.

3. How is *Adaptive Logic* Generated? (focusing on adaptive 'intelligence' ...)

   (a) a general 'adaptive key' with *material* and *behavioral* facets is identified in 'levers'. Thus, *levers* afford a basis for further logical analysis (i.e., a *subjectively grounded* 'computational trope'),

   (b) this *adaptive key* is next deconstructed to mark three lever classes and three key computational roles, that naturally afford/generate **numerous** adaptive options,

   (c) those computational roles are then mapped in relation to Shannon signal entropy, to mark natural 'entropic types' that join to initiate a sense-making interpretive ('entropically generative' or *creative*) system,

   (d) a natural scalable example of this interpretive system is then given in the advent of lever-based 'simple machines and beyond'.

   (e) Step 3's novelty lies in: (i) the joint modeling of diverse levered roles, (ii) to derive a continuous *general adaptive logic*, (iii) that naturally bridges to signal entropy.

4. How is Adaptivity *Selectively Optimized*? (given many adaptive outputs ...)

   (a) myriad adaptive options thus exist (per above), that are now reduced by the *happenstance* of 'evolution by natural selection' (e.g., problem of 'uncontrolled variables'),

   (b) only *functional reduction* can optimize those options, driven by natural selection,

   (c) to frame that 'evolutionary landscape' classic threefold selection pressure and agent responses are shown as entangled functional roles,

   (d) as such, *happenstance* is also reframed as a general 'agent+force = result' (2–3) logic, for a basic *reducing model*, or an 'interpretive process' that reduces 'many *subjectives*' into 'the **objective**',

   (e) *reductive logic* is then shown to hold a 2–3 topology of ... 3232 ... as an extensible 'fractal key', for a naturally scalable adaptive continuum,

   (f) next, that *fractal key* is explored in relation to chaos theory as a way to structurally/computationally model happenstance and logical reduction,

   (g) lastly, that *reductive process* is framed as a 'base cognitive psychology' that conveys nominal intelligence.

   (h) Step 4's novelty is in: (i) the joint modeling of selection dynamics and agent responses, (ii) to detail a continuous dualist-triune topology, that also (iii) frames a *base adaptive psychology* as 'adaptive intelligence'.

The implication of this analysis is that designing an HLAI(+) likely requires a sequence of computational roles, rather than a one-step (top-down) algorithmic model. Also, using this step-wise view implies a range of 'interpretive tendencies', *adjacent possibilities* [20], or *stepping-stones* [35] typical to chaos theory, rather than firm predictive results. Such a model can still aid human inventiveness, but more likely in a non-autonomous HLAI+ role. Also, this computational view implies that an HLAI would not 'consciously experience' worldly events, unless specifically programmed to model existential risks to a 'Self', as with actual living agents. This analysis covers *general adaptive logic*, but does not address existential risk modeling. Finally, this study focuses on defining a *simple adaptive logic* (SAL), rather than targeting 'complex (higher-order) adaptive systems' (CAS). More detail is available in the video and papers linked below.

A   Appendix: Supplementary Material

The video and papers listed here provided added detail on the above step-wise analysis.

Title: *THE 'HARD PROBLEM' OF CONSCIOUSNESS* — names flaws in one of the more popular/well-known philosophical views, from among the many philosophical views noted in the first paragraph of Sect. 2.

Link: https://issuu.com/mabundis/docs/hardproblem.

Abstract: To frame any *meaningful* model of information, intelligence, 'consciousness', or the like, one must address a claimed Hard Problem (Chalmers, 1996) — the idea that such phenomenal roles fall beyond scientific views. While the Hard Problem's veracity is often debated, basic analogues to this claim still appear elsewhere in the literature as a 'symbol grounding problem' (Harnad, 1990), 'solving intelligence' (Burton-Hill, 2016), Shannon and Weaver's (1949) 'theory of meaning', etc. As such, the 'issue of phenomena' or *innate subjectivity* continues to hold sway in many circles as being unresolved. Also, direct analysis of the Hard Problem seems rare, where researchers instead typically offer related-claims asserting that: (1) it is a patently absurd view unworthy of study, or (2) it presents a fully intractable issue defying clear exploration, but with little clarifying detail. Debate on 'the claim' thus endures while clarity remains absent. This essay takes a third approach, that of directly assessing the Hard Problem's assertion *contra* natural selection in the formation of human consciousness. It examines Chalmers's logic and evidence for this view, taken from his articles over the years. The aim is to set an initial base where it then becomes possible to attempt resolution of the aforementioned 'issue of phenomena' (8 pages: 4,000 words).

Title: *ONE PROBLEM - ONE THOUSAND FACES*: IS4IS 2015 (International Society for Information Studies, conference presentation) — gives a broad abstract view of the model's basic approach, and further details the first bullet point in the step-wise model (Sect. 3) above.

Link: https://vimeo.com/140744119.

Abstract: This video (23 min) gives a broad view of *a priori* notions of information. It names an initial general 'theory of meaning' and 'theory of information' that emphasize scalable **primitive** *subjective* and *objective* facets. In brief, the model synthesizes Shannon entropy, Bateson's different differences, and Darwinian selection (an S-B-D model) to derive *meaningful information* across diverse disciplines.

In the video: Basic issues and questions are framed (2:30 min). Known meaning-ful metadata traits are detailed (2:30 min). Next, metadata's role is fully decon-structed in remaining minutes to name universal *a priori* facets. Lastly, the model is re-constituted 'from the ground up' to present a fully synthesized S-B-D *a priori* view. Text for the video voice-over can also be read or downloaded at: http://issuu.com/mabundis/docs/oneprob.fin

Title: *A GENERAL THEORY OF MEANING: Modeling informational fun-daments* — details the second bullet point in Sect. 3.
Link: https://issuu.com/mabundis/docs/abundis.tom.
Abstract: This essay targets a meaningful void in information theory, as named by Shannon and Weaver (1949). It explores current science (i.e., the standard model in physics, the periodic table, etc.) in relation to information and consciousness. It develops a 'bridge' to join these topics by framing *mean-ingful* information, or a 'natural/core informatics'. The study posits a general theory of meaning, where three types of informational meaning are detailed. As such, the model uses type theory to re-frame classic conflicts that arise across diverse informational roles, with Bateson-like (1979) 'differentiated differences' (or *types*) as informational fundaments (12 pages; 5,700 words).

Title: *NATURAL MULTI-STATE COMPUTING - Engineering evolution: Simple machines and beyond* — supports the third bullet point in Sect. 3.
Link: https://issuu.com/mabundis/docs/multistate.
Abstract: This essay covers *adaptive logic* in humans and other agents, and complements a related 'general theory of meaning' (Abundis, 2016). It names informational roles needed for minimal adaptivity as a *direct experience*, versus the 'reasoning by analogy' typical of artificial intelligence. It shows how levers, as a computational trope (adaptive template), typify *meaningful adaptive* traits for many agents and later afford the advent of simple machines. To develop the model: (1) Three lever classes are shown to compel a natural informatics in diverse agents. (2) Those lever classes are next deconstructed to derive a 'scalable creativity'. (3) That creative logic is then detailed as holding three *entropically generative* computational roles. (4) Lastly, that adaptive logic is used to model tool creation. Thus, the analysis frames systemic creativity (natural disruptions and evolution) in various roles (discrete, continuous, and bifurcations) for many agents, on diverse levels, to depict a 'general *adaptive* intelligence' (16 pages; 6,600 words).

Title: *SELECTION DYNAMICS AS AS ORIGIN OF REASON: Causes of cognitive information - a path to 'Super-Intelligence'* — covers the fourth bullet point in Sect. 3.
Link: https://issuu.com/mabundis/docs/lgcn.fin.4.15.
Abstract: This study explores 'adaptive cognition' in relation to agents striving to abide *entropic forces* (natural selection). It enlarges on a view of Shannon (1948) information theory and a 'theory of meaning' (Abundis, 2016)

developed elsewhere. The analysis starts by pairing classic selection pressure (*purifying*, *divisive*, and *directional* selection) and agent acts (as *flight*, *freeze*, and *fight* responses), to frame a basic model. It next details ensuing environs-agent exchanges as marking *Selection Dynamics*, for a 'general *adaptive* model'. Selection Dynamics are then shown in relation to chaos theory, and a fractal-like topology, for an initial computational view. Lastly, the resulting *dualist-triune topology* is detailed as sustaining many evolutionary and cognitive roles, thus marking an extensible adaptive informational/cultural fundament (13 pages: 5,700 words).

References

1. Bateson, G.: Mind and Nature: A Necessary Unity. Dutton, New York (1979)
2. Boyden, E.: Engineering revolutions. In: The 2016 World Economic Forum, Davos, Switzerland, World Economic Forum, February 2016
3. Burton-Hill, C.: The superhero of artificial intelligence. The Guardian, February 2016
4. Carroll, S.: Moving naturalism forward. In: An interdisciplinary workshop, Stockbridge, MA, Division of Physics, Mathematics, and Astronomy, California Institute of Technology, October 2012
5. Chalmers, D.J.: The Conscious Mind: In Search of a Fundamental Theory. Oxford University Press, Oxford (1998)
6. Chapman, D.: General definition of information: GDI (Floridi). http://www.intropy.co.uk/2010/04/general-definition-of-information-gdi.html (2010)
7. Blythe, M.: The Theory of Multiple Intelligences. Clinchy and Howard Gardner, Frames of mind (1984)
8. Deacon, T.W.: Incomplete Nature: How Mind Emerged from Matter. W.W. Norton & Co., New York (2013)
9. Daniel, C.: The Brain and Its Boundaries. Times Literary Supplement. Denett, London (1991)
10. Dennett, D.C.: Consciousness Explained. Little Brown and Co., Boston (1991)
11. Dennett, D.C.: Aching voids and making voids. Q. Rev. Biol. **88**, 321–324 (2013)
12. Floridi, L.: Semantic conceptions of information. In: Zalta, E.N. (ed.) The Stanford Encyclopedia of Philosophy. Metaphysics Research Lab, Stanford University, Spring 2017th edn. (2017)
13. Fodor, J.: What are trees about? London Rev. Books **34**(10), 34 (2012)
14. French, R.M.: Catastrophic forgetting in connectionist networks. Trends Cogn. Sci. **3**(4), 128–135 (1999)
15. Horgan, J.: Scientific Seeker Stuart Kauffman on free will, god, ESP and other mysteries. https://blogs.scientificamerican.com/cross-check/scientific-seeker-stuart-kauffman-on-free-will-god-esp-and-other-mysteries/ (2015)
16. ICLR: Workshop track. In: International Conference on Learning Representation. In: ICLR, Out of Nearly 160 'Speculative Proposals' Submitted, Only 2 Covered HLAI, April 2017
17. Joshepson, B.: Biological organisation as the true foundation of reality. In: 66th Lindau Nobel Laureates talks, Cambridge, UK, University of Cambridge, July 2016
18. Karpthy, A.: Alphago, in context. Medium, May 2017

19. Kauffman, S.: Beyond the stalemate: conscious mind-body - quantum mechanics - free will - possible panpsychism - possible interpretation of quantum enigma (2014). https://arxiv.org/abs/1410.2127. Accessed 21 Oct 2014 (this version, v2)
20. Kauffman, S.A.: Investigations. Oxford University Press, New York (2003)
21. Koch, C.: Consciousness: Confessions of a Romantic Reductionist. MIT Press, Cambridge (2012)
22. Lecun, Y., Bengio, Y., Hinton, G.: Deep learning. Nature **521**, 436–444 (2015)
23. Legg, S., Hutter, M.: Universal intelligence: a definition of machine intelligence. Minds Mach. **17**(4), 391–444 (2007)
24. Marcus, G.: Is artificial intelligence stuck in a rut? In: Intelligent machines, EmTech DIGITAL, MIT Technology Review, March 2017
25. McGinn, C.: Can Anything Emerge from Nothing?. New York Review of Books, New York (2012)
26. Peterson, G.R.: Demarcation and the scientific fallacy. Zygon J. Relig. Sci. **38**(4), 751–761 (2003)
27. Popper, K.R.: Conjectures and Refutations: The Growth of Knowledge, 4th edn. Routledge & Kegan Paul, London (1972)
28. Robinson, H.: Dualism. In: Zalta, E.N. (ed.) The Stanford Encyclopedia of Philosophy. Metaphysics Research Lab, Stanford University, Winter 2016th edn. (2016). See notes on 'property dualism'
29. Rosa, M.: Good AI (2017). https://www.roadmapinstitute.org
30. Searle, J.: The Mystery of Consciousness: An Exchange. The New York Review of Books, New York (1995)
31. Searle, J.: Biological Naturalism (2004)
32. Searle, J.: Consciousness in artificial intelligence. In: Talks at Google. Google Inc., Mountain View (2015)
33. Shannon, C.E.: A mathematical theory of communication. Bell Syst. Tech. J. **27**(3), 379–423 (1948)
34. Claude, E.: Shannon and Warren Weaver. Advances in a mathematical theory of communication. University of Illinois Press, Urbana (1949)
35. Stanley, K.O., Lehman, J.: Why Greatness Cannot be Planned: The Myth of the Objective. Springer International Publishing, Switzerland (2015)
36. Stubenberg, L.: Neutral monism. In: Zalta, E.N. (ed.) The Stanford Encyclopedia of Philosophy. Metaphysics Research Lab, Stanford University, Winter 2016th edn. (2016). See notes on dual aspect
37. AIXI (2017). https://wiki.lesswrong.com/wiki/AIXI
38. Wolfram, S.: A new kind of science: a 15-year view (2017). http://blog.stephenwolfram.com/2017/05/a-new-kind-of-science-a-15-year-view/#more-13536

Author Index

Printe
By Boo